RC 672

The Open University

Understanding Cardiovascular Diseases

D1379977

This publication forms part of an Open University course SK121 *Understanding cardiovascular diseases*. Details of this and other Open University courses can be obtained from the Student Registration and Enquiry Service, The Open University, PO Box 197, Milton Keynes MK7 6BJ, United Kingdom: tel. +44 (0)845 300 60 90, email general-enquiries@open.ac.uk

Alternatively, you may visit the Open University website at http://www.open.ac.uk where you can learn more about the wide range of courses and packs offered at all levels by The Open University.

To purchase a selection of Open University course materials visit http://www.ouw.co.uk, or contact Open University Worldwide, Michael Young Building, Walton Hall, Milton Keynes MK7 6AA, United Kingdom for a brochure: tel. +44 (0)1908 858793; fax +44 (0)1908 858787; email ouw-customer-services@open.ac.uk

The Open University
Walton Hall, Milton Keynes
MK7 6AA

First published 2007

Edited and designed by The Open University.

Typeset by SR Nova Pvt Ltd, Bangalore, India.

Printed and bound in the United Kingdom by the University Press, Cambridge.

ISBN 978 0 7492 2677 0

1.1

THE SK121 COURSE TEAM

Course Team Chair and Academic Editor

Duncan Banks, Department of Life Sciences, Faculty of Science

Course Managers

Darran Dawes, Department of Chemistry, Faculty of Science

Simone Pitman, Department of Chemistry, Faculty of Science

Course Team Assistant

Helen Copperwheat, Department of Life Sciences, Faculty of Science

Course Team Authors

Duncan Banks (Chapters 7 and 9)

Tom Heller, Faculty of Health and Social Care (Chapters 3 and 4)

David Male, Department of Life Sciences, Faculty of Science (Chapters 5, 6, 8 and 10)

Kerry Murphy, Department of Life Sciences, Faculty of Science (Chapter 2)

Vicky Taylor, Department of Life Sciences, Faculty of Science (Chapter 1)

Academic Readers

Duncan Banks

Tom Heller

David Male

Kerry Murphy

Claire Rothwell, Staff Tutor, Faculty of Science

Vicky Taylor

External Course Assessor

Jeremy Pearson, Professor of Vascular Biology, King's College London and Associate Medical Director, British Heart Foundation

Media Project Manager

Rafael Hidalgo

Editor

Joe Buchanan

Design

Chris Hough

Illustration

Steve Best

DVD-ROM Production

Will Rawes

Video Production

Marcus Bailey, East Anglian Ambulance NHS Trust, Locality Manager

Sarah Carr, Angel Eye Producer

Martin Chiverton, LTS Producer

James Clenaghan, Camera DOP/Lights

Jenny Dobbs, Production Assistant

Ben Hole, Angel Eye Director/Editor

Andrew Stronnach, Head of Communications, Norfolk and Norwich University Hospital NHS Trust

Jonathan Wyatt AMBS, Sound

Course Website

Nicola Heath

Picture Researcher

Martin Keeling

Rights Executives

Sarah Gamman

Martin Keeling

Indexer

Jane Henley

Consultants

Richard Heller, Emeritus Professor, Faculty of Population Health, University of Manchester (co-author Chapters 3 and 4)

Elizabeth Parvin, Department of Physics and Astronomy, Faculty of Science (co-author Chapter 7)

Alison Prust, General Practitioner, Isle of Jura (co-author Chapters 8 and 10)

Other Contributors

The Course Team would like to thank the following people for their involvement in the production of SK121:

Critical readers: Mary Edmonds, Lecturer, Homerton School of Health Studies

Video participants and production: Marcus Bailey, Jonathan Dermott, Barbara Phelps, Phil Sweeney

Developmental testers: Peter Culleton, Noel Eastman, Gill Ewing, David Henley, Sonja Hilborne-Clarke, Tina Milledge, Gill Mitan, Anne Moore, Jacky Shapley, Marion Swan, Eileen Wass

Thanks are also due to:

Sarah Wayte and Nigel Williams, University Hospitals Coventry and Warwickshire

Marcus Bailey, East of England Ambulance NHS Trust (filming, photographs and advice)

Malcolm Sperrin, Royal Berkshire NHS Foundation Trust (photographs)

Richard Wellings, University Hospital Walsgrave, University Hospitals Coventry and Warwickshire NHS Trust (photographs and advice)

Jonathan Ellis, Milton Keynes General NHS Trust (photographs and advice)

John Jameson, Glenfield Hospital, University Hospitals of Leicester NHS Trust (photographs)

CONTENTS

CHAPTER 1

INTRODUCTION TO CARDIOVASCULAR DISEASES

Learning Outcomes

When you have completed this chapter you should be able to:

1.1 Define and use, or recognise definitions and applications of, each of the terms printed in **bold** in the text.

1.2 Describe, in general terms, the different types of cardiovascular diseases, making clear the difference between the terms cardiovascular diseases (CVDs) and coronary heart disease (CHD).

1.3 Identify different areas of the body likely to be affected by cardiovascular diseases.

1.4 Locate information on the internet. Understand and interpret data on disease occurrence.

1.5 Recognise the importance of historical and geographical factors in the changing profile of cardiovascular disease incidence worldwide.

1.6 Identify and list a number of risk factors that contribute to the development of cardiovascular diseases.

1.1 Introduction

Welcome to the first chapter of the course *Understanding cardiovascular diseases*; we hope you find studying with us a valuable experience. This chapter will encourage you to develop some of the skills that will be needed throughout the study of this course. You will be introduced to the whole of the course text and its associated materials, including the interactive Multi-ed Cardiology program. This chapter also provides an introductory overview of some of the diseases of the heart and circulation (the **cardiovascular system**) and their medical management. This should help you get used to the medical terminology that you will soon become familiar with during your study. The initial chapters provide an introduction to the anatomy and physiology of the cardiovascular system. Then you will study the risk factors for developing cardiovascular diseases and some of the patterns of the diseases that point the way towards methods of preventing them. The whole course aims to help you study the subject of cardiovascular diseases within a social and global context.

This course text, with its case studies and the associated multimedia resources, will help you to develop your knowledge and understanding of the characteristic symptoms and development of some of the diseases of the heart and circulation. By the end of the course, you will also have a broader idea of how they can be diagnosed using a variety of techniques. The course material will also help you discover how a range of cardiovascular diseases can be treated and managed through medicines, surgery and lifestyle modification – and you may even have made some changes to your own cardiovascular risk factors!

1.2 People and cardiovascular diseases

You may be studying this course because you – or a member of your family or a friend – have been personally affected by cardiovascular diseases in some way. You may be professionally involved in looking after people with one of these diseases. Perhaps you are interested in health issues in general. Whatever your motivation or underlying reasons for studying this course, you will gain valuable insights into the extent of cardiovascular diseases and their treatment in the early twenty-first century. What you learn about avoiding or delaying cardiovascular diseases may also be incorporated into your own lifestyle for a healthier future for you and your family.

In this course you will be introduced to a number of people who have been affected by some aspect of cardiovascular disease. These are fictional characters who have been created to help your studies. You will learn about their clinical history, their subsequent treatments and the outcome of these treatments. This should help to place your new knowledge into context, helping you to understand why certain treatments are chosen for individuals and – equally importantly – what people can do to help themselves.

1.3 What are cardiovascular diseases? A simple introduction

Cardiovascular diseases (CVDs) is a 'catch all' phrase used to describe a variety of diseases of the heart and blood circulatory system. The main types of CVD are listed in Table 1.1, along with commonly used alternative descriptions. (Also see Box 1.1.) In Figure 1.1, CVDs are indicated in association with the particular body area where they mainly occur. Remember that this is just an introduction; when you get to Chapter 2, it will guide you in detail through the anatomy and physiology of the heart and blood circulation system in its healthy state. In later chapters (Chapters 5 and 6) you will learn about various aspects of each cardiovascular condition and how they develop. For now, it is useful to become more familiar with some of the more common terms that you will be encountering and their general definitions. To help you with any

Table 1.1 The major types of cardiovascular diseases, together with acronyms and/or commonly used alternative names.

Disease	Abbreviations and alternative names
cardiovascular diseases	CVDs
angina pectoris	angina, chest pain
arrhythmia	irregular heart beat
atherosclerosis	hardened arteries, furred up arteries
congenital defects	birth heart/valve defects
coronary heart disease	CHD, heart disease
heart failure	acute or chronic heart failure, congestive heart failure
hypertension	elevated or high blood pressure
ischaemia	ischæmia, ischemia
myocardial infarction	MI
rheumatic heart disease	(see Chapter 6)
stroke	cerebrovascular disease

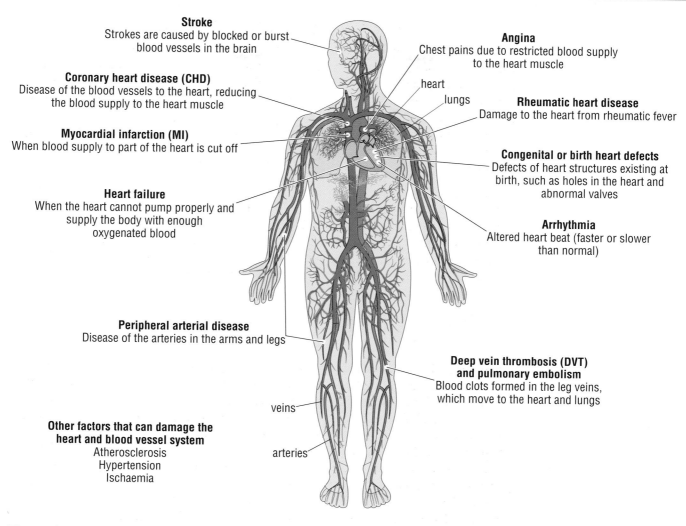

Stroke
Strokes are caused by blocked or burst blood vessels in the brain

Coronary heart disease (CHD)
Disease of the blood vessels to the heart, reducing the blood supply to the heart muscle

Myocardial infarction (MI)
When blood supply to part of the heart is cut off

Heart failure
When the heart cannot pump properly and supply the body with enough oxygenated blood

Peripheral arterial disease
Disease of the arteries in the arms and legs

Other factors that can damage the heart and blood vessel system
Atherosclerosis
Hypertension
Ischaemia

Angina
Chest pains due to restricted blood supply to the heart muscle

heart

lungs

Rheumatic heart disease
Damage to the heart from rheumatic fever

Congenital or birth heart defects
Defects of heart structures existing at birth, such as holes in the heart and abnormal valves

Arrhythmia
Altered heart beat (faster or slower than normal)

Deep vein thrombosis (DVT) and pulmonary embolism
Blood clots formed in the leg veins, which move to the heart and lungs

veins

arteries

Figure 1.1   Outline of the human body indicating the particular body area generally associated with the various cardiovascular diseases.

new medical terms, this course has an accompanying glossary which contains definitions for all of the words printed in bold in the text. Be sure to refer to it as you work your way through the course, when you come across new or unfamiliar terms.

Box 1.1 CVD or CHD?

You may have heard statistics about how many people are killed by cardiovascular diseases (CVDs): one in three people in the UK, one in four men and one in three women in the USA, or similar such figures for elsewhere in the world. So what are CVDs and how do they differ from heart disease or even coronary heart disease (CHD), which you will have heard used?

Firstly, CVDs describes a number of different diseases of the heart and circulatory system, including CHD and stroke. This is why the course and this chapter refer to cardiovascular diseases in the plural, as opposed to referring to a single disease.

So it should not be too surprising to learn that there is no simple cause of CVDs. Reassuringly though, there are a wide range of drugs and medical procedures available for CVD patients. There are also many contributing lifestyle factors that have been identified, which can be modified to either reduce the risk of developing CVDs or to help those living with it. You will learn about these throughout this course.

Occasionally in scientific literature and on the internet, the acronym CVD is also used to describe cerebrovascular disease (stroke). Be careful when you research the subject not to confuse this condition with cardiovascular diseases.

The following are broad definitions that may be useful in familiarising yourself with the range of CVDs and are here for you to return to at any time during the course to use as a reminder. You will undoubtedly come across variations as you read about them on the internet and in other texts.

Vascular refers to blood vessels (arteries, veins, and smaller vessels, all of which you will read about in Chapter 5) and **vasculature** refers to the arrangement of blood vessels within the body.

Atherosclerosis (hardened or furred-up arteries) is due to the accumulation of fatty material within the blood vessel wall, which can lead to narrowing of the vessel and restriction of blood flow.

Ischaemia is a restriction in the blood supply within the blood vessels, with resultant tissue damage.

Angina pectoris describes chest pains due to ischaemia, often experienced during exercise.

Coronary heart disease (CHD) is the most common form of heart disease, which involves a reduction in the blood supply to the heart muscle by narrowing or blockage of the coronary arteries. It is often characterised by atherosclerosis in the coronary arteries, angina pectoris and myocardial infarction, leading to acute heart failure.

Myocardial infarction (MI) occurs when the blood supply to part of the heart is cut off. If the blood flow to the heart is not restored, that part of the heart will die, causing disability or death. Myocardial infarction is the main cause of acute heart failure.

Heart failure is a medical condition resulting from heart disease and is often misunderstood. It describes when the organ cannot pump efficiently and is unable to generate blood flow sufficient to meet the demands of the body, either at rest or during exercise. **Congestive heart failure** is the term generally used when there is peripheral swelling due to fluid build-up (**oedema**; see Section 6.2).

Heart attack is the common name for acute heart failure, which is most often due to myocardial infarction following blockage of a coronary artery, but which also may be caused by other events that disturb the organised spread of electrical activity in the heart (e.g. arrhythmia, electrocution).

Myocardial infarction, heart failure and heart attack are terms that are often used interchangeably when they actually have different meanings. Chapter 6 will discuss this in more detail.

Arrhythmia is an uncontrolled, disordered or irregular heart beat. It can be faster or slower than normal.

Palpitations are when a distinct heart beat can be felt, and may be normal, faster or slower than usual. This is not necessarily a problem; for example, they can be caused by certain medications or simply by drinking too much caffeine in a short space of time!

Blood pressure (see Section 2.7) is a measure of the force generated by the beating of the heart pressing blood against the walls of the arteries as it is pumped around the body. A blood pressure measurement shows the higher systolic pressure – when the heart contracts – and the lower diastolic pressure – when the heart relaxes.

Normal adult blood pressure should be less than about 140/90 mmHg (systolic/ diastolic), as in the first pale orange zone in the bottom left-hand corner of Figure 1.2. (Section 2.7 gives more detail on the measurement process and what the result means.) If your blood pressure is consistently measured by medical staff as over 140/90 mmHg (the orange central zone or red outer zone of Figure 1.2), or over 140/80 mmHg if you have diabetes (see Section 1.5.1), you will be considered to have elevated or high blood pressure, known as **hypertension**. Consistently high blood pressure is a risk factor for many cardiovascular diseases. The excess pressure can damage the lining of an artery, allowing blood clots to form and cause blockages.

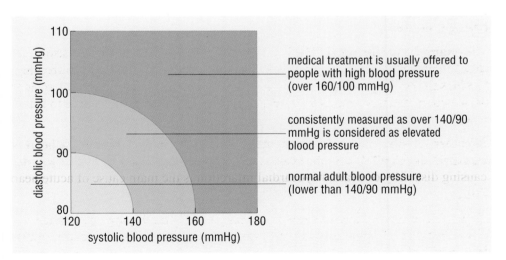

Figure 1.2 The relationship between systolic and diastolic blood pressure. The zones of blood pressure measurement indicate whether the readings are generally normal or elevated. Health care professionals also consider other symptoms and illnesses an individual has when determining whether medical treatment is needed.

Strokes are caused by either blocked or burst blood vessels in the brain. By reducing high blood pressure to within the normal range, nearly half of all strokes can be prevented. Strokes are not covered in this course or text in detail – they vary according to the area of brain affected and there is not the space to cover the required brain anatomy or neuroscience. Strokes can kill or cause major disability, although full recovery is possible after a minor stroke.

Other rarer forms of heart disease are those that some people may be born with, known as **congenital heart defects**. Examples include problems with the heart valves or heart beat rhythm, and these are more likely to be encountered in younger people. They can cause long-term problems and even death (if undiagnosed) for people with these conditions. Sometimes you hear news stories about previously healthy children or young adults dying suddenly, especially following strenuous sports activities such as football matches (see Box 1.2).

Box 1.2 Sudden heart death in the young

SADS is another acronym that is used interchangeably, but this time for two descriptions of the same condition: Sudden Arrhythmic Death Syndrome and Sudden Adult Death Syndrome. The first is more accurate because SADS can affect children too.

There are a number of different causes of sudden heart death in young people, but sometimes no cause is found when a young person dies. This happens in about 1 in 20 cases in the UK (up to 500 per year). It is thought that a proportion of cases may be caused by a fast, uncontrolled heart beat (arrhythmia). One identified arrhythmia has been called long QT syndrome, which describes a lengthening of the time it takes the heart's electrical system to recharge, leaving the individual susceptible to an abnormal heart beat rhythm. (The normal physiology is covered in Chapter 2 and cardiac arrhythmias in Chapter 6.)

If the condition is diagnosed in time, a miniature **defibrillator** (to restart the heart) may be fitted or drugs can be taken (for the rest of the individual's life) to slow down the heart rate. Without treatment, the brain becomes deprived of oxygen, causing fainting – or, rarely, collapse and death.

As long QT syndrome can be genetically inherited and may be brought on by exercise, it has been suggested that all young athletes should be screened for the condition (Cardiac Risk in the Young, 2003).

1.3.1 There's a lot of it about: the global picture of cardiovascular diseases

Who is affected by cardiovascular diseases?

Cardiovascular diseases are the main cause of premature death (before the age of 75) in the UK, across Europe and the USA – indeed, across many parts of the world (Figures 1.3 and 1.4). One third of global deaths in 2002 were from cardiovascular diseases: 16.7 million people (World Health Organization (WHO) figures: Mackay and Mensah, 2004; see Figure 1.3). However, the burden is not shared equally between the developed and developing world, or even within European states, as you will see in the next section.

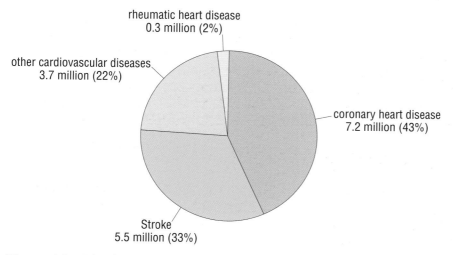

Figure 1.3 Pie chart showing the proportion of global deaths from various cardiovascular diseases in 2002.

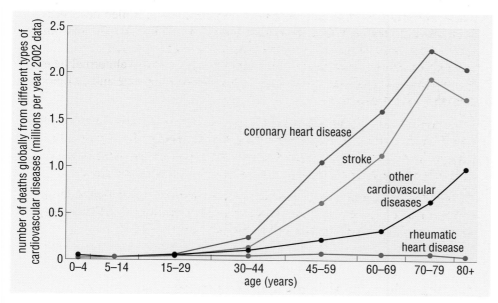

Figure 1.4 The number of deaths per year throughout the world for different types of cardiovascular diseases subdivided by age into different groups. As you can see, in early adulthood coronary heart disease and stroke become the common causes of cardiovascular deaths for large numbers of people.

Activity 1.1 Interpreting coronary heart disease deaths from a world distribution map

Suggested study time 10 minutes

Using Figure 1.5, find three countries with the highest numbers of deaths from coronary heart disease (more than 500 000) and then three countries with the lowest numbers (fewer than 1000; exclude the no data countries).

Look at your own country and decide whether it has a high or low occurrence of coronary heart disease.

Comment

You should be aware that the number of deaths from coronary heart disease in 2002 varied greatly between different countries. There are numerous reasons for these differences and you will start to learn about some of these in the following sections.

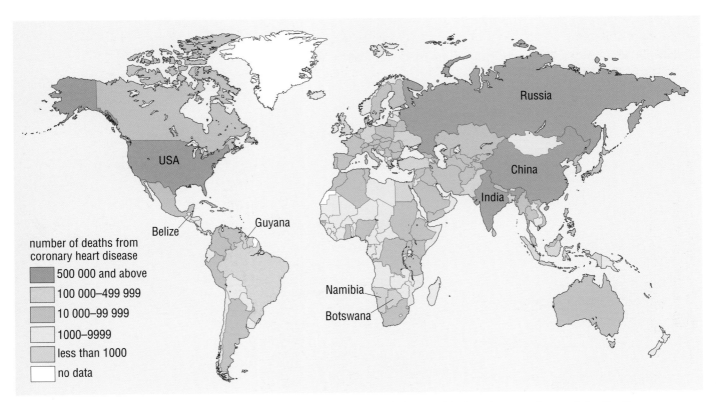

Figure 1.5 Coronary heart disease knows no borders: a map of the world showing numbers of deaths from coronary heart disease in 2002.

1.3.2 Decline of cardiovascular diseases in Western society?

Cardiovascular diseases may be the main cause of death across most of the world, but the mortality (death) rates have actually been declining since the 1970s in most industrialised countries.

> '…CHD mortality decreased by more than 50% between 1981 and 2000 in England and Wales. Approximately 40% of the UK decrease was attributable to the combined effects of modern cardiological treatments and almost 60% to [a] reduction in major risk factors, particularly smoking. This is consistent with the majority of other studies in the United States, Europe, Scotland and New Zealand.'
>
> (Unal et al., 2004)

For the USA, Figure 1.6 shows the decline in heart attacks in its population over 25 years to 2005. The reasons for all these declines are not straightforward, but may be due to improved prevention, diagnosis and treatment. These include:

- changes in cardiovascular risk factors, such as reduced smoking in adults, lower blood pressure and lower blood cholesterol levels (covered in Chapter 3)

- development and access to medical treatments, such as thrombolysis, aspirin and statins (covered in Chapter 8), and surgical treatments, such as coronary artery bypass surgery and angioplasty to widen blocked blood vessels (covered in Chapter 9).

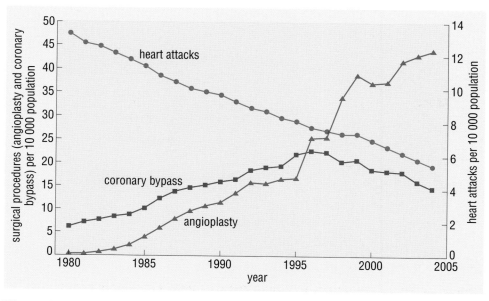

Figure 1.6   The numbers of heart attacks and surgical procedures (angioplasty and coronary bypass) per 10 000 of the population in the USA between 1980 and 2005.

● From Figure 1.6, you will see that, in 1990, 11 people per 10 000 of the population in the USA had angioplasty surgery. By 1995, this had increased to 17 people per 10 000. What was the figure in 2000?

● About 37 people per 10 000 of the population had angioplasty surgery in 2000.

Although this decline in cardiovascular disease deaths sounds encouraging, the same researchers from the above quoted study also identified some adverse trends which would be expected to lead to more cardiovascular diseases in the future:

> 'The adverse trends in obesity, diabetes, and physical inactivity together contributed ~8000 additional deaths in 2000. These canceled out 2 decades of improvement in cholesterol. Furthermore, continuing deteriorations are expected.'

(Unal et al., 2004)

The 2005 statistics confirm that cardiovascular disease rates are falling in most northern, southern and western European countries, but the decline is slower or there is even an increase in central and eastern European countries (see Figure 1.7; Petersen et al., 2006). It is anticipated that over 80% of the future increases in coronary heart disease will be in developing countries (Mackay and Mensah, 2004). The death rate from coronary heart disease is not falling so fast in South Asian people in the UK as in the rest of the UK population (Lip et al., 2007). So although many improvements have been made to the diagnosis, treatment and prevention of cardiovascular diseases, there is no time to be complacent: there are also other socioeconomic and risk factors at work that can just as easily reverse these encouraging declines.

Figure 1.7 The percentage change in coronary heart disease death rates in men and women aged 35 to 74 over a 10-year period (1988–1998) in selected countries.

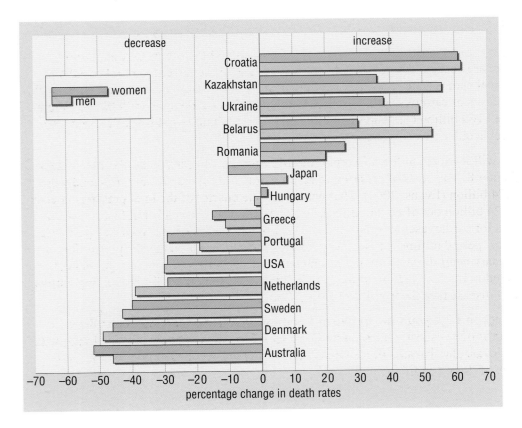

How confident can you be that statements of medical statistics are true – for example, 'approximately 43% (43 men in every 100) of deaths in men in Europe are due to cardiovascular diseases'? What exactly do such statements mean? Identifying the cause of death is not an exact science, and medical practitioners may make a mistake. Moreover, there may be a greater tendency in some countries than others to identify the cause of death as a cardiovascular disease. Such effects can mask, accentuate or confuse genuine differences between countries in the occurrence of cardiovascular diseases. Often, such statements are more informative when a range is given, such as '30–50% of deaths in men are caused by cardiovascular diseases'. Such ranges may relate to true differences between countries, as well as to accuracy or bias in the diagnosis. It is important to look carefully at the meaning of such general statements to establish where and when they may be applicable.

Even given perfect diagnosis or data, statements on disease occurrence still require careful analysis if they are based on a sample of the whole population. For example, if a statement is made concerning smokers and is based on the incidence of cardiovascular diseases in a sample of 1000 smokers, can you be sure that the results seen with the sample of 1000 smokers apply to the whole population of smokers? This is where statistical methods are used which aim to show whether a result seen in a study is truly applicable to the population as a whole. These methods frequently generate a value called P (the P-value, a probability), which indicates how likely the result is to be wrong. For example, if you read that a study has shown that $P < 0.01$ (probability P less than 0.01), it shows that in more than 99% of cases the results from the sample indicate what is happening in the wider population. The probability that the conclusions of the study do not apply – that is, they are incorrect for the population as a whole – is less than 1%.

1.3.3   Economic impact of cardiovascular diseases

The economic costs of cardiovascular diseases are wide-ranging and increasing. There are costs to the individual and their family, to the government (especially if medical care is state-funded) and to the country's economy if time is lost from work. The costs of cardiovascular diseases within the European Union in 2005 are estimated to be €169 billion (169 thousand million) per year. Over two thirds of the costs are direct health care costs (Petersen et al., 2006).

You will learn about the different types of drugs used in cardiovascular medicine in Chapter 8. The costs of prescribing cardiovascular drugs for 2002 in England were £1.74 billion (Evans, 2004). That was about one quarter of the total prescribing costs (£1.74 billion out of £6.84 billion). In Chapter 4, you will read about more current costs for cardiovascular drugs and see how their patterns of use have changed over a short period of time. In the UK, prescribing costs in relation to the prevention of coronary heart diseases are increasing nationally, with significant cost pressures related to implementation of the National Service Framework for preventing coronary heart disease (see Section 1.6.1; Evans, 2004).

In Section 1.3.1 you were introduced to the global cost of cardiovascular diseases in terms of lives lost to these conditions. However, many people are also living with cardiovascular diseases or disabled in some way due to the debilitating effects of some of these conditions.

The World Health Organization (WHO) produces world data tables detailing, by country, the total population and the deaths from heart disease and other cardiovascular diseases (plus some major risk factors) (WHO, 2006). There are also figures for the 'healthy years of life lost' (DALYS: disability-adjusted life years), and these give an indication of the disease burden within the population.

Activity 1.2   Using the world data tables for cardiovascular diseases

Suggested study time 15–20 minutes

The world data tables for 2002 produced by WHO (2006) are available on the course website. Find the row of data for the UK, which had a population of roughly 60 million in 2002. You can calculate the actual number of healthy years of life lost due to coronary heart disease for the UK (DALYS lost) in 2002 as being:

$$
\begin{aligned}
\text{DALYS lost} &= 59\,068\,000 \times (7 \text{ per } 1000) \\
&= 59\,068\,000 \times (7/1000) \\
&= 59\,068\,000 \times 0.007 \\
&= 413\,476 \text{ years}
\end{aligned}
$$

Pick another country with a similar population – for example, Thailand (62 million), Turkey (70 million), France (60 million) or Italy (57 million) – and repeat the above calculation using the data for that country. Compare the answer you get with the answer for the UK.

If you haven't done so already, take a look at the data from your own country.

Comment

This activity should have exercised your mathematical skills and showed the number of healthy years lost due to the development of coronary heart disease in different countries. The differences observed between countries with similar-sized populations should stimulate you to think about the wider implications on, for example, their health services and economies.

1.4 Studying cardiovascular diseases

1.4.1 Using medical terminology: building a glossary

As you start studying a medical subject, it is useful to be familiar with the sort of terminology you will come across. Often there are similar-sounding terms with different meanings, e.g. hypo and hyper. There is medical jargon that needs deciphering, e.g. hypertension means high blood pressure. Likewise, the same acronyms can be used for different things, which can cause frustration (e.g. the two different uses of the acronym CVD – see Box 1.1 for a reminder). To help you with the medical terminology, this course has an accompanying glossary.

Be sure to refer to it as you work your way through the course when you come across new or unfamiliar terms or when you need to revise them.

Many medical, scientific and technical terms are derived from other languages, such as Greek, Latin, Sanskrit and German. Understanding specialised terms can be made much easier with some knowledge of how complex words are made up of simpler ones. The study of the origins of words is called etymology; etymologies, while not being definitions, are interesting demonstrations of how our words have formed from other words and why the original words were chosen. For example, 'cardiomyopathy' breaks down into 'cardio' (heart), '-myo-' (muscle) and '-pathy' (disease).

Activity 1.3   Using the course glossary

Suggested study time 20 minutes

Pick five unfamiliar words from the following list and look them up in the course glossary: angina, arrhythmia, bradycardia, cardiology, electrocardiogram, epidemiology, ischaemia, myocardium, pulmonary, tachycardia, thrombosis.

Use the glossary to find out what the difference is between the two (very similar) words atherosclerosis and arteriosclerosis.

Activity 1.4   Using the Multi-ed Cardiology program to decipher some medical jargon: introducing and explaining syncope

Suggested study time 30 minutes

To help plan your study, an icon printed in the margin of this book indicates the activities, such as this one, which require you to use the DVD-ROM provided as part of your course materials. You are also given guidance on the likely length of time you will need to complete activities. The actual time you take may depend on various factors, but as you work through the course you will get a feel for whether the given estimates are realistic for you personally.

The Multi-ed Cardiology program contains animations and resources such as summary sheets which will help reinforce your understanding of the material in this course. As well as using it when prompted in activities such as this one, it will also be useful as a reference and revision resource.

There are four animations to watch at this point to introduce and explain syncope. From the DVD Guide program, follow the links to Multi-ed Cardiology, and then navigate to Animations | Condition | Syncope. Watch the animations in order by selecting their names from the resulting list.

Once you have done this, navigate to Resources | Leaflets | Syncope. Here you will find a document summarising the information you have just watched and listened to.

Comment

You now know how to access and use the Multi-ed Cardiology program, so you can make use of this resource throughout the rest of this course and your study of cardiovascular diseases.

Now you have started to get to grips with some of the terminology (and, more importantly, you know where to get help with any unfamiliar terms: the glossary and the Multi-ed Cardiology program), you can move on to study the biology of the heart and circulation with confidence (Chapter 2). As you work your way through this course, remember that you can return at any time to the Multi-ed Cardiology program and view any of the animations to consolidate your knowledge. Some of the activities in this course will refer you to specific animations to help you understand the material you are studying.

Following your study of Chapter 2, you will have a sound foundation of the cardiovascular system. From there you will move on to find out about cardiovascular disease risk factors and incidence throughout the world.

1.5 Risk factors

Health is generally considered to be the absence of disease. However, the absence of any symptoms of disease may cause us to mistakenly believe we are healthy. We can't see inside our arteries to know how blocked up they are with fatty deposits without specialised equipment (as described in Chapter 7), but that doesn't mean it isn't gradually happening.

In your study of Chapters 3 and 4 you will be able to read in detail about some of the known risk factors that relate to cardiovascular diseases. For now, let's consider some of the general issues. You may consider that your heart is healthy. What are your chances, as a member of the general population, of developing cardiovascular diseases now, next year or in 20 years' time? What are your risk factors for developing a heart problem in the future, and what can you do to minimise them? These appear to be simple questions, but what is the difference between chance and risk?

Chance is the likelihood of something happening (or not happening) randomly. It is not something that can be controlled. What determines who will succumb to cardiovascular diseases within the population has been studied scientifically. Rather than being just down to chance, it may be described in terms of risk factors (covered in Chapter 3).

Risk has a connotation of something bad possibly (but not definitely) happening. Everyone has an **absolute risk** of developing cardiovascular diseases, or any other disease over their lifetime. We can express an individual's risk in a variety of ways: a 1 in 10 risk can also be written as a 10% risk or as a risk of 0.1. The absolute risks for men and women in Europe are actually much higher; approximately 43% of deaths in men and 55% of deaths in women in Europe are due to cardiovascular diseases (Petersen et al., 2006). Chapter 3 gives many more examples of risk and what it means.

There are some activities and lifestyle choices that increase an individual's risk of disease. These can also be calculated and combined with their absolute risk. An assessment of **relative risk** in **epidemiology** (the study of the distribution of diseases in populations and their causes) looks at, for example, the risk of cardiovascular diseases occurring in smokers relative to the risk of cardiovascular diseases occurring in non-smokers, comparing two probabilities. There is no assessment of how bad the cardiovascular diseases are or even if smoking is the cause, but for whatever reasons, the risk of cardiovascular diseases in smokers is found to be greater than in non-smokers. You will be guided through calculating risk factors for individuals in Chapter 3. To summarise, chance relates to the whole population and the likelihood of developing cardiovascular diseases, but risk can be specifically calculated for a subset of the population, such as smokers or those with pre-existing diabetes.

There are many scientific studies that have looked at a whole host of lifestyle risk factors for cardiovascular diseases, such as smoking, raised blood cholesterol and elevated blood pressure. (Others are listed in Table 1.2.) Unlike chance, once identified, a modifiable risk factor can be acted upon to reduce its possible negative effect on health or future health, hence reducing the risk of developing cardiovascular diseases. Many of these factors can also be termed modifiable risk factors because they can be changed through personal choice (but often not without considerable effort!).

You read about both decreasing and increasing rates of cardiovascular diseases in Section 1.3. Even though some major risk factors have been identified from studies that date back to the 1940s (see Chapter 3), and although some reductions in cardiovascular diseases have been achieved based on these investigations, changes in society and global factors since then have led to the emergence of new or more prevalent risk factors. Why is it that cardiovascular diseases are expected to continue increasing throughout certain areas of the world? The habits or 'lifestyle risk factors' of people and populations have changed over recent years, often described as becoming more 'Westernised'. The trend has been towards the consumption of more energy-dense but nutrient-poor food, such as saturated fats and *trans* fatty acids (see Box 1.3 later), salt and refined carbohydrates, and a correspondingly lower consumption of fresh fruit and vegetables. At the same

Table 1.2 Cardiovascular risk factors can be separated into three broad categories: biological risk factors that are non-modifiable; biological risk factors that are modifiable by treatment or altered lifestyle; and lifestyle factors that are modifiable.

Biological risk factors: non-modifiable	Biological risk factors: modifiable by treatment or altered lifestyle	Lifestyle risk factors: modifiable
age (increasing)	high blood cholesterol	smoking
male	high blood pressure (hypertension)	diet (unhealthy or unbalanced)
family history (genetic)	overweight and obesity	inactivity (sedentary lifestyle)
race/ethnicity	diabetes (Type 2)	excessive alcohol consumption
diabetes (Type 1)	psychosocial factors, e.g. stress, depression, anger	

time, many societies have reduced their physical activity, perhaps due to more time spent watching television, playing computer games and other sedentary activities, rather than on physical or outdoor activities. At the same time, there has been more travel taking place in cars and other motorised vehicles rather than by bicycle or walking.

There are also some biological risk factors that are not modifiable (Table 1.2). These include gender, increasing age, any genetic disorders and some diseases, e.g. Type 1 diabetes (see Section 1.5.1). Type 2 diabetes and its precursor, insulin resistance, can be modified to some extent during their early stages.

Some of the modifiable risk factors could fall equally well into the biological or lifestyle risk category, especially if they have arisen as a result of lifestyle. Examples are: hypertension due to a diet high in salt; high blood cholesterol due to a diet high in saturated fat; being overweight or obese due to excessive or indiscriminate eating behaviour; and Type 2 diabetes developed following weight gain. The development of such risk factors may be unavoidable, but with medical management they may be influenced positively.

In the following case study, where you are introduced to Winifred Fowler, you will start to investigate how an individual may consider their lifestyle in relation to their cardiovascular disease risk. You will follow her treatment throughout the course.

Case Study 1.1   Winifred Fowler

Winifred Fowler is a bus driver in Norwich. She is 61 and will be retiring soon. Winifred is counting the years to finishing work, but with one of her children at college, the family still needs her income. She recently had a medical examination, arranged by her employer, and was found to have high blood pressure. Winifred smokes at least 20 cigarettes a day, spends most of her time sitting down and snacks on chocolate and sweets. She has to keep to a tight bus schedule, working the 2 to 8 p.m. shift, so lunch is often a takeaway bacon roll or a portion of chips with plenty of salt from the café on the way to her bus depot.

Activity 1.5   Risk factors and simple ways of changing them

Suggested study time 10–15 minutes

Make a list of the modifiable risk factors that Winifred could change to improve her overall health and reduce her risk of cardiovascular diseases. For each one that you have listed, write a sentence identifying at least one way in which she could change.

Comment

You should have been able to identify at least a few modifiable risk factors that Winifred could work towards changing. These might have included: reducing or giving up smoking; reducing or replacing her snacks with healthy options; improving her general diet; reducing her salt intake; and taking up exercise to counteract the amount of time she sits during her working day.

1.5.1 Diabetes as a risk factor

One risk factor – diabetes –requires special attention with regard to cardiovascular diseases. **Diabetes mellitus** is a condition in which the blood glucose level is higher than it should be for a healthy individual. If it remains that way, over time, it will cause numerous medical problems, including cardiovascular diseases. Cardiovascular diseases are responsible for up to four-fifths of the deaths of people with diabetes. The risk factors you are becoming familiar with are greater for people with diabetes; they have a 2- to 3-fold increased risk of atherosclerosis and a 3- to 5-fold increased risk of heart failure. As well as a doubling of cardiovascular disease risk, the risk of death from coronary heart disease for people with diabetes is 2 to 4 times higher than average.

The word 'diabetes' comes from the Greek for 'siphon'. A siphon removes liquid, and diabetes is used to describe disorders that remove liquid from the body, as the 'external' symptoms include excessive thirst and the production of large amounts of urine. The word 'mellitus' is Latin for 'honeyed'. Diabetes mellitus, therefore, describes a condition that produces 'sweet urine'. This production of sweet urine occurs as the end result of a high blood glucose level. Diabetes mellitus has been known for thousands of years, but it is rapidly increasing in occurrence in modern times. From now on, throughout the course, the term diabetes will be used to describe diabetes mellitus.

There are several types of diabetes, but we are only interested in the two most common: **Type 1** and **Type 2**. Worldwide, about 90% of people with diabetes have Type 2 and about 10% have Type 1. Type 2 diabetes was previously called non-insulin-dependent diabetes. People with Type 2 diabetes produce insulin (unlike Type 1), but it may be in insufficient amounts and/or their cells may be resistant to the action of insulin (insulin resistance). Because insulin directs glucose into cells from the bloodstream, glucose will be left to build up in the blood if there is not enough insulin or if cells are resistant to its actions. In people without diabetes, blood glucose levels are kept tightly controlled. Type 2 diabetes may be present for many years before a clinical diagnosis is made. This is because some people may have few obvious symptoms, and others do not see their thirst or getting up at night to pass urine as a problem. Having diabetes for several years before a diagnosis is made can mean that complications of diabetes, including cardiovascular diseases that take years to develop, may therefore already be present at the time of diagnosis. Obesity and lack of exercise are two particularly important environmental factors thought to be contributing to the rapidly increasing numbers of people worldwide with Type 2 diabetes. Although it has previously been considered to be a condition of adults, particularly those over 40 years old, it is now occurring with increasing frequency in younger people, including adolescents.

This section has introduced you to the concept of risk factors and the possibility that they can be altered through either lifestyle modification or medical intervention. When you reach Chapter 3, you will be looking in more detail at how they are studied by investigators known as **epidemiologists**. Then in Chapter 4 you will read about how preventive measures can be undertaken at all levels ranging from the individual to the population level.

Box 1.3 Fats

Fats, also known as **lipids**, are important components of living tissues, and are used by the body for making cell membranes and for storing energy. Fats come in a variety of different biochemical types, which may be obtained from the diet or can be synthesised within the body. Many cells of the body can convert certain types of fat into others, but by preference, fats will be obtained from the diet, if available. The fatty acids that cannot be synthesised by the body and therefore must be obtained from the diet are called **essential fatty acids**. To understand the different types of fat (see Figure 1.8), and how the body can make use of them, you need to know about the building blocks from which they are made.

Fatty acids can be classified as **saturated** or **unsaturated**, depending on their chemical structure. Generally, complex fats that include unsaturated fatty acids are more fluid than those containing saturated fatty acids, because their tails do not pack together so neatly. However, in one group of unsaturated fatty acids, *trans* **fatty acids**,

the kink(s) which are present in more abundant unsaturated fats are minimal. So, like saturated fats, the compounds formed from them also have lower fluidity. The precise position(s) of the special chemical bond(s) which produce the kinks in an unsaturated fatty acid is indicated by its biochemical nomenclature, e.g. omega-3 fatty acids. The pattern of kinks is also fundamental to the kinds of more complicated molecules that can be built from fatty acids.

Fatty acids and cholesterol are transported around the body in the blood or the lymph (clear fluid that bathes tissues), in association with specific types of proteins that link them together and prevent them from sticking to other molecules. Some are just attached to a protein in the blood called albumin, but larger and more complex combinations of lipids and protein are called **lipoproteins**. Different types of lipoprotein are classified according to their density, which reflects their lipid and protein composition. They may be high-density lipoproteins (**HDL**), low-density lipoproteins

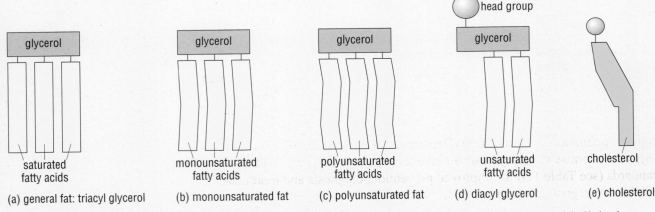

(a) general fat: triacyl glycerol (b) monounsaturated fat (c) polyunsaturated fat (d) diacyl glycerol (e) cholesterol

Figure 1.8 The chemical structures of fats (lipids). (a) Many fats are formed by three fatty acids linked together by a molecule of glycerol. Each of the fatty acids has a long tail (**acyl** groups), so this compound is called a **triacylglycerol** (often called a **triglyceride**). The length of the acyl groups can vary, as can their chemical type. (b) **Monounsaturated** fats have a particular chemical bond which produces a kink in the acyl groups. (c) **Polyunsaturated** fats have a number of kinks, which vary in number and position. (d) The lipids present in cell membranes are usually **diacylglycerols**, in which one of the fatty acids is substituted with a completely different type of molecule – generically called a 'head group'. (e) **Cholesterol** is not a fat, but its structure is functionally similar to the fatty acids, so it can sit in cell membranes in a similar way to them. The liver can synthesise cholesterol, but in practice most is derived from the diet.

(LDL) or very low-density lipoproteins (VLDL). Fat is less dense than protein, so, as an example, LDL has a higher proportion of cholesterol and saturated fatty acids than HDL. Dietary fats are transported in the blood to the liver as the very large lipoproteins called chylomicrons. Those that reach the liver are processed and may be converted to other fatty acids before the blood carries them on to other tissues. The liver also acts as a way-station (store) for fats from the tissues that are to be used as a source of energy or for synthesising cell membranes.

1.6 Prevention is better than cure

Prevention strategies for cardiovascular diseases are often referred to as primary or secondary. This distinction is made because recommendations for the patient are slightly different, depending on whether cardiovascular diseases have already been established. Primary prevention involves preventing the onset of disease in individuals without symptoms. Secondary prevention refers to the prevention (or delay) of death or recurrence of disease in those with symptoms.

For all coronary heart disease patients who die within a month of the onset of symptoms, about three more have died before even reaching hospital. This emphasises the need to recognise the warning signs and work on prevention of the causes of cardiovascular diseases. The health problems caused by cardiovascular diseases worldwide have led to a great deal of research into both causes and treatment. (The scale and depth of the research can be demonstrated by searching various resources on the internet, such as PubMed (National Center for Biotechnology Information, 2007).) There is now better evidence to guide the prevention, diagnosis and treatment of coronary heart disease than there is for most other major diseases, and in the UK this has led to the development of guidelines for the health service.

1.6.1 The National Service Framework

National Service Frameworks are long-term strategies for tackling major health issues and important diseases, especially improving specific areas of care, e.g. coronary heart disease, cancer and diabetes. They set measurable goals within set timeframes. The National Service Framework for coronary heart disease in England, published in March 2000 (Department of Health, 2000), sets out a strategy to modernise coronary heart disease services over 10 years. It details 12 standards (see Table 1.3) for improved prevention, diagnosis and treatment, for rehabilitation goals, and to secure fair access to high-quality services.

The 2006 progress report for England states that:

> 'We continue to make good progress towards our Public Service Agreement mortality target for cardiovascular disease (CVD) with a 35.9% reduction, against a target of 40% by 2010.'

> (Department of Health, 2007)

Table 1.3 The 12 standards that make up the National Service Framework for coronary heart disease in England. (NHS, National Health Service.)

Target	Standard	Description
Reducing heart disease in the population	1	The NHS and partner agencies should develop, implement and monitor policies that reduce the prevalence of coronary risk factors in the population, and reduce inequalities in risks of developing heart disease.
	2	The NHS and partner agencies should contribute to a reduction in the prevalence of smoking in the local population.
Preventing CHD in high-risk patients	3	General practitioners and primary care teams should identify all people with established cardiovascular disease and offer them comprehensive advice and appropriate treatment to reduce their risks.
	4	General practitioners and primary health care teams should identify all people at significant risk of cardiovascular disease but who have not developed symptoms and offer them appropriate advice and treatment to reduce their risks.
Heart attack and other acute coronary syndromes	5	People with symptoms of a possible heart attack should receive help from an individual equipped with and appropriately trained in the use of a defibrillator within 8 minutes of calling for help, to maximise the benefits of resuscitation should it be necessary.
	6	People thought to be suffering from a heart attack should be assessed professionally and, if indicated, receive aspirin. Thrombolysis should be given within 60 minutes of calling for professional help.
	7	NHS Trusts should put in place agreed protocols/systems of care so that people admitted to hospital with proven heart attack are appropriately assessed and offered treatments of proven clinical and cost-effectiveness to reduce their risk of disability and death.
Stable angina	8	People with symptoms of angina or suspected angina should receive appropriate investigation and treatment to relieve their pain and reduce their risk of coronary events.
Revascularisation	9	People with angina that is increasing in frequency or severity should be referred to a cardiologist urgently or, for those at greatest risk, as an emergency.
	10	NHS Trusts should put in place hospital-wide systems of care so that patients with suspected or confirmed coronary heart disease receive timely and appropriate investigation and treatment to relieve their symptoms and reduce their risk of subsequent coronary events.
Heart failure	11	Doctors should arrange for people with suspected heart failure to be offered appropriate investigations (e.g. electrocardiography, echocardiography) that will confirm or refute the diagnosis. For those in whom heart failure is confirmed, its cause should be identified – treatments most likely to both relieve their symptoms and reduce their risk of death should be offered.
Cardiac rehabilitation	12	NHS Trusts should put in place agreed protocols/systems of care so that, prior to leaving hospital, people admitted to hospital suffering from coronary heart disease have been invited to participate in a multidisciplinary programme of secondary prevention and cardiac rehabilitation. The aim of the programme will be to reduce their risk of subsequent cardiac problems and to promote their return to a full and normal life.

A similar framework was published for Wales in July 2001 (The National Assembly for Wales, 2001) and outlined five standards. Other countries worldwide are likely to have or be developing their equivalent National Service Framework for coronary heart disease and other cardiovascular diseases and be at various stages of implementation.

In Section 1.3.3 the substantial economic costs of cardiovascular diseases were introduced. Box 1.4 reports the success of physicians in the USA in lowering the national average blood pressure values to slightly below those in some Western European countries. They have achieved this with more interventions and drug treatment. This presumably also has higher cost implications, at least initially – as is currently being experienced with the National Service Framework for coronary heart disease in England. The obvious question that follows is to ask whether prevention would be cheaper than intervention. If so, how can it be done at different levels: globally, nationally, individually? Chapter 4 looks at these issues in detail, but in Sections 1.6.3, 1.6.4 and 1.6.5 we will start to consider some of them.

Box 1.4 Keeping the blood pressure of nations under control

A recent study reveals that people living in the USA have lower blood pressure than some of their Western European counterparts (in the UK, France, Germany, Spain and Italy; Wang et al., 2007).

US doctors administer hypertension treatment earlier and more aggressively than doctors in Western Europe. By doing this, they say they can reduce the cost of health care for patients by decreasing their chances of developing cardiovascular diseases (mainly MIs and strokes).

The US patients in this study had an average blood pressure slightly lower than the combined blood pressure average of Western Europeans. Of the 21 000 US patients with hypertension, 63% had their blood pressure under control and met the recommended blood pressure target of 140/90 mmHg. This was a significantly larger percentage than the other countries featured in the study. Furthermore, 32% of US patients with inadequately controlled hypertension received increased doses of medication, compared with only 14 to 26% of Western European patients.

1.6.3 Education, education, education

We have already listed some of the main modifiable risk factors, such as smoking and excessive alcohol consumption.

● Try to recall two other major modifiable risk factors.

● The risk factors could be diet (unhealthy or unbalanced) and inactivity. Look back at Table 1.2 for a full list.

There are current awareness campaigns in mainly developed countries, originating from many quarters, ranging from the government to health charities as well as via celebrity chefs, which try to improve the food that children and young people eat. In parallel, there are efforts to engage younger people in more physical activity. Both of these initiatives aim to avoid future health problems, whether they are cardiovascular and/or related to obesity. Both help practically by improving current health and by educating children to opt for healthier diets and lifestyles as they grow.

1.6.4 Obesity and cardiovascular diseases

Obesity and being overweight are well-known as risk factors for cardiovascular diseases. Carrying excess body fat predisposes individuals to developing elevated blood cholesterol and diabetes (see Section 4.12). You will begin to appreciate that many of the modifiable risk factors for cardiovascular diseases are interlinked. This means that influencing one, such as reducing the amount of stored lipids in the body, may have a positive effect in reducing the risk associated with high blood cholesterol levels and hypertension.

Obesity is an issue that increasingly needs to be addressed in developing countries, as well as in the developed or 'Westernised' world. Type 2 diabetes used to be described as a mainly adult disease, but that is changing as the incidence of obesity is increasing in young people, including children (see Figure 1.9 for England). This trend extends across the globe – even in countries such as Thailand and China, home to traditionally slender people. While awareness of the problem is growing, there is very limited guidance on what can be done to reverse or stem the problem.

Measures of adiposity

The amount of lipid stored within the body – an individual's adiposity – can be indirectly measured. Body shape (e.g. 'apple' or 'pear' shapes), waist-to-hip ratio, waist circumference and body mass index (BMI; see Box 4.8) are all used to classify obesity and being overweight, although BMI is the most common.

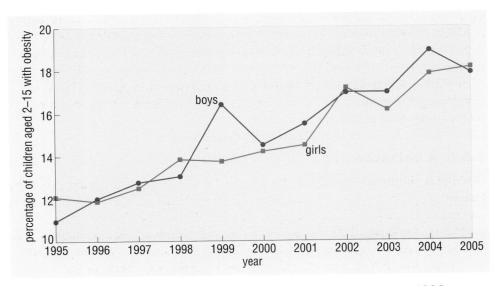

Figure 1.9   The increase in obesity in children in England between 1995 and 2005.

Everyone should aim to have a body weight within the normal range for their height. In Chapter 4 – and later in Chapter 10 – we look at the BMI and weight management. Slightly different ranges apply between populations due to different body shapes. It is worth noting that there is increasing scientific evidence that excess abdominal adiposity may be more associated with cardiovascular disease risk than the general degree of adiposity throughout the body (Iacobellis and Sharma, 2007). Thus where the lipid is stored within the body may have more bearing on cardiovascular disease risk than how much lipid is stored. Some scientists and clinicians are now suggesting that the waist-to-hip ratio or the waist circumference should be used in conjunction with BMI when considering cardiovascular disease risk factors.

In general, people who are overweight need to reduce their calorie intake in a balanced way and to increase the amount of exercise that they take in order to burn up calories. Moderate physical activity is generally considered to be 30 minutes of activity per day, e.g. taking a brisk walk. Exercise in itself improves blood glucose control, even when no weight changes are occurring, so it is equally important for people who are not overweight to take regular moderate exercise to maintain cardiovascular health.

1.6.5 What can individuals do?

Whatever age they are, men, women and children can all do something to try to prevent future cardiovascular diseases in themselves or their families by eating a balanced diet (see Section 1.6.6), taking more exercise and modifying their lifestyles to reduce any other known risk factors (see Chapters 3 and 4). If cardiovascular diseases are pre-existing, there are still numerous areas in which improvements can be made; Chapter 10 deals with these in detail, including through case studies.

In most people, hypertension is not associated with any symptoms, although a small proportion of patients will experience symptoms such as headaches, blurry vision, or shortness of breath. The only way to be sure that your blood pressure is within normal limits is to have it regularly measured by your doctor or nurse. In between visits to your health care provider, you can also monitor your blood pressure at home with a calibrated sphygmomanometer (see Section 2.7 and Figure 2.12). At the same time, everyone can help to prevent themselves from developing hypertension by eating a healthy diet (see Chapter 10) and getting plenty of physical activity or exercise.

1.6.6 A balanced diet

Our diet is simply what we eat and drink. Diet does not mean that we are trying to lose weight, although sometimes this is necessary. What we eat is very important, particularly in people with diabetes (as you found out in Section 1.5). Our wellbeing is influenced by whether or not we eat a balanced diet. A balanced diet (see Section 3.14) is one in which all the food groups are eaten in the quantities and proportions required by an individual to maintain health and normal body weight, given their level of activity. A low-fat diet and a good source of antioxidants are often recommended for individuals with cardiovascular diseases. It is advised that all people with cardiovascular diseases should see a dietician to discuss their dietary needs. The recommended balanced diet should be based on the principles of a healthy diet that anyone could eat, and these recommendations are covered in Chapter 10.

1.6.7 Special circumstances?

Individuals can only attempt to alter risk factors they are aware of and need to be informed about what is relevant to them. Women and men have different considerations, and ethnic background can also have an influence on susceptibility to cardiovascular diseases. Such considerations require improved awareness based on reliable knowledge from scientific studies (see Box 1.5 on B vitamins). In Section 3.2 you will find out more about how women have extra protection from cardiovascular diseases during their reproductive years, due to their higher concentrations of the **hormone** oestrogen. (A hormone is a chemical messenger that travels via the blood.) However, this 'protection' may give women and their doctors less reason to suspect cardiovascular diseases and their gradual development may go unnoticed. Cardiovascular diseases remain the main cause of death in women in all European countries (Petersen et al., 2006), the USA (American Heart Association, 2006) and in many other countries. Even simply the awareness of cardiovascular disease risk has been found to be lower in black and Hispanic women compared with white women (around 30%, compared with nearly 70%) with more than 50% of all respondents (average age of 50) confused about how to embark on cardiovascular disease prevention strategies (Christian et al., 2007).

Box 1.5 To supplement with B vitamins or not to supplement with B vitamins?

Some women take **antioxidant** dietary supplements because initial studies suggested they would lower the risk of developing a serious cardiovascular disease. A large medical study – the Women's Antioxidant and Cardiovascular Study (WACS) – is underway in the USA and it is designed to investigate whether the vitamins B_6, B_{12}, C and E, folic acid and beta-carotene reduce the risk of cardiovascular disease episodes specifically in women. The researchers have recruited nearly 5500 female health professionals throughout the country who are over 40 years old and have either an existing cardiovascular disease or a minimum of three cardiovascular disease risk factors. Seven years into the study, the investigators have found no differences between women receiving supplements and women taking a **placebo** (a 'dummy pill' with no active ingredient) in terms of the cardiovascular disease events that had been experienced during that time period: 15% for both groups. This study is the fourth large investigation that has found no benefit of taking B vitamins and folic acid to specifically avoid cardiovascular diseases in women and their use is not now recommended for this purpose alone.

Ethnicity is important in terms of health care because patterns of cardiovascular disease risk factors vary by ethnic group. In some situations, this is also complicated by socioeconomic status. In some cases, moving to live in different countries – from rural China to urban USA, for example – dramatically alters disease and cardiovascular disease risk. In contrast, South Asian people from the Indian subcontinent or East Africa have higher incidences of coronary heart disease regardless of whether or not they are indigenous to the area (Lip et al., 2007). African-American people have higher incidences of stroke – but, somewhat surprisingly, lower rates of coronary artery disease – in families with a number of members with diabetes (Freedman et al., 2005). These examples highlight the need for further extensive studies on cardiovascular disease risk factors in individuals from different ethnic backgrounds and localities. In Chapter 3 you will be calculating risk factors for various individuals using the ETHRISK calculator that takes into account known ethnic differences for cardiovascular diseases.

1.7 Early warning signs

Many people are familiar with chest pain as an early warning sign of an impending heart attack (see Figure 1.10). However, chest pain can also be a symptom of something completely unrelated to cardiovascular diseases. As well as chest pain, there are other equally important symptoms of cardiovascular diseases. The early warning signs that may lead a doctor to refer a patient to a hospital cardiology centre (**cardiology** is the medical study of the heart) include pain, weakness, fatigue, breathlessness, oedema (especially in the ankles or legs) and arrhythmia.

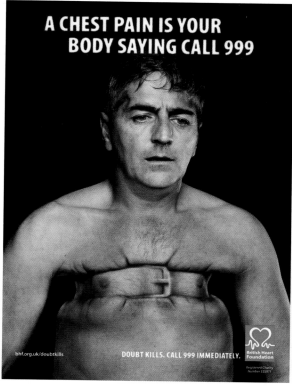

Figure 1.10   Graphic advertising campaigns are used to try to get the important messages about cardiovascular diseases across to the general public. In the UK, 999 is the main telephone number for contacting the emergency services; the EU standard 112 can also be used.

Activity 1.6   Finding out about chest pain and its causes

Suggested study time 25 minutes

Read the article 'Chest Pain' by Cohn and Cohn (2002), available on the course website.

Create a list of all the causes of chest pain that are mentioned in this article. Add any others that you may be aware of. Highlight all the terms you are not familiar with and then look them up using other resources you have already made use of in this chapter – for example, the glossary and the Multi-ed Cardiology program.

Some symptoms are common to several cardiovascular diseases – these include developing hypertension and early atherosclerosis which may not result in any early or obvious signs. While we are mainly concerned with the blood vessels supplying the heart in this course, atherosclerosis can develop in almost all major arteries, leading to the formation of blood clots, the whole process being called atherothrombosis. In the brain, this can lead to strokes, and in the arms and legs it is known as peripheral arterial disease. This will be covered in more detail in Section 5.5.1.

Cholesterol is an important component of cell membranes, and although the body can make its own, much of our cholesterol is obtained from the modern diet. A high cholesterol level in the blood is a major risk factor for the development of atherosclerosis and eventually coronary heart disease. Two types of cholesterol measurements are routinely taken: LDL and HDL (refer back to Box 1.3). You may come across these described in the popular media as 'bad' (LDL) cholesterol and 'good' (HDL) cholesterol. Too much LDL cholesterol or too little HDL cholesterol are warning signs for developing cardiovascular diseases – see Table 1.4 for the reference levels of cholesterol in the blood. (The limits vary slightly between countries.)

The unit 'mmol/l' (millimoles per litre) here refers to the amount of substance – counted out as numbers of molecules or particles – in a given volume of blood. The unit 'mg/dl' (milligrams per decilitre) is used less frequently in this context and refers to the mass of substance – commonly referred to as weight – in a given volume of blood.

It is worth pointing out here to avoid confusion that there is only one type of cholesterol, but it can be transported by combining with proteins in a number of

Table 1.4 Reference levels of cholesterol in the blood: figures from the UK, Europe and USA. (<, less than; >, more than.)

Type	UK (mmol/l)	Europe (mmol/l)	USA (mmol/l)	Level
total cholesterol	<5.2	<5.0	<6.2 (240 mg/dl)	ideal
	5.2 to 6.2			borderline
	>6.2			high risk
LDL cholesterol	<3.4	<3.0	<3.8 (160 mg/dl)	ideal
	3.4 to 4.1			borderline
	4.2 to 4.8			high risk
	>4.9			very high risk
HDL cholesterol	>1.6	>1.0 (men) >1.2 (women)	>1.0 (40 mg/dl)	ideal
	<0.9			some risk
triglycerides (fasting)	<1.7	<1.7	<2.3 (200 mg/dl)	

different ways, e.g. via HDL, LDL and other lipoprotein complexes. In general practice, doctors can use the ratio (fraction) of a patient's total cholesterol to HDL cholesterol ratio (TC : HDL) and the 'Sheffield table' (based on the Framingham risk assessment method covered in Chapter 3) to estimate cardiovascular disease risk for primary prevention (Wallis et al., 2000). Its use is not appropriate for secondary prevention – that is, in people with established cardiovascular diseases such as MI and angina.

● Which type of cholesterol-carrying lipoprotein complex contains the most cholesterol and transports it around the body: LDL or HDL?

● LDL carries more cholesterol. (Refer back to Box 1.3 if you weren't sure.)

1.8 When things go wrong

Despite efforts to avoid them, heart disease, heart failure and heart attacks do occur – sometimes with warning symptoms and sometimes without. In Chapter 6, you will find out about different conditions leading to heart disease and the tests that are then used by cardiologists (doctors specialising in the heart) to determine the cause and guide the subsequent treatment. Special tests that are carried out in cardiology departments may include blood pressure measurements, blood tests, electrocardiography, angiography, echocardiography and nuclear imaging – all of which will be covered in later chapters.

Less than a century ago, little could be done to treat high blood pressure and other cardiovascular diseases. Today, medical and surgical interventions are available to reduce damage and disability as well as delay death. Once under the care of the cardiologist in the hospital setting or discharged to the care of a family medical practitioner, the cardiac patient will receive treatment according to established protocols which you will learn about in Chapters 8 and 9.

Outside the medical setting, first aid for acute heart conditions can be life-saving and it is useful for everyone to be aware of the current guidelines.

1.8.1 Cardiopulmonary resuscitation (CPR)

The immediate treatment given when the heart stops beating is **cardiopulmonary resuscitation (CPR)**. (**Pulmonary** refers to the lungs.) Outside the hospital setting, first aid is required in the first instance. It is important to keep the heart beating artificially by CPR to circulate oxygenated blood to the brain, otherwise irreversible brain damage can be caused within minutes.

The Red Cross, an international charity, publishes the commonly adopted first aid guidelines and these have recently been revised (see Figure 1.11). They do occasionally make adjustments to them, so it is important to try to keep your knowledge current by visiting their website (British Red Cross, 2007) or refreshing any first aid qualifications you have every few years.

Figure 1.11 The current (2007) first aid guidelines recommended by the British Red Cross, available from their website.

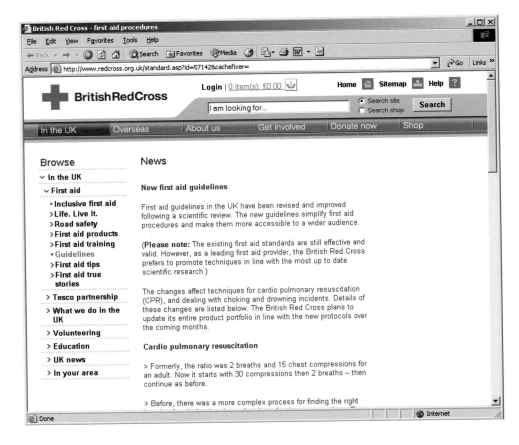

1.9 Immediate treatment of cardiovascular diseases

Treatment obviously depends on the severity of cardiovascular diseases at presentation and any safety considerations. Medications (pharmaceutical drugs) are available to treat many of the symptoms and slow the progression of cardiovascular diseases. Some are used for specific purposes, whereas others are useful for a range of cardiovascular diseases, details of which are given in Chapter 8. In certain circumstances, individuals may not be able to take one type of medication and will be prescribed something else to serve the same function. The type of treatment will certainly depend on where in the world the patient is taken ill, due to availability and costs (see Figure 1.12).

Immediate treatment following an MI is required to minimise further damage to the heart cells and restore blood circulation. As soon as possible, drugs to prevent blood clotting are administered, as long as there are no medical reasons contravening this. After further assessment, other treatments may be required. Many effective surgical devices have been developed to treat cardiovascular disease complications and are now in routine use, including:

- pacemakers (to artificially maintain the heart's rhythm)

- implantable defibrillators (to restart the heart)

- coronary angioplasty followed by placement of stents (to widen blocked vessels)

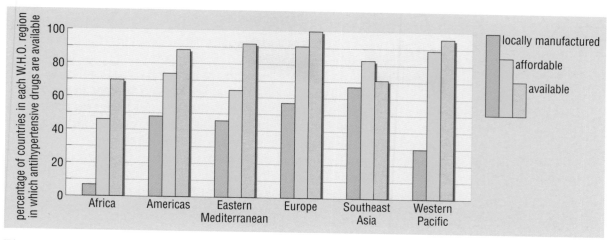

Figure 1.12   The availability and/or affordability of antihypertensive medications in different regions of the world (WHO data; Mackay and Mensah, 2004).

- prosthetic heart valves (to replace faulty or diseased valves)
- patches to mend holes or tears in the heart muscle, and other interventions that are covered in Chapter 9.

Technological advances also mean that many of these procedures are being used and further developed so that they involve only minor surgery, leading to safer outcomes for patients. More invasive but often life-saving and life-enhancing operations that are also carried out include coronary artery bypass and – as a last resort – artificial hearts and heart transplantation, again covered in Chapter 9. The development and use of such impressive surgical advances reduce disability and death from cardiovascular disease complications and improve the quality of life for patients, but they do incur higher health care costs.

Despite such encouraging advances in cardiovascular disease treatment options, there are still substantial numbers of people worldwide who would benefit from treatment but are not receiving it. Whereas 1 in 2 people with high blood pressure in the USA are receiving treatment, only a quarter of those over 20 years old with blood cholesterol levels of more than 6.2 mmol/l are on cholesterol-lowering drugs (Mackay and Mensah, 2004). As you started to discover in Section 1.5, the quality of treatment received by people of different ethnicities, socioeconomic backgrounds and even gender show marked disparity. Research in these areas is ongoing, so if you are interested you can keep your knowledge current with developments via the internet or publications.

1.10 Long-term treatment, and living with cardiovascular diseases

The longer-term medical treatment of patients with identified cardiovascular diseases or significant cardiovascular disease risk factors could involve any or all of the following interventions: monitoring; medical management of risk factors; the use of medications for secondary prevention; and various stages of surgical management.

1.10.1 Secondary prevention using drugs

Extensive research has been carried out into the use of drugs to help limit damage and minimise deterioration of an established heart or circulatory condition. The use of four main drug categories together reduces the risk of an MI, a stroke or cardiovascular disease death over the next 2 years by 75% in patients with previous coronary heart disease or stroke (2002 figures from Mackay and Mensah, 2004). In Chapter 8 you will study in detail the therapeutic drugs used to treat cardiovascular diseases. Such secondary prevention of cardiovascular diseases has been formalised into a set of recommendations for doctors in the UK by the National Institute for Health and Clinical Excellence (NICE). This is an independent organisation responsible for providing national guidance on promoting good health and preventing and treating ill health in the population.

NICE produces guidance in three areas of health (public health, health technologies and clinical practice) through centres of excellence. The Centre for Clinical Practice develops the clinical guidelines or recommendations, based on the best available scientific evidence, on the appropriate treatment and care of people with specific diseases and conditions, such as hypertension, chronic heart failure and diabetes. To look at one in more detail, read the following summary on the treatment of high blood pressure and then work through the flowchart in Figure 1.13.

The NICE clinical guideline on hypertension (National Institute for Health and Clinical Excellence, 2007) covers:

- how doctors should find out whether someone has high blood pressure
- how doctors should assess someone's risk of developing problems with their heart or blood vessels, such as a heart attack or stroke
- how lifestyle factors such as smoking, diet and exercise can affect blood pressure
- the use of medicines to lower blood pressure
- how high blood pressure should be monitored.

These recommendations apply to primary care – treatment by a GP or practice nurse. They do not apply to hospital care. This guideline does not look at screening for hypertension (routine checking of blood pressure in healthy people to detect early disease), hypertension during pregnancy or the specialist management of secondary hypertension (where the high blood pressure is happening because of another medical problem).

1.10.2 Issues with medications

Most pharmaceutical drugs will have side effects – unwanted and sometimes unexpected effects, in addition to the medical benefits expected with the drug's use (see Chapter 8). All prescription drugs are accompanied by an information sheet outlining possible side effects. Such unwanted effects can cause problems with patient compliance: despite being prescribed certain

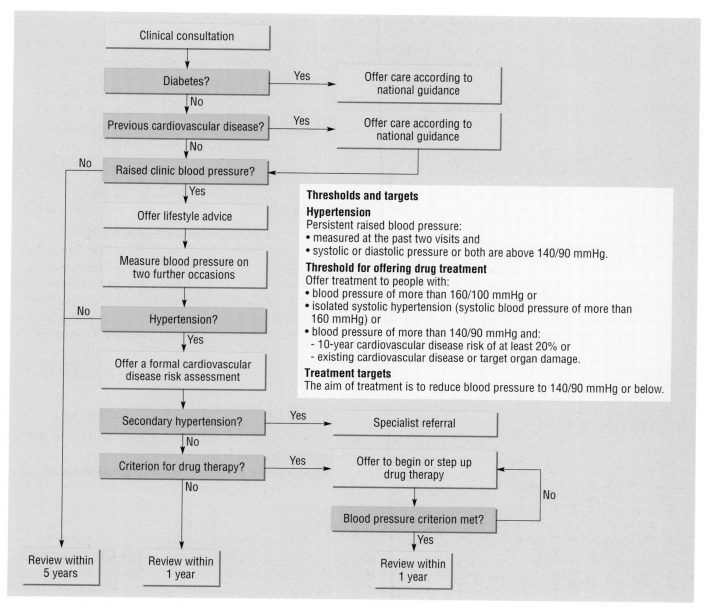

Thresholds and targets

Hypertension
Persistent raised blood pressure:
• measured at the past two visits and
• systolic or diastolic pressure or both are above 140/90 mmHg.

Threshold for offering drug treatment
Offer treatment to people with:
• blood pressure of more than 160/100 mmHg or
• isolated systolic hypertension (systolic blood pressure of more than 160 mmHg) or
• blood pressure of more than 140/90 mmHg and:
  - 10-year cardiovascular disease risk of at least 20% or
  - existing cardiovascular disease or target organ damage.

Treatment targets
The aim of treatment is to reduce blood pressure to 140/90 mmHg or below.

Figure 1.13   Clinical guidelines or recommendations by NICE, based on the best available scientific evidence, on the appropriate treatment of individuals with hypertension.

drugs or drug combinations, patients will either not take their drugs or not take them in accordance with the suggested schedule. Sometimes the lack of patient compliance may simply be an issue of the patient forgetting to take their medication.

> 'For [the cholesterol-lowering drug] simvastatin, the evidence is that marginally better lowering of total and LDL cholesterol comes from taking the tablets in the evening than in the morning.'

However,

> 'There is an inverse relationship between patient compliance and both number of drugs and number of doses per day, and there can be further loss in compliance when medication regimens are changed. What is really important is that the patient takes the drug reliably, and if that is easier with morning dosing, the extra 10 to 13% reduction in LDL-cholesterol potentially achieved with evening dosing is probably worth foregoing. An evening dose is more easily forgotten.'

> (Bandolier, 2005)

1.10.3 When surgery is required

For some cardiovascular disease patients, surgery may be carried out as an emergency procedure or become an inevitable progression, following on from drug therapy (Chapter 8). There are various degrees of surgery carried out, ranging from the fairly routine and minorly invasive procedure of coronary angioplasty to the major life-saving heart (or heart and lung) transplant. Various procedures will be described in detail in Chapter 9 and the involvement of the medical specialists required will be outlined. While it is important to understand all of the detail of surgical procedures and how the cardiac surgical team work together, it is also equally important to consider surgery from the position of the cardiovascular disease patient.

For some individuals, simply having a blood sample taken is a stressful procedure, so the psychological as well as the physiological effects of any minor or major surgical procedures need to be considered. In addition, how a patient recovers and embraces the required lifestyle management and complies with further ongoing drug therapy can be influenced by psychosocial factors. Psychologists have found from studies of patients recovering from MI that depressed patients were 3 times more likely to die within a year than those who were not depressed, unrelated to the initial severity of their disease (Frasure-Smith et al., 1999). The same authors published another study showing that depressed patients who thought that they did not get enough support at home had the highest death rates. From a more positive angle, researchers on the Recurrent Coronary Prevention Project, which randomly allocated over 1000 MI patients to receive either routine medical care or the same care with additional counselling about risk factors or group therapy with behaviour modification, found a 44% reduction in the incidence of second MIs in the latter group (Friedman, 1989).

> 'By choice or default, physicians, nurses and allied health professionals are the ones who need to take responsibility for systematically and effectively addressing patients' psychosocial needs… There aren't enough psychologists who are trained in the ins and outs of life with cardiovascular illness. It's a huge area of unmet need.'

> (Wayne Sotile, Wake Forest University Cardiac Rehabilitation Program; quoted in Clay, 2001)

While this quotation is just an opinion, it nevertheless makes an important point. It emphasises that health care professionals can provide support and advice on recovery and coping skills that are beneficial to cardiovascular disease patients, in addition to standard medical care.

Following successful surgery, it remains essential to control the symptoms and further development of cardiovascular diseases, all of which will be covered in Chapter 10.

1.10.4 How things change

Despite the advances made in cardiac care over the previous century, it is thought that the global epidemic of cardiovascular diseases is both increasing (see Table 1.5) and shifting from developed to developing countries (Mackay and Mensah, 2004). While treatments are available for some cardiovascular disease patients, prevention must remain a priority through the reduction of known risk factors. Whether or not people have already been diagnosed with cardiovascular diseases, taking account of the risk factors and minimising them where possible should result in positive changes and improved health in individuals and their families.

Table 1.5 Predictions of global cardiovascular disease deaths in the early twenty-first century.

CVD/CHD deaths	2010	2020	2030
annual number of CVD deaths	18.1 million	20.5 million	24.2 million
CVD deaths as a percentage of all deaths	30.8%	31.5%	32.5%
CHD deaths as a percentage of all deaths of men	13.1%	14.3%	14.9%
CHD deaths as a percentage of all deaths of women	13.6%	13.0%	13.1%

1.11 Summary of Chapter 1

By the time you reach the end of this course you will be very familiar with cardiovascular diseases, their development and their diagnosis. You will also know their treatment and many of the cardiovascular disease risk factors – what they are and how they can be influenced positively to minimise cardiovascular diseases. You will understand the overall importance of a balanced diet, regular exercise and weight management (guided by adiposity measurements) throughout life, to maintain cardiac and vascular health. You will also be able to explain the negative effect of behaviours such as smoking and drinking too much alcohol. You should have an appreciation of the 'bigger picture' and see how all these factors combine to influence our cardiovascular health that in itself will affect our relationships and our daily lives, at home and at work.

Questions for Chapter 1

Question 1.1 (Learning Outcomes 1.4 and 1.5)

Referring to Figure 1.6, state how many people per 10 000 of the North American population had heart attacks in (i) 1990; (ii) 1995; (iii) 2000. Make sure that you are reading from the correct y-axis (labelled 'heart attacks per 10 000 population').

Question 1.2 (Learning Outcome 1.3)

Name two distinct areas of the body that may be affected by the deposit of fatty plaques in the blood vessels.

Question 1.3 (Learning Outcome 1.6)

What factors increase the risk of someone developing cardiovascular diseases?

Question 1.4 (Learning Outcome 1.6)

Produce a table of risk factors for cardiovascular diseases (using your answers to Question 1.3), separating them into three columns of modifiable (biological and lifestyle) and non-modifiable (biological) risk factors. Explain your reasoning for which category you have placed the risk factor diabetes.

Place a tick alongside any risk factors that you have identified as being relevant to yourself or someone else you know. Suggest what measures you can take to positively influence any modifiable risk factors.

Question 1.5 (Learning Outcomes 1.1 and 1.3)

List three different causes of chest pain.

Question 1.6 (Learning Outcomes 1.2 and 1.6)

Distinguish between primary and secondary prevention strategies for developing cardiovascular diseases. Suggest why this distinction is important in relation to cardiovascular disease treatment.

Question 1.7 (Learning Outcome 1.6)

Explain why preventive measures (i.e. reduction of risk factors) are still required following any surgical treatment for cardiovascular diseases.

Question 1.8 (Learning Outcomes 1.2, 1.3 and 1.6)

Explain why monitoring blood pressure and blood cholesterol levels are important in the management of cardiovascular diseases.

References

American Heart Association (2006) 'Heart disease and stroke statistics – 2006 update: A report from the American Heart Association Statistics Committee and Stroke Statistics Subcommittee', *Circulation*, **113**, pp. e85–e151.

Bandolier (2005) *Statins: when should you take the tablet?* [online] Available from: http://www.jr2.ox.ac.uk/bandolier/booth/cardiac/stattime.html (Accessed April 2007).

British Red Cross (2007) *First aid guidelines in the UK* [online] Available from: http://www.redcross.org.uk/standard.asp?id=57142&cachefixer= (Accessed April 2007).

Cardiac Risk in the Young (2003) *When a young person dies suddenly* [online] Available from: http://www.sads.org.uk (Accessed April 2007).

Christian, A. H., Rosamund, W., White, A. R. and Mosca, L. (2007) 'Nine-year trends and racial and ethnic disparities in women's awareness of heart disease and stroke: an American Heart Association national study', *Journal of Women's Health*, **16**, pp. 68–81.

Clay, R. A. (2001) *Research to the heart of the matter* [online] Available from: http://www.apa.org/monitor/jan01/coverheart.html (Accessed April 2007).

Department of Health (2000) *National Service Framework for coronary heart disease*, Chapter 4 [online] Available from: http://www.dh.gov.uk/en/Publicationsandstatistics/Publications/PublicationsPolicyAndGuidance/DH_4094275 (Accessed May 2007).

Department of Health (2007) *The coronary heart disease National Service Framework: shaping the future: progress report 2006* [online] Available from: http://www.dh.gov.uk/en/Publicationsandstatistics/Publications/PublicationsPolicyAndGuidance/DH_063168 (Accessed April 2007).

Evans, N. (2004) 'Managing the cost of cardiovascular prevention in primary care', *Heart*, **90**, suppl. IV, pp. iv26–iv28.

Frasure-Smith, N., Lesperance, F., Juneau, M., Talajic, M. and Bourassa, M. G. (1999) 'Gender, depression, and one-year prognosis after myocardial infarction', *Psychosomatic Medicine*, **61**, pp. 26–37.

Freedman, B. I., Hsu, F. C., Langefeld, C. D., Rich, S. S., Herrington, D. M., Carr, J. J., Xu, J., Bowden, D. W. and Wagenknecht, L. E. (2005) 'The impact of ethnicity and sex on subclinical cardiovascular disease: the Diabetes Heart Study', *Diabetologia*, **48**, pp. 2511–2518.

Friedman, M. (1989), 'Type A behavior: its diagnosis, cardiovascular relation and the effect of its modification on recurrence of coronary artery disease', *American Journal of Cardiology*, **64** (6), pp. 12C–19C.

Iacobellis, G. and Sharma, A. M. (2007) 'Obesity and the heart: redefinition of the relationship', *Obesity Reviews*, **8**, pp. 35–39.

Lip, G. Y. H., Barnett, A. H., Bradbury, A., Cappuccio, F. P., Gill, P. S., Hughes, E., Imray, C., Jolly, K. and Patel, K. (2007) 'Ethnicity and cardiovascular disease prevention in the United Kingdom: a practical approach to management', *Journal of Hypertension*, **21**, pp. 183–211.

Mackay, J. and Mensah, G. (eds) (2004) *The Atlas of Heart Disease and Stroke*, Geneva, World Health Organization.

The National Assembly for Wales (2001) *Tackling coronary heart disease in Wales: implementing through evidence* [online] Available from: http://www.wales.nhs.uk/publications/coronary-heart-disease-e.pdf (Accessed June 2007).

National Center for Biotechnology Information (2007) *PubMed* [online] Available from: http://www.ncbi.nlm.nih.gov/entrez/query.fcgi (Accessed April 2007).

National Institute for Health and Clinical Excellence (2007) *Hypertension: management of hypertension in adults in primary care* [online] Available from: http://www.nice.org.uk/guidance/CG34#summary (Accessed April 2007).

Petersen, S., Peto, V., Rayner, M., Leal, J., Luengo-Fernandez, R. and Gray, A. (2006) *European cardiovascular disease statistics*, London, British Heart Foundation.

Swanton, K. and Frost, M. (2007) *Lightening the Load: Tackling Overweight and Obesity*, London, National Heart Forum.

Unal, B., Critchley, J. A. and Capewell, S. (2004) 'Explaining the decline in coronary heart disease mortality in England and Wales between 1981 and 2000', *Circulation*, **109**, pp. 101–107.

Wallis, E. J., Ramsay, L. E., Ul Haq, I., Ghahramani, P., Jackson, P. R., Rowland-Yeo, K. and Yeo, W. W. (2000) 'Coronary and cardiovascular risk estimation for primary prevention: validation of a new Sheffield table in the 1995 Scottish health survey population', *British Medical Journal*, **320**, pp. 671–676.

Wang, Y. R., Alexander, G. C. and Stafford, R. S. (2007) 'Outpatient hypertension treatment, treatment intensification, and control in Western Europe and the United States', *Archives of Internal Medicine*, **167**, pp. 141–147.

World Health Organization (2006) *World data tables* [online] Available from: http://www.who.int/cardiovascular_diseases/en/cvd_atlas_29_world_data_table.pdf (Accessed April 2007).

CHAPTER 2

A GUIDE TO THE CARDIOVASCULAR SYSTEM

Learning Outcomes

When you have completed this chapter you should be able to:

2.1 Define and use, or recognise definitions and applications of, each of the terms printed in **bold** in the text.

2.2 Describe and illustrate the basic anatomical components of the heart.

2.3 Explain the series of mechanical and electrical events that give rise to a heart beat.

2.4 Explain the physiological mechanisms that regulate cardiac output and blood pressure.

2.5 Describe how blood pressure is measured and relate systolic and diastolic values to the pumping action of the heart.

2.1 Introduction

The central player in this course and the focus of this chapter is the heart. The aim of this chapter is to provide you with a basic toolkit that will allow you to navigate and to understand the anatomical and physiological processes that regulate a healthy heart.

The heart beating in your chest is about the size of a closed fist and weighs between 250 and 350 g – less than a standard jar of strawberry jam! The modest size and weight of a human heart belies its incredible strength and endurance. The heart of a person aged 72 will have already beaten approximately 2500 million times. The relentless beating heart has fascinated people for centuries. The ancient Greeks believed the heart was the seat of intelligence. Others thought it was a source of emotions. Of course, such fancies are no longer believed, but as will be shown later, emotions can affect our hearts.

While reading this chapter, bear in mind that the heart does not work alone. It is part of the cardiovascular system, a network that includes miles of blood vessels (described in more detail in Chapter 5). Day and night, the tissues of the body take in nutrients and oxygen and excrete wastes. Because the cells that make up our tissues can only exchange these molecules over a short distance, some means of changing and renewing the local tissue environment is necessary. The blood is the agent of change, the source of new nutrients and a fresh supply of oxygen, and the vehicle for removing wastes. The cardiovascular system provides the transport infrastructure that keeps the blood continuously flowing, to maintain the conditions essential for life.

The heart is the powerhouse of the cardiovascular system, the pump that pushes blood through the blood vessels. However, before you find out more about the heart, you will first examine the blood.

2.2 The blood

The blood is considered by some to be the very essence of life itself. Long before the advent of modern medicine, blood was viewed as magical: an elixir that held the mystical force of life, because life departed when it was drained from the body. Today, centuries later, blood still has enormous importance in the practice of medicine. Clinicians examine it more often than any other tissue when trying to determine the cause of a disease or an ailment. In an adult human, blood accounts for approximately 7 to 9% of body weight. So for a person weighing 70 kg, some 5 to 6 litres of blood circulate around the body.

The blood transports nearly everything that must be carried from one place to another within the body. Every living cell needs a continuous supply of oxygen, nutrients and a means to remove waste products; performing these needs is the primary function of the blood. Blood is a fluid comprising red blood cells (**erythrocytes**; see Figure 2.1), several types of white blood cell (**leukocytes**) and **platelets**, all suspended in a yellowish or straw-coloured liquid called **plasma**. The components of blood and their diverse functions are summarised in Table 2.1.

Erythrocytes are also called red blood cells because they contain **haemoglobin**, which is red. Haemoglobin is a large protein containing four groups of a globular (spherical) protein called globin and four groups of a pigmented iron-containing complex called haem. Each haem group contains an atom of iron, and each atom of iron can combine with an oxygen molecule – so a single haemoglobin molecule can carry up to four molecules of oxygen. An average erythrocyte contains about 280 million haemoglobin molecules, giving each cell a theoretical oxygen-carrying capacity of over a billion oxygen molecules.

● What do you think is the main function of the erythrocytes?

● To transport oxygen and deliver it to the body's tissues.

It is the haemoglobin in the erythrocytes that plays a central role in delivering oxygen to the tissues of the body. When all four oxygen-binding sites are occupied by oxygen, the haemoglobin is described as being saturated. Haemoglobin in this state is called **oxyhaemoglobin** and is bright red. The association of oxygen with haemoglobin is a loose one and oxyhaemoglobin releases its cargo of oxygen readily,

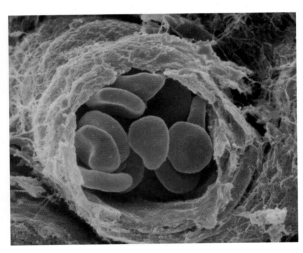

Figure 2.1 False-colour scanning electron micrograph of a group of red blood cells (erythrocytes). They are travelling through an arteriole, which is a small branch of an artery. In a litre of blood, there are normally 5 trillion (5 million million) red blood cells. Each erythrocyte is about 7 μm (7 millionths of a metre) in diameter.

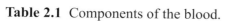
Table 2.1 Components of the blood.

Constituent	Description and function
Cellular components	
erythrocytes (men have 4.5–6.5 million per ml of blood; women have 3.8–5.8 million per ml of blood)	Small biconcave disc-shaped cells produced in the bone marrow. They transport oxygen and the waste product carbon dioxide.
leukocytes, also known as white blood cells (approximately 7000 per ml of blood in a healthy individual)	Involved in the immune response. Depending on the type of leukocyte, they can produce antibodies, release agents that facilitate the immune response and remove bacteria and debris by engulfing them.
platelets (approximately 250 000 per ml of blood)	Involved in blood clotting, the process that prevents the loss of blood from damaged blood vessels.
Plasma composition	
water	90–95% of the plasma is water, which maintains the normal hydration of the body. Also acts as the transport vehicle for many essential **ions** (which are charged atoms, important in many biochemical processes in the body). Involved in the transfer of heat around the body.
plasma proteins	Albumin represents about 60% of all plasma proteins and regulates the passage of water and diffusible solids through the capillary wall. Fibrinogen represents 4% of all plasma proteins, essential for blood clotting. Globulins represent 36% of plasma proteins, involved in a variety of functions including the immune response, and the transport of lipids and fat-soluble vitamins.
plasma ions (electrolytes)	Sodium (Na^+), chloride (Cl^-), potassium (K^+), calcium (Ca^{2+}), iodide (I^-), magnesium (Mg^{2+}) and phosphate (PO_4^{3-}) ions. These behave as an electrically conductive medium.
nutrients	Glucose (the sugar most widely used in the body) is a source of energy. Amino acids are required for the production of proteins. Lipids are components of cell membranes and can be used as a fuel store.
hormones	Chemical messengers released into the blood, where they are then transported to their target tissue/organs.
waste products	Metabolic waste products, including lactate and nitrogenous waste from protein metabolism (urea, the chemical that makes urine yellow) and from nucleic acids (uric acid).
gases	The main gases dissolved in plasma are: oxygen, transported by the erythrocytes with a small amount dissolved in the plasma; nitrogen, carried exclusively in the plasma; carbon dioxide, carried by erythrocytes and the plasma, both in solution and as bicarbonate ions (HCO_3^-).

especially under those conditions found in active tissue where oxygen is needed. Haemoglobin depleted in oxygen is dark red.

The readiness of haemoglobin to give up its cargo of oxygen depends on the prevailing conditions in the tissue. Active tissue tends to be warmer, produces more carbon dioxide and consumes local oxygen at a greater rate. Each of

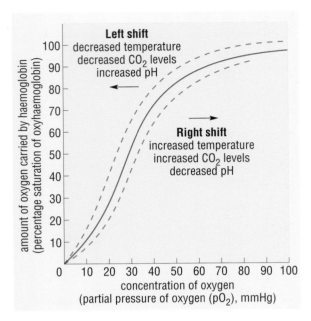

Figure 2.2 The oxygen dissociation curve for haemoglobin at 37 °C (normal body temperature). The relationship between the oxygen saturation of haemoglobin and the concentration of oxygen is affected by changes in carbon dioxide levels, temperature and pH.

these factors influences the ability of haemoglobin to release oxygen. This property is shown graphically in Figure 2.2 and is called the oxygen dissociation curve. You will notice that the amount of oxygen carried by haemoglobin (expressed here as percentage saturation) is directly related to the concentration of oxygen (expressed as the partial pressure for oxygen (pO_2), with units in mmHg); the higher the oxygen concentration, the higher the level of saturation. The 'flat top' of the curve means that very little oxygen is released from haemoglobin when the oxygen concentration is between 60 and 100 mmHg, a range which corresponds to the concentration of oxygen found in oxygenated arterial blood. However, this relationship rapidly changes as the concentration of oxygen falls. The 'steep part' of the graph illustrates an important property of haemoglobin, in that it can release large quantities of oxygen for a relatively small decrease in oxygen concentration.

The dissociation curve is sensitive to the conditions of the tissues, and is shifted to the right when carbon dioxide levels rise, the tissue temperature increases or/and the pH of the blood falls. (A falling pH means that the blood is getting more acidic.) Each of these indicates that the tissue activity has increased and therefore the tissue requires more oxygen. Shifting the curve to the right liberates more oxygen from the haemoglobin. Conversely, when carbon dioxide levels are low, the temperature falls and/or the pH rises, the oxygen dissociation curve for haemoglobin is shifted to the left, making it less likely that oxygen will be released. The level of oxygen saturation found in venous blood returning to the heart is typically about 70%.

Erythrocytes are unusual in that they do not possess a cell nucleus. Their membranes are highly flexible, an important property that allows them to deform and squeeze through even the smallest of blood vessels in the body – and, on occasion, even through vessel walls. In contrast, leukocytes, which lack haemoglobin, appear white (hence the term white blood cells) and can be divided into several discrete subpopulations.

Erythrocytes, which outnumber white blood cells by 750 : 1, have a comparatively short lifespan of about 120 days and are continuously replaced by a process called **haematopoiesis**. The production of erythrocytes is regulated by the hormone **erythropoietin**, which stimulates a population of cells in the bone marrow, called precursor cells, to produce new erythrocytes. These precursor cells are found mainly in the bone marrow of the pelvis, sternum (breastbone), vertebrae and skull. Normally, the number of erythrocytes circulating in the body is fairly constant. This is because the blood marrow produces them at the rate at which they are destroyed, a process under the control of a homeostatic **negative feedback** mechanism.

Negative feedback is a control mechanism used widely in physiological systems. You will come across several examples of this in the regulation of the cardiovascular system. It is a form of feedback control in which the system responds in an opposite direction to the perturbation. It provides a mechanism for maintaining stability and is the basis of homeostasis, the means of returning the system to its original condition. The same concept of homeostatic control by negative feedback is used in all modern central heating systems. The temperature is set and regulated by the thermostat, a device that measures temperature. In most homes, the thermostat is set at 21 °C. When the temperature falls below this level, the thermostat detects the decrease and sends a signal to the boiler to heat water and pump it throughout the house, where the radiators heat the rooms. The heating of the house will eventually raise the temperature to 21 °C. When the temperature exceeds this set level, the thermostat then sends another signal to the boiler and pump to stop heating. This is an example where temperature, using negative feedback, regulates its own temperature range.

The hormone erythropoietin is made mainly by cells in the kidney, where it is secreted into the bloodstream and transported to the bone marrow. The erythropoietin-producing cells are sensitive to the oxygen-carrying capacity of the blood and secrete erythropoietin when the oxygen content of the blood falls. As more erythrocytes enter the circulation, the increase in oxygen-carrying capacity is detected by the erythropoietin-producing cells; consequently, these cells reduce their secretion of erythropoietin. Here, the oxygen concentration of the blood has a negative feedback effect on the production of erythropoietin.

● People often donate blood to the blood transfusion service. What do you think happens to circulating levels of erythropoietin after a donation of blood?

● The removal of blood from the circulation reduces the total number of circulating erythrocytes and thereby reduces the oxygen-carrying capacity of the blood. The erythropoietin-producing cells respond by increasing their secretion of erythropoietin, increasing the levels of this hormone circulating in the blood.

Each erythrocyte will travel a distance of about 1200 km before being removed from the circulation. This process is called haemolysis and is carried out by phagocytic ('cell-eating') cells specialised for this purpose. These phagocytic cells are found mainly in the spleen, bone marrow and liver.

Red and white blood cells, as well as platelets (about which you will learn more in Chapter 5), can be separated from the plasma by centrifuging a blood sample (spinning at high speed) in a small test tube. This compacts the erythrocytes at the bottom of the test tube. By measuring the height of the column of compacted erythrocytes relative to the total height of the column of spun blood, the volume percentage occupied by the packed erythrocytes can be determined; this is called the **haematocrit**. The normal haematocrit is about 45%.

● Athletes have been known to 'cheat' by injecting themselves with erythropoietin. How might this alter the haematocrit of such an individual?

● Erythropoietin boosts the production of red blood cells, increasing the quantities circulating in the blood and resulting in a higher haematocrit.

● How might an increase in the number of erythrocytes alter the properties of the blood?

● Erythrocytes contain haemoglobin, the protein involved in the transport of oxygen. An increase in the number of erythrocytes will increase the ability of the blood to deliver oxygen to active muscles and other organs (hence improving performance). The viscosity of the blood is also increased, and this is potentially harmful.

Activity 2.1   Blood composition

Suggested study time 15 minutes

Use the Multi-ed Cardiology program, introduced in Chapter 1, to test your understanding of Section 2.2 by reviewing the section on the blood.

The two animations to watch, 'The blood' and 'The blood circulation', can be found by navigating to Animations | Condition | Anatomy. The second of these animations also contains information which will aid your understanding of the next section of this chapter.

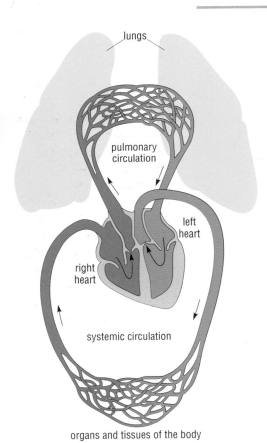

Figure 2.3   Simple schematic diagram showing the parallel circulation to the lungs (the pulmonary circulation) and the rest of the body (the systemic circulation).

2.3 The heart: structure and blood flow

As mentioned in the introduction to this chapter, the heart is the powerhouse of the cardiovascular system, the pump that drives blood through the network of blood vessels. In fact, the heart consists of two pumps that serve two parallel cardiovascular circuits: one that serves the lungs and another that serves the rest of the body (see Figure 2.3).

The heart is a large four-chambered muscular bag, sitting at an angle in the ribcage. In order to appreciate how the heart works, remind yourself of the primary function of the cardiovascular system: to deliver oxygen and nutrients and to remove carbon dioxide and other waste products. During inspiration (breathing in), the lungs are filled with air, of which roughly 21% is oxygen. To collect this inspired oxygen, the blood has to be pumped around the lungs by the heart. Oxygenated blood from the lungs, which is bright red because oxygen has bound to the haemoglobin, returns to the heart and is then pumped around the body to supply the tissues. Blood returning from the body to the heart is rich in waste products such as carbon dioxide and is depleted of oxygen. This oxygen-depleted blood (dark red in colour) is termed deoxygenated blood and is pumped through the lungs to release carbon dioxide and, of course, to collect more oxygen. The design of the heart and associated blood vessels ensures that blood going to the lungs is kept separate from that going around the body.

● Why do you think the separation of oxygenated blood from the deoxygenated blood is important?

● To maintain an adequate supply of oxygen to the tissues of the body, it is essential not to mix the oxygenated blood with the deoxygenated blood. If they were allowed to mix, then the efficiency with which oxygen can be collected from the lungs would be reduced, compromising the ability of the heart to deliver sufficient oxygen to the rest of the body.

The heart prevents the mixing of oxygenated blood with deoxygenated blood by using two separate but parallel circuits of blood vessels: the **pulmonary circulation** and the **systemic circulation**. Because of its four-chamber design, the heart can serve both circuits at once, using its two pumps to simultaneously push blood from one circuit through one half of its structure and blood from the other circuit through its other half.

The musculature of a heart is called the **myocardium** ('myo-' means 'muscle'; '-cardium' means 'of the heart'). As you can see in Figure 2.4, the left and right sides of the heart are separated by a muscular wall (called the **septum**), and each side is divided into a small chamber, the **atrium** (plural atria), and a larger chamber, the **ventricle** (plural ventricles). The atria are connected to the ventricles via a valve that ensures a one-way flow of blood. Deoxygenated blood returns from the body through two main 'great' veins, the **inferior** and **superior vena cava** (plural venae cavae; shown in Figures 2.4 and 2.5). These veins drain into the right atrium,

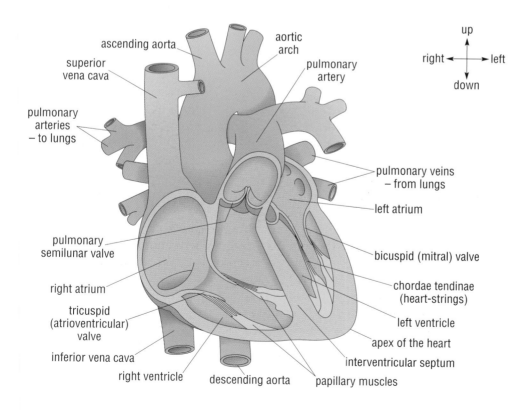

Figure 2.4   Gross anatomy of the human heart. The heart is shown in cross-section, illustrating the position of the atria, ventricles and major veins and arteries. Note that the outer muscle wall of the left ventricle is thicker than that of the right ventricle, and that the heart shown here is rotated so that the relative sizes of the chambers are reversed.

a thin-walled chamber that expands with little resistance as the blood enters. Blood from the right atrium flows into the right ventricle, which is separated from the atrium by the **tricuspid valve** – also known as the **atrioventricular valve** (Figures 2.4 and 2.5). The tricuspid valves are supported by the strong tendinous cords or **chordae tendinae** ('heart strings'), which pass from the papillary muscles at the base of the ventricles to the ventricular surface of the valve flaps (Figure 2.4). The cords act like the guy ropes of a tent, preventing the pressure within the ventricles inverting the valves into the atria. You can imagine the valve operating in a manner similar to a swing door that only opens in one direction. When blood enters the right atrium, the valve opens and blood flows into the right ventricle. When the ventricles contract, the back pressure of the blood forces the valve to close. Under normal conditions, the papillary muscles hold the cords in place to prevent any backflow of blood into the atria.

● Why is it important that the blood is prevented from flowing back into the right atrium by the tricuspid valve?

Figure 2.5 The movement of blood through the human heart – the cardiac cycle. (a) Blood flows into the heart, first entering the atria and then filling the ventricles. During this part of the cycle, the atrioventricular valves are open. This part of the cardiac cycle is called ventricular filling. (b) The ventricles begin to contract. (c) The arteries begin filling as blood is forcefully pumped out of the ventricles. (d) Blood moves away from the heart. (e) The start of atrial filling. Note the cyclical nature of muscular activity in the heart pumping blood into – and receiving blood from – the blood vessels. Red denotes oxygenated blood and blue denotes deoxygenated blood.

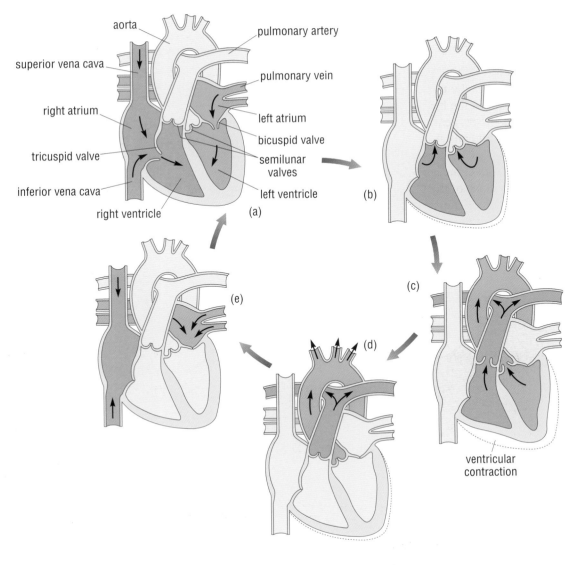

54

● Without a tricuspid valve, contraction of the heart would force the blood back into the right atrium and into the main veins (venae cavae), mixing it with blood returning to the heart from the body and thereby reducing the pumping efficiency of the heart.

All blood leaving the heart is pumped into arteries. (You will learn more about the properties of arteries and veins in Chapter 5.) The blood leaving the right ventricle is pumped into the **pulmonary artery**, which is the only artery in the body that carries deoxygenated blood. This artery branches into two smaller vessels, one serving each lung. Blood is prevented from turning back into the ventricle by a one-way valve in the pulmonary artery. The cusps of the valve are half-moon shaped, so it is called the pulmonary **semilunar valve**. There is also a semilunar valve in the other main artery leaving the heart, the **aorta**. When the heart contracts, the pulmonary semilunar valve is forced open and blood is forced out of the right ventricle into the pulmonary artery. At the end of the contraction phase, the ventricle relaxes and the valve closes, preventing blood draining back into the ventricle. The mechanism of valve opening and closure is illustrated in Figure 2.6. Blood from the pulmonary artery enters the blood vessels that supply the lungs, where it releases the waste carbon dioxide and collects oxygen. The oxygenated blood from the lungs passes back through the heart before it is pumped around the rest of the body. Blood from the lungs returns to the left side of the heart through the four large pulmonary veins (two from each lung) and enters the left atrium.

From the left atrium, blood flows into the left ventricle through the **bicuspid valve** (also known as the **mitral valve**). When the heart contracts, the blood in the ventricle is forced out of the heart and into the main artery of the systemic circulation, the aorta. This blood is oxygenated and it is this blood that supplies the tissues of the body with oxygen. Again, any flow of blood back into the atrium is prevented by the bicuspid valve. Backflow of blood from the aorta to the ventricle is prevented by another semilunar valve, the aortic semilunar valve. Both the ventricles have much thicker walls than those of the atria, and the left ventricle has a thicker muscular wall than the right ventricle. (The importance of this difference will be discussed in Section 2.7.) Contraction of the ventricular muscles is responsible for the main pumping action of the heart and the delivery of blood to the pulmonary and systemic circuits. Figure 2.5 illustrates the flow of blood through the four chambers of the heart.

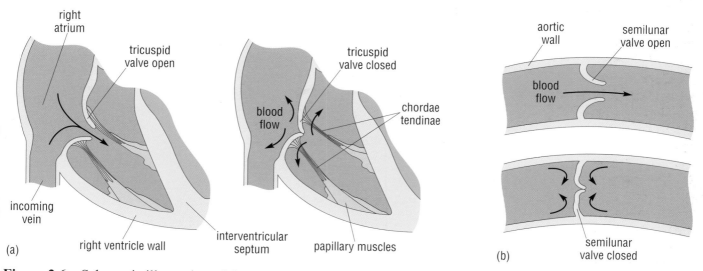

Figure 2.6   Schematic illustration of the valve mechanisms for the (a) tricuspid and bicuspid valves and (b) semilunar valves.

The heart is encased in the pericardium, a double-walled sack filled with fluid ('peri-' means 'around'). The outer pericardial membrane is attached to the connective tissue that separates the two lungs, and this attachment helps keep the heart in its correct position within the chest cavity. The pericardial fluid provides lubrication between the walls of the pericardium and allows the heart to glide smoothly within the pericardium during each heart beat. (Inflammation of the pericardium is called pericarditis and will be discussed further in Section 6.6.)

Activity 2.2   Blood flow and the heart

Suggested study time 15 minutes

Now use the Multi-ed Cardiology program to review the sections on the anatomy of the heart, the flow of blood through the chambers of the heart and the heart valves.

The two animations to watch, 'The structure of the heart' and 'How the blood flows in the heart', can be found by navigating to Animations | Condition | Anatomy.

2.4 What is a heart beat?

So far, the terms 'pumping', 'beating' and 'contracting' have been used – but what do they really mean? Clearly, the activity of the heart, at one level, can be seen as a mechanical event: the movement of muscle that brings about the pumping action of the heart. However, the mechanisms that initiate and regulate the movement of heart muscle are actually a series of electrical events.

Like all muscles in the body, heart muscle is electrically excitable. It is a collection of interconnected muscle cells (also known as muscle fibres) that, when at rest, maintain a small electrical potential difference (voltage) of about –90 mV (1 mV is one thousandth of a volt) between the inside and outside of the cell. This electrical difference is called the resting membrane potential. Heart muscle contracts when this membrane potential becomes less negative, as the result of a process called **depolarisation**. An important property of some of these cardiac muscle cells is that they are self-excitable: they are able to initiate their own depolarisation and, in doing so, cause the heart muscle to contract. The depolarisation is in the form of an electrical signal called the **cardiac action potential**, and an example is shown in Figure 2.7.

Importantly, cardiac muscle cells are highly interconnected, facilitating the rapid spread of action potential throughout the muscle, allowing the heart to contract in a coordinated manner.

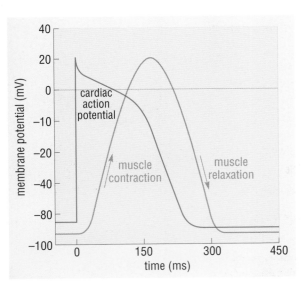

Figure 2.7 The cardiac action potential generated in the heart muscle cells of the ventricles is shown in relation to the subsequent contraction of the ventricular muscle in this stylised graph.

While, for the purposes of this course, it is not necessary for you to grasp the complex biophysics that underlies the cardiac action potential, it is important that you are aware that ions are involved in both the maintenance of the resting membrane potential and the process of depolarisation.

Ions are atoms or molecules that have either lost or gained electrons; when they have gained electrons, ions are negatively charged. The ions involved in regulating the electrical properties of the heart are ions of sodium (Na), potassium (K) and calcium (Ca). The atoms these ions came from have all lost electrons, and therefore the ions carry positive charges. (Na and K have lost one electron each and are written as Na^+ and K^+, respectively; Ca has lost two electrons and hence is written as Ca^{2+}.) Any change in the concentrations of these ions in the blood can affect the ability of the heart to function correctly.

The ability of heart muscle to depolarise and contract is intrinsic; that is, it is a property of the heart muscle and does not depend on the nervous system for instruction. This property is called **autorhythmicity**. You may have seen re-enactments of human sacrifice showing a priest holding a beating heart freshly excised from a sacrificial victim!

2.4.1 The coordination of contraction

The sequence of excitation that produces coordinated contraction of the heart is an exquisitely choreographed process. It depends on the activity of a series of specialised groupings of autorhythmic cardiac muscle cells that initiate and pace the rate at which the heart beats. The first group of cells (called a node) is embedded in the wall of the right atrium, close to where the superior vena cava enters the heart. These cells form the **sinoatrial node** (SAN); because they determine the rate at which the heart beats, these cells are often referred to as the heart's **pacemaker** (see Figure 2.8).

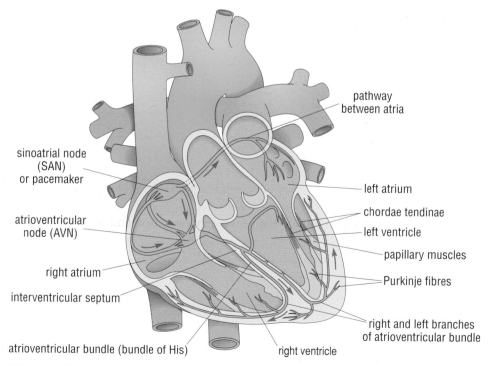

Figure 2.8   Transmission of electrical activity (red arrows) through the heart, responsible for the coordinated contraction of the atria and ventricles. Note the location of the sinoatrial node (SAN), the atrioventricular node (AVN) and the bundle of His.

Contraction of the heart is initiated by electrical activity in the SAN. A wave of electrical activity then spreads from the node and permeates throughout the right and the left atria, causing them to contract. When the wave reaches the junction between the atria and the ventricles, a second group of specialised pacemaker cells, located at the **atrioventricular node** (**AVN**), come into play. Here the speed of electrical conduction slows, so transmission between the atria and ventricles is delayed briefly. This delay allows the atria to complete their contraction before the ventricles are activated and is called the AVN delay.

● Why is the delay between atrial and ventricular contractions important?

● This delay ensures that most of the blood in the atria is ejected into the ventricles. Should the ventricles contract during atrial contraction, the valves between the atria and ventricles will close, preventing the efficient transfer of blood from the atria.

The cells of the AVN are connected to a bundle of modified cardiac muscle fibres known as **Purkinje fibres**, illustrated in Figure 2.8. The Purkinje fibres form a long bundle called the **atrioventricular bundle**, also known as the **bundle of His**, which runs down the septum between the ventricles. The speed at which the wave of electrical activity is conducted increases as it passes along the bundle of His, ensuring that the wave of electrical activity radiates throughout the ventricles, allowing them to contract in a unified manner.

If the SAN is removed from the heart and observed, it will continue to contract at a rate equivalent to 80–85 beats per minute. Tissue taken from the remaining atria is also capable of beating, but instead of beating at a similar rate to the SAN, the atrial tissue beats at a slightly slower rate. Likewise, tissue taken from the ventricles is also able to beat, but at an even slower rate than atrial tissue. So while different regions of the heart possess the ability to contract at their own innate rate, it is important to appreciate that the overall contraction rate of a healthy heart is determined by the activity of the SAN, a rate which is referred to as the **sinus rhythm**.

2.4.2 The electrocardiogram (ECG)

The human body is a good conductor of electricity, and the electrical activity of the heart during contraction can be measured. This is done by attaching electrodes to the surface of the body, as shown in Figure 2.9, and using a machine called an electrocardiograph to record heart activity. The graphic recording obtained using an electrocardiograph is called an **electrocardiogram** (**ECG**). The ECG represents the composite activity of the pacemaker nodes of both the heart and the cardiac muscle. Figure 2.10 shows a typical recording from a healthy individual. A normal ECG has three distinguishable waves called deflection waves. The first wave, the **P wave**, lasts for about 0.08 s and represents the wave of depolarisation

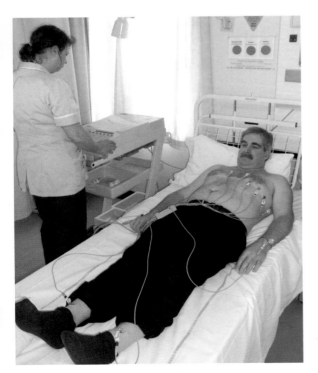

Figure 2.9 A middle-aged man undergoes electrocardiographic investigation. Note the attachment of recording electrodes to the chest.

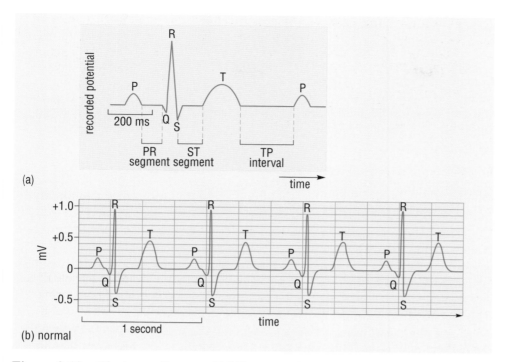

Figure 2.10   Electrocardiogram (ECG) traces: (a) a stylised representation and (b) a trace of a healthy individual.

arising from the SAN, which then spreads throughout the atria. Approximately 0.1 s after the P wave begins, the atria contract. The large **QRS complex** represents the wave of ventricular depolarisation that precedes the contraction of the ventricles. This wave has a much more complicated shape because the ventricles are larger and the directional path taken by the wave of electrical activity is more complex. The average duration of the QRS complex is also about 0.08 s. The **T wave** is caused by ventricular repolarisation. During this period, the membrane potential of the ventricular muscle cells returns to the resting state and the muscle relaxes. (Look again at Figure 2.8.) In some cases, a U wave (not shown) is also seen, which corresponds to the slow repolarisation of the papillary muscles which attach the chordae tendinae to the ventricle wall.

Activity 2.3   Electricity and the heart

Suggested study time 15 minutes

At this stage of this chapter it will be useful for you to use the Multi-ed Cardiology program to review the sections on the electrical activity of the heart and the ECG.

The first animation to watch, 'The electrical activity of the heart', can be found by navigating to Animations | Condition | Anatomy. The second animation, 'Electrocardiogram (ECG)', can be found by navigating to Animations | Investigations.

2.4.3 The cardiac cycle in more detail

One complete heart beat takes about 0.8 s and is called the cardiac cycle. It consists of a period of muscle contraction, a period referred to as **systole** (pronounced with three syllables, as in 'mystery') and a period of relaxation, referred to as **diastole** (pronounced with four syllables, as in 'catastrophe'). The normal number of cardiac cycles per minute ranges from 60 to 80 in a resting adult. Taking 75 as an example, each cycle lasts 0.8 s and has the following sequence of phases:

*   atrial systole: contraction of the atria

*   ventricular systole: contraction of the ventricles

*   complete cardiac diastole: relaxation of the atria and ventricles.

The cardiac cycle is marked by a succession of pressure and blood volume changes in the heart related to the contraction and relaxation of the atria and ventricles. The convention when discussing the cardiac cycle is to start with the period of atrial filling as shown in Figure 2.5a, a period when the heart is in a state of complete rest or **complete cardiac diastole**. During this period, the pressure in the heart is low. Blood returning to the heart via the venae cavae and pulmonary veins flows passively into the atria and through the open atrioventricular valves in the ventricles. Approximately 70% of ventricular filling occurs during this period. The remaining 30% is forced into the ventricles during **atrial systole**. The contraction of the atria compresses the blood they contain, causing a sudden but slight rise in atrial pressure, propelling the residual atrial blood into the ventricles. During this phase, the ventricles are still relaxed in their diastolic state, and now have the maximum volume of blood they will contain in the cardiac cycle. This volume is known as the **end diastolic volume**. The atria relax at this stage of the cycle, entering atrial diastole, which is sustained throughout the rest of the cardiac cycle.

As the atria relax, the ventricles begin their period of contraction (**ventricular systole**). The ventricular pressure rises sharply, closing the atrioventricular valves. For a brief period, the blood in the ventricles is trapped within the chamber, unable to leave, the volume remaining constant; this period is called the **isovolumetric contraction phase**. Importantly, ventricular pressure continues to increase and eventually reaches a point where it exceeds the pressure in the large arteries leaving the heart. At this point, the isovolumetric contraction phase ends and ventricular pressure forces open the semilunar valves, allowing blood to be ejected from the ventricles into the pulmonary arteries and aorta. This phase of ejection is called the **ventricular ejection phase** and the blood pressure within the aorta normally reaches 120 mmHg. Blood pressure will be returned to in Section 2.7.

The final phase of the cardiac cycle is the period of ventricular relaxation. During this period, the blood remaining in the ventricles, a volume called the **end systolic volume**, is no longer compressed by the ventricular walls. The pressure within the ventricles rapidly falls and the higher pressure in the aorta and pulmonary arteries forces the semilunar valves to close. Once again, for a brief period, the ventricles are closed chambers.

●   What state are the atria in during the period of ventricular systole?

●   During ventricular systole, the atria are in diastole – they are relaxed.

During ventricular systole, the relaxed atria are being filled by blood returning to the heart via the venae cavae and pulmonary veins. The atrial pressure rises, and when the pressure on the atrial side of the atrioventricular valves exceeds that on the ventricular side, the atrioventricular valves open and the cycle begins once more with ventricular filling.

By this point in this chapter, you will have formed the opinion that blood pressure is a major factor in determining the flow of blood through the heart. Indeed, blood flow through the heart is controlled entirely by pressure changes; changes that reflect the alternating contraction and relaxation of the heart muscle and the opening and closing of the heart valves. Blood flows down its own pressure gradient, much in the same way as water flows through the water mains.

2.4.4 Heart sounds

The heart valves play a critical role in determining the efficient flow of blood through the heart and connecting vessels. All of us, at sometime or other, will have been asked to allow a nurse or doctor to listen to our heart through our chest using a stethoscope. The sound heard is described as 'lub-dup', and two lub-dups are heard during each heart beat ('lub-dup, pause, lub-dup' per cycle). The lub-dup sound is produced by the percussive closure of the heart valves. The first lub-dup corresponds to the sudden closure of the atrioventricular valves and is generally louder, longer and more resonant than the second lup-dup, which is produced by the closure of the semilunar valves. By varying the position of the stethoscope over the heart, it is possible to distinguish the sound of each valve as it closes. You will learn in Chapters 6 and 7 how heart sounds can be used to diagnose heart defects.

Activity 2.4   Listening to heart sounds

Suggested study time 20 minutes

Follow the links on the DVD Guide program to the 'Heart sounds' audio clips. Listen to the recordings of heart sounds from:

- someone who has 'normal' heart sounds
- someone who has valvular heart disease with regurgitation.

Regurgitation is a way in which heart valves may fail and will be discussed in more detail in Chapter 6. See if you can recognise the normal 'lub-dup' sounds found in the normal recording in the person with valvular heart disease.

Why should the presence of valvular disease be associated with the change in heart sound?

Comment

Under normal circumstances, the heart sounds are generated by the beating heart and the resultant flow of blood through it. When a health care professional uses a stethoscope to listen for these sounds, important information can be provided about the condition of the heart. In addition to the 'lub-dup' sounds, a variety of other sounds may be present. These include heart murmurs generated by the disturbed flow of blood due to physiological or pathological processes. In the second recording, regurgitation allows blood to flow back through a valve when it is supposed to be closed.

2.5 The control of heart rate: the autonomic nervous system

You learned in Section 2.4.1 that the SAN plays a central role in determining the rate at which the heart beats. However, you will know from your own experience that your heart rate is not constant but can vary dramatically, depending on your emotional state and level of physical activity. So how is this achieved? The rate at which the heart beats is controlled both by the nervous system and by circulating hormones. The SAN is innervated (receives a nervous input) by the autonomic nervous system, along which nervous messages travel without our voluntary input. Sympathetic and parasympathetic nerves lead to the SAN and originate in the two regions of the brain involved in the regulation of heart rate. The sympathetic nerves originate in the **vasomotor centre**, located in the brain's medulla (hindbrain), but reach the heart via the spinal cord, as shown in Figure 2.11. Sympathetic nerves release a chemical messenger (neurotransmitter) called noradrenalin which excites the heart, making it beat faster. In contrast, the parasympathetic nerves slow the heart. These nerve fibres originate in the **cardio-inhibitory centre**, which is also located in the medulla, and descend to the heart in the **vagus nerve**. These fibres use acetylcholine as their neurotransmitter.

● In Section 2.4.1, you discovered that the SAN beats at a rate of 80–85 beats per minute when placed in a dish, and that the average heart rate is approximately 75 beats per minute. Can you explain why the average heart rate is slower than the intrinsic rate of the SAN?

● The SAN sets the rate for the heart. If the heart beats at a slower rate than the intrinsic rate of the SAN, then the SAN must have been slowed by the action of the parasympathetic nerves.

The SAN is under a sustained level of inhibition (tonic inhibition) from the parasympathetic vagus nerve. This means that the activity of the SAN is continuously held 'in check' by the parasympathetic system (called vagal restraint).

● What would happen to heart rate if the vagal supply to the heart was cut?

● The SAN would no longer be under vagal restraint. Consequently, the heart would beat faster – at the intrinsic rate of the SAN.

● In a normal person, what do you think happens if there is an increase in the activity of the vagus nerve?

● Vagal restraint is increased and the heart rate is slowed.

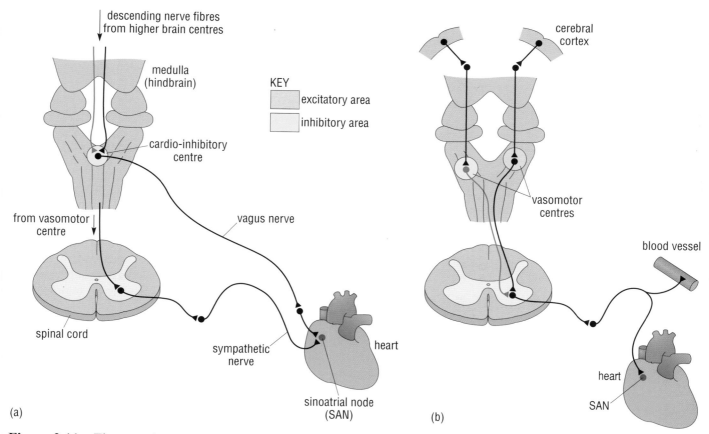

Figure 2.11 The neural control of heart rate. This schematic illustration shows (a) the innervation of the sinoatrial node (SAN) by nerves from the cardio-inhibitory centre and (b) the vasomotor centres in the brain.

Circulating hormones, such as adrenalin or noradrenalin, can also increase heart rate by their direct excitatory action on the SAN. Most people have experienced moments of acute stress or fright when their heart seems to be pounding in their chest at a heightened rate. This is because of the action of adrenalin and noradrenalin, which are released into the bloodstream at such times to prepare our bodies to fight or for flight. Indeed, this response, which is mediated by the sympathetic nervous system, is often referred to as the 'fright, fight or flight' reflex.

2.6 Cardiac output

Cardiac output is the amount of blood pumped out of each ventricle in one minute. The calculation of cardiac output depends on the volume of blood pumped out of the heart during one beat or cycle, the **stroke volume**, and the number of times the heart beats in a minute, i.e. the heart rate. In general, stroke volume is correlated with the force of ventricular contraction and is explained further in Section 2.6.1.

Cardiac output = stroke volume × heart rate

- Under normal resting conditions for an adult, the heart rate is about 75 beats per minute and the stroke volume is about 70 ml. Use these values to calculate cardiac output.

- Cardiac output = 70 ml × 75 beats per minute

    = 5250 ml per minute

    = 5.25 litres per minute

The normal adult blood volume is about 5 litres, so in one minute the entire blood supply of the body passes through each side of the heart.

Cardiac output is highly variable. From the equation above, it can be seen that changes in either stroke volume or heart rate will affect the pumping power of the heart. The difference between the resting cardiac output and the maximum output of the heart is called the cardiac reserve, and for average individuals this is four to five times the resting cardiac output. In fitter individuals, such as trained athletes, the reserve can be as much as seven times the resting level.

2.6.1 Regulation of stroke volume

The stroke volume is the difference between the end diastolic volume, the amount of blood that collects in a ventricle during diastole, and the end systolic volume, the volume of blood left in the ventricle after is has contracted. The end diastolic volume is largely determined by the duration of the ventricular diastole and by venous pressure (which will be examined further in Section 2.7). The end systolic volume is determined by arterial blood pressure and the force of ventricular contraction.

An amazing property of heart muscle is that its force of contraction is related to the degree it is stretched before it contracts. (This is known as **Starling's law** and is a property of the muscle fibres.) If the end diastolic volume is large, the greater stretching of the ventricular muscle wall will result in a more forceful contraction. Conversely, if the end diastolic volume is small, the muscle wall is stretched less and the subsequent contraction is weaker.

Although the size of the end diastolic volume is the major intrinsic factor determining the stroke volume, other extrinsic factors (factors from outside the heart) can also affect the force with which blood is ejected from the ventricles. One such factor is **contractility**, an increase in contractile strength of the muscle that is independent of the degree of ventricular stretching. Contractility is under the control of the sympathetic nervous system (direct neural control) and is also affected by the levels of adrenalin and noradrenalin circulating in the bloodstream (hormonal control). Factors that increase the contractility of the heart are called positive inotropic agents, and those that reduce contractility are termed negative inotropic agents. These agents will feature later in the course.

2.6.2 Venous return

As mentioned above, the amount of blood returning to the heart (**venous return**) is also a major determinant of the end diastolic volume, and hence of the stroke volume. While the heart is the powerhouse of the cardiovascular system, the pumping action of the heart alone is not sufficient to return the blood, ejected from the ventricles, to the atria. Other factors are also involved. The veins have valves that prevent the backflow of blood, especially when standing. The contraction of the skeletal muscle surrounding the deep veins also assists in pumping blood towards the heart. In the legs, this pumping action is called the skeletal muscle pump. Also, during breathing, the expansion of the chest creates a negative pressure within the chest, helping to draw blood towards the heart. In addition, when the diaphragm descends during inspiration, it increases the pressure within the abdominal cavity, pushing blood towards the heart. Finally, the position of the body and gravity can also aid venous return.

2.7 Blood pressure

You have read so far that the flow of blood within the heart and the cardiovascular system is a function of blood pressure (blood flows down a pressure gradient). Indeed, as you will see in the final sections of this chapter, the mechanisms that regulate cardiac output are essentially involved in maintaining this pressure gradient. Blood pressure is the force exerted by the blood on the surface of the inner walls of the blood vessels, and the average blood pressure is determined by the rate of blood flow and the resistance to blood flow. The systemic arterial blood pressure (usually referred to as the arterial blood pressure) is the result of the blood discharged from the left ventricle into the aorta. When the left ventricle contracts and pushes blood into the aorta, the pressure produced within the arterial system is called the **systolic blood pressure**, and in resting adults it is about 120 mmHg. During complete cardiac diastole, when the heart is at rest after the ejection of blood, the pressure within the arteries is much lower and is called **diastolic blood pressure**, usually about 80 mmHg in resting adults. (The unit of pressure used traditionally to measure blood pressure is expressed in millimetres (mm) of mercury (Hg) and refers to the height of a column of mercury traditionally attached to the device used to measure blood pressure.) Arterial blood

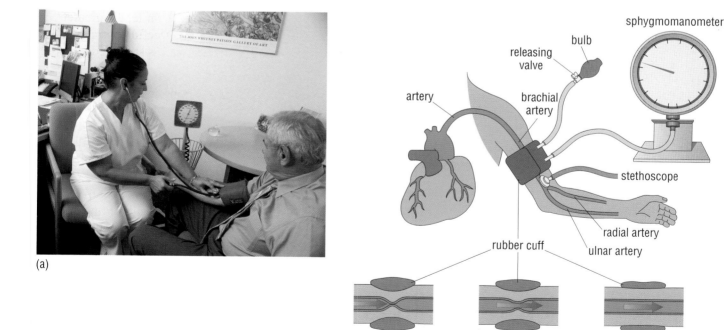

Figure 2.12 (a) Measurement of blood pressure using a sphygmomanometer. (b) The pressure in the cuff is increased until the blood flow stops, and then the flow gradually returns as the cuff is slowly deflated.

pressure is measured with a sphygmomanometer (Figure 2.12) and is expressed with the systolic pressure written above the diastolic pressure:

Blood pressure = 120/80 mmHg

Blood pressure is measured by wrapping a cuff round the upper arm and inflating it to compress the brachial artery, blocking the flow of blood into the arm (see Figure 2.12a). The cuff is then slowly deflated, gradually reducing the pressure applied to the arm until a point is reached when blood starts to flow once more through the brachial artery. By listening through a stethoscope held over the brachial artery (Figure 2.12), it is possible to hear the blood starting to flow into the arm, and the cuff pressure at this point corresponds with the arterial systolic blood pressure. The cuff is then deflated further until the blood flows freely through the artery at a cuff pressure that corresponds to the diastolic blood pressure. The difference between the systolic and diastolic blood pressure is called the pulse pressure. The cyclic surge in pulse pressure is often used to facilitate heart rate measurement. There are several points in the body where arteries lie close to the skin, at which it is possible to sense pulse pressure using a fingertip. A commonly used site is the inner wrist; here, the radial artery runs beneath the skin.

Of course, it should be noted that the blood pressure measurement described here is a method for measuring arterial pressure within the systemic circulation.

● Look again at Figure 2.4. You will notice that the left ventricle has a greater muscle mass than the right ventricle. How might this influence arterial blood pressure in the pulmonary circulation?

● Because there is less muscle mass pumping an equivalent volume of blood into the pulmonary circuit, the pulmonary arterial pressure is likely to be less than that produced in the systemic circuit.

The arterial blood pressure in the pulmonary circuit is about 14 mmHg – a fraction of that in the systemic system.

Activity 2.5   Blood pressure

Suggested study time 40 minutes

Now use the Multi-ed Cardiology program to review the sections related to blood pressure, watching four animations in total.

The first three animations to watch, 'What is blood pressure?', 'What causes blood pressure?' and 'How is blood pressure diagnosed?', can be found by navigating to Animations | Condition | Hypertension (blood pressure). The final animation to watch, 'Blood pressure', can be found by navigating to Animations | Living with.

Now follow the links on the DVD Guide program to the section on the measurement of blood pressure. Play the short video and work through the interactive questions to test your understanding of how blood pressure is measured.

Case Study 2.1 Katerin Wilcox

Katerin Galina Sergeyevna was born in the USSR in 1936 and came to the UK on a cultural exchange programme in the early 1950s to study at the Royal College of Music. Here she met and married Brian Wilcox, becoming a British naturalised subject in 1962, during the heights of the Cuban missile crisis. Sadly, Brian died in a car accident in 1973. Since then, Katerin has lived a meagre life on a limited widow's pension supplemented by a small income from giving violin lessons on Thursday evenings.

Recently, Katerin has been suffering from a series of severe headaches, which she feels have also affected her vision, making it difficult to read her violin music. She also feels very lethargic and has the occasional nosebleed. The headaches become so debilitating that she visits her GP. During the consultation, her GP takes her blood pressure and discovers that it is high. She refers Katerin to the local hospital so that further tests can be done to identify the cause of her condition.

2.7.1 Physiological control of blood pressure

Your blood pressure and heart rate can vary depending on your level of activity, but it is important that blood pressure is kept within normal limits. If it becomes too high, blood vessels can be damaged; if it is too low, the blood flow through the organs of the body may be compromised. (The kidneys, heart and brain are particularly vulnerable.)

Blood pressure is determined by cardiac output and the resistance to blood flow within the cardiovascular system (the **peripheral resistance**). In short, factors that affect stroke volume, heart rate and peripheral resistance can impact upon blood pressure.

While the blood vessels of the cardiovascular system will be discussed more fully in Chapter 5, it is necessary at this stage to introduce the concepts of vasodilation and vasoconstriction, the vascular properties that determine peripheral resistance. The arterioles (see Section 5.1) have a wall of smooth muscle that can either contract or relax. Contraction causes vasoconstriction and increases peripheral resistance. Relaxation, on the other hand, causes vasodilation and lowers peripheral resistance. The arteriole smooth muscle is under the control of the sympathetic nervous system, and is sensitive to local conditions (see Chapter 5) and circulating hormones.

Heart rate, stroke volume (e.g. contractility) and peripheral resistance can be altered in response to changes in blood pressure. There are receptors that monitor blood pressure (**baroreceptors**) located in the aorta and in one of the main arteries that carries oxygenated blood to the brain. (Here, the baroreceptors reside in the carotid sinus, a small protrusion in the wall of the carotid artery in the neck.) The baroreceptors detect small changes in blood pressure and relay this information back to the vasomotor and cardio-inhibitory centres in the brain. The information is processed, and the output to the SAN via the sympathetic and vagus nerves is altered accordingly (affecting contractility, regulated by the sympathetic system, and heart rate). The sympathetic output to the arteriolar smooth muscle is also altered (regulating peripheral resistance). This is known as the **baroreceptor reflex** (an example of a feedback mechanism) and is illustrated in Figure 2.13.

The cardiovascular centres in the brain also receive input from other receptors that monitor the levels of carbon dioxide and oxygen in the blood and are sensitive to changes in acidity. These receptors, called **chemoreceptors**, are located in the carotid and aortic bodies, found in the carotid artery and the aorta. They are primarily involved in the regulation of breathing, but during periods of severe cardiovascular disturbance can influence the output of the cardiovascular centres.

2.8 Coronary circulation

Because of the thickness of the muscular heart walls, the blood flowing through the chambers of the heart is unable to supply the needs of the heart. Instead, the heart

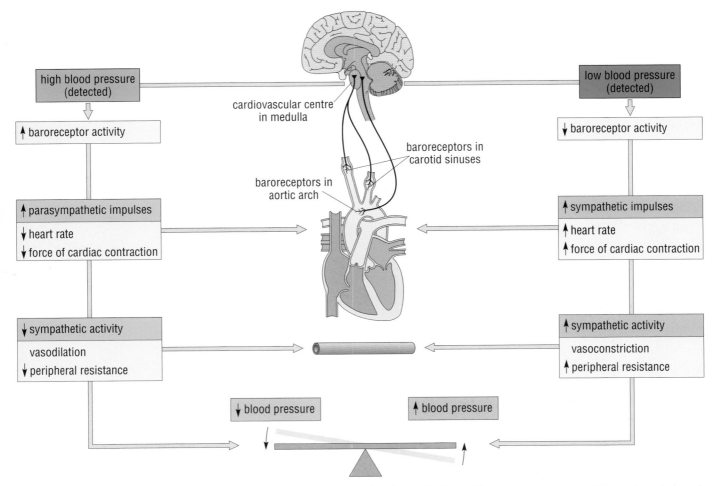

Figure 2.13 Schematic representation of the negative feedback regulation of heart rate, contractility and peripheral resistance via the baroreceptor reflex (feedback mechanism).

relies on its own circulatory system called the **coronary circulation**, and you will learn later in this course that this system is central to a host of cardiac problems.

The heart muscle is supplied by two coronary arteries which branch off from the aorta as it leaves the heart. Between 4 and 5% of the output of the left ventricle enters the coronary circulation. The coronary arteries branch within the wall of the heart, forming a capillary bed, allowing oxygen and nutrients to reach the cardiac cells and remove waste products. The coronary capillaries drain into the coronary veins, and these in turn drain into the **coronary sinus** that returns the blood to the main circulation through a valve-regulated opening which drains directly into the right atrium.

2.9 Summary of Chapter 2

Having completed this chapter, you should now be equipped with a sound working knowledge of the homeostatic mechanisms involved in regulating cardiac output and blood pressure. You should also have a solid grounding in the anatomical components of the heart and a functional understanding of how neural activity and hormonal influences affect heart function.

Questions for Chapter 2

Question 2.1 (Learning Outcomes 2.1, 2.2 and 2.3)

Describe the journey taken by one drop of blood from the time it enters the right atrium until it leaves the left ventricle.

Question 2.2 (Learning Outcomes 2.1 and 2.3)

Draw a normal ECG trace. Label and explain the significance of the deflections.

Question 2.3 (Learning Outcomes 2.1, 2.3 and 2.4)

Define Starling's law of the heart and the property of contractility. How do they differ?

Question 2.4 (Learning Outcome 2.4)

How does the autonomic nervous system influence cardiac function?

Question 2.5 (Learning Outcome 2.4)

Assume that your heart rate is 72 beats per minute and your stroke volume is 70 ml. Calculate your cardiac output in litres per hour. What factors influence cardiac output?

Question 2.6 (Learning Outcomes 2.4 and 2.5)

How do baroreceptors contribute to the regulation of blood pressure?

Further reading

If you would like to read further, please refer to the following publications.

Waugh, A. and Grant, A. (2006) *Ross and Wilson: Anatomy and Physiology in Health and Illness* (10th edition), London, Churchill Livingstone.

Widmaier, E. P., Raff, H. and Strang, K. T. (2005) *Vander's Human Physiology: Mechanisms of Body Function* (10th edition), Boston, McGraw-Hill.

CHAPTER 3

RISK FACTORS AND SOCIAL DISTRIBUTION OF CARDIOVASCULAR DISEASES

Learning Outcomes

When you have completed this chapter you should be able to:

3.1 Define and use, or recognise definitions and applications of, each of the terms printed in **bold** in the text.

3.2 Understand the concept of risk in relation to coronary heart disease.

3.3 Outline some important features of the social distribution of cardiovascular disease.

3.4 Explain how research into cardiovascular disease risk factors can be carried out.

3.5 Identify some factors that might increase an individual's risk of developing cardiovascular disease.

3.1 Introduction

In this chapter you will be encouraged to think about some of the risk factors and the social distribution of cardiovascular disease. The chapter will not teach you all about every possible risk factor. However, it will demonstrate some of the interesting epidemiological features of cardiovascular disease, and, importantly, will introduce you to some of the ways in which this information has been uncovered through diligent research.

Within the chapter you will notice that statistical information has been presented in a number of different ways, with the use of tables and graphs. If you are not familiar with this way of presenting information, this chapter will help you to learn about some of these techniques.

This chapter is linked closely to Chapter 4. In the present chapter, you will start to consider some of the risk factors for cardiovascular disease. In Chapter 4, you will learn what can be done to change the damaging risks and social distribution of this common health problem.

3.2 What are risk factors?

The story starts in a small town in Massachusetts, USA, at the end of the 1940s. In Framingham, some far-sighted researchers wanted to find out what causes some people to develop heart disease and hypertension whereas others remain healthy. They asked the whole population to agree to be studied (Figure 3.1). The key in any study such as this is to have a good **research question** to ask, i.e. a **hypothesis** to test. The investigators were the first to popularise the concept that there are some characteristics that individual people have that put them at an increased risk of

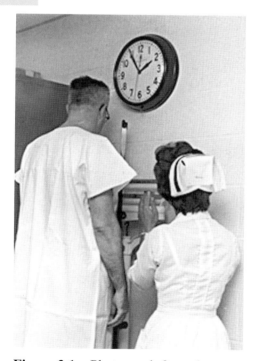

Figure 3.1 Photograph from the archives of the Framingham research study. For several decades this study has continued to provide essential information about the ways in which individuals and populations develop heart disease and hypertension.

developing heart disease or hypertension. These characteristics have become known as **risk factors**.

Case Study 3.1   The Framingham heart study

The town of Framingham in Massachusetts, USA, has become the site of a remarkable long-term research project conducted by the National Heart, Lung and Blood Institute and Boston University. Over 5200 healthy residents, men and women, aged between 30 and 62 living in the town have been studied since the end of the 1940s to see what their experience of heart disease would be and what 'risk factors' would contribute to their **morbidity** and **mortality** from cardiovascular disease.

In 1971, a further 5124 children of the original cohort were recruited into a second, 'offspring' study. These two studies have already generated a wealth of scientific data and established the most important risk factors for coronary heart disease (Box 3.1), and demonstrated the importance of modifying lifestyle factors in order to protect against cardiovascular disease.

A third generation of participants is now included in the study: the grandchildren of the first volunteers. The study across these generations and the collection and analysis of **DNA** from all the participants in the study will lead to new insights about the role of **genetic factors** (see Section 3.4) in the metabolism of cholesterol and the development of cardiovascular disease.

There are a number of characteristics that are comparatively easy to identify that increase the risk of both high blood pressure and cardiovascular disease. Being a man rather than a woman, and being older rather than younger, are the most readily identifiable causes of increased risk of heart disease and hypertension. Figure 3.2 shows that coronary heart disease rates rise fairly steeply with

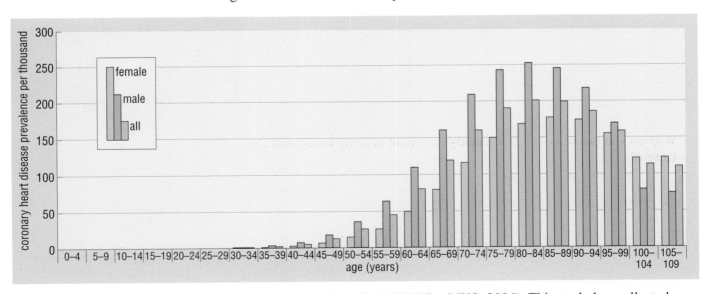

Figure 3.2   Graph taken from a detailed research study called PRIMIS+ (NHS, 2006). This study has collected details of health and disease from 1302 primary care practices (general practices) in the UK. The graph is a bar chart and shows the differing experience of men and women. Because the data have been collected from primary care records, they may underestimate the recording of cardiovascular disease, especially in women. Other studies have shown a sharper rise in women's incidence of cardiovascular disease after the menopause.

increasing age. (Note: **incidence** is the rate at which new cases of disease arise over a specified time period, whereas **prevalence** is the rate of disease in a population at a specific single time.) Also, until old age, being a man involves a risk of heart disease equivalent to that of a woman approximately 10 years older. Because individuals cannot do anything about either age or gender, it is usual to consider these factors in a different category, commonly termed **non-modifiable risk factors**.

The risk factors which the Framingham investigators identified as predictors of cardiovascular disease (and which have been added to by many other later studies) included the presence of hypertension, having a high level of cholesterol in the blood, being overweight, being physically inactive and, most importantly, being a cigarette smoker. This type of study indicates factors that are associated with the later development of cardiovascular disease and may not be causal. A number of newer risk factors have been discussed more recently, but those listed in Box 3.1 have stood the test of time and are still considered to be the major factors associated with the later development of cardiovascular disease. Most importantly, these risk factors are all sensitive to being changed by individuals in order to reduce their risks. Hence they are called the **modifiable risk factors**. The 'weight' given to each factor will be a little different according to the type of person and the population being studied. Later in this chapter you will be encouraged to study how to calculate these risk factors.

Box 3.1 Principal modifiable risk factors for cardiovascular disease

- Raised blood cholesterol
- Raised blood pressure (hypertension)
- Physical inactivity
- Smoking
- Poor nutrition
- Being overweight or obese
- Type 2 diabetes

● Why do you think that it is particularly important to study modifiable risk factors?

● People have an opportunity to change their modifiable risk factors, but are stuck with their non-modifiable ones.

The risk factors for hypertension are a little different and are less well understood. Age remains top of the list of the non-modifiable risk factors, and it seems that being overweight and having an excessive alcohol intake are important among the modifiable risk factors.

For some people there are no apparent 'causes' of high blood pressure. It is just bad luck that their blood pressure is high. They might be a regular attendee at the gym, eat a sensible diet and keep their weight within the 'normal' range, but still develop high blood pressure.

You will see from Table 3.1 that, as cholesterol levels increase in an individual, their risk of death from heart disease increases relative to those whose cholesterol levels are below average. This social distribution is also seen for blood pressure, where each increase in blood pressure category is followed by an increase in heart disease deaths. The higher the cholesterol levels, the greater the risk. In Section 3.6, it will be shown that risk in one group can be compared to that in another as 'relative risk'. If the relative risk is greater than 1, the risk is higher than in the comparison group; if it is less than 1, it is lower. One extra issue to consider is that there are not many people in the population with the highest level of risk. So when a 'population approach' is used, it can be calculated that those at highest risk individually, i.e. with a risk 3.5 times greater than those below average, account for only 10% of all the deaths in the population attributable to raised cholesterol levels. This is because there are so few people at this very high risk level – an important consideration when prevention strategies are considered in Chapter 4. Cardiovascular risk between different populations is also linked to their cholesterol level. Thus populations with generally low cholesterol levels, such as in rural China, will have a lower incidence of cardiovascular disease than that experienced in northern Europe, where cholesterol levels are significantly higher.

Table 3.1 Relative risk of death from heart disease for populations with elevated cholesterol levels, in the three years after measurement.

Cholesterol levels	Relative risk of death in the 3 years after measurement (compared with those with low cholesterol levels)	Population size (from doctor's patient base of 10 000)	Percentage of all deaths attributable to raised cholesterol levels
very high	3.46	326	10
high	2.59	979	18
just above average	1.75	1912	17

3.3 Why are women so superior?

In Figure 3.2 you noted that women had a lower incidence of cardiovascular disease than men at all ages until they are well past the **menopause**. This **gender differential** remains one of the most interesting epidemiological questions (Barrett-Connor, 1997). Is the difference caused by unhealthier lifestyles in men? A small proportion of the difference is attributable to smoking, alcohol intake and dietary factors, but even after these factors have been taken into account a substantial difference remains. Are men harmed by stresses within their workplace? Probably not, because there are few differences in cardiovascular disease experience when women who work outside the home are compared with those who do not work outside the home. Are there differences in social support and protective networks for men and for women? Although there is some evidence that social support is **cardioprotective**, it isn't enough to explain all of the difference. So, is it all down to hormones? It is probable that some of the difference can be explained by circulating levels of **oestrogen**. Oestrogen is a hormone that circulates in high levels in women before the menopause.

It increases blood flow in the coronary arteries and controls some of the ways in which lipids such as cholesterol are used and deposited within the body. Post-menopausal women at each age have significantly greater levels of cardiovascular disease than pre-menopausal women of the same age. More recent research seems to indicate that the way that fats are distributed within the coronary arteries is different in men and women. Whereas men tend to develop atheroma and plaques (see Section 5.6), women before the menopause may develop a different condition which causes their coronary arteries to spasm. This may not be apparent when the coronary blood vessels are X-rayed.

Activity 3.1   Gender differences in cardiovascular disease

Suggested study time 20 minutes

Study the gender differences in the experience of coronary heart disease shown in Figure 3.2. What do you notice about the difference as age increases? Figure 3.11 (later) also shows that the recent rate of decline of death rates from coronary heart disease in England is much more pronounced among men. Why do you think this might be happening?

Comment

It is possible that women simply do not associate heart disease as something that they, individually, would suffer from. If they get chest pain they might ascribe it to other causes such as indigestion. Doctors are also geared up to expect men to have angina or coronary heart disease, but may not diagnose or treat women in the same way. Also, as indicated above, women's hearts may not behave in the same way as men's, and diagnostic testing may be less sensitive or throw up false abnormalities.

'… in many cases heart disease is a fundamentally different disease in many women in ways that we need to pay attention to.'

(Merz, 2006)

Case Study 3.2   Martha Childs

Martha is 48 years old. She is Afro-Caribbean and was born in Trinidad. She came to the UK as a child with her parents as migrants from the Caribbean. When she was 23, she married and now has one teenaged child. Currently, she works as a receptionist in council offices and helps in a charity shop at weekends. Although she does walk the half mile to work on most days, in reality her life is fairly sedentary. Her busy lifestyle means that she can't always have regular meals and she eats high-fat snacks fairly frequently.

She really isn't keen on doctors or orthodox medical treatments. Recently, she has been experiencing menopausal symptoms including hot flushes and swollen legs. She has had to decide whether to visit her doctor and discuss the use of hormone replacement therapy (HRT) or continue with the herbal treatment she has been buying over the counter.

Martha's decision is not easy. During and after the menopause, some women use hormone replacement therapy (HRT) to counter symptoms that accompany this phase of life (McPherson, 2004). However, it seems as though HRT has some complicated actions on cardiovascular disease, and the treatment has undergone a transition in perception from 'presumed benefit to potential harm' (Herrington and Howard, 2003). Although HRT has a beneficial effect on the lipid concentrations circulating in the blood, it apparently increases the risk of cardiovascular disease. Tucker (2003) estimates that, in the USA alone, with the excess risk associated with prescribing HRT, you could expect 1370 incident cases of breast cancer, 1200 cases of coronary heart disease, 1370 strokes and 1370 pulmonary embolisms each year.

● What factors might affect a woman's choice about taking HRT?

● A woman has to make an individual decision with regards to her personal risk factors. She has to decide if the possible risks of HRT outweigh the problems from current symptoms she may be experiencing. As new research evidence on the risks and benefits of taking HRT emerges, an individual's decision may become even more complicated.

The discussion so far has focused on the risk factors for individual people, but it is also important to realise that there are risks that can be identified for whole populations. Later in the chapter you will be able to learn how some populations have higher chances of developing cardiovascular disease and hypertension than other populations. In this way, it can be considered that an individual's risk can partly be explained by the population into which that person has been born, or moves to.

3.4 Genes and heart disease

In common with many other conditions and diseases, there is a genetic predisposition to having heart disease or hypertension. Both conditions can be demonstrated to run in families. There are to date very few specific **genetic markers** found to be associated with either heart disease or hypertension, but the search continues in a number of research projects around the world (Cohen, 2006; Topol et al., 2006). Marfan syndrome (Case Study 3.3) is an example of a genetic condition that may have specific effects on the cardiovascular system. Several **genes** have been reported to be associated with hypertension and heart disease, but it is not yet known what the impact of each specific gene might be on any particular individual. More details about genetic variation can be found in Box 3.2.

Case Study 3.3	**Marfan syndrome: genetics and vascular disease**

Marfan syndrome is a rather complicated condition that affects a small number of people (probably about one in 5000). People with this condition may develop problems with many organs throughout their bodies, including their bones, eyes and blood vessels. The condition is caused by a defect in one of the genes that produces **fibrillin**. This protein is an important part of many supporting structures throughout the body and particularly occurs in the wall of every artery. The largest artery in the body, the aorta, is often affected by this condition and it can develop an aneurysm because of the lack of supporting tissues. Everyone with Marfan syndrome has a defect in the same gene, but each family seems to have its own specific mutation (Byers, 2004). For reasons that are not yet well understood, the genetic problems have **variable penetrance**, which means that not every person with the same genetic problem goes on to develop the same physical or clinical problems. Detailed study of the genetics behind this condition is starting to help the understanding of the way in which problems with genetic control mechanisms can manifest themselves in various vascular diseases.

At least part of the reason for cardiovascular disease to be found at high levels in particular families is that risk factors also tend to run in families. For example, a family lifestyle may be identified with poor attention to exercise, or a high dietary fat intake that might be the norm for all members of that family. One genetic condition that has been well established as a cause of increased levels of cardiovascular disease is the inheritance of defective **fat metabolism**, which leads to a high cholesterol level. This is called **familial hypercholesterolaemia**. Approximately 5% of people who develop coronary heart disease before the age of 55 have been found to have abnormal genes that control the amount of fat in their blood (Vergopoulos et al., 2002). DNA testing can identify those individuals in the family who have the defective gene. In addition, it has been discovered that carriers of a particular genetic variant of a protein called **apolipoprotein E** do seem to be at increased risk of developing cardiovascular disease (Eicher et al., 2002; Song et al., 2004). This protein works in the liver and is associated with circulating levels of cholesterol and its various **metabolites**. Those with the 4 variant of this protein have a slightly increased risk of developing cardiovascular disease and it is also associated with a form of dementia (Alzheimer's disease).

Box 3.2 Genetic variation

Our genes contain all the information that is needed to make us as human beings and they also determine our individual characteristics. Genetic information is encoded in DNA and the genes in different humans are more than 99% identical. The remaining 1% of DNA, which differs between individuals (**genetic variation**), determines not just physical appearance but also whether a person is more susceptible or less susceptible to particular diseases. DNA itself does not produce an individual's characteristics, but it contains the information (i.e. it encodes) for the proteins which do.

Genes are packaged into **chromosomes** which are found in the nucleus of every cell in the body. Humans have two copies of each of 22 chromosomes; one copy is inherited from the mother and one from the father. Each cell also has two chromosomes (X and Y) which determine gender. Women have two X chromosomes and men have one X and one Y chromosome. Each chromosome has between a few hundred and a few thousand genes. However, any particular gene will always be located on a specific chromosome. For example, one gene that causes high levels of cholesterol in the blood is located on chromosome 19 and it encodes a protein that affects how cells take up cholesterol and fats (LDLs; see Figure 3.3).

What is the nature of genetic variation between individuals? The genetic information contained in the DNA is written using only four letters – A, C, G and T – where each letter corresponds to a molecule called a nucleotide arranged linearly on the chromosome. For example, a piece of a gene might read …AGGTCCACCTGTTT… and so on for millions of nucleotides. Let us suppose that in another person this piece of genetic code reads …AGG**G**CCACCTGTTT…, so the fourth nucleotide varies (either T or G) between people. This is called a **single nucleotide polymorphism** (**SNP**, pronounced 'snip'). SNPs may cause individuals to have different characteristics, either because they produce different variants of an encoded protein, or because they produce more, less or none of that protein. Sometimes a gene may contain a few extra nucleotides inserted or deleted, which affects the structure of the encoded protein. Different variants of a protein may be more active, less active or totally inactive, but genetic variation often has no functional effect at all.

Genetic variation may also result from people missing whole genes (deletions) or having extra copies (duplications) on a single chromosome. The effect that genetic variants will have on disease susceptibility will depend on what the gene encodes and what other genes the person has, including the other copy of the gene in question. The effects of genetic variation also depend on a person's lifestyle.

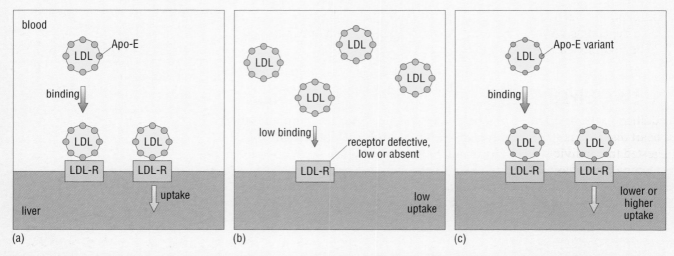

Figure 3.3 Uptake from the blood to the liver of low-density lipoproteins (LDLs), which carry fats and cholesterol. (a) Normally, LDLs have a coating of apolipoprotein E (Apo-E) and are taken up by cells in the liver by binding to their LDL receptors (LDL-R). (b) In a person with a defective or absent LDL receptor, LDLs are not taken up by the liver, so the levels of LDL and cholesterol in the blood are very high (familial hypercholesterolaemia). (c) People may have different variants of Apo-E, some of which are taken up more efficiently or less efficiently, resulting in lower or higher levels of LDL in the blood, respectively.

More recently, scientists have identified the first gene that is a confirmed cause of cardiovascular disease in humans (Wang et al., 2003). Scientists at the Cleveland Clinic studied the genetic makeup of a family from Iowa, USA, who had extremely high levels of cardiovascular disease. In this family, almost everybody developed cardiovascular disease and went on to have a heart attack. By looking at their genes in detail, a genetic variation was found on a particular chromosome (chromosome 15, long arm 26) which was not present in the members of the family who had healthy hearts. Further research showed that the problem with the gene affected the way in which coronary arteries protect themselves from atheroma. This leads to the build-up of plaques that narrow the coronary arteries (Section 5.6).

Although genetic conditions such as Marfan syndrome may have considerable personal and familial implications, the role of genetic influences on heart disease should be kept in context. As you will learn later in this course, so much is known about the behavioural characteristics that cause heart disease that enormous improvements in health can be gained by comparatively simple lifestyle changes. Even if there were some major genetic factors to be uncovered, their effects will still be modified by lifestyle or behaviour. In other words, people with specific genetic problems leading to an increased risk of cardiovascular disease will still need to heed lifestyle advice in order to improve their chances of avoiding excess risk. The large decline in cardiovascular disease that has been apparent in recent years – in developed countries, at least – encourages the search for better ways of behaviour change, not a more intensive search for genetic causes.

● Which factors may determine whether a particular gene produces an effect?

● A particular gene or variants of the gene will have an effect on disease susceptibility dependent on the other genes the person has. The effect will also depend on what the gene encodes and, of course, environmental and behavioural factors always play their part as well.

3.5 Low birth weight and cardiovascular disease

In addition to the main lifestyle influences and the range of genetic risk factors for heart disease that have already been introduced (Box 3.1), it has been suggested that individuals who have a low birth weight have an increased risk of developing cardiovascular disease and high blood pressure in later life (Fall et al., 1995; Figure 3.4). This hypothesis has attracted considerable opposition, with some researchers doubting the link and challenging the evidence behind the

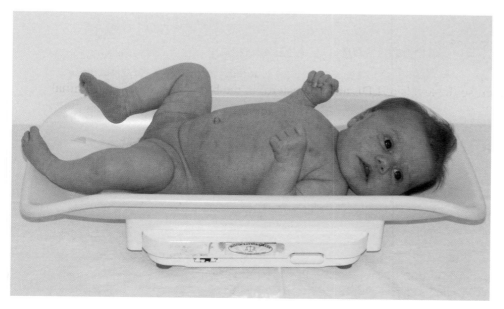

Figure 3.4 Babies of low birth weight seem to have a higher risk of developing cardiovascular disease in later life. This baby seems perfectly normal and will have a reduced cardiovascular disease risk compared with babies of low birth weight.

hypothesis (Paneth and Susser, 1995). However, the most comprehensive, recent review focusing on the proposed link found evidence that:

> '...larger infant size is associated with reduced rates of IHD [ischaemic heart disease] in adult men: those who were of smaller size in infancy experienced greater mortality and morbidity from IHD as adults. No association was demonstrated in women, but there was evidence from a single study that greater gain in BMI in the first 2 years is associated with reduced rates of IHD in both men and women.'

> (Fisher et al., 2006)

It remains one of the most intriguing puzzles to try to explain the reasons for this connection, which was first proposed by the epidemiologist David Barker (Barker, 1992). The suggested link has been called the 'Barker hypothesis'. Barker himself believes that the link between low birth weight and the increased rates of cardiovascular disease in later life reflects the long-term consequences of undernutrition during the development of the baby in the womb (Barker, 1998).

Activity 3.2   Low birth weight and cardiovascular disease

Suggested study time 10 minutes

What reasons can you suggest for the link between low birth weight and a higher incidence of cardiovascular disease in the future?

Comment

People of low birth weight are more likely to become overweight as children and later as adults. This in itself might lead to higher rates of cardiovascular disease. It is possible that when a baby is born apparently undernourished, the parents and other carers overcompensate and tend to give the infant too much nutrition, leading to the established problems associated with being overweight.

3.6 Understanding the nature of risk, for individuals, families and populations

In order to understand the nature of risk, it is necessary to explore how risk is measured. For example, say the chance of dying of heart disease each year in men aged 40–49 is 2 per 1000 in the population, and that in men aged 50–59 it is 6 per 1000 in the population. The older group clearly has triple the death rate of the younger group. Thus the relative risk (the higher rate divided by the lower rate) is calculated as 3. But of every 1000 men aged 50–59, there are only 4 more deaths in a year than among the younger age group. This is the **absolute difference**, sometimes called the **risk difference**.

By careful consideration and measurement of a number of risk factors, it is possible to divide the population into many different risk groups. Those at one end of the spectrum may have as much as 90 times the risk of those at the other end, even after considering (adjusting the statistics) for differences in age and gender.

Box 3.1 listed the major risk factors for cardiovascular disease. However, the list did not mention that having had a heart attack greatly increases the chance of having another. This is one of the strongest predictors.

After having your first heart attack, the risk of having a heart attack in the next year is from five to ten times higher than if you are free of heart disease. This has given rise to the notion that the potential benefits of prevention may be greater in those who have already had a heart attack than in the general population. The prevention of disease in those who have never had that disease is called **primary prevention**, and the prevention of a subsequent disease event in those who have already had some evidence of the disease is called **secondary prevention**. You might think that reversing a high risk in a few people with that risk may result in saving more lives than reversing a low risk in many people. In fact, Gemmell and his colleagues have established that, based on treatment levels at the time of their study (Gemmell et al., 2006), the opposite is true: a little prevention for the general population is likely to result in preventing more heart attacks than targeting either those at high risk or those with previous heart disease.

- What is the difference between primary and secondary prevention?

- Secondary prevention is associated with lowering the risk of disease after a heart problem has already been diagnosed. Primary prevention aims to stop the disease establishing itself in the first place.

3.7 Salt and blood pressure

Salt, including table salt, is sodium chloride (NaCl), which is found naturally in sea water. There is compelling evidence that higher levels of salt intake are associated with higher levels of blood pressure (Figure 3.5). The first observations of this came from studying different population groups. In the 1960s, Louis Dahl, a keen observer, demonstrated that blood pressure levels followed average salt intake in five different populations (Dahl, 1972). A much larger version of this study was repeated in the 1980s using 52 different populations (Intersalt Cooperative Research Group, 1988). This study also concluded that in populations where blood pressure increased a large amount with age, salt intake was higher. In addition, Figure 3.6 demonstrates that when blood pressure levels were measured among individuals within these populations, salt again correlated with their blood pressure levels (over 10 000 people took part). All salt consumed is eventually excreted, and it is easier to measure salt excretion than intake (because so much salt is hidden in manufactured foodstuffs). The authors of the study concluded:

> 'These results support recommendations for reduction of high salt intake in populations for prevention and control of adverse blood pressure levels.'

> (Elliot et al., 1996)

Figure 3.5 People who eat an excessive amount of salt have an increased chance of developing high blood pressure in the future.

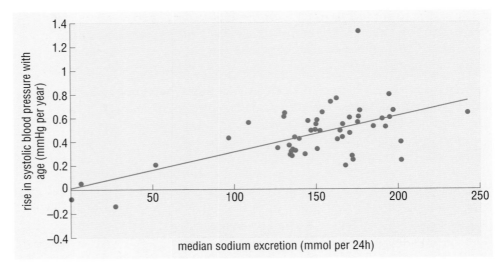

Figure 3.6 Scatter diagram and regression line showing the relationship of systolic blood pressure rise with age and median 24-hour sodium excretion. The data are from the Intersalt study of 52 populations (1988).

The scatter diagram in Figure 3.6 plots two different factors against each other. The amount by which systolic blood pressure increases with age is one factor and the median (a form of average) sodium excretion over 24 hours is the other factor. Both measurements were taken for each population. It can be seen that, in general, those populations with a low measurement for one factor have a low measurement for the other factor, and that those with a high measurement for one factor have a high measurement for the other factor. The regression line is a statistical way of summarising this relationship between the two factors for all the populations examined.

3.8 Calculating risk for individuals

There are a number of comparatively easy ways of calculating cardiovascular risk for individuals, many of which can be found on the internet. These have mostly been generated from data produced by large research trials, such as the Framingham heart study. Recently, the risk associated with the ethnicity of the individual has been incorporated into these calculations.

The ETHRISK calculator (Brindle et al., 2006) has been developed as a modified Framingham risk calculator which can also be used for British black and minority ethnic groups. The calculator should be used for people aged 35–74 without diabetes and with no previous history of cardiovascular disease.

Activity 3.3   Calculating individual cardiovascular risk

Suggested study time 45 minutes

You will be able to calculate the risk for different people using the ETHRISK calculator, available from the DVD Guide program.

Consider a Caucasian man aged 53, with blood cholesterol of 5.8 mmol/l (HDL cholesterol 2.3 mmol/l) and blood pressure of 160 mmHg systolic, 95 mmHg diastolic. Assuming he is a non-smoker, his risk of having cardiovascular disease at some time in the next 10 years is 9%; if he is a smoker, his risk rises to 16%.

(Note that 'general population' gives the standard Framingham study estimate, including all ethnic groups. This is the option to choose for Caucasian people.)

Spend some time playing with different permutations. For example, what cardiovascular disease risk would the person in the calculation have if they were female?

Please remember that calculating possible future risks of potentially serious health problems can raise sensitive issues. If you are worried about the results that this calculation uncovers, for you or for people close to you, please seek professional advice.

Now use the ETHRISK calculator to calculate the cardiovascular risk factors for the people in the case studies in this book, completing the bottom row of Table 3.2.

Table 3.2 ETHRISK calculations.

	Mr Kamal Patel*	**Winifred Fowler**	**Katerin Wilcox**	**Martha Childs**
Ethnic group	Bangladeshi	Caucasian	Caucasian (born in the former USSR)	Afro-Caribbean (born in Trinidad)
Gender	male	female	female	female
Age	53	61	71	48
Systolic blood pressure	160	150	170	140
Total cholesterol	5.8	6.7	6.0	6.4
HDL cholesterol	2.3	2.0	1.9	3.2
Current smoker?	no	yes	no	yes
10-year risk of cardiovascular disease				

*See Case Study 3.4.

Comment

Using the ETHRISK calculator can only ever give an approximate risk score for any individual. By changing the parameters, you should have started to get a feeling for the size of risk that different lifestyle factors contribute to the total risk. This particular calculator has been designed to help demonstrate the differences in risk that are related to the person's ethnic background. You may have tried to enter the same physiological parameters into the calculator and then changed the ethnicity of the person… perhaps with surprising results.

Case Study 3.4   Mr Patel's risk of cardiovascular disease

Mr Kamal Patel is 53 years old. His parents came to the UK from Bangladesh a couple of years before he was born and he has lived in South London all his life. Recently, he decided to leave his job as a clerk in an insurance firm and set up his own mail-order business selling specialist electronic components. The business requires him to work long hours and it is starting to make a small profit. He takes almost no exercise and for relaxation tends to watch football on satellite television. His diet is mainly Western.

According to the ETHRISK calculator, Mr Patel has a 14% risk of having cardiovascular disease over the next 10 years. This is obviously an average estimated risk and doesn't take into consideration his rather sedentary lifestyle. If he were to start smoking, his risk would rise to 25%.

Although people who have come to the UK from South Asia have a higher risk of developing cardiovascular disease than the indigenous British population, the risk is not the same for all ethnic groups (Lip, 2007). Bangladeshi people fare worse than people from Pakistan and India (Kuppuswamy and Gupta, 2005). Box 3.3 lists some of the factors that have been suggested as the reason why there is an excess risk of cardiovascular disease in people who come to the UK from South Asia. Children from South Asian families who come to Britain show early evidence of increased risk of cardiovascular disease compared with Caucasian white children (Whincup et al., 2002).

Box 3.3 Possible reasons for increased rate of cardiovascular disease in people who come to the UK from South Asia

- Adopting a Western lifestyle has an adverse affect on metabolic and vascular function in people from different ethnic backgrounds, including the way in which insulin, lipids and homocysteine (see Section 3.16) are metabolised
- The cumulative effects of disadvantaged socioeconomic status
- Poor diet lacking in potentially protective fresh fruit and vegetables
- Lack of exercise and high smoking rates

3.9 Researching risk factors

In this chapter you have been learning about cardiovascular disease and hypertension risk and will have noticed that just about all the information and knowledge about the subject has come from research studies. It is also clear that there are still a large number of unanswered questions which require considerable further investigation. So research is of fundamental importance to the subject area and aims to provide practical answers that can help individuals live longer, healthy lives. This section will help you find out more about the research methods that are necessary to help us understand more about cardiovascular disease and its risk factors.

Returning to the Framingham heart study, it is apparent that it has become one of the most sophisticated and sustained research studies of disease causation ever initiated. As you learned before, one of the key reasons that the Framingham heart study continues to be so successful is that it asked good questions and collected appropriate data right from the outset. Planning is always the key to good research. Where do the research questions (or hypotheses) come from? They may come from careful observations of people with the disease, or from people who have the problem themselves seeking answers. They may come from an understanding of basic biology or physiology (how the body works), biochemistry (what the body is made up of) or **pathology** (how the body changes with disease). The questions should make sense in terms of both basic science and clinical observation. The best studies come from the best questions – although you also have to use the correct methods!

● Why do you think that it is important to continue to undertake research on risk factors associated with cardiovascular disease?

● All the risk factors for the development of cardiovascular disease have not yet been determined or quantified. Cardiovascular diseases continue to be among the most significant causes of death and serious illness throughout the world. Research methodology in population health is continually improving and methods of diagnosing disease are also becoming increasingly sophisticated.

The Framingham heart study had the advantage of taking a population that was, at the time of recruitment, free of disease and following its members for many decades to see what happens to them. This is called a longitudinal, prospective or **cohort** study (Figure 3.7), because it studies people's development over a sustained period of time.

Less effective methods of researching the causes of cardiovascular disease are to take people who have already developed the disease (cases) and compare them with those who have remained free of the disease (controls). This type of study – using the **case/control design** – can give useful clues, but the research has to be carefully designed in order to avoid introducing bias into the results.

The most satisfactory evidence about whether a proposed risk factor is really a cause of cardiovascular disease is to remove the risk factor and see if the amount of disease is reduced. In order to be sure that any change in the level of disease that may have occurred following the removal in the risk factor level has resulted from that removal, a comparison with people whose risk factors have not been changed is required. These studies are very difficult to design and carry out.

One of the most famous of all cohort studies looks at British doctors and has followed them for over 50 years (Doll et al., 2004). This study provided the first conclusive proof of the

Figure 3.7   Cohort studies are named after cohorts, groups of Roman legionaries that continued without new members until the last of them had died (or maybe retired if they were allowed to do so).

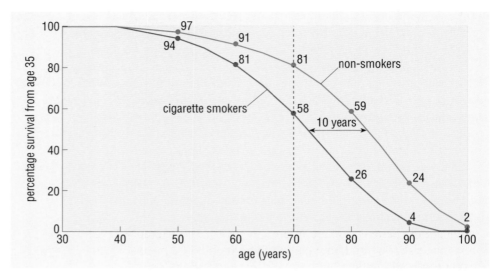

Figure 3.8 A study which followed a cohort of more than 34 000 male British doctors for many years revealed an enormous difference in the age of death between those who smoked and those who didn't. The figures along the curves give the percentage of the sample alive at the end of each decade.

link between cigarette smoking and lung cancer (Doll and Hill, 1954), but it also revealed interesting features about cardiovascular disease. Throughout this course, you will come to recognise that smoking is the dominant risk factor for cardiovascular disease. Doll and his colleagues recruited a cohort of over 34 000 doctors, 30% of whom were smokers at the beginning of the study. Figure 3.8 shows the differences in survival between those doctors who smoked and those who didn't. The difference is very striking; on average, doctors who didn't smoke lived 10 years longer than those who did. In the cohort study, smokers were found to have an excess mortality from 11 different causes. Although the greatest relative risk for smokers was for lung cancer, a smaller relative risk for heart disease (because cardiovascular disease is so common in the population) means that this contributed to the biggest number of deaths (7628).

Activity 3.4 Relative and absolute risk

Suggested study time 20 minutes

Consider a study of 1000 people which followed them over 10 years after examining their blood pressure. Say that, on the original examination, 100 had high blood pressure and 900 did not. Over the next 10 years, 10 of those with high blood pressure develop cardiovascular disease, as did 18 of those without high blood pressure. Calculate the risk of cardiovascular disease in those with and without high blood pressure on original examination.

Comment

The absolute risks are calculated as:

High blood pressure   10/100 get cardiovascular disease = 10%

Blood pressure not high   18/900 get cardiovascular disease = 2%

So the risk difference is:

10% − 2% = 8%

and the relative risk is:

10%/2% = 5

If you are a person with high blood pressure, or are the health professional advising the patient, you are interested in the risk difference, a measure of absolute risk. So you know that, without high blood pressure, only 2 out of 100 people will get cardiovascular disease but, with high blood pressure, 10 out of 100 will get it – thus the extra risk is 8%. If you are a researcher, you are interested in relative risk – how many more times it is likely to get cardiovascular disease with the risk factor than without. However, this is not much use to decision making as a patient: a very low risk multiplied by 5 may still be a very low absolute risk, whereas a high risk multiplied by 5 is still a high risk for that individual.

Also bear in mind the population perspective. Although having high blood pressure increases your risk of cardiovascular disease, most of the disease cases occur in those without the risk factor (18 out of a total of 28 heart attacks in this population of 1000 people).

3.10 Global patterns of cardiovascular disease

Some years ago it was common to consider cardiovascular heart disease as a 'disease of affluence'. This is nowadays clearly incorrect. The way in which cardiovascular disease relates to wealth and poverty should be considered from two different perspectives: the distribution of heart disease within populations and between populations. Within all populations in the developed world, those at the top end of the social distribution (which can be defined according to income, education or occupation) invariably have a lower risk of cardiovascular disease than those at the bottom end. In fact, there is a clear gradation of risk across the social spectrum, which will be explored later in this chapter.

In the developing world, the situation is changing rapidly and the patterns of disease have become rather complex. Until fairly recently, the main causes of illness and premature death in the poorest countries of the world were infectious diseases such as cholera and tuberculosis, which were associated with poverty and malnutrition. The majority of people in these underdeveloped countries never lived long enough to develop the chronic diseases such as cardiovascular disease, associated with older age. However, along with economic development and increasing affluence among some members of society, diseases such as cardiovascular disease have rapidly become significant causes of illness. This change in social distribution of ill health as countries undergo economic development has come to be called **epidemiological transition**. In a further cruel twist of fate, some developing countries may now have the old social distribution of infectious disease and malnutrition among the poorest members of their society while those at the top have a similar social distribution of degenerative illness, including high rates of cardiovascular disease, to that experienced in developed countries. The pattern continues to become more complex when new infectious diseases such as HIV/AIDS are introduced, and when infections (such as malaria and tuberculosis) that were thought to be largely under control develop **resistant** strains and become a significant problem again.

3.11 Global burden of chronic disease

Although chronic diseases such as cardiovascular disease occur in both developed (high-income) and developing (low-income) countries, more people die in the developing countries of these conditions:

> '35 million people will die (worldwide) in 2005 from heart disease, stroke, cancer, and other chronic diseases. Only 20% of these deaths will be in high-income countries – while 80% will occur in low-income and middle-income countries. The death rates from these potentially preventable diseases are higher in low-income and middle-income countries than in high-income countries, especially among adults aged 30–69 years.'

> (Strong et al., 2005)

Figure 3.9 shows the global distribution of total deaths projected for the year 2005. Cardiovascular diseases can be seen to contribute 30% of the total. By the year 2020, it is estimated that cardiovascular diseases will cause 25 million deaths, or 37% of total deaths worldwide (Neal et al., 2002).

Figure 3.9 Projected global distribution of total deaths (58 million) by major cause, 2005. Each sector of the pie chart makes a graphic representation of the percentage of deaths from various causes. Cardiovascular diseases are the single biggest killer worldwide.

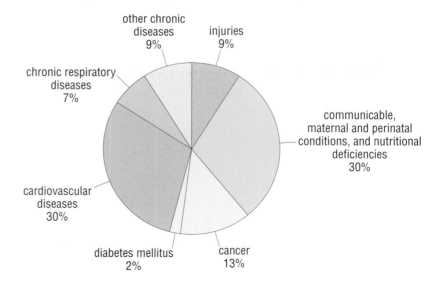

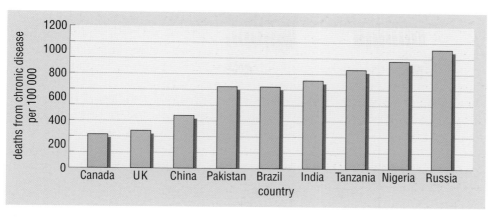

Figure 3.10   Age-standardised death rates (2005 estimates), shown in the 30–69 age group, for chronic diseases in developing countries are greater than those in developed countries. This bar chart shows that death rates in developed countries from chronic diseases are 4 or 5 times lower than comparable rates found in developing parts of the world.

● How are the ways of preventing cardiovascular disease in developing countries different from those applicable in more developed countries?

● The principles of cardiovascular disease prevention remain exactly the same throughout the world. However, there may be fewer resources available to provide preventive services or to tackle established health problems among the population within developing nations.

Bernard Choi and his colleagues (Choi et al., 2005) have attempted to look even further ahead – into the twenty-second century – and foresee an even more depressing picture where 'diseases of comfort', including cardiovascular disease, dominate the world scene and become an even greater public health problem for future generations. In their opinion, the 'rising tide of obesity and physical inactivity' is caused by an increasingly worldwide culture in which technological 'advances' make it difficult for individuals to remain free of heart disease.

There are variable death rates from cardiovascular and other chronic diseases in different countries. The variability probably relates to the fact that in poor countries the population does not have the resources to indulge in healthy lifestyles. In addition, health services in very poor countries will not be able to cope with the increasing scale of the burden of these illnesses. Figure 3.10 shows the **age-standardised death rates** for ages 30–69 from chronic diseases (per 100 000) in various countries during 2005.

3.12 Time trends

Although the total global outlook for the numbers of people developing cardiovascular disease is not necessarily encouraging, recent research has demonstrated that the death rates from cardiovascular disease have been falling fast in many developed countries (Strong et al., 2005). Death rates from cardiovascular disease have fallen by up to 70% over the last 30 years

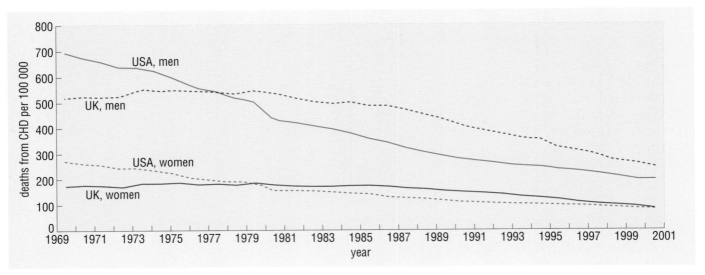

Figure 3.11 Age-standardised death rates from coronary heart disease for men and women in the UK and the USA between 1968 and 2000. The steepness of the lines on this graph indicates the rates of decline in deaths from cardiovascular disease. The rate of decline among women is much less, although from a lower starting point, than that experienced by men over the same period of time.

in Australia, Canada, Japan, the UK and the USA. Between 1970 and 2000, 14 million deaths due to cardiovascular disease were averted in the USA alone. During the same period, the numbers of deaths averted in Japan and the UK were 8 million and 3 million, respectively.

In England, coronary heart disease mortality has continued to fall (Department of Health, 2004). Figure 3.11 shows the trend in coronary heart disease mortality for men and women below the age of 65.

3.13 Social patterns of cardiovascular disease

Research has consistently shown that an individual's risk of developing cardiovascular disease is linked to several key social factors: social class, educational attainment, employment status and income (Leyland, 2005). People with less money and fewer achievements in life will tend to have a greater risk of developing cardiovascular disease. Lawlor et al. (2006) found that it is the individual's early-life socioeconomic position that largely determines the later experience of many chronic diseases, including cardiovascular disease. This finding confirmed the previous work by Davey Smith et al. (1997), who studied 5766 men growing up and then working in the West of Scotland. This research demonstrated the importance of social factors at different stages of life, and especially during childhood, when explaining the later experience of cardiovascular disease. Of course, some of the gradient is associated with the uptake of risky behaviour, such as smoking, poor diet and inadequate exercise, which seems more prevalent in people in poorer social categories. When studies analyse the data, taking account of the greater prevalence of risky behaviour at the less-educated end of the social spectrum, the social factors persist as being associated with higher risk. The reasons for this are the topic of much current research.

Case Study 3.5 British civil servants and coronary heart disease

It seems as though British civil servants have proved to be ideal research animals in the study of cardiovascular disease. For many years, a large number (6895 male and 3413 female) of civil servants between 35 and 55 years of age have been followed to see what factors in their lives could explain their eventual development of cardiovascular disease – or what had protected them from it. The study called 'Whitehall II' has revealed many interesting features. The study considered their traditional risk factors, such as cigarette smoking, blood pressure and alcohol intake. In addition, many factors relating to their working lives were studied, such as the strain that their job involved and the level of decisions that needed to be taken within their working lives (Kuper and Marmot, 2003). Highly demanding jobs with low decision latitude and increased job strain are associated with increased risk of cardiovascular disease.

'… giving people a stronger say in decisions about their work, providing them with more variety in work tasks or developing leadership may improve long-term health.'

(Kuper and Marmot, 2003)

3.14 Dietary patterns and cardiovascular disease

The link between diet and cardiovascular disease has been established through detailed research over many years. Recently there has been considerable focus on the **Mediterranean diet** in which monounsaturated fats largely replace saturated fats (Figure 3.12). Perhaps as important as the shift away from saturated fat content are the large amount of olive oil consumed and the interactions between all the various components of the diet. It now appears that the Mediterranean diet has considerable benefit with regards to lowering the risk of cardiovascular disease and also has a positive influence on cancer occurrence and total mortality rates (Trichopoulou, 2005).

A recent trial among older European people demonstrated that an adoption of the Mediterranean diet is associated with a longer life expectancy (Trichopoulou et al., 2005). The people on the trial who adhered most successfully to the positive components of a Mediterranean diet and ate more vegetables, fruits, fish and olive oil had a 7% reduction in mortality compared with those who ate more meat and dairy products.

Figure 3.12 Key elements of a Mediterranean diet.

Further research is continuing in order to determine what parts of the Mediterranean diet might be beneficial for cardiac health and apparently protect people from cardiovascular disease. At present, two theories seem to hold the most likely explanation, as described below.

3.14.1 Lipid intake profile

The Mediterranean diet relies largely on plant foods and unsaturated fats. It seems as though the elimination from the diet of saturated and *trans* fatty acids, which can be found in meat products and industrially produced food, might be particularly important. In addition, monounsaturated fat intake, from using olive oil, might have specific protective qualities. The proportion of the Mediterranean diet that comes from oily fish, which contains **omega-3 fatty acids**, may also be significant (Brunner, 2006).

3.14.2 Antioxidant content of the diet

Antioxidants are found in many of the fruits and vegetables that are components of the Mediterranean diet. Vitamins E, C and beta-carotene are antioxidants, as are carotenoids, flavonoids, selenium and magnesium. They may help the way in which potentially harmful fats are metabolised in the body. In particular, these circulating compounds may be able to protect the body, including blood vessels, against damage.

3.15 Stress and the risk of cardiovascular disease: truth and myths

There has been a great deal written on stress and cardiovascular disease, and the debates on this subject illustrate the ebb and flow of epidemiological research.

Most of the ideas surrounding this proposed link have changed over time. You may have heard of type A behaviour, characterised by people rushing around exhibiting 'time urgent' behaviour. There has been debate about whether this is something with which they are born, or if it is acquired. A number of publications in the past did suggest a causal link between **psychosocial factors**, such as type A behaviour, and cardiovascular disease, but this has not been borne out by recent studies. However, recent reviews of longitudinal prospective studies (Hemingway and Marmot, 1999) seem to agree that some psychological and psychosocial factors do predict the development of heart disease – particularly depression and lack of social support, as depicted in Figure 3.13. More recently, the Whitehall II study in Case Study 3.5 found that those civil servants who were persistently worried about their ability to pay their bills and buy appropriate food and clothing for their families had an increased experience of cardiovascular disease (Ferrie et al., 2005). The study found that the greater the individual's economic difficulties, the higher their incidence of coronary events.

A study in 52 developing countries (Interheart, 2004) found that people who have had a heart attack are more likely to report stress at work and at home, as well as financial stress, than people who had not had a heart attack. This type of study is called a case/control study. It is subject to many possible biases. The potential

Figure 3.13 Key psychosocial factors contribute to stress.

bias which is most likely here is that the patients were studied after, not before, their heart attack. The evaluation of stress was based on their interpretation. Having had a heart attack may well have influenced the way the questions were answered.

The link between psychosocial factors (including stress) and cardiovascular disease continues to be explored. Three different mechanisms have been proposed that might explain the possible link. Firstly, psychological stress might be associated with an increase in damaging health-related behaviours. It is possible that people under stress might smoke more, indulge in comfort eating and neglect any potentially protective physical activity. Secondly, there may be direct links between physiological changes that are associated with stress, such as the release of certain hormones – adrenalin and corticosteroids, for example – that might directly affect the heart and the coronary arteries. Thirdly, people under stress might neglect to seek appropriate medical attention and they might also have less well developed social support mechanisms.

3.16 Metabolic factors and the risk of cardiovascular disease

3.16.1 Metabolic syndrome, diabetes and cardiovascular disease

In other parts of the course, you will be able to study in more detail some of the metabolic aspects that relate to the way in which pathological processes within blood vessels, including the coronary vessels around the heart, are controlled by a variety of hormones and other circulating natural chemicals. **Metabolic syndrome** is the name given to a cluster of criteria that together increase an individual's risk of developing cardiovascular disease (Sundström et al., 2006; see Figure 3.14).

Figure 3.14 Diagram illustrating the various factors that are thought to contribute to metabolic syndrome. The relationships between the various factors are complex. People with any of these problems are more likely also to develop another condition from this cluster. Some researchers believe that this interrelated group of health problems is a manifestation of a single pathological process.

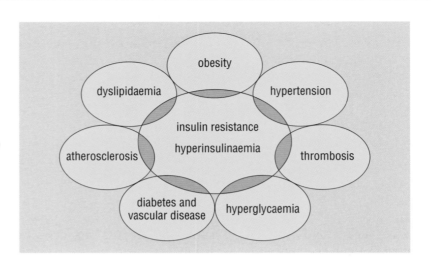

Although there are several definitions of metabolic syndrome, it is usually associated with **impaired glucose metabolism**, high blood pressure, abnormally high lipid levels in the blood and a degree of obesity. Although these factors independently increase the risk of cardiovascular disease, it appears that the combination is particularly damaging to the cardiovascular system:

> 'The presence of the metabolic syndrome increased the risk for total and cardiovascular mortality by 40%, when established cardiovascular disease risk factors were taken into account.'

> (Sundström et al., 2006)

(See also Figure 3.15.) Various population studies have estimated that between 22 and 39% of the adult population of developed countries can be considered to have metabolic syndrome. This 'epidemic' seems to be growing all the time (Tonkin, 2004). Of course, the percentage of people in any population who develop this condition relates to a number of factors, including their diet, their smoking habits and other damaging behaviours, and is also influenced by ethnicity.

The way in which glucose and insulin are metabolised in the body seems to be important in the development of cardiovascular disease. **Insulin resistance** is considered to be the underlying factor that links metabolic syndrome and Type 2 diabetes.

Figure 3.15 Coronary heart disease mortality in men with and without metabolic syndrome. As the time since diagnosis passes, more people with metabolic syndrome die than comparable people without this condition.

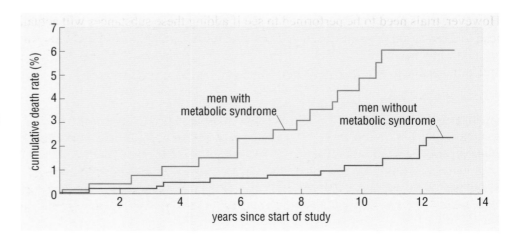

Both Type 1 and Type 2 diabetes are significant risk factors for calculating the future development of cardiovascular disease. Indeed, cardiovascular complications are the principal cause of death among people with Type 1 and Type 2 diabetes: 60% of people with Type 2 diabetes and 67% of people with Type 1 diabetes (compared with 35% of the general population) die from cardiovascular causes (Watkins, 2003). Good control of blood sugar does protect diabetic people to some extent, but even when blood sugar is well controlled diabetes remains a major cause of **microvascular** and **macrovascular** problems.

Women with diabetes are more at risk than men with diabetes. For women, the relative risk of fatal cardiovascular disease associated with diabetes is 50% higher than for men (Huxley et al., 2006). Developing diabetes seems to counter the hormonal advantages of being female that have already been discussed. The reasons behind this gender-related difference seem to be associated with different attitudes towards diabetes and vascular complications among the women themselves and the reduced awareness of health care professionals looking after them. Thus one study found that fewer women than men were on appropriate protective treatment such as aspirin or lipid-lowering medication and received less aggressive treatment for blood pressure management (Huxley et al., 2006).

3.16.2 'New' risk factors

Homocysteine/folate

There are a number of areas of current research which look promising in the search for the causes of cardiovascular disease. There continues to be a need to look for 'new' risk factors, particularly those which have the potential for later prevention. Dietary **folic acid** (one of the B vitamins) is one of these candidates. **Homocysteine** is an **amino acid** containing sulfur. It has been found that high circulating levels of homocysteine in the blood predict the development of cardiovascular disease in a number of studies of different types and in different populations. Folic acid has been shown to reduce levels of homocysteine and it has been predicted that:

> '…lowering homocysteine concentrations by 3 μmol/l from current levels (achievable by increasing folic acid intake) would reduce the risk of ischaemic heart disease by 16%.'

> (Wald et al., 2002)

However, trials need to be performed to see if adding these substances will actually lead to a reduction in cardiovascular disease. A recent trial (Bonaa et al., 2006) did not show any benefit from dietary manipulation. So the jury is still out on folic acid and homocysteine (Wald et al., 2006).

C-reactive protein

C-reactive protein is a marker of inflammation in the body. It is part of the immune system: proteins that our bodies make when faced with various threats such as infections. It has been found to be associated with an increase in the risk of cardiovascular disease in a number of studies (e.g. Danesh et al., 2004; Ranjit et al., 2007). Again, the evidence is unclear, and it is too early to be confident that inflammation and its markers such as C-reactive protein really do have an important role in causing cardiovascular disease. Of course, just finding that a factor is more common in those with a disease than in those without the disease – finding that there is an association – does not necessarily imply that there is cause and effect. There is a whole range of factors to be taken into account when deciding if an association implies causality. However, finding an association is a good start!

3.17 Summary of Chapter 3

In this chapter you have been introduced to some of the important risk factors associated with the development of cardiovascular disease. You have also learned about some of the patterns of cardiovascular disease that can be determined through epidemiological research. The way in which research is conducted in this subject area has also been explored. Most individuals are in control of their own behaviour and have risk factors that are subject to change (modifiable), and it is these that will be studied in greater detail in the next chapter, which will focus on prevention.

Questions for Chapter 3

Question 3.1 (Learning Outcomes 3.2, 3.3 and 3.5)

Which risk factor is particularly important for determining the future development of cardiovascular disease? How have risk factors for cardiovascular disease been determined?

Question 3.2 (Learning Outcomes 3.2, 3.3, 3.4 and 3.5)

In what ways do you think that women's experience of cardiovascular disease is different from that of men?

Question 3.3 (Learning Outcome 3.3)

Describe some of the differences in chronic disease patterns, including cardiovascular disease, that occur as countries develop economically.

Question 3.4 (Learning Outcomes 3.3 and 3.5)

In which ways might the Mediterranean diet affect the development or progress of cardiovascular disease?

Question 3.5 (Learning Outcomes 3.3 and 3.5)

How is salt intake associated with cardiovascular disease?

References

Barett-Connor, E. (1997) 'Sex differences in coronary heart disease: Why are women so superior?', *Circulation*, **95**, pp. 252–264.

Barker, D. (1992) *Fetal and Infant Origins of Adult Disease*, London, BMJ Publishing Group.

Barker, D. (1998) *Mothers, Babies and Health in Later Life*, Edinburgh, Churchill Livingstone.

Bonaa, K., Njolstad, I., Ueland, M., Schirmer, H., Tverdal, A. and Steigen, T. (2006) 'Homocysteine lowering and cardiovascular events after acute myocardial infarction', *New England Journal of Medicine*, **354**, pp. 1578–1588.

Brindle, P., May, M., Gill, P., Cappuccio, F., Agostino, R., Fischbacher, C. and Ebrahim, S. (2006) 'Primary prevention of cardiovascular disease: a web-based risk score for seven British black and minority ethnic groups', *Heart*, **92**, pp. 1595–1602.

Brunner, E. (2006) 'Oily fish and omega 3 fat supplements', *British Medical Journal*, **332**, pp. 739–740.

Byers, P. (2004) 'Determination of the molecular basis of Marfan syndrome: a growth industry', *Journal of Clinical Investigation*, **114**, pp. 161–163.

Choi, B., Hunter, D., Tsou, W. and Sainsbury, P. (2005) 'Diseases of comfort: primary cause of death in the 22nd century', *Journal of Epidemiology and Community Health*, **59**, pp. 1030–1034.

Cohen, J. (2006) 'Genetic approaches to coronary heart disease', *Journal of the American College of Cardiology*, **48** (9), suppl. A, pp. A10–A14.

Dahl, L. (1972) 'Salt and hypertension', *American Journal of Clinical Nutrition*, **25**, pp. 231–234.

Danesh, J., Wheeler, J., Hirschfield, G., Eda, S., Eiriksdottir, G., Rumley, A., Lowe, G., Pepys, M. and Gudnason, V. (2004) 'C-reactive protein and other circulating markers of inflammation in the prediction of coronary heart disease', *New England Journal of Medicine*, **350**, pp. 1387–1397.

Davey Smith, G., Hart, C., Blane, D., Gillis, C. and Hawthorne, V. (1997) 'Lifetime socioeconomic position and portability: prospective observational study', *British Medical Journal*, **314**, pp. 547–552.

Department of Health (2004) *Winning the war on heart disease: the National Service Framework for coronary heart disease: progress report 2004* [online] Available from: http://www.dh.gov.uk/assetRoot/04/07/71/58/04077158.pdf (Accessed November 2006).

Doll, R. and Hill, B. (1954) 'The mortality of doctors in relation to their smoking habits: a preliminary study', *British Medical Journal*, **228**, pp. 1451–1455.

Doll, R., Peto, R., Boreham, J. and Sutherland, I. (2004) 'Mortality in relation to smoking: 50 years' observations on male British doctors', *British Medical Journal*, **328**, pp. 1519–1528.

Eichner, J., Terence Dunn, S., Perveen, G., Thompson, D., Stewart, K. and Stroehla, B. (2002) 'Apolipoprotein E polymorphism and cardiovascular disease: a HuGE review', *American Journal of Epidemiology*, **155**, pp. 487–495.

Elliot, P., Stamler, J., Nichols, R., Dyer, A., Stamler, R., Kesteloot, H. and Marmot, M. (1996) 'Intersalt revisited: further analyses of 24 hour sodium excretion and blood pressure within and across populations', *British Medical Journal*, **312**, pp. 1249–1253.

Fall, C., Vijayakumar, M., Barker, D., Osmond, C. and Duggleby, S. (1995) 'Weight in infancy and prevalence of coronary heart disease', *British Medical Journal*, **310**, pp. 17–20.

Ferrie, J., Martikainen, P., Shipley, M. and Marmot, M. (2005) 'Self-reported economic difficulties and coronary events in men: evidence from the Whitehall II study', *International Journal of Epidemiology*, **34**, pp. 640–648.

Fisher, D., Baird, J., Payne, L., Lucas, P. Kleijnen, J., Roberts, H. and Law, C. (2006) 'Are infant size and growth related to burden of disease in adulthood? A systematic review of literature', *International Journal of Epidemiology*, **35**, pp. 1196–1210.

Gemmell, I., Heller, R., Payne, K., Edwards, R., Roland, M. and Durrington, P. (2006) 'The potential population impact of the UK Government strategy for reducing the burden of coronary heart disease in England: comparing primary and secondary prevention strategies', *Quality and Safety in Health Care*, **15**, pp. 339–343.

Heller, R. (2005) *Evidence for Population Health*, Oxford, Oxford University Press.

Hemingway, H. and Marmot, M. (1999) 'Psychosocial factors in the aetiology and prognosis of coronary heart disease: systematic review of prospective cohort studies', *British Medical Journal*, **318**, pp. 1460–1467.

Herrington, D. and Howard, T. (2003) 'From presumed benefit to potential harm: hormone therapy and heart disease', *New England Journal of Medicine*, **349**, pp. 519–521.

Huxley, R., Barzi, F. and Woodward, M. (2006) 'Excess risk of fatal coronary heart disease associated with diabetes in men and women: meta-analysis of 37 prospective cohort trials', *British Medical Journal*, **333**, pp. 73–78.

Interheart (2004) 'Effect of potentially modifiable risk factors associated with myocardial infarction in 52 countries: case-control study', *Lancet*, **364**, pp. 937–952.

Intersalt Cooperative Research Group (1988) 'Intersalt: an international study of electrolyte excretion and blood pressure: results for 24-hour urinary sodium and potassium', *British Medical Journal*, **297**, pp. 319–328.

Kuper, H. and Marmot, M. (2003) 'Job strain, job demands, decision latitude, and risk of coronary heart disease within the Whitehall II study', *Journal of Epidemiology and Community Health*, **57**, pp. 147–153.

Kuppuswamy, V. and Gupta, S. (2005) 'Excess coronary heart disease in South Asians in the United Kingdom', *British Medical Journal*, **330**, pp. 1223–1224.

Lawlor, D., Sterne, J., Tynelius, P., Davey Smith, G. and Rasmussen, F. (2006) 'Association of childhood socioeconomic position with cause-specific mortality in a prospective record linkage study of 1,839,384 individuals', *American Journal of Epidemiology*, **164**, pp. 907–915.

Leyland, A. (2005) 'Socioeconomic gradients in the prevalence of cardiovascular disease in Scotland: the roles of composition and context', *Journal of Epidemiology and Community Health*, **59**, pp. 799–803.

Lip, G., Barnett, A., Bradbury, A., Cappuccio, F, Gill, P., Hughes, E., Imray, C., Jolly, K. and Patel, K. (2007) 'Ethnicity and cardiovascular disease prevention in the United Kingdom: a practical approach to management', *Journal of Human Hypertension*, **21**, pp. 183–211.

McPherson, K. (2004) 'Where are we now with hormone replacement therapy?', *British Medical Journal*, **328**, pp. 357–358.

McPherson, K., Britton, A. and Causer, I. (2002) *Coronary Heart Disease: Estimating the Impact of Changes in Risk Factors*, Norwich, National Heart Forum/The Stationery Office.

Merz, C. (2006) 'A gender difference in heart disease: variant in women called hard to detect', *Washington Post*, 1 February, pp. A08.

Neal, B., Chapman, N. and Patel, A. (2002) 'Managing the global burden of cardiovascular disease', *European Heart Journal Supplements*, **4**, suppl. F, pp. F2–F6.

NHS (2006) *PRIMIS+* [online] Available from: http://www.primis.nhs.uk (Accessed March 2007).

Paneth, N. and Susser, M. (1995) 'Early origin of coronary heart disease (the 'Barker hypothesis')', *British Medical Journal*, **310**, pp. 411–412.

Ranjit, N., Diez-Roux, A., Shea, S., Cushman, M., Seeman, T., Jackson, S. and Ni, H. (2007) 'Psychosocial factors and inflammation in the multi-ethnic study of atherosclerosis', *Archive of Internal Medicine*, **167**, pp. 174–181.

Song, Y., Stampfer, M. and Liu, S. (2004) 'Meta-analysis: Apolipoprotein E genotypes and risk for coronary heart disease', *Annals of Internal Medicine*, **141**, pp. 137–147.

Strong, K., Mathers, C., Leeder, S. and Beaglehole, R. (2005) 'Preventing chronic diseases: how many lives can we save?', *Lancet*, **366**, pp. 1578–1582.

Sundström, J., Riserus, U., Byberg, L., Zethelius, B., Lithell, H. and Lind, L. (2006) 'Clinical value of the metabolic syndrome for long term prediction of total and cardiovascular mortality: prospective, population based cohort study', *British Medical Journal*, **332**, pp. 878–882.

Tonkin, A. (2004) 'The metabolic syndrome: a growing problem', *European Heart Journal Supplements*, **6**, pp. A37–A42.

Topol, E., Smith, J., Plow, E. and Wang, Q. (2006) 'Genetic susceptibility to myocardial infarction and coronary heart disease', *Human Molecular Genetics*, **15**, review issue 2, pp. R117–R123.

Trichopoulou, A. (2005) 'Modified Mediterranean diet and survival: EPIC-elderly prospective cohort study', *British Medical Journal*, **330**, pp. 991–995.

Trichopoulou, A., Corella, D., Martinez-Gonzalez, M., Soriguer, F. and Ordovas, J. (2005) 'The Mediterranean diet and cardiovascular epidemiology', *Nutrition Reviews*, **64**, pp. S13–S19.

Tucker, G. (2003) Comments from reviewer, *Climacteric*, **6**, pp. 310–314.

Vergopoulos, A., Knoblauch, H. and Schuster, H. (2002) 'DNA testing for familial hypercholesterolaemia: improving disease recognition and patient care', *American Journal of Pharmacogenomics*, **2**, pp. 253–262.

Wald, D., Law, M. and Morris, J. (2002) 'Homocysteine and cardiovascular disease: evidence on causality from a meta-analysis', *British Medical Journal*, **325**, pp. 1202–1206.

Wald, D., Wald, N., Morris, J. and Law, M. (2006) 'Folic acid, homocysteine, and cardiovascular disease: judging causality in the face of inconclusive trial evidence', *British Medical Journal*, **333**, pp. 1114–1117.

Wang, L., Fan, C., Topol, S., Topol, E. and Wang, Q. (2003) 'Mutation of MEF2A in an inherited disorder with features of coronary heart disease', *Science*, **28**, pp. 1578–1581.

Watkins, P. (2003) 'Cardiovascular disease, hypertension and lipids', *British Medical Journal*, **326**, pp. 874–876.

Whincup, P., Gilg, J., Papacosta, O., Seymour, C., Miller, G., Alberti, K. and Cook, D. (2002) 'Early evidence of ethnic differences in cardiovascular risk: cross sectional comparison of British South Asian and white children', *British Medical Journal*, **324**, pp. 635–641.

CHAPTER 4

PREVENTING CARDIOVASCULAR DISEASES

Learning Outcomes

When you have completed this chapter you should be able to:

4.1 Define and use, or recognise definitions and applications of, each of the terms printed in **bold** in the text.

4.2 Understand the role of a population approach to the reduction of cardiovascular disease.

4.3 List the main ways that cardiovascular disease can be prevented in individuals.

4.4 Explain the primary importance of smoking cessation in the prevention of cardiovascular disease in individuals.

4.5 Outline the role of diet in the prevention of cardiovascular disease.

4.6 Discuss how exercise may be a feature of cardiovascular disease risk reduction for individuals.

4.1 Introduction

In Chapter 3 you studied some of the dominant patterns and risk factors that relate to cardiovascular disease. In this chapter the focus will switch to prevention. Of course, there is a very direct link between causation and prevention: when the cause of a disease becomes widely known, prevention can be attempted by tackling or altering the cause. At an individual level, if someone is aware that a habit or lifestyle factor is a known cause of cardiovascular disease for them in the future, they have an opportunity to prevent this increased risk to their health by adjusting their lifestyle or changing that potentially harmful habit. However, prevention also works at other levels. In Chapter 3 you were made aware of population as well as individual risk of developing cardiovascular diseases. This chapter will focus on some of the ways in which cardiovascular disease can be prevented at several different levels, ranging from governmental down to the individual. Firstly, some of the issues that relate to the prevention of cardiovascular disease in whole populations will be examined.

4.2 Who has the responsibility for prevention? Government-level intervention

The habits of people within a population can, to some extent, be controlled by the actions of their government. The best example of this, particularly in relation to cardiovascular disease, is the way in which various governments attempt tobacco control. The most common types of government activity are through the use of taxation, by banning smoking in public places, by banning tobacco advertising and choosing to finance health education campaigns, usually through the mass media.

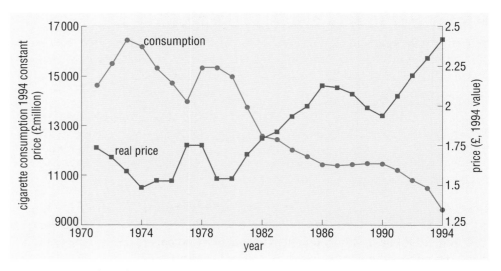

Figure 4.1 The relationship between consumption (pounds sterling in millions at 1994 values) and real price (pounds sterling at 1994 values) of a typical pack of cigarettes in the UK from 1971 to 1994. From this figure, it can be seen that consumption of cigarettes falls as the real price is increased through higher taxation.

4.2.1 Taxation policy

As demonstrated in Figure 4.1, as the price of cigarettes rises, consumption falls:

> '…price increases are the most effective and cost-effective tobacco control measure, especially for young people and others on low incomes, who are highly price responsive. A price rise of 10% decreases consumption by about 4% in high-income countries.'

(Joosens and Raw, 2006)

For governments, this may not be a simple issue and they will be keen not to alienate significant sectors of their electorate by imposing punitive taxation. In addition, geographic variations between countries in the price of tobacco products may lead to the emergence of smuggling (Wiltshire et al., 2001) and even the growth of organised crime involved in the international movement of tobacco products (Jamrozik, 2006).

Recent research in four developed countries (Hyland et al., 2006) has shown that people who smoke full-price cigarettes are more likely to attempt to quit their habit than those who purchase low-price or untaxed cigarettes.

So it is not a simple task for governments to decide the level of taxation that they should apply to tobacco products. As the taxation levels rise, there is usually a growth in illegal activity (Figure 4.2) to circumvent the tax, and the intended outcome – a reduction in tobacco consumption – might not happen at all.

Figure 4.2 If the price of 'legal' cigarettes grows too high then the temptation for illegal sources of supply, particularly in deprived neighbourhoods, becomes much greater.

4.3 Smoking and passive smoking

Smoking is the single most important cause of cardiovascular disease. Any preventive activity for whole nations, communities or individuals that manages to decrease the amount of tobacco consumed will also reduce the incidence of cardiovascular disease.

Giving up smoking is a great way to reduce your risk of cardiovascular disease. The longer that people have given up smoking, the greater their reduction in risk. Within a year of smoking cessation, the excess cardiovascular mortality due to smoking is halved; within 15 years, the absolute risk is almost the same as in people who have never smoked (Edwards, 2004).

However, cutting down the amount of tobacco consumed is nowhere near as effective as stopping smoking altogether. Norwegian researchers (Tverdal and Bjartveit, 2006) have shown that heavy smokers who halved their daily tobacco intake failed to reduce their risk of death from cardiovascular disease or other causes. A study of over 50 000 smokers for 21 years revealed that the risk of dying from cardiovascular disease increases dramatically as soon as an individual starts smoking even as few as four cigarettes each day. Although it may seem counterintuitive, the only certain way of reducing risk is to stop smoking altogether. It seems as though cutting down on tobacco use has hardly any evidence-based beneficial effect at all.

4.3.1 Passive smoking

In Section 4.1 you started to learn about the way in which governments can act to increase the price of tobacco products so that smoking, particularly among young people, is a less attractive option. Governments also have an opportunity to create an environment in which smoking is restricted. This has become increasingly important as evidence continues to grow about the dangers of inhaling other people's smoke, commonly called **passive smoking**.

Case Study 4.1 Environmental tobacco smoke

Environmental tobacco smoke seems to be especially hazardous. Even a small exposure to second-hand tobacco smoke has a large effect on the risk of developing cardiovascular disease (Barnoya and Glantz, 2005). Comparatively slight exposure to environmental tobacco smoke results in increased platelet aggregation and causes the endothelial cells lining the coronary arteries to dysfunction, contributing to narrowing of the arteries and a reduction in blood flow (Otsuka, 2001).

> 'Evidence is rapidly accumulating that the cardiovascular system – platelet and endothelial function, arterial stiffness, atherosclerosis, oxidative stress, inflammation, heart rate variability, energy metabolism, and increased infarct size – is exquisitely sensitive to the toxins in second-hand smoke.'
>
> (Barnoya and Glantz, 2005)

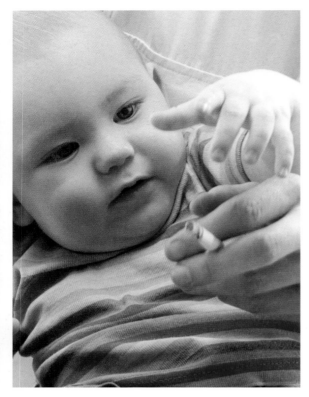

Figure 4.3 Passive smoking has become increasingly unacceptable because of the known harmful effects of second-hand smoke on susceptible others, particularly small children.

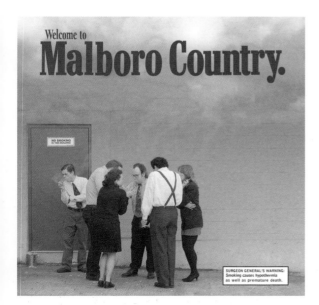

Figure 4.4 Sometimes humour is the best way to drive home the point.

● Why do you think passive smoking might be particularly harmful?

● The chemicals contained in second-hand smoke include those that come from the smouldering tobacco that is produced between puffs. Environmental tobacco smoke contains over 4000 chemicals, including over 50 compounds that are known or probable human carcinogens (National Cancer Institute, 1999). It's not surprising that it has the capacity to induce cardiovascular disease as well.

In terms of prevention, the breakthrough for the introduction of tobacco control policies has come from the evidence that exposure to other people's smoke greatly increases the risk to an individual's health. While it may be acceptable to behave in a way that will harm your own health, it is unacceptable to behave in a way that will harm others (Figure 4.3). Smoking in pregnancy harms the growing fetus. In childhood, having parents who smoke increases chest diseases; in adulthood, having a partner who smokes increases the risk of heart disease and lung cancer. The argument about occupational exposure to cigarette smoke by bar workers and others has been crucial in the drive to ban smoking in public places.

4.3.2 Banning smoking in public places

A growing number of European governments have attempted to reduce tobacco consumption through the imposition of bans on smoking in public places. In March 2004, the Republic of Ireland became the first European country to impose an outright ban on smoking in workplaces, including bars and restaurants. Because of the popular success of this measure, several other European governments have taken the same steps, including Norway, Scotland, Italy, France, Wales, Northern Ireland and, most recently, England. This is an excellent example of a 'population approach', which has in part been brought about by popular campaigns against smoking (Figure 4.4). Although it is early days, there is growing evidence that banning smoking in public places leads to a reduction in smoking rates in the general population and in heart attack rates.

4.4 Can cardiovascular disease be prevented in whole populations?

There have been a number of population approaches to the prevention of cardiovascular disease. The most famous of these is the North Karelia project. This began in Finland in the province of North Karelia (Figure 4.5) as far back as 1972 and was followed by other cardiovascular disease prevention

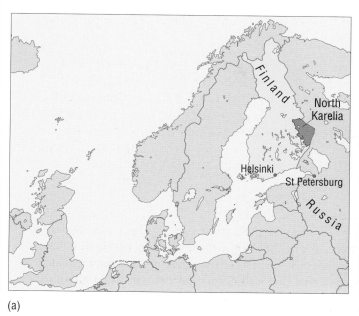

(a)   (b)

Figure 4.5   North Karelia's (a) remoteness and (b) natural beauty belie the fact that, in the 1970s, it had one of the highest heart disease rates in the world.

activities throughout Finland. The stimulus was pressure from the community in response to the knowledge that Finland in general, and North Karelia in particular, had one of the highest heart disease rates in the world.

A comprehensive approach to the reduction of risk factors for cardiovascular disease was taken and considerable resources were used in an attempt to demonstrate that the high levels of cardiovascular disease experienced in this community were not inevitable. Almost all health workers in the area received additional training in ways to help people reduce their individual risk profile for cardiovascular disease. Other organisations, such as sports facilities and a wide range of community groups, were targeted for health promotion activities. Some of these activities were innovative, including competitions to see which groups could lower their cholesterol levels furthest – and smoking reduction contests as well. Local suppliers of foodstuffs also became involved in the project, helping to promote low-fat and low-salt alternatives and to encourage healthy diets.

Results showed that the project appeared to be successful over the long term. Risk factor rates decreased in the project area and the consumption of fruit and vegetables increased considerably, whereas butter consumption, for example, dropped dramatically. Interestingly, the consumption of cigarettes fell among men but increased among women, as shown in Table 4.1. The project appeared to be successful with regards to the levels of cardiovascular disease in the community. For example, cardiovascular mortality rates for men aged 35–64 decreased 57% from 1970 to 1992 (Vartiainen et al., 2000). The difficulty has been in deciding whether this dramatic decrease was due to the programme itself. Risk factor levels and heart disease rates both fell after the programme was started, but this was a demonstration project rather than a research study and there was no good comparison group. Comparisons were made with similar communities and it did appear that the change was greater in North Karelia, although improvements

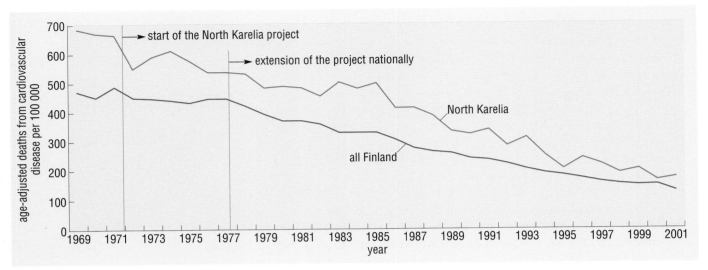

Figure 4.6 Cardiovascular disease mortality in all Finland and in the province of North Karelia, 1969–2002 (men aged 35–64).

Table 4.1 Risk factor changes in North Karelia, 1972–1997 (men and women aged 30–59).

Year	Men			Women		
	Percentage smoking	Cholesterol (mmol/l)	Blood pressure (mmHg)	Percentage smoking	Cholesterol (mmol/l)	Blood pressure (mmHg)
1972	52	6.9	149/92	10	6.8	153/92
1977	44	6.5	143/89	10	6.4	141/86
1982	36	6.3	145/87	15	6.1	141/85
1987	36	6.3	144/88	16	6.0	139/83
1992	32	5.9	142/85	17	5.6	135/80
1997	31	5.7	140/88	16	5.6	133/80

occurred in all communities (Pekkanen et al., 1995). Figure 4.6 shows the decline in cardiovascular disease mortality in the province of North Karelia and compares it with the decline in the whole of Finland over the same period. Both rates seem to fall over the period of study, but the previously excessive rate in North Karelia has almost approached the Finnish average by the new millennium.

Activity 4.1   How effective was the North Karelia project?

Suggested study time 20 minutes

Look carefully at Figure 4.6, which shows coronary heart disease mortality in all Finland and in the province of North Karelia from 1969 to 2002. What are the major features shown in this figure? How convinced are you that the fall in heart disease in North Karelia was due to the prevention programme? Also consider the data presented in Table 4.1. Pick out some of the trends that are shown in the data. For example, what is happening to the smoking rates among women in this area over time?

Comment

Figure 4.6 shows clearly that cardiovascular disease mortality fell rapidly in North Karelia during the years since the start of the project. However, it also shows that this decline in mortality was also happening throughout Finland at the same time. At the start of the project, cardiovascular disease mortality in North Karelia does seem to be considerably higher than in the rest of Finland, and at the end of the project there is not much difference.

Of course, it can never be proven that the steeper fall in cardiovascular disease death rates in North Karelia has been directly the result of the preventive work done within the project. If people throughout Finland started to change their habits as a result of wider societal concerns, then the areas with the highest rates of cardiovascular disease would be likely to suffer the most rapid drop in mortality, irrespective of the special projects available to people in North Karelia. On the other hand, any information disseminated by the North Karelia project would be bound to leak out into other areas and help everybody in Finland consider the ways they could change their lifestyle in order to reduce their risk of developing cardiovascular disease.

The figures in Table 4.1 clearly show a rise in the percentage of women smoking. This rose from 10% in 1972 to 16–17% between 1987 and 1997. Presumably this was not the effect of the preventive health programmes, rather reflecting a more general societal trend throughout Finland at that time.

Case Study 4.2   Heartbeat Wales

In the UK, the most comprehensive population-based programme designed to combat the high rate of cardiovascular disease has been the Heartbeat Wales project (Tudor-Smith et al., 1998).

This project used a wide range of coordinated community-level interventions in an attempt to modify the cardiovascular-disease-associated behavioural risks. Many innovative projects were undertaken, including special television programmes to alert people to the risks they might be taking and promoting ways they would be able to reduce those risks. One of the most interesting features of Heartbeat Wales was the way in which the project involved food producers and retailers to ensure that healthy food was promoted at the point of sale and was available for those people who wanted to make changes to their diets. Other projects within the overall programme focused on smoking cessation and regular exercise.

The programme appeared to be very successful in bringing about the reduction of behavioural risks for cardiovascular disease (Smith et al., 1994). However, the project compared the programme area against a **reference area** with similar socioeconomic characteristics as those found in Wales. There were similar changes and reductions in the levels of behavioural risks in both areas.

A number of other population-wide approaches to cardiovascular disease prevention have been tried as well as those in Finland and Wales. In the USA, the Stanford Five-City Project seemed to have considerable success in reducing cardiovascular heart disease risk (Farquhar et al., 1990), but even this project was not able to reduce the actual cardiovascular disease event rates to a greater extent than those experienced in the control populations.

● How might the positive effects of health education campaigns spread to areas that have not been specifically targeted?

● In most modern societies, it is virtually impossible to isolate specific campaigns. Health education messages, particularly those delivered through the mass media, will always spread much wider than just to their target audience.

There may be other technical reasons for the apparent difficulty in establishing the benefit of population-level interventions that are aimed at the reduction of cardiovascular disease. How is it that so much is known about the causes of cardiovascular disease, but researchers have been unable to provide convincing evidence that interventions at the population level can be beneficial? Some answers may lie in technical reasons associated with research design. For example, in order to demonstrate a positive effect for the intervention project, the length of time for which researchers would have to follow people to be able to show a benefit would need to extend to many years. In addition, very large numbers of people would have to be recruited for the projects themselves, as well as for control groups. In this context the problem of 'contamination' of the control groups has been discussed (Tudor-Smith et al., 1998). Contamination means that unanticipated events have gone on in the control areas so that comparison with the areas of the project becomes problematic.

Throughout developed nations there has been a consistent fall since the Second World War in cardiovascular disease risk factors as well as a decline in morbidity and mortality from cardiovascular disease. This means that in the control areas people are changing their behaviour and experiencing a lower rate of cardiovascular disease, but these phenomena are taking place for reasons other than the introduction of specific population-wide health promotion projects.

4.5 Population approaches to the reduction of hypertension

Every living human being has a blood pressure that can be measured and recorded. If each individual's blood pressure is plotted on a graph, the **distribution** can be shown. The shape of the distribution curve for blood pressure is shown in Figure 4.7. Most biological variables are distributed in a similar fashion.

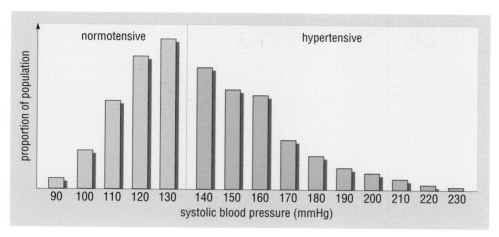

Figure 4.7   The distribution of systolic blood pressure measurements throughout a given population. At some point, it has to be decided which readings are considered abnormal and above which a label of 'hypertensive' is given. Some people will have very high blood pressure readings and be towards the right-hand end of the **bell-shaped curve**. You will notice that all those with a systolic blood pressure greater than 140 mmHg have been defined as 'hypertensive' in the data summarised by this figure.

● Why do you think the systolic reading of 140 mmHg was chosen in Figure 4.7 to define hypertension?

● This level is largely arbitrary. Although cardiovascular risk does increase with higher blood pressure readings, there is no point at which a specific risk kicks in and below which can be considered 'safe'. The systolic reading of 140 mmHg seems perfectly reasonable and has been chosen as a convenient figure largely through clinical experience.

Geoffrey Rose, a British epidemiologist, suggested that greater benefit to the health of the population could be gained by reducing a risk factor for the whole population by a small amount rather than focusing just on people with high levels of that particular risk factor (Rose, 1985, 1992). Unfortunately, as described in Box 4.1, this theory has been difficult to demonstrate in practice.

Box 4.1 Is the population approach effective?

Although the theory behind multiple-risk-factor interventions and population-based approaches to the reduction of cardiovascular disease remains strong, in practice the effectiveness of these complex programmes has been hard to prove. None of the major community-based studies within developed countries, such as the Stanford Heart Disease Prevention Program, the Stanford Five-City Project or the Minnesota Heart Health Program, detected significant changes in cardiovascular risk factors or disease events (Ebrahim and Davey Smith, 2001).

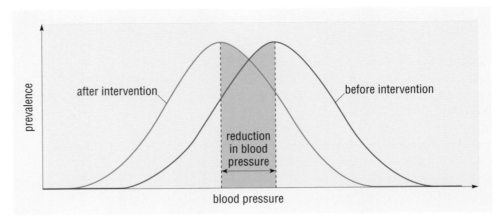

Figure 4.8 Systolic blood pressure distributions before and after population-level interventions.

Figure 4.8, which shows systolic blood pressure distributions before and after population-level intervention, demonstrates the theory that has come to be called the 'population approach' to prevention. You can see that if you shift the whole distribution of blood pressure 'to the left', the average blood pressure of the population is reduced. At the same time, the proportion of the population which has high levels is reduced. The figure shows the potential reduction in cardiovascular disease as well as in stroke that would occur if average blood pressure levels were to be reduced by even modest amounts. You may remember that in Chapter 3 you learned how different populations have different blood pressure and salt levels. One prevention strategy would be to reduce the salt intake of the whole population. This would theoretically achieve a 'shift to the left' in the population's blood pressure. Although experimental reduction of salt intake has not been attempted in whole populations, it has been estimated that reducing the average diastolic blood pressure in the population of the USA by 2 mmHg would result in a 17% decrease in the prevalence of hypertension (Stamler, 1991). This would be a true population approach to prevention. Unfortunately, there is as yet no evidence in real life that such an approach is effective.

Geoffrey Rose developed his theory at a time when risk factor calculation and indeed treatment of people with a high level of cardiovascular disease risk was not well developed. With the introduction of more modern approaches to **multiple risk evaluation** and the use of highly effective cholesterol-lowering drugs, as well as the development of more effective ways of controlling blood pressure, the balance between population approaches and 'high-risk' approaches (see Section 4.6) may have shifted significantly – as shown by a recent analysis of Canadian data (Manuel et al., 2006).

4.6   Can cardiovascular disease be prevented in individuals?

In Chapter 3 you learned about some of the risk factors that may be present in individuals that have been identified by assessing the individual's future chance of developing cardiovascular disease. The theory behind the prevention of disease in individuals is called the 'high-risk' approach, contrasting with the population approach discussed above. This approach targets those individuals within the population who are at greatest risk – but identifying these individuals does present a series of challenges.

4.6.1   Capacity to benefit

It is becoming clearer that risk factors are not simply present or absent in individuals. For example, some years ago it was considered that people either had hypertension or did not. But there is now common acceptance that there is a continuum of cardiovascular disease related to blood pressure. Hypertension is increasingly being defined as:

> '…the blood pressure level above which there would be substantial (or clinically significant) benefits from lowering blood pressure.'

> (Jackson et al., 2005)

The same concept of a continuum of cardiovascular disease related to lipid levels in the blood can be applied to the definition of **hyperlipidaemia** (elevated blood lipid levels). For this reason, most people throughout the developed world and increasing numbers in developing nations would actually be included in **capacity to benefit** definitions of hypertension and hyperlipidaemia. Virtually everyone would benefit from attention to their lifestyle features and would benefit from reduced blood cholesterol and blood pressure readings.

Information on individual prevention has been accumulated by research involving **clinical trials**. This involves offering people something like a pill or specific advice (such as smoking cessation) and comparing any resulting change in the patients given the pill or advice with those who have not been given it. Drug companies are very keen to show that their drugs are effective, as this will increase sales. So there have been many clinical trials sponsored by commercial drug companies which test medication that may be effective in cardiovascular disease. Most of these trials are among patients who have already sought medical help, either for the disease itself or for its risk factors.

Sometimes clinical prevention trials attempt to reduce just one risk factor such as high blood cholesterol, high blood pressure or smoking. Other, more complex trials attempt to reduce more than one to follow the theory (Chapter 3) that the more risk factors individuals have, the greater their risk of getting heart disease. Unfortunately, doctors and other clinical workers are not very accurate at quantifying cardiovascular disease risk factors for individuals (Box 4.2). Individual risk factors seem to aggregate in the same people. This is partly because those who are obese, for example, are also likely to be physically inactive and to have high blood pressure and low levels of the 'good' (HDL) cholesterol.

Box 4.2 Estimating coronary risk: how good are the professionals?

Clinicians, both generalists and specialists, have been found to be poor at quantifying cardiovascular risk (McManus et al., 2002). Knowledge of risk is generally not very good. When presented with the hypothetical case of a person with raised cholesterol, they overestimated the risk that the person would have a heart attack within the next five years by more than three times the actual risk, and also overestimated the benefits of treatment by approximately the same amount. This appears to be a good reason for using one of the readily available research-based cardiovascular risk prediction devices such as the ETHRISK calculator you were introduced to in Section 3.8.

A combined approach is to look at a strategy which, rather than deciding between primary and secondary types of prevention and between the population and high-risk approaches, uses **baseline risk** as the defining characteristic for attempts at prevention. This is assessed by algorithms that include age, gender, smoking status, blood pressure, cholesterol levels and other behavioural or disease risk factors (Manuel et al., 2006).

- Why do you think that health professionals may not be very good at estimating an individual's cardiovascular risk?

- Some professionals might have been trained before risk factor analysis was widely acknowledged and not be entirely familiar with this concept. Most health professionals only see people with established disease and this might also tend to distort their estimates.

4.7 Can medication help to prevent cardiovascular disease?

There are many trials apparently providing further evidence that lowering blood cholesterol and blood pressure, often using medication, results in fewer people having heart attacks and dying. Every few months, another such trial is published.

Jackson and his colleagues published a review of the effectiveness of drug-based medication designed to reduce blood cholesterol and blood pressure (Jackson et al., 2005). They conclude that, although medication aimed at reducing one particular risk factor – for example, tablets that lower blood pressure or reduce circulating cholesterol – may indeed lower those values, they seem to be of little clinical relevance when considered in isolation from the individual's absolute cardiovascular risk prediction scores:

> 'Separate management guidelines for raised blood pressure and blood cholesterol need to be replaced by integrated cardiovascular risk management guidelines.'

> (Jackson et al., 2005)

4.7.1 Statins

Statins are chemicals that interrupt cholesterol synthesis in the liver. You will learn about them in more detail in Chapter 8. Technically, they are 3-hydroxy-3-methylglutaryl coenzyme A reductase inhibitors, and according to some analysts they are 'the most successful cardiovascular drugs of all time' (Shepherd, 2006). As well as lowering the amount of potentially harmful circulating cholesterol, they may even help to clear up the fatty deposits of atherosclerosis that have been previously deposited in the major vessels, such as coronary, cerebral and peripheral arteries. A list of the claims made for these remarkable chemical compounds is given in Box 4.3.

> 'This constellation of benefits with little side effect penalty has resulted in the comparison of statins with antibiotics in the global battle against cardiovascular disease.'
>
> (Shepherd, 2006)

Box 4.3 Claims made for the use of statins

- Atheroma regression
- Retards the progress of diabetes
- Slows the progress of chronic renal (kidney) failure
- Prevents MI
- Reduces the incidence of recurrence of MI
- Enhances cerebral and coronary blood flow
- Improves outlook for people with familial hyperlipidaemia

The commercial success of statins is continuing. Figure 4.9 shows that there has been an enormous growth in the number of prescriptions in England for this class of drug over recent years. This rapid growth in prescriptions may have been partially checked by the recent introduction of over-the-counter availability for these drugs in the UK (Filion et al., 2006).

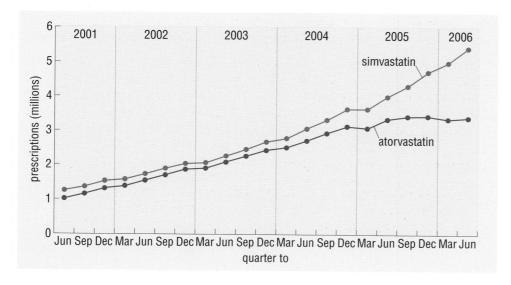

Figure 4.9   Trends in prescribing statins in general practice in England. This graph shows the rapid rise in the number of prescriptions for the two most commonly prescribed statins in England since 2001.

The number of prescriptions for statins trebled between 2001 and 2006 to a total of 9.7 million prescriptions each quarter in England alone. The cost of these drugs has increased over this period by 41% to £141 million each quarter (Prescription Pricing Authority, 2006). The debate about the effectiveness and **cost-effectiveness** of this type of medication continues (Figure 4.10). Heller et al. (2001a,b) queried whether this expenditure is of benefit to individuals with raised cholesterol levels but without known coronary heart disease. A **meta-analysis** of **randomised controlled trials** (Thavendiranathan et al., 2006) concluded that using statins in people without known cardiovascular disease produces such limited benefits that it may not be cost-effective. A meta-analysis is a statistical technique which takes all relevant (and well-designed) studies on a topic and arrives at a composite result using data from all the trials. The analysis, which took the results from seven trials involving nearly 43 000 adults aged from 55 to 75, found that 60 people would need to take statins for an average of 4.3 years to prevent one serious cardiovascular event. Moreover, there are considerable problems associated with chemical approaches to prevention (Box 4.4), and statin use did not improve the overall risk of dying from cardiovascular disease or from other causes:

> '…statins have not been shown to provide an overall health benefit in primary prevention trials.'

> (Therapeutics Initiative, 2003)

Figure 4.10   There is always a balance between personal gain from a particular treatment and the need to consider public or community benefit – for example, when expensive medication is required to treat a medical condition.

Box 4.4 Problems with chemical approaches to prevention

All medication carries with it the potential problems of **side effects** and **adverse reactions**. The types of chemicals designed for preventive action all have their own risks and benefits. For example, this is the entry (written for doctors and containing some technical terms) in the British National Formulary that gives some of the adverse effects of statins:

'Reversible myositis [muscle swelling and injury] is a rare but significant side effect of the statins. The statins also cause headache, altered liver-function tests (rarely, hepatitis), paraesthesia [a sensation of tingling or numbness in the skin], and gastro-intestinal effects including abdominal pain, flatulence, constipation, diarrhoea, nausea and vomiting. Rash and hypersensitivity reactions (including angioedema and anaphylaxis) have been reported rarely.'

(British National Formulary, 2007)

The effectiveness of the use of statins on people who are known to have heart disease or who have had a major coronary event such as an MI has different parameters (secondary prevention) and will be explored later in this chapter and in Chapter 8.

4.8 Could there be a single pill for preventing cardiovascular disease?

The ultimate technological solution for preventing cardiovascular disease has been proposed by Wald and Law (2003). These two London professors have suggested that the combined benefits of several types of medication taken by everyone aged 55 years and over, whether they had cardiovascular disease or not, would lead to a reduction in the prevalence of the disease by more than 80%. So a single pill (Figure 4.11) could, in theory, bring these benefits to so many. Table 4.2 lists the proposed constituents of the 'polypill'.

The cost of prescribing the polypill for the entire population has come under scrutiny (Franco et al., 2006). The greatest benefits would be obtained if the polypill were to be given to everyone at high risk of cardiovascular disease in addition to everyone over the age of 55. This strategy only becomes cost-effective if the medication can be produced and distributed at a low price. In addition, the generalised use of medicines in this way stands the risk of **medicalising** the entire population and also exposes otherwise healthy people to the risk of harmful effects from the combination of chemicals contained in the polypill.

Figure 4.11 People with cardiovascular disease are often prescribed a number of medications to manage the symptoms.

Table 4.2 Proposed polypill constituents.

Drug type	Drug action
aspirin	blood-thinning and anti-platelet agent
statin	reduces levels of harmful lipids
thiazide diuretic	reduces blood pressure
beta-blocker	reduces blood pressure
ACE inhibitor	reduces blood pressure
folic acid	reduces levels of homocysteine

● What side effects do you think might be associated with the use of the polypill?

● Each pharmaceutical chemical contained within the polypill has potentially serious side effects. Of course, the combination of active chemical ingredients might also create problems. However, each constituent would be included at a dose lower than if each single therapy were used, and this would have the effect of minimising potential adverse drug effects.

Because this proposal would involve large segments of the population becoming 'patients' and having to take pills for many years, an alternative approach has been suggested – the 'polymeal' (Franco et al., 2004; Box 4.5). The beneficial effects may be similar to those associated with the proposed 'polypill', but with the active ingredients all coming from food products.

Box 4.5 The proposed polymeal

In response to the proposed polypill, other researchers have suggested that a comparative beneficial effect could be achieved by an 'evidence-based diet' containing specific foodstuffs with proven cardio-protective ingredients (Franco et al., 2004). The polymeal would contain:

• wine
• fish
• dark chocolate
• fruits and vegetables
• almonds
• garlic.

4.9 Does alcohol cause cardiovascular disease or protect against it?

Many epidemiological studies have appeared to show the protective effects of moderate alcohol consumption, and there are plausible explanations (see Box 4.6) for this possible effect. Originally, this was called the 'French paradox' because

French people seem to develop less heart disease than could be expected by calculating their other risk factors. Some studies have also suggested that the pattern of drinking is as important as the quantity of alcohol consumed. For example, a study in Denmark (Tolstrop et al., 2006) followed 28 448 women and 25 052 men and found that, for men, the lowest risk of developing coronary heart disease events was among those who drank moderate amounts of alcohol each day. This same finding was not shown in the women who took part in the study. But is the relationship between drinking alcohol and reduced risk for coronary heart disease **causal**? Comparing the drinking group with people who drink no alcohol at all can be problematic because the group of total abstainers might include people who were already ill with other conditions or ex-alcoholics who are abstaining for medical reasons. Similarly, the moderate use of alcohol might be linked with other healthy behaviours such as having more social contacts or eating a better diet.

Box 4.6 Possible biological mechanisms for the potentially cardioprotective effects of alcoholic drinks

Polyphenols contained in alcoholic drinks, such as red wine, result in the following conditions which reduce an individual's risk of developing cardiovascular disease:

- a beneficial effect on HDL cholesterol levels
- lower plasma fibrinogen, which would otherwise tend to produce clotting in the coronary arteries
- reduced platelet aggregation.

4.9.1 Heavy drinking and cardiovascular disease

There seems to be little doubt that heavy drinking does cause cardiovascular disease, along with a wide range of other physical, psychological and social problems (Alcohol Concern, 2006). Some of these adverse effects are outlined below.

Hypertension

High blood pressure is associated with a high intake of alcohol (Svetkey, 2005), although reducing alcohol intake in people who are already hypertensive may not always be successful (Cushman et al., 1998). Approximately 5–7% of people diagnosed with hypertension are heavy drinkers.

Sudden death

High alcohol intake is also a cause of several different heart arrhythmias, including atrial fibrillation, atrial flutter and various other rhythm disturbances (see Section 6.4). The arrhythmias are caused by increased secretion of various hormones as well as a sudden rise in fatty acids in the blood in addition to the action of **acetaldehyde**, which is a primary breakdown product of alcohol. In the most severe cases, typically during an alcoholic binge after a period of relative abstinence, sudden death can occur. This is sometimes called 'holiday heart syndrome' (Ettinger et al., 1978).

Alcoholic cardiomyopathy

If individuals drink heavily for many years, a serious heart condition called **alcoholic cardiomyopathy** can develop. The enlarged heart that has been observed at the autopsy of heavy drinkers was previously thought to be due either to contaminants in the alcoholic beverages or from vitamin deficiencies that are often associated with people who drink to excess. More recently, the directly toxic effect of alcohol on the heart has been recognised (Piano, 2002). Individuals drinking 7 to 8 units of alcohol each day for 5 years run the risk of developing this serious condition in which the mass of the heart is increased while the ventricles dilate and the walls of the heart chambers become thinner and less effective, eventually leading to heart failure.

It would appear that stopping drinking heavily is a good way of preventing cardiovascular disease.

Case Study 4.3 Martha Childs' comfort eating of chocolate

Martha lives a very active life with a family, a volunteer job and an almost full-time job. She often doesn't give herself time for a proper meal and she snatches a quick snack when she can. On many occasions, these snacks are not healthy options, with lunch comprising a chocolate bar.

Is this good or bad for her cardiovascular health? Unfortunately, chocolate bars are very high in calories and this diet will tend to maintain her weight in the 'obese' category. However, chocolate contains a complex mixture of chemicals. In its commercial form, it is usually mixed together with various fats and sugars that together make up the familiar chocolate bars that are widely available (Figure 4.12). It would be hard to make a case for a diet that contained too many of these products, especially as some of the beneficial chemicals may be destroyed in the manufacturing process. However, the basic substance, cocoa, as derived from the cocoa bean may well contain constituent chemicals, including antioxidants, that have beneficial effects.

Flavonoids are **phenolic phytochemicals** that are found in many different foods such as tea, oat bran, almond skins and in cocoa itself. It might be that these naturally occurring chemicals are the common link that seems to give cardiovascular benefit from the Mediterranean diet, and the daily consumption of small amounts of alcohol, tea and cocoa itself. Cocoa-derived polyphenols have been shown to dilate arteries and change the way platelets work (Ferri and Grassi, 2003), whereas other researchers have found that the chemicals in chocolate can lower blood pressure, reduce inflammation and improve the levels of circulating lipids in the blood (Ding et al., 2006).

In an experiment that must be close to the heart of all 'chocoholics', Taubert et al. (2003) fed 100 g of dark chocolate each day for 14 days to a group of elderly people with high blood pressure, whose blood pressure was observed to fall. The same effect was not noted when they were switched to white chocolate.

Figure 4.12   Some types of chocolate may be good for us.

In Chapter 3 you were introduced to the way that various cardiovascular disease risk factors can be studied by following a cohort of people for many years and observing what happens to them. In Zutphen, in the Netherlands, researchers followed a group of elderly men in an attempt to discover which features in their lives affected their future health. Cocoa intake certainly seems to be a relevant factor. Those elderly men who ingested the most cocoa also had the lowest blood pressures and the lowest cardiovascular mortality over the 15 years of the study (Buijsse et al., 2006).

4.10 Does being vegetarian help to prevent cardiovascular disease?

There is a continuing debate between vegetarians and omnivores in an attempt to determine which type of diet is most healthy. If you take away aspects of the debate that relate to the ethics of killing animals for human use, the health-related interchange goes something like this:

> 'Vegetarians can't possibly get sufficient nutrients to keep themselves healthy. They are particularly at risk from deficiency problems, with trace elements, vitamins and probably iron being best provided by a balanced diet that contains meat.'

Advocates of a vegetarian diet might retort:

> 'Meat-based diets themselves may well be deficient in plant-based protective constituents such as phytochemicals and may also have harmful excesses of damaging lipid products.'

So what is the truth and how might it be possible to throw light on this subject?

Once again, there is evidence from epidemiological studies that can be used to determine what sorts of diet are most likely to protect against cardiovascular disease. Hu (2003) reviewed all the studies that explored the link between diet and cardiovascular disease and came to the following conclusion:

> 'Evidence from prospective cohort studies indicates that a high consumption of plant-based foods such as fruit and vegetables, nuts, and whole grains is associated with a significantly lower risk of coronary artery disease and stroke. The protective effects of these foods are probably mediated through multiple beneficial nutrients contained in these foods, including mono- and polyunsaturated fatty acids, n-3 [omega-3] fatty acids, antioxidant vitamins, minerals, phytochemicals, fiber, and plant protein.'
>
> (Hu, 2003)

(See also Figure 4.13.) For both vegetarian diets and those containing meat products, there can be no doubt that a balance of different classes of foodstuff is important. No single food group contains all the things that are necessary for a healthy diet, especially for preventing cardiovascular and other chronic diseases. Even plant-based diets are not necessarily healthy unless the right types of carbohydrates and fats are the predominant sources of energy (Hu, 2003). It certainly appears that the health benefits of fruit and vegetables come from rather complex interactions, combinations and synergy between the various constituents (Liu, 2003):

> '...the additive and synergistic effects of phytochemicals in fruit and vegetables are responsible for their potent antioxidant and anticancer activities, and that the benefit of a diet rich in fruit and vegetables is attributed to the complex mixture of phytochemicals present in whole foods.'
>
> (Liu, 2003)

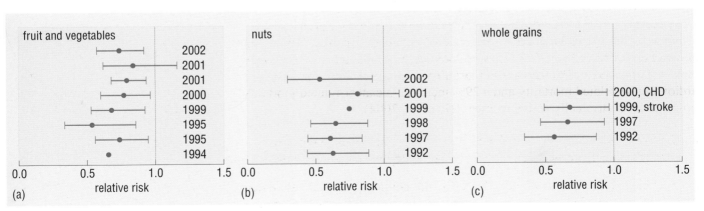

Figure 4.13 Visual representation of the results from a large number of prospective cohort studies (labelled by year) of cardiovascular disease and consumption of (a) fruit and vegetables, (b) nuts and (c) whole grains (also labelled by cardiovascular disease studied). In these graphs, a relative risk of 1 means that there is neither an increase nor a decrease in risk. Below 1, the risk is lower; above 1, the risk is higher. In all these graphs, the risk of cardiovascular disease is lower among those who have vegetarian diets, who eat nuts or who eat whole grains.

4.11   Does increasing physical activity reduce the risk of cardiovascular disease?

Later in the course you will be able to learn more about the benefits of exercise for people who have confirmed cardiovascular disease or who have had an MI. The preventive activity that can be taken in the presence of confirmed disease is called secondary prevention. There have been a number of studies looking at the positive effects of increased physical activity following a heart attack (for example, see Briffa et al., 2006). This increased physical activity is often undertaken in the context of a general cardiac **rehabilitation** programme (see Section 10.7.2) and it can be difficult to separate out the effect of exercise on its own. A review (Jolliffe et al., 2001) found that, for people who had had a heart attack, taking part in a cardiac rehabilitation programme reduced the chance of cardiac death and total mortality significantly. The effect of exercise was also beneficial in the absence of other aspects of rehabilitation. Together, these research studies indicate that cardiac rehabilitation including exercise should be a part of the routine care of people who have had a heart attack.

The evidence for the protective effect of exercise before an individual develops cardiovascular disease (primary prevention) has also been established (Thompson et al., 2003; Warburton et al., 2006). Physical activity does seem to be really good for human beings in general and not just those at risk of cardiovascular disease. The list of chronic diseases for which there is evidence for positive protective effects of sustained physical exercise also includes diabetes, cancer of the colon, breast cancer, osteoporosis, osteoarthritis and depression:

> 'An increase in physical fitness will reduce the risk of premature death, and a decrease in physical fitness will increase the risk. The effect appears to be graded, such that even small improvements in physical fitness are associated with a significant reduction in risk.'
>
> (Warburton et al., 2006)

The effects of physical exercise on reducing the risk of developing cardiovascular disease have been shown in a large number of studies. Being fit or physically active seems to be associated with a greater than 50% reduction in risk. On the other hand, physically inactive women aged between 30 and 55 (and followed up for more than 20 years) who took less than 1 hour of exercise each week 'experienced a 52% increase in mortality from all causes, a doubling of cardiovascular related mortality and a 29% increase in cancer-related mortality compared with physically active women' (Hu et al., 2004).

● Can you think of any biological mechanisms that could explain the way in which increased physical activity might lead to improved cardiovascular health?

● Warburton et al. (2006) suggest the following possible mechanisms. There will be improved body composition that will be of particular importance to people who are obese. Also an improved lipoprotein profile will result, including reduced triglyceride and LDL cholesterol levels and an increase in HDL cholesterol levels. Glucose metabolism will also be improved and blood pressure will be reduced. Blood coagulation will be better controlled and coronary artery blood flow will be improved. In addition, psychological wellbeing is generally improved with greater levels of exercise.

Box 4.7　How is fitness measured?

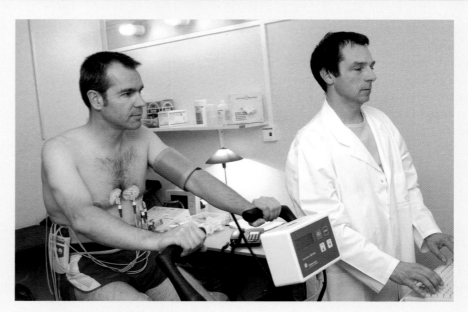

Figure 4.14　Heart fitness test.

In the measurement of physical fitness, it has become standard practice to distinguish between aerobic and anaerobic types of activity.

Anaerobic fitness is concerned with the body's ability to produce energy without the use of oxygen. Maximum anaerobic power can be measured by assessing an individual's all-out effort while running or jumping, in which muscles create or use energy sources within the body.

Aerobic fitness can be measured by estimating the individual's maximum amount of oxygen that can be used by the working muscles (**VO_2 max**). Because this is not easy to measure directly, aerobic fitness is usually estimated using the heart rate during graduated exercise such as cycling or running on a treadmill (Figure 4.14; see also Section 7.4.3). A lower heart rate for a given workload is thought to represent a higher level of aerobic fitness.

The energy demands of tissues will be discussed in greater detail in Section 5.3.

4.11.1　How much physical activity, and for how long?

Various official organisations, such as the American College of Sports Medicine and the Center for Disease Control and Prevention in the USA (Thompson et al., 2003), have recommended that benefit from physical activity will be gained if people undertake 30 minutes or more of moderate-intensity physical activity such as brisk walking on most, or preferably all, days of the week. As the person gets used to one level of activity, they should be encouraged to increase this in order to maintain the maximum benefit. Unfortunately, the exercise has to be maintained throughout the person's entire life. Even people who have been extremely fit in the past go back to average levels of cardiovascular risk if they do not maintain their exercise regimes.

4.12 Obesity and cardiovascular disease

Obesity is the term that is commonly used when excessive fat builds up in the body. Box 4.8 shows how we can categorise this using the **body mass index (BMI)**. Unfortunately, obesity can have serious health problems for the individual because many organs of the body may be affected and function poorly. This seems especially true of the fat that builds up within arteries which can lead to reduced blood flow and damage to the heart and other organs.

Fat can be distributed in different ways throughout the body, and it appears that the type of fat that builds up around the waist is more likely to be associated with increased risk of cardiovascular disease than fat elsewhere in the body (Han, 2006).

In terms of prevention, it would appear self-explanatory that individuals and whole populations should avoid becoming obese.

4.12.1 How is obesity measured?

Box 4.8 The body mass index

Whether or not an adult is overweight or obese can be estimated using the body mass index (BMI). BMI is calculated by dividing someone's mass (in kg; commonly referred to as their weight) by their height (in metres) multiplied by itself:

$$BMI = \frac{mass\ (kg)}{height\ (m) \times height\ (m)}$$

A BMI of 20–24.9 kg/m^2 is a healthy one, 25–29.9 kg/m^2 is overweight and 30 kg/m^2 or more indicates obesity. This measurement was established by the Belgian scientist Adolphe Quételet and was previously called Quételet's Index. Note that it does not apply to athletes, children, pregnant women or lactating women.

Waist circumference is probably a better indicator of the most harmful type of fat distribution because it relates more directly to the presence of fat around the organs (Han, 2006).

You will revisit the BMI during the discussion on weight management in Section 10.2.3.

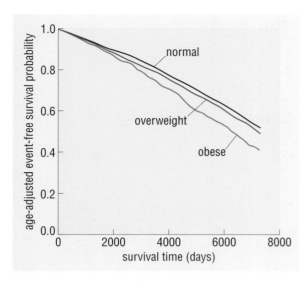

Figure 4.15 Age-adjusted event-free survival in men for cardiovascular death or hospital admission.

Obesity is a risk factor in coronary heart disease (Rao et al., 2001) and is associated with several risk factors that you have already studied. People carrying significant amounts of excess weight are more likely to develop metabolic syndrome, glucose intolerance, diabetes, hypertension and hyperlipidaemia... but is obesity also an independent risk factor? The Framingham heart study, introduced in Chapter 3, showed that people carrying excess body fat had more coronary arterial disease episodes than those who remained at their 'ideal weight', independent of any other factors. More recently, the long-term cardiovascular consequences of obesity have been followed up in Glasgow (Murphy et al., 2006). This 20-year study of more than 15 000 men and women found that obesity is associated with a broad range of fatal and non-fatal cardiovascular events: heart failure, venous problems, atrial fibrillation and, probably, stroke. Figure 4.15 shows how the men in the study fared over time. Overweight people had survival rates just below those with normal body weights. Obese people survived for shorter periods of time than people of the same age but with normal body weights. It is worth noting that the steadily increasing level of overweight and obesity observed in developed countries – particularly among younger people – is likely to reverse the recent decline in cardiovascular mortality.

Case Study 4.4   Is Mr Patel obese?

Mr Kamal Patel is 1.64 m tall and his weight is 78 kg. His body mass index can therefore be calculated to be 29. Does this make him obese?

This BMI would put him in the overweight category if he had a Caucasian ethnic background. With a BMI of 30 or over, he would be considered to be obese. However, some commentators (Kuppuswamy and Gupta, 2005) feel that the normal ranges for independent risk factors for cardiovascular disease should be lowered for people from South Asia. The World Health Organization (2004) has also focused on this issue, and their recommendations would suggest that any person of South Asian ethnicity with a BMI of over 27.5 should be in the 'higher high-risk' (obese) group.

Waist circumference is even more closely related to cardiovascular risk than BMI. A waist measurement of 100 cm for men (93 cm for women) corresponds to a BMI of 30, the 'obese' range for Caucasian people. However, the percentage of body fat – and, perhaps even more importantly, the distribution of body fat – may be different for various ethnic groups. Overweight and obese men from South Asia often have their body fat distributed in a pattern known as 'abdominal obesity', and this has been linked with excessive abdominal fat content and greatly increased cardiovascular risk.

Mr Patel needs help to lose weight and reduce his waist circumference from its current 101 cm.

4.13 Secondary prevention for people with known cardiovascular disease

Having one heart attack greatly increases the risk of another. People who have had a heart attack or who have known cardiovascular disease are at special risk and should be targets for prevention advice. In the UK, the government has set targets for the care of people with, or at risk of, heart disease – National Service Frameworks (Department of Health, 2000; see Section 1.6.1). However, there is incomplete awareness of these targets, which are not being fully implemented. Research has shown that going from current preventive practice to 'best practice' as defined in the National Service Frameworks would in theory save a large number of lives among those who have already had a heart attack (Gemmell et al., 2005). Both drug-based (such as increasing the use of statins and blood-pressure treatment) as well as lifestyle interventions (such as increasing exercise and stopping smoking) are important in meeting these targets.

Should medical and public health resources concentrate more on primary prevention or on secondary prevention? Currently, most prevention efforts are aimed at secondary prevention as people with cardiovascular disease come to the attention of doctors and other health professionals. Further research has demonstrated that meeting government targets for primary prevention would (in theory again) save even more lives than meeting secondary prevention targets (Unal et al., 2005; Gemmell et al., 2006). This of course depends on whether effective prevention programmes can be implemented:

> 'Compared with secondary prevention, primary prevention achieved a fourfold larger reduction in deaths (between 1981 and 2000 in England and Wales). Future coronary heart disease policies should prioritise population-wide tobacco control and healthier diets.'

> (Unal et al., 2005)

4.14 Summary of Chapter 4

The simplest way for individuals to consider the prevention of cardiovascular disease is to study the list of known risk factors such as the ones identified in Chapter 3 and make sure that action is taken on all these factors. This might be effective at an individual level, but as soon as community or population interventions are considered a wide range of new issues need to be taken into account. Since the 1980s, there has been a significant fall in the incidence of cardiovascular events in developed countries. Changes in lifestyle as well as the introduction of newer forms of treatment and more effective preventive medication have all played their part in bringing about this substantial improvement. The relative contribution of each of these factors remains the subject of considerable debate and there is growing uncertainty whether these possible changes will continue into the future.

> 'Currently the dramatic rises in obesity (and hence diabetes) threaten to cancel out the benefits of recent positive trends in cholesterol, blood pressure, and smoking in the youngest groups. The party may soon be over.'

> (Capewell, 2006)

This chapter has demonstrated that it is hard to plan and implement strategies for the reduction of these known risk factors and is then difficult to determine if these interventions have been effective.

Questions for Chapter 4

Question 4.1 (Learning Outcome 4.2)

Why is the population approach to smoking reduction more effective than an approach targeted at susceptible individuals in reducing the incidence of cardiovascular disease?

Question 4.2 (Learning Outcomes 4.2 and 4.4)

Why is passive smoking so dangerous and what do you think action at governmental level can do about it?

Question 4.3 (Learning Outcome 4.3)

What are the main ways that individuals can protect themselves against the development of cardiovascular disease?

Question 4.4 (Learning Outcomes 4.3 and 4.5)

What is the role of diet in the prevention of cardiovascular disease?

Question 4.5 (Learning Outcomes 4.3 and 4.6)

How important is exercise in the prevention of cardiovascular disease? How might the beneficial effects of exercise be determined?

References

Alcohol Concern (2006) *Factsheet: health impacts of alcohol* [online] Available from: http://www.alcoholconcern.org.uk/files/20060320_121128_Health%20 effects%20pullout%20version%203%20March%202006.pdf (Accessed October 2006).

Barnoya, J. and Glantz, S. (2005) 'Cardiovascular effects of secondhand smoke', *Circulation*, **111**, pp. 2684–2698.

Briffa, T., Maiorana, A., Sheerin, N., Subbs, A., Oldenburg, B., Sammel, N. and Allan, R. (2006) 'Physical activity for people with cardiovascular disease: recommendations of the National Heart Foundation of Australia', *Medical Journal of Australia*, 184, pp. 71–75.

British National Formulary (2007) *Statins* [online] Available from: http://www. bnf.org/bnf/bnf/53/33422.htm?q=%22statin22 (Accessed April 2007).

Buijsse, B., Feskens, E., Kok, F. and Kromhout, D. (2006) 'Cocoa intake, blood pressure, and cardiovascular mortality: the Zutphen Elderly Study', *Archives of Internal Medicine*, **166**, pp. 411–417.

Capewell, S. (2006) 'Predicting future coronary heart disease deaths in Finland and elsewhere', *International Journal of Epidemiology*, **35**, pp. 1253–1254.

Cushman, W., Cutler, J., Hanna, E., Bingham, S., Follmann, D., Harford, T., Dubbert, P., Allender, P., Dufour, M., Collins, J., Walsh, S., Kirk, G., Burg, M., Felicetta, J., Hamilton, B., Katz, L., Perry, H., Willenbring, L., Lakshman, R. and Hamburger, R. (1998) 'Prevention and Treatment of Hypertension Study (PATHS): effects of an alcohol treatment program on blood pressure', *Archives of Internal Medicine*, **158**, pp. 1197–1207.

Department of Health (2000) *National Service Framework for coronary heart disease* [online] Available from: http://www.dh.gov.uk/en/Publicationsandstatistics/ Publications/PublicationsPolicyAndGuidance/DH_4094274 (Accessed February 2007).

Ding, E., Hutfless, S., Ding, X. and Girotra, A. (2006) 'Chocolate and prevention of cardiovascular disease: a systematic review', *Nutrition and Metabolism*, **3** (2) [online] Available from: http://www.nutritionandmetabolism.com/content/3/1/2 (Accessed November 2006).

Ebrahim, S. and Davey Smith, G. (2001) 'Exporting failure? Coronary heart disease and stroke in developing countries', *International Journal of Epidemiology*, **30**, pp. 201–205.

Edwards, R. (2004) 'The problem of tobacco smoking', *British Medical Journal*, **328**, pp. 217–219.

Ettinger, P., Wu, C., De La Cruz, C., Weisse, A., Ahmed, S. and Regan, T. (1978) 'Arrhythmias and the 'Holiday Heart': alcohol-associated cardiac rhythm disorders', *American Heart Journal*, **95**, pp. 555–562.

Farquhar, J., Fortman, S., Flora, J., Taylor, C., Haskell, W., Williams, P., Maccoby, N. and Wood, P. (1990) 'Effects of community-wide education on cardiovascular disease risk factors: The Stanford Five-City Project', *Journal of the American Medical Association*, **262**, pp. 359–365.

Ferri, C. and Grassi, G. (2003) 'Mediterranean diet, cocoa and cardiovascular disease: a sweeter life, a longer life, or both?', *Journal of Hypertension*, **21**, pp. 2231–2234.

Filion, K., Delany, J., Brophy, J., Ernst, P. and Suissa, S. (2006) 'The impact of over-the-counter simvastatin on the number of statin prescriptions in the United Kingdom: a view from the General Practice Research Database', *Pharmacoepidemiology and Drug Safety*, **16**, pp. 1–4.

Franco, O., Bonneux, L., de Laet, C., Peeters, A., Steyerberg, E. and Mackenbach, J. (2004) 'The polymeal: a more natural, safer, and probably tastier (than the polypill) strategy to reduce cardiovascular disease by more than 75%', *British Medical Journal*, **329**, pp. 1447–1450.

Franco, O., Steyerberg, E. and de Laet, C. (2006) 'The polypill: at what price would it become cost effective?', *Journal of Epidemiology and Community Health*, **60**, pp. 213–217.

Gemmell, I., Heller, R., McElduff, P., Payne, K., Butler, G., Edwards, R., Roland, M. and Durrington, P. (2005) 'Population impact of stricter adherence to recommendations for pharmacological and lifestyle interventions over one year in patients with coronary heart disease', *Journal of Epidemiology and Community Health*, **59**, pp. 1041–1046.

Gemmell, I., Heller, R., McElduff, P., Payne, K., Butler, G., Edwards, R., Roland, M. and Durrington, P. (2006) 'Potential population impact of the UK government strategy for reducing the burden of coronary heart disease in England: comparing primary and secondary prevention strategies', *Quality and Safety in Health Care*, **15**, pp. 339–343.

Han, T. (2006) 'Assessment of obesity and its clinical complications', *British Medical Journal*, **333**, pp. 695–698.

Heller, T., Heller, R., Pattison, S. and Fletcher, R. (2001a) 'Treating the patient or the population? Judging the benefit of treatment of individual patients', *Western Journal of Medicine*, **175**, pp. 35–37.

Heller, T., Heller, R., Pattison, S. and Fletcher, R. (2001b) 'Treating the patient or the population? Judging the benefit of treatment to society as a whole', *Western Journal of Medicine*, **175**, pp. 104–107.

Hu, F. (2003) 'Plant-based foods and prevention of cardiovascular disease: an overview', *American Journal of Clinical Nutrition*, **78**, suppl., pp. 544S–551S.

Hu, F. B., Willett, W. C., Li, T., 'Stampfer, M. J., Colditz, G. A. and Manson, J. E. (2004) Adiposity as compared with physical activity in predicting mortality among women', *New England Journal of Medicine*, **351**, pp. 2694–2703.

Hyland, A., Laux, F., Higbee, C., Hastings, G., Ross, H., Chaloupka, F., Fong, G. and Cummings, K. (2006) 'Cigarette purchase patterns in four countries and the relationship with cessation: findings from the International Tobacco Control (ITC) Four Country Survey', *Tobacco Control*, **15**, suppl. 3, pp. iii59–iii64.

Jackson, R., Lawes, C., Bennett, D., Milne, R. and Rodgers, A. (2005) 'Treatment with drugs to lower blood pressure and blood cholesterol based on an individual's absolute cardiovascular risk', *Lancet*, **365**, pp. 434–441.

Jamrozik, K. (2006) 'Policy priorities for tobacco control', *British Medical Journal*, **328**, pp. 1007–1009.

Jolliffe. J., Rees, K. and Taylor, R. (2001) 'Exercise-based rehabilitation for coronary heart disease', *Cochrane Database Systematic Review*, **1**, CD001800.

Joosens, L. and Raw, M. (2006) 'The tobacco control scale: a new scale to measure country activity', *Tobacco Control*, **15**, pp. 247–253.

Kuppuswamy, V. and Gupta, S. (2005) 'Excessive coronary heart disease in South Asians in the United Kingdom: the problem has been highlighted but much more needs to be done', *British Medical Journal*, **330**, pp. 1223–1224.

Liu, R. (2003) 'Health benefits of fruit and vegetables are from additive and synergistic combinations of phytochemicals', *American Journal of Clinical Nutrition*, **78**, suppl., pp. 517S–520S.

Manuel, D., Lim, J., Tanuseputro, P., Anderson, G., Alter, D., Laupacis, A. and Mustard, C. (2006) 'Revisiting Rose: strategies for reducing coronary heart disease', *British Medical Journal*, **332**, pp. 659–662.

McManus, R., Mant, J., Meulendijks, C., Salter, R., Pattison, H., Roalfe, A. and Hobbs, R. (2002) 'Comparison of estimates and calculations of risk of coronary heart disease by doctors and nurses using different calculation tools in general practice: cross-sectional study', *British Medical Journal*, **324**, pp. 459–464.

Murphy, N., MacIntyre, K., Stewart, S., Hart, C., Hole, D. and McMurray, J. (2006) 'Long-term cardiovascular consequences of obesity: 20-year follow-up of more than 15,000 middle-aged men and women (the Renfrew–Paisley study)', *European Heart Journal*, **27**, pp. 96–106.

National Cancer Institute (1999) 'Health effects of exposure to environmental tobacco smoke: the report of the California Environmental Protection Agency', *Smoking and Tobacco Control Monograph no.10*, Bethesda, MD, National Cancer Institute, pp. 359–425.

Otsuka, R. (2001) 'Acute effects of passive smoking on the coronary circulation in healthy young adults', *Journal of the American Medical Association*, **286**, pp. 436–441.

Pekkanen, J., Tuomilehto, J., Uutela, A., Vartiainen, E. and Nissinen, A. (1995) 'Social class, health behaviour, and mortality among men and women in eastern Finland', *British Medical Journal*, **311**, pp. 589–593.

Piano, M. (2002) 'Alcoholic cardiomyopathy: incidence, clinical characteristics and pathophysiology', *Chest*, **121**, pp. 1638–1650.

Prescription Pricing Authority (2006) *PCT prescribing report, July–September 2006: lipid-regulating drugs: prescribing guidance and discussion points,* [online] Available from: http://www.ppa.org.uk/systems/pctreports/pctreport_20062.pdf (Accessed February 2007).

Rao, S., Donahue, M., Pi-Sunyer, F. and Fuster, V. (2001) 'Obesity as a risk factor in coronary artery disease', *American Heart Journal*, **142**, pp. 1102–1107.

Rose, G. (1985) 'Sick individuals and sick populations', *Bulletin of the World Health Organisation*, **79**, pp. 990–996.

Rose, G. (1992) *The Strategy of Preventive Medicine*, Oxford, Oxford University Press.

Shepherd, J. (2006) 'Who should receive a statin these days? Lessons from recent clinical trials', *Journal of Internal Medicine*, **260**, pp. 305–319.

Smith, C., Moore, L., Roberts, C. and Catford, J. (1994) 'Health-related behaviours in Wales, 1985–1990', *Health Trends*, **26**, pp. 18–21.

Stamler, R. (1991) 'Implications of the INTERSALT study', *Hypertension*, **17**, suppl. 1, I16–I20.

Svetkey, L. (2005) 'Management of prehypertension', *Hypertension*, **45**, pp. 1056–1061.

Taubert, D., Berkels, R., Roesen, R. and Klaus, W. (2003) 'Chocolate and blood pressure in elderly individuals with isolated systolic hypertension', *Journal of the American Medical Association*, **290**, pp. 1029–1030.

Thavendiranathan, P., Bagai, A., Brookhart, M. and Choudhry, N. (2006) 'Primary prevention of cardiovascular diseases with statin therapy: a meta-analysis of randomised controlled trials', *Archives of Internal Medicine*, **166**, pp. 2307–2313.

Therapeutics Initiative (2003) *Therapeutics Letter 48: Do statins have a role in primary prevention?* [online] Available from: http://www.ti.ubc.ca/PDF/48.pdf (Accessed December 2006).

Thompson, P. D., Buchner, D., Piña, I. L., Balady, G. J., Williams, M. A., Marcus, B. H., Berra, K., Blair, S. N., Costa, F., Franklin, B., Fletcher, G. F., Gordon, N. F., Pate, R. R., Rodriguez, B. L., Yancey, A. K. and Wenger, N. K. (2003) 'Exercise and physical activity in the prevention and treatment of atherosclerotic cardiovascular disease', *Circulation*, **107**, pp. 3109–3116.

Tolstrop, J., Jensen, M., Tjonneland, A., Overvad, K., Mukamal, K. and Gronbaek, M. (2006) 'Prospective study of alcohol drinking patterns and coronary heart disease in women and men', *British Medical Journal*, **332**, pp. 1244–1248.

Townsend, J., Roderick, P. and Cooper, J. (1994) 'Cigarette smoking by socioeconomic group, sex and age: effects of price, income and health publicity', *British Medical Journal*, **309**, pp. 923–927.

Tudor-Smith, C., Nutbeam, D., Moore, L. and Catford, J. (1998) 'Effects of the Heartbeat Wales programme over five years on behavioural risks for cardiovascular disease: quasi-experimental comparison of results from Wales and a matched reference area', *British Medical Journal*, **316**, pp. 818–822.

Tverdal, A. and Bjartveit, K. (2006) 'Health consequences of reduced daily cigarette consumption', *Tobacco Control*, **15**, pp. 472–480.

Unal, B., Critchley, J. and Capewell, S. (2005) 'Modelling the decline in coronary heart disease deaths in England and Wales, 1981–2000: comparing contributions from primary prevention and secondary prevention', *British Medical Journal*, **331**, pp. 614–617.

Vartiainen, E., Jousilahti, P., Alfhan, G., Sundvall, J., Pietinen, P. and Puska, P. (2000) 'Cardiovascular risk factor changes in Finland 1972–1977', *International Journal of Epidemiology*, **29**, pp. 49–56.

Wald, N. and Law, M. (2003) 'A strategy to reduce cardiovascular disease by more than 80%', *British Medical Journal*, **326**, pp. 1419–1423.

Warburton, D., Nicol, C. and Bredin, S. (2006) 'Health benefits of physical activity: the evidence', *Canadian Medical Association Journal*, **174**, pp. 801–809.

Wiltshire, S., Bancroft, A., Amos, A. and Parry, O. (2001) '"They're doing people a service": qualitative study of smoking, smuggling and social deprivation', *British Medical Journal*, **323**, pp. 203–207.

World Health Organization (2004) 'Appropriate body-mass index for Asian populations and its implications for policy and intervention strategies', *The Lancet*, **363**, pp. 157–163.

VASCULAR DISEASES

5.1 Introduction

In Chapter 2, you looked at the role of the heart in pumping blood around the body. The right ventricle pumps blood through the lungs, where it picks up oxygen; the left ventricle pumps the freshly oxygenated blood through the other tissues of the body. This chapter looks at the circulatory system in more detail, to explain how the blood supply to different tissues is controlled according to the requirements of each tissue. To understand vascular disease, you first need to look at how blood flow is controlled normally.

5.2 The vascular tree

The branching network of vessels that distribute blood is called the vascular tree. The anatomical structure of different vessels within the tree varies according to their position and functions (Figure 5.1). All blood vessels are lined on the

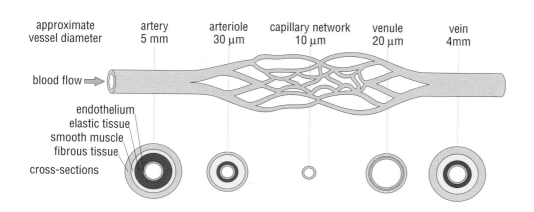

Figure 5.1 Blood vessels vary greatly in diameter and in the thickness of the vessel wall. All vessels have an internal lining of endothelium. Arteries and arterioles have thicker walls than venules and veins, due to the relatively thick layers of elastic tissue and smooth muscle. All vessels except capillaries have an outer layer of fibrous tissue.

inside surface with a layer of **endothelial cells**. These cells are flattened, which facilitates the smooth flow of blood within the vessels, and this internal layer of cells is called the **endothelium**. Although endothelium is similar in all parts of the vascular tree, endothelial cells do have some functional differences, depending on where they are located. One function of these cells is to prevent the blood from clotting inside the vessels (see Section 5.7), and another is to help control how much blood flows through each capillary network (see Section 5.3).

Arteries are subjected to higher blood pressure than any other vessels and the blood flow in them is pulsatile, meaning that the blood pressure and the rate of blood flow vary with the pumping action of the heart. Arteries have layers of muscular and elastic tissue in their wall, which allows the vessels to expand with the contraction of the ventricle (systole), and contract again as the ventricle refills (diastole). This is a special type of muscle called smooth muscle; unlike muscles that move parts of the body, we do not have any voluntary control over it.

Box 5.1 Types of muscle

There are three basic types of muscle. **Skeletal muscles** move parts of the body, and we have voluntary control over what they do. **Smooth muscle** is present in many tissues – for example, in the gut. It may contract, but we do not have voluntary control over what it does. It is also present in the walls of larger blood vessels. **Heart muscle** is the third, specialised type of muscle.

Arterioles are smaller vessels that distribute the blood into the network of capillaries (capillary beds). They too have layers of muscle in the wall; this is very important, because it controls how much blood goes into the capillary beds.

Capillaries are the smallest blood vessels in the body, having an internal diameter hardly larger than the diameter of a single red blood cell. They have a very thin wall, lacking muscle and elastic tissue. The internal surface is lined with a single layer of **capillary endothelial cells** and there are a few structural cells in the wall, which help to stop these tiny vessels from collapsing. The thin wall is perfect for allowing nutrients and oxygen to diffuse from the blood into the tissues, and to allow waste products and carbon dioxide to diffuse from the tissues into the blood. In one person, the internal surface area of the capillaries is equivalent to several tennis courts.

Venules collect blood from the capillary networks. The blood pressure in these vessels is low, and they do not pulse. Consequently, they need very little elastic tissue in their walls. However, they do have one special function. White blood cells belonging to the immune system migrate out of the blood by crossing the wall of venules, moving into tissues in order to patrol the body and protect against infection.

Veins are the larger collecting vessels. They may run deep in tissues such as muscles, or superficially, just beneath the skin. Veins have valves to prevent the blood from running backwards or pooling. Although there is very little residual pressure in the veins to push blood forwards, the contraction of muscles around them squeezes them so that blood does move forward. Eventually, the veins drain into the largest vein, the vena cava, which leads back to the heart.

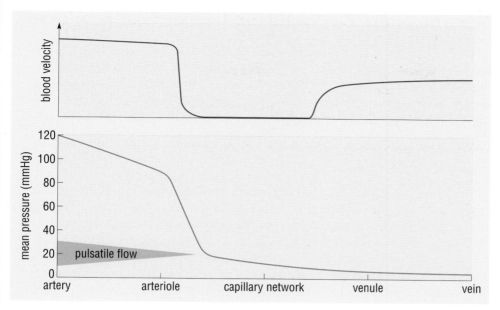

Figure 5.2   Blood pressure and the flow rate of the blood vary along the vascular tree. Pressure and flow rate are pulsatile in the arteries and larger arterioles, but pressure and velocity fall rapidly in smaller arterioles. Blood flows slowly in capillaries, but velocity increases as the blood drains into venules and veins.

Figure 5.1 shows how the vessels get progressively smaller as the blood flows from the heart to the capillaries. The pressure within the vessels drops and the pulse also disappears by the time the blood has reached the capillaries (Figure 5.2).

In general, each artery supplies just one area of the body, and each arteriole supplies the blood to one area within that tissue. If the blood supply in one artery is suddenly blocked or the artery is severed, then the tissue supplied by that artery will have no blood supply. Arteries may also become gradually blocked. The narrowing of vessels is called **stenosis**, and it may develop over a period of months or years, as a result of vascular disease. If the blood supply to an area is reduced, due to the narrowing of an artery, the body can occasionally compensate by widening the artery so that it is sufficiently large again.

The endothelium of the capillaries generally allows free exchange of oxygen, nutrients and waste products between the blood and the tissues. This is also true for larger molecules such as hormones, although the rate of exchange is generally faster for smaller molecules. There are, however, some areas of the body where the movement of molecules between the blood and tissue is restricted – the capillaries in these areas have barrier properties. The most important tissue with barrier properties is the brain, and the physiological effect is called the **blood–brain barrier**.

In the brain, the specialised endothelial cells prevent the free exchange of molecules between blood and tissues. Oxygen can still reach the brain tissue by diffusion, but many nutrient molecules (e.g. glucose) require transporters to take them across the endothelium. In addition, the brain endothelium has a system for excluding many toxic molecules. Unfortunately, this system also prevents many potentially useful drugs from getting into the brain, but that is another story.

5.3 The energy demands of tissues, and how they are supplied

Recall that the primary function of the blood supply is to deliver oxygen and nutrients to tissues. This raises a number of questions. What level of supply does a tissue actually need to get sufficient oxygen and nutrients? How does the blood supply adapt to the demands of a tissue? What happens if a tissue receives insufficient oxygen and nutrients? How long can a tissue cope with an inadequate blood supply, before irreversible damage occurs? This section is concerned with answers to these questions.

Tissues need energy to carry out their functions, and ultimately they need some energy just to stay alive. The energy is provided mostly by biochemical reactions in which carbohydrates are combined with oxygen, in a series of steps, and the energy released at each stage is trapped, so that it can be used for specific functions. The major carbohydrate carried in the blood to be used as a source of energy is the sugar **glucose**. At each step of the reaction, the energy released is trapped by the generation of a molecule called **ATP** (adenosine triphosphate). ATP acts as a way of exchanging energy between different reactions within cells. You can think of ATP as a kind of energy-money. If you did not have money, it would be very difficult to trade between different shops and businesses; if there was no ATP, cells would find it very difficult to transact their business. The name for all the chemical reactions and transactions that cells carry out is **metabolism**. **Aerobic metabolism** describes the series of reaction in which carbohydrates combine with oxygen to generate ATP.

It is also possible for cells to produce ATP without using oxygen (**anaerobic metabolism**), but the reactions are much less efficient because they produce less ATP from the same amount of glucose. In addition, the reactions result in the build-up of potentially harmful acids in the tissues. Nor do cells have to use glucose to generate energy. For example, heart muscle is surprisingly versatile and normally uses other carbohydrates and fatty acids as well as glucose – indeed, it tends to use whatever is most readily available. Although cells can break down other molecules, it is less efficient than using glucose. So supplying glucose and oxygen to a cell from the blood is the most effective way of providing it with energy. Some muscle cells can store oxygen, bound to a pigment called myoglobin, which is related to haemoglobin and gives red meat its colour. However, this store is limited and can extend the aerobic metabolism of a muscle cell for only a few minutes if it is not re-supplied from the blood.

When a cell runs out of ATP, it can no longer stay alive and so is dead. ATP is continually being synthesised and used up. This turnover time depends on the type of cell and how active it is, but typically ATP will turn over in a period of less than a minute.

5.3.1 Which tissues use most energy?

The energy demands of tissues vary considerably. It will not surprise you that active muscles require a lot of energy, and this includes heart muscle. Less obvious is the fact that the brain also requires a great deal of energy, partly to maintain its continuous electrical activity, and partly to maintain its complex cellular structure. Conversely, tissue such as fat (adipose tissue) requires very little energy to maintain itself. Some tissues – for example, a leg muscle – have very variable energy requirements, depending on what they are doing. Normally, the blood supply to each tissue is matched to the energy demand of that tissue, by adjusting the amount of blood that flows through it. There are exceptions to this general rule – for example, the blood flow to the skin may increase during light exercise to dissipate heat. However, the blood supplied to muscle, including heart muscle, is essentially demand-led.

● Identify two ways in which the blood supply to a tissue could be increased: one is a long-term solution and the other a short-term solution.

● Increasing the number of capillaries present in a tissue is a long-term solution. Increasing the amount of blood that flows into existing capillary beds is a short-term solution.

Problems may arise if the energy demand of the tissue is greater than the capacity of the blood to supply it. This condition is called ischaemia (an inadequate blood supply). The amount of blood that is required by the heart varies.

● Under what circumstances would the energy demand of the heart be greatest?

● The energy demand of the heart is greatest when it is pumping the greatest blood volume, which happens when a person is taking exercise and skeletal muscles have a high energy demand.

When a person is exercising, the energy demand of active muscles may increase up to 100-fold, and this demand is met by increasing the volume of blood that flows through the muscle. In turn, the cardiac output (the total volume of blood flowing from the heart) may increase up to fourfold. As a result, the heart muscle itself has a corresponding increased demand for blood supply from the coronary circulation. Table 5.1 shows how the blood supply to different organs is redistributed in a person taking exercise. Notice how the blood supply can partly be redistributed. The supply to the brain is fully maintained, but the supply to some other organs, such as the kidney, can be reduced.

Table 5.1 Redistribution of blood supply to tissues during exercise.

Organ/tissue	Volume of blood (ml/min)		
	at rest	during light exercise	during heavy exercise
skeletal muscle	1200	4500	22 000
heart muscle	250	350	1000
brain	750	750	750
kidney	1100	900	250
cardiac output	5800	9700	25 700

● Using the data in Table 5.1, work out what percentage of the total cardiac output goes to heart muscle at rest and during exercise.

● The values are 4.3% at rest, 3.6% for light exercise and 3.9% for heavy exercise ((1000/25 700) × 100). Notice how the proportion of the cardiac output supplied to the heart muscle (coronary supply) is always ≈4%, even as the cardiac output varies between 5800 and 25 700 ml/min.

A leg muscle needs a fairly small amount of energy just to stay alive, but needs more energy to carry out its function. It is perfectly possible for such a tissue to stop its normal function for a while. However, this is not an option for the heart and brain – these organs must carry out their normal function in order for a person to stay alive. It is not enough for them just to survive, so any interruption in the blood supply to these critical organs rapidly leads to serious consequences.

5.3.2 Adjusting the blood flow to the energy demands of tissues

The principal way of adjusting blood flow to the requirements of the tissue is to change the amount of blood flowing through capillaries in the tissue, which is controlled by the arterioles. If the layer of smooth muscle in the wall of an arteriole contracts, then the interior of the vessel is reduced in diameter and less blood can flow through. Sometimes this may cause the blood supply in an entire capillary bed to shut down. (Additionally, some tissues have small interconnecting vessels between the arterioles and the venules which allow blood to bypass the capillaries.) If, on the other hand, the arteriolar smooth muscle relaxes, then it allows an increase in blood flow in the capillaries. The amount of blood that flows through a tissue is called the **perfusion**.

To summarise, the perfusion of a tissue is controlled by its arterioles, but if the perfusion of the tissue is insufficient to supply its energy demands, then ischaemia develops. So, to understand ischaemia and how it can be corrected, you need to look at what controls the smooth muscle in the arterioles.

There are two ways of controlling the arterioles:

* the tissues, and particularly the endothelium, produce signalling molecules (mediators) that act on local arterioles

* the nervous system can also affect the smooth muscle in the arterioles – one part of the nervous system innervates blood vessels and can modulate the contraction and relaxation of the smooth muscle in blood vessel walls.

The relative importance of these two mechanisms varies depending on the tissue. For heart muscle and the brain, perfusion is almost entirely determined by mediators produced by the local tissues in response to the energy demand of that tissue. In contrast, for tissues such as the gut and kidney, the activity of the nervous system in controlling the arterioles is at least as important as the locally produced mediators.

● Can you see any relationship between the way blood supply is controlled (i.e. the balance between local and nervous system control) and the type of tissue?

- The heart and brain are essential organs in which blood supply must be maintained, and their perfusion is controlled by local energy demand. The gut and kidney are organs that may change their activity and energy demand, in response to external events – see, for example, the reduction in kidney perfusion during heavy exercise (Table 5.1).

The major mediator produced by the endothelium that affects vascular smooth muscle is **nitric oxide** (NO). Before it was properly identified, this mediator was called endothelial cell-derived relaxing factor, which describes exactly what it does.

- Will NO cause an increase or a decrease in the blood flow in a capillary bed? Why?

- It causes an increase, because relaxation of the arteriolar smooth muscle allows more blood to flow into the capillaries.

Figure 5.3 illustrates how the perfusion of capillary beds is controlled. Mediators and drugs that cause arterioles to open are called **vasodilators**. When a person is treated with glyceryl trinitrate to alleviate symptoms of heart disease, the drug works by stimulating the production of NO. This decreases the resistance of arterioles throughout the body, and hence tends to lower blood pressure, which in turn reduces the load on the heart. Endothelium also produces the vasodilator **prostacyclin**. Both NO and prostacyclin are produced in response to blood flowing rapidly over the endothelial surface and they also have an important role in preventing blood clotting. In some circumstances, the endothelium can produce mediators that cause the smooth muscle to contract, one of which is **endothelin**. Overproduction of endothelin can contribute to high blood pressure, vascular disease and heart failure. Mediators and drugs which reduce perfusion are called **vasoconstrictors**. Limiting the production or the effects of endothelin is one potential way of treating vascular disease.

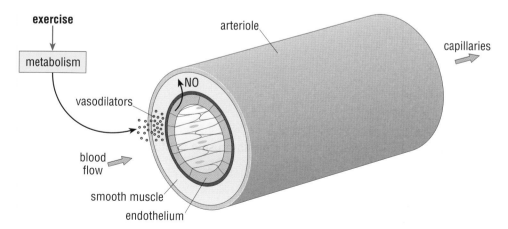

Figure 5.3 Blood flow into capillary networks is controlled by arterioles. Shear forces caused by blood flow on the endothelium cause the release of NO. Exercise causes the release of vasodilator molecules as a result of metabolism in muscle tissue. Mediators from both the endothelium and the vasodilators cause relaxation of the smooth muscle (vasodilation) and an increased blood supply to the capillaries.

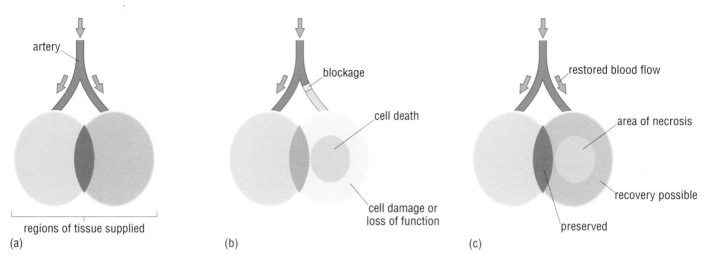

Figure 5.4 Ischaemia, recovery and necrosis. (a) The regions of tissue (green, left; blue, right) are both supplied by the artery, and there is an area (shown in the centre) which may be supplied by either branch of the artery. (b) If the right-hand branch is blocked, the blue area becomes ischaemic. Cells in the centre of the area die, and those around may be damaged or lose function. Cells that are also supplied by the other branch may continue to function. (c) If the blood supply is restored in the right-hand branch, damaged cells may recover, but dead cells cannot do so and the area of necrosis is cleared up by macrophages from the immune system.

As noted above, tissues need some energy just to stay alive. What happens if the tissue does not even get the minimal level of blood required for this to happen? In this case, the cells that do not receive sufficient blood supply will die, a process called **necrosis**. This most often happens when the blood supply to a tissue is suddenly blocked (see Section 5.8), and it affects just the area that is supplied by the artery that has been blocked. An area of dead cells within an organ is called an **infarct**. At the edge of the area supplied by the blocked artery, cells may receive sufficient supply from surrounding capillary beds to survive, even if they cannot function properly (Figure 5.4). This is very important, because cells that have not died may recover if they are re-supplied with blood, whereas the cells that have died can never recover. Dead cells and cell debris in the area of necrosis will be removed by cells of the immune system. Following an MI or a stroke, a primary aim is always to get the surviving cells to recover their function.

The metabolic demands of the tissue are also critical in determining how much blood flows into that tissue. This effect appears to be mediated by molecules produced in the tissue by metabolism, acting directly on the arterioles, rather than by the shortage of oxygen itself. In the coronary circulation, virtually all of the available oxygen is used during the passage of blood through the capillaries. Consequently, with no reserve oxygen in the blood, the only way of increasing oxygen supply is to increase blood flow.

5.3.3 Ischaemia produces pain

What happens if the arteries supplying a tissue have narrowed to such a degree that they cannot supply sufficient blood, regardless of whether the arterioles are open? In this case, ischaemia causes pain. If it affects the heart, it produces angina, a crushing pain or feeling of constriction in the chest that usually lasts for several minutes. However, the symptoms of angina can be very variable and can differ greatly between individuals; men tend to be more often and more seriously affected than women. Surprisingly, ischaemia does not always produce angina, although angina in the chest is most often due to ischaemia caused by narrowing of the coronary arteries. A less common cause of angina is muscular spasms in the arterioles that supply the heart, but this tends to affect younger people and women more often than men.

Ischaemic pain may occur in other parts of the body. Section 5.5 looks at peripheral arterial disease, which may cause narrowing of arteries in the legs. In this case, excessive exercise causes pain in the leg muscles which generally resolves after a few minutes of resting the muscle. Other organs can also be affected. For example, narrowing of the vessels that supply the kidney can lead to kidney failure.

5.3.4 Severe ischaemia causes cell death

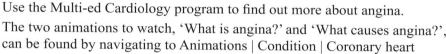

Activity 5.1   Understanding angina

Suggested study time 30 minutes

Use the Multi-ed Cardiology program to find out more about angina.

The two animations to watch, 'What is angina?' and 'What causes angina?', can be found by navigating to Animations | Condition | Coronary heart disease. After you have watched these sections, answer the following questions.

(a) What is the medical term for insufficient blood supply to the heart?

(b) What two types of event can induce an attack of angina?

(c) What is the typical duration of an attack of angina?

(d) In what part of the body is angina felt?

(e) The narrator gives two possible underlying causes of ischaemia. What are they?

(f) How do these two underlying causes result in ischaemia?

(g) Does atheroma always result in angina?

Comment

(a) Insufficient blood supply to the heart is called cardiac ischaemia.

(b) Physical exercise and emotional stress can induce angina.

(c) Angina typically lasts from a few seconds to a few minutes, but it is very variable between individuals.

(d) Angina is usually felt in the chest, but also in the neck, jaw, arms and upper back. It can also produce the symptoms of indigestion.

(e) Atherosclerotic plaques and arrhythmias are possible underlying causes of ischaemia.

(f) The narrowing of an artery means that insufficient blood can pass through it to the tissue. An arrhythmia means that the heart is unable to pump as efficiently, which affects the circulation to all tissues, including itself.

(g) A moderate narrowing of arteries due to atheroma does not itself cause ischaemia and angina, but it may progress to atherosclerosis and severe narrowing, which does cause ischaemia.

Case Study 5.1   Mr Patel's bout of angina

Mr Patel has had a busy day and has taken several deliveries of electronic components from his suppliers, which he has put in his office upstairs. After he has signed for the last delivery he suddenly realises that two boxes are missing. He quickly runs upstairs to check what is missing. As he does so, he starts to get a pain in the chest which radiates into his neck. This has happened several times before, and he knows exactly what to do. He lies down on the bed and takes a glyceryl trinitrate tablet that his doctor has prescribed for chest pains. He puts the tablet under his tongue; within a few minutes, the pain starts to subside and he finds he can breathe more easily. His wife Anika finds him 10 minutes later sitting at his desk taking stock of the components, and on the telephone to his supplier. He tells her what has happened and that he is feeling OK now. 'Well, Kamal,' she says, 'there is no need to shift everything upstairs at soon as it arrives, you know – they're not going to disappear once you've signed for them. Take it more steadily.'

Activity 5.2   Understanding angina continued

Suggested study time 30 minutes

Now watch the two animations 'How is angina diagnosed?' and 'How is angina treated?', which can also be found in Animations | Condition | Coronary heart disease. After you have watched these sections, answer the following questions.

(a) What type of test is carried out with people walking on a treadmill? Why is a treadmill used?

(b) What does a coronary angiogram determine?

(c) What five types of drug are mentioned as potential treatments for angina?

(d) How does glyceryl trinitrate work?

(e) What two surgical procedures are mentioned as potential treatments for angina?

(f) Apart from drugs and surgery, what other way of treating angina is highlighted?

Comment

(a) An electrocardiogram (ECG) is carried out while subjects are on the treadmill. The treadmill is used to exercise the subjects, so that the ECG can be determined when the heart rate and cardiac output are increased above the resting state.

(b) A coronary angiogram looks at the arteries supplying the heart, to determine where they might be blocked.

(c) Anti-platelet drugs, beta-blockers, nitrates, calcium channel blockers and potassium channel openers are all potential treatments for angina.

(d) Glyceryl trinitrate improves the circulation throughout the body, and the blood supply to the heart itself.

(e) Angina can be potentially treated by coronary angioplasty and by a coronary artery bypass.

(f) Lifestyle modifications, such as stopping smoking, can also treat angina.

5.4 Changes in the vascular tree

The previous section showed how the local blood supply can vary in response to the energy demand of the tissues. However, blood supply can also be adjusted to the requirements of the tissue by increasing or decreasing the number of vessels. The formation of new blood vessels (**angiogenesis**) is a very important process which takes place when damaged tissues are repaired and then re-supplied with blood. Lack of oxygen is a major stimulus for angiogenesis. However, it takes days or weeks for new vessels to grow, so this process cannot compensate for the sudden loss of blood supply to a tissue. Nevertheless, over time, ischaemia does induce the growth of new vessels. This effect is seen in the muscles of athletes: over a period of weeks, the number of vessels in the muscles increases and this is matched by a number of other physiological changes that make aerobic metabolism in those muscles more efficient. These changes allow the oxygen in the blood to be used more effectively, so an athlete at rest will have a slightly lower cardiac output than an untrained person.

These effects are not just of interest to athletes. Gentle exercise increases the number of capillaries in heart muscle. For this reason, progressive gentle exercise is often used in people with heart disease and in the recovery period following a heart attack, in order to improve the perfusion of the heart muscle. In addition, the increased metabolic efficiency caused by exercise means that the cardiac output needed for a particular level of activity is somewhat lower than in a person who does not exercise.

Blood vessels also change to a limited degree with age. It is difficult to interpret the microscopic changes in the vessels of older people to say what effects this might have. However, the observations show that capillaries tend to be longer, but less dense and with a thicker **basal lamina** – the layer of extracellular proteins which lies underneath cells such as the endothelium. This suggests that it will take longer for capillaries to re-grow in older people than in younger people, and the supply of nutrients to the tissues will also be slower.

In some tissues, ischaemia may stimulate the formation of larger vessels that cross-connect between two arteries or between two veins. When a cross-connecting vessel is formed, it is called an **anastomosis**, and it can allow blood to bypass a blockage. In the heart, this natural form of bypassing occurs only to a very limited extent, because each coronary vessel is normally only able to supply its own area. When surgery is carried out to replace arteries (coronary artery bypass graft), the grafted artery is put alongside the original blocked artery, to bypass the narrowed vessels.

5.5 Pathological changes in blood vessels

Blood vessels are affected by a variety of diseases and conditions. Some changes may be related to age and others to diseases that affect other organs of the body, and in some cases the blood vessels themselves are selectively affected. The symptoms of these changes are almost always related to the reduced supply of blood to tissues supplied by the vessels.

5.5.1 Atherosclerosis and peripheral arterial disease

The most common condition that affects blood vessels is atherosclerosis, which is the narrowing of an artery caused by the build-up of fatty deposits in the arterial wall. The deposits are called **atheroma** and they tend to be localised in particular regions of particular arteries, especially where the vessels branch. An area of the artery wall affected by atheroma is called an **atheromatous plaque**, and these plaques may vary in size from a few millimetres to more than 1 cm (Figure 5.5). How plaques develop is considered in Section 5.6.

Atherosclerosis should probably not be considered as a disease, but as a condition that develops with age. Arteries may be narrowed by up to 70% without producing symptoms. The rate at which atherosclerosis develops is enormously variable, depending on the individual, their genetic makeup and lifestyle. Post-mortem examination of fit young men who have died of accidents often shows that their arteries have atheromatous plaques. Even in childhood, streaks of fatty deposits, up to 1 cm long, are present beneath the endothelium of the arteries. There is good evidence that these fatty streaks are the precursors of atheromatous plaques, implying that the development of atherosclerosis takes place from childhood onwards.

Although atherosclerosis in the coronary arteries is a major health concern, it does occur in other vessels too. For example, atherosclerosis in the aortic arch and in the blood vessels supplying the brain is a major cause of stroke. Atherosclerosis can also occur in arteries supplying other tissues, where it is called **peripheral arterial disease**.

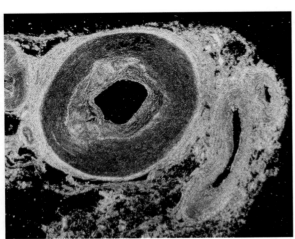

Figure 5.5   Cross-section of an atherosclerotic artery.

- If a person had peripheral arterial disease in the arteries that supply the legs, what effect would you expect this to have?

- Such people fatigue quickly and develop pain in their legs during exercise.

The term for this condition is **intermittent claudication**, and it tends to be particularly prevalent in diabetic people and smokers. It can be detected by the large drop in blood pressure between the arm (conventional blood pressure measurement) and in the ankle. In severe cases, ulcers or gangrene may occur.

There have been several theories put forward over the last 150 years to explain how atherosclerosis develops. The great nineteenth-century pathologist Rudolf Virchow (Figure 5.6) first proposed that it was due to cells dividing in the arterial wall, proteins and lipids entering the plaque from the blood, a low-grade inflammation, and a repair process. Interestingly, the idea that inflammation is an important component of atherosclerosis has come right back into mainstream thinking in the last 15 years.

Figure 5.6   Rudolf Virchow (1821–1902), famed German pathologist.

5.5.2 Inflammation and vasculitis

When tissues become damaged, the body attempts to clear up the damage, replace cells that have died and repair anything that cannot be replaced. **Inflammation** is the process by which the body clears up damage and starts the process of repair. Inflammation may take place in response to infection, in which case it occurs alongside an immune response against the infectious agent. However, this section is concerned with the inflammation that takes place in response to tissue damage but which is not due to infection.

The cells that are responsible for clearing up dead cells and cell debris are **phagocytes**. They internalise (phagocytose) debris and break it down into its simplest components. There are resident phagocytes distributed in virtually all tissues of the body. Additional, wandering phagocytes may enter the tissues from the blood, particularly in an area of inflammation. One type of white blood cell called a **monocyte** migrates from the blood into the tissue, where it transforms into a **macrophage**, a large mobile phagocyte. There is nothing abnormal about this process – cells of the body die surprisingly frequently, and it is essential that there is some means of clearing them away. Macrophages are particularly important in the development of atheromatous plaques, where they occur in large numbers.

As well as clearing up debris, macrophages can also phagocytose and kill bacteria. For this purpose, they produce a variety of toxic molecules, which are normally directed against the phagocytosed bacteria. However, if these molecules leak out of the macrophage and into the tissues, they can equally well cause tissue damage. Macrophages therefore need to make a proportionate response, which can be anything from the quiet phagocytosis of a dead tissue cell to a powerful reaction aimed at eliminating a bacterial infection. In other words, the process of inflammation varies considerably in strength, depending on what caused it – but potentially it can do more harm than good.

In atherosclerosis, there is a low level of inflammation associated with the development of the atheromatous plaques. In a few conditions, severe inflammation occurs in the arterial walls. The ending '-itis' is used to indicate that something is inflamed, so **vasculitis** describes a condition where there is severe inflammation of arteries or veins and **angiitis** is used for inflammation of capillaries. Although it is not nearly as common as atherosclerosis, vasculitis can be very serious and fatal if not treated.

There are more than 20 different types of autoimmune vasculitis. Some affect capillaries, some medium-sized vessels and others the largest vessels. All of these conditions are rare, and they are subdivided according to which types of vessels they affect. Sometimes the vasculitis follows on from infection, but in many conditions the underlying causes are not known. In some individuals, the immune system recognises components of the body as foreign and mounts a reaction against them. This is called an autoimmune reaction (an immune reaction against self). The inflammation that accompanies vasculitis can lead to narrowing of the arterioles and damage, as macrophages and other white blood cells migrate into the vessel wall. It can also lead to bleeding and scarring in tissues such as the kidney and lung.

For the most part, it is not known exactly why the immune system is attacking the person's own tissue, and often it is not known exactly which molecules in the tissue are the target of the attack. Treatment for these conditions is therefore pragmatic, and aimed at suppressing the immune response (immunosuppression) and maintaining the functions of the affected organs. Early diagnosis and aggressive immunosuppressive treatment is often the best option.

5.5.3 Aneurysms

Blood vessels may develop local dilations in the wall, called an **aneurysm**. This occurs most often in the aorta and in areas affected by atherosclerosis, and is exacerbated by hypertension. An aortic aneurysm can be felt as a pulsating mass in the abdomen and can be life-threatening if it ruptures. Aneurysms also develop in Marfan syndrome (see Case Study 3.2).

An aneurysm may be harmless. However, it is a sign of weakness in the vessel wall, and in some cases the aneurysm can erode the vessel wall, leading to bleeding, which is potentially serious. In addition, the presence of an aneurysm means that blood does not flow smoothly through the vessel, but with disturbed flow and spiralling vortices. As you will see in Section 5.7, disturbed blood flow tends to promote blood clotting, and this in itself is potentially dangerous. For these reasons, aneurysms are often treated by surgery, which reinforces the vessel wall.

5.5.4 Varicose veins and spider veins

Varicose veins are one of the most readily visible changes in blood vessels (Figure 5.7a). Veins located beneath the skin, particularly in the legs, become dilated and tortuous and often appear blue–black. The changes are caused by

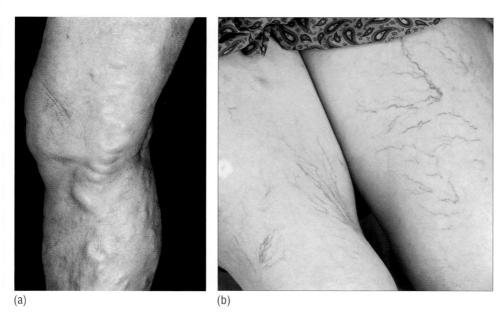

(a)   (b)

Figure 5.7   Two common changes in superficial veins: (a) varicose veins, here on a leg, and (b) spider veins.

blood accumulating in the leg veins instead of flowing through the valves into the major veins. This tends to put pressure on the valve at the bottom of the affected segment of vein; this pressure often progressively increases, worsening the condition. As the veins enlarge and blood fails to return to the heart, the condition can lead to so-called venous insufficiency. Fluid accumulates in the tissues, which become tender to touch and there is often a dragging pain in the affected limb(s).

Women seem to be more susceptible to varicose veins than men, and the condition is often exacerbated around the time of menstruation. Some people are more susceptible to the condition, particularly the rare individuals who were born without valves in their veins. Problems arise if the vessels break and blood leaks into the skin tissue, or if the stationary blood starts to clot inside the vein. Such blood clotting is called **phlebitis**; the process and the hazards associated with clotting in veins is explained more fully in Section 5.7. Varicose veins may be treated with pressure stockings or by surgery, and the aim is to reduce the pain and the risks associated with phlebitis, not just for cosmetic reasons.

Spider veins are clusters of small vessels just beneath the skin, occurring most frequently on the legs (Figure 5.7b) but sometimes on the face. They are not particularly associated with pressure, but with the female hormone oestrogen. They are more common in women who are pregnant, taking the oral contraceptive pill or having oestrogen replacement therapy.

Aortic dissections occur where the layers of the artery wall peel away from each other. These can be painful and, like aneurysms, life-threatening.

5.6 The development of atheromatous plaques

Atherosclerosis develops over many years, but it is usually only in middle age that it may produce the symptoms of ischaemia or lead to a heart attack. Figure 5.8 illustrates our understanding of how atheromatous plaques develop. The steps can be summarised as follows.

- Fatty deposits, appearing initially as fatty streaks, accumulate in the arterial wall.

- Fat, particularly LDL cholesterol trapped in the vessel wall, becomes oxidised.

- Macrophages migrate into the area, where they attempt to phagocytose the fat. They become progressively filled with fat globules, so taking on a foamy appearance and becoming **foam cells**.

- With macrophages unable to break down the fat, it continues to build up, causing narrowing of the artery.

- Fibrous cells now divide in the vessel wall between the fat deposits and the endothelium, forming a **fibrous cap**.

- Smooth muscle cells may grow into the shoulders of the plaque, giving it some rigidity.

- The central area of the developing plaque may become so full of fat that cells cannot survive inside it, forming a pool of cell debris and fat accumulation called the **necrotic core** of the plaque.

- The irregular flow of blood through the artery and the damage to the endothelium may promote blood clotting inside the artery.

- The fibrous cap may rupture through the endothelium, which may eventually lead to repair of the damaged arterial wall, with the production of scar tissue. Rupture of the cap can also cause blood clots to form.

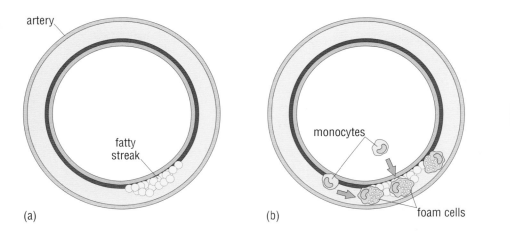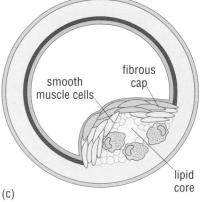

Figure 5.8   Development of an atheromatous plaque. (a) Fatty streaks appear in the walls of arterioles. (b) As lipids continue to accumulate, monocytes migrate in from the vessel or the tissue and phagocytose the lipid, becoming foam cells. (c) The lipid core becomes necrotic as a fibrous cap forms on the developing plaque and smooth muscle cells grow into the shoulder of the plaque, which is now partly blocking the artery.

These steps will be described in more detail, but in this progression two major phases can be distinguished:

- A steady build-up of the plaques and narrowing of the artery
- A phase in which cells die and the fibrous cap may rupture, leading to serious damage and repair of the artery. Rupture of the cap may also trigger blood clotting inside the vessel (see Section 5.7).

The first phase is called **stable atherosclerosis** and the second phase **unstable atherosclerosis**. It is by no means certain that a stable atheromoatous plaque will become unstable. However, the unstable plaque is potentially much more dangerous than the stable plaque and it is very difficult to predict if or when a plaque will become unstable.

In a similar way, doctors distinguish between stable angina and unstable angina. **Stable angina** develops slowly and causes discomfort or pain in the chest with exercise, which is relieved after a few minutes by rest. **Unstable angina** tends to get noticeably worse over shorter time periods, occurs more frequently with exercise and may occur at rest. The recovery period is much more variable. Unstable angina is sometimes called pre-MI angina, which describes the problem precisely. It is an intermediate stage between stable angina and an MI. Consequently, changes in the pattern of a person's angina or a rapid increase in the severity of the symptoms are always treated seriously.

● Does Mr Patel have stable angina or unstable angina?

● He appears to have stable angina. The condition came on after exercise and was alleviated within a few minutes by resting. It was no worse than on previous occasions.

It is very difficult to be certain exactly how the changes in atheromatous plaques relate to symptoms of angina. Nevertheless, it is generally assumed that rupture of a plaque in the coronary arteries will very probably cause progression to unstable angina, and potentially lead to a heart attack. In other words, unstable atheromatous plaques are associated with unstable angina.

Case Study 5.2   Mr Patel's angina worsens

Mr Patel is watching the football on television with his son Faruk. It is a particularly exciting cup game, made more so by the fact that Mr Patel supports Chelsea, whereas Faruk supports Arsenal, who are one goal up with 10 minutes left to play. In the final minutes Mr Patel starts to get chest pains. He takes his glyceryl trinitrate tablets but, unlike earlier occasions, the pain does not subside quickly. The game is quickly forgotten, as the pain does not wear off until 2 hours later. His wife Anika and Faruk are both worried about him and encourage him to go and see the doctor the next day. He thinks it was severe indigestion from something he ate, as they had had a big family meal together just before the match. Even so, he is a bit concerned; despite the fact that he was expecting to visit his mother the next day, he calls the local surgery, telling them what happened and intending to arrange an appointment for the following week. His doctor says that she will see him immediately.

● What do you think has happened to Mr Patel? What could have caused the change in his angina?

● Mr Patel's angina appears to have become unstable. The immediate event is probably caused by the formation of a blood clot within a coronary artery. This could have resulted from the rupture of an atheromatous plaque.

5.6.1 Rupture of an atheromatous plaque

An atheromatous plaque extends into the artery's interior, and so a stress is exerted on it by the blood flowing past. The fatty core of the plaque is inherently weak, although it may be strengthened by smooth muscle cells and the fibrous tissue in the cap. The presence of macrophages also presents a particular problem. These cells do not contribute to the strength of the plaque. One of their functions is to clear away and digest dead tissues; to do this, they secrete digestive enzymes that contribute to the tissue damage, and further weaken the plaque. Unpredictably, the fibrous cap of the plaque may break through (rupture) the endothelium, releasing cell debris and lipid and allowing the blood to come in contact with the tissues in the arterial wall (Figure 5.9).

● What would happen to blood that comes into contact with cells in the arterial wall? Why?

● The endothelium normally inhibits blood clotting, but if the plaque ruptures, this protective layer of cells is missing. Blood coming into contact with tissue from the arterial wall is more likely to clot.

Plaque rupture in a coronary artery may itself lead to a heart attack, but if the person recovers the artery will start to repair itself with additional fibrous tissue, leaving an artery that is narrower and scarred.

The next sections look in more detail at how atherosclerosis develops, and relate the development to the risk factors that you learned about in Chapter 3.

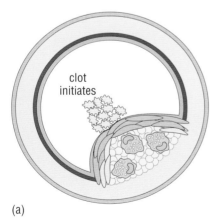
(a)

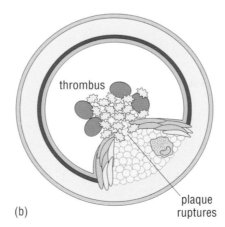
(b)

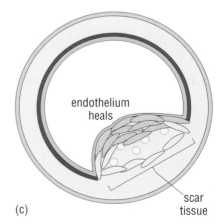
(c)

Figure 5.9   Rupture and healing of an atheromatous plaque. (a) Blood clotting is initiated on the atheromatous plaque. (b) The plaque ruptures and the endothelium is damaged, exposing the underlying tissue and lipid, which strongly promote clotting. The blood clot (thrombus) may be released into the circulation. (c) The artery may heal with scar tissue and a regrown layer of endothelium.

5.6.2 Atherosclerosis and fat

Exactly why fatty deposits should accumulate in patches (streaks and plaques) in the walls of arteries is not known. Nevertheless, it is easy to see why a diet high in fat and cholesterol would lead to the faster accumulation of these deposits. Fats are carried in the blood as lipoproteins (LDL, HDL, etc.), and some people have naturally higher levels of circulating fat, regardless of their diet. This is partly due to genetic differences in the proteins that associate with the fat, and the way fat is taken up and used in cells of the body (see Section 3.4). However, regardless of a person's propensity to synthesise cholesterol, the more fat and cholesterol that a person eats, the higher the levels of these in the blood, at least after meals.

The type of fat that accumulates in an atheromatous plaque also affects its biomechanical properties. The softer the core of plaque, the more stress is exerted on the fibrous cap by the pulsatile blood flow. Accumulations of saturated fats are difficult for macrophages to break down, and they may be toxic for smooth muscle cells and other cells in the arterial wall, so contributing to loss of cells that give the plaque mechanical stability. Types of fat called *trans* fatty acids are also more difficult for macrophages to break down, because they do not occur naturally in large amounts. Cholesterol is another molecule that is not normally broken down in the body but is removed by the liver. In summary, the collections of fatty deposits and cholesterol are not easily removed by the macrophages.

5.6.3 Atherosclerosis and inflammation

The presence of macrophages and foam cells in the plaques indicates an important link between atherosclerosis and inflammation. The mediators that attract macrophages into the arterial wall are called chemokines and it is worth noting that there are genetic differences between people in these signalling systems – some variants make an individual more susceptible to cardiovascular disease than others. One of the preventive treatments for cardiovascular disease is aspirin, which acts as an anti-inflammatory drug, although its effect in reducing blood clotting is equally important. Interestingly, psychological stress often reduces the activity of macrophages, by the action of certain hormones (corticosteroids). However, stress also increases blood pressure, which offsets any beneficial effects it might have for cardiovascular disease.

5.6.4 Atherosclerosis, blood pressure and smoking

Chapter 3 showed how smoking and high blood pressure both increase the risk of cardiovascular disease. High blood pressure causes increased stress on the vessel wall, so making it more likely that a plaque will rupture and chronic high blood pressure also stiffens arteries, making them less elastic. Even before this stage, however, minor damage to the vessel wall caused by high blood pressure can lead to endothelial cell damage and accumulation of macrophages.

Smoking results in lower levels of oxygen in the blood. This means that the amount of blood required by a tissue to supply its oxygen demand is greater, which in turn will put higher demands on the heart to pump blood. Lower oxygen levels and higher carbon monoxide levels in the blood of smokers, along with the toxic chemicals in cigarette smoke, can all lead to cell damage. It is not clear exactly where the critical damage caused by smoking occurs in cardiovascular disease. However, it seems likely that the endothelial cells may be particularly affected. Recall that endothelial cells prevent blood clotting as well as producing both NO and prostacyclin, which causes arterioles to dilate and thereby reduces blood pressure.

In addition to cell damage, smoking causes an increase in the LDL : HDL cholesterol ratio in the blood, so exacerbating the effects of a high-fat diet, and chemicals in smoke can contribute to the oxidation of LDL cholesterol. This illustrates the complicated way in which a single risk factor such as smoking can produce its effects in several ways in the body, both in the short term and in the long term, and also shows how several risks can act together to accelerate the progression of atherosclerosis.

● Give two reasons why Mr Patel might have developed severe angina when he was watching a football match on television.

● The excitement of the match leads to the production of the hormone adrenalin, which has the effect of increasing blood pressure and heart rate. This would put more stress on the plaque, so that it is more likely to rupture.

In addition, adrenalin promotes blood clotting, which may also have occurred in this attack of angina.

5.7 Blood clotting

Atherosclerosis does not by itself result in an MI. Often, the narrowing of the arteries caused by the plaques is compensated by an increase in the diameter of the blood vessel so that blood flow to the tissue is maintained. However, atherosclerosis can promote the formation of blood clots inside the arteries, and it is the combination of the atherosclerosis and the blood clot that is particularly dangerous. The process by which a blood clot (**thrombus**, plural thrombi) forms is called **thrombosis**, and the combination of atherosclerosis and thrombosis is called **atherothrombosis**. It is important to distinguish between atherosclerosis, which is a process that occurs progressively in all individuals with age, from atherothrombosis, which is often pathological.

Blood clotting is a normal process needed to stop bleeding following an injury. However, if blood clots form inside blood vessels, this is potentially dangerous. Blocking the blood supply to a tissue causes cells in the tissue to die, if an adequate blood supply is not restored soon (see Section 5.3.2).

Normally, blood clots do not develop inside arteries, because the endothelial cells that line the inside of the blood vessel specifically prevent it from happening – they are said to be anti-thrombotic, because they inhibit thrombosis. Not all cells have this property, and when blood comes in contact with other cells following injury, clotting is promoted. In order to understand how thrombosis occurs in arteries, and how it can be prevented, it is necessary to understand something of the mechanism by which it occurs.

5.7.1 Blood clot formation

A blood clot is formed by two main components:

- platelets circulating in the blood
- a meshwork of protein fibres formed by the blood clotting system.

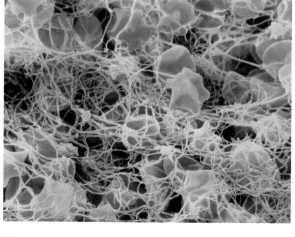

Figure 5.10   Composition of a blood clot.

The meshwork of proteins traps both the platelets and red blood cells (Figure 5.10), which is fine to stop bleeding, but can equally well make a plug inside a blood vessel that blocks blood flow.

Platelets, also called **thrombocytes**, are cellular elements formed by the fragmentation of a large cell present in bone marrow called a megakaryocyte. They are released into the blood from the bone marrow and are much smaller than other cells in the blood, such as red blood cells. They do not have a nucleus, but they do have a cell membrane, and they are present in the blood in very large numbers. When they are triggered by contact with a suitable surface, platelets become activated. They change shape and aggregate, binding to each other and to areas of the blood vessel wall, particularly where the endothelial cells are absent or damaged.

There are several triggers for platelet activation. Proteins of the basal lamina that are exposed where endothelial cells are missing can directly activate the platelets. In addition, when a platelet becomes activated it releases signalling molecules that cause other platelets to become activated. Consequently, the initial activation of one platelet can lead to a chain reaction in which many further platelets bind to each other, linking into the clot. One of these triggering factors released at sites of platelet activation is adenosine diphosphate (ADP), and another is thromboxane-A2 (TxA2). You will find out more about these two factors when considering how platelet aggregation can be inhibited (see Section 8.2.7). The process by which platelets stick together involves so-called 'adhesion molecules' on the platelet surface, which act like a molecular glue. Interfering with this molecular glue is another way of preventing platelet aggregation. Indeed, there are a variety of drugs that inhibit platelet aggregation and they belong to the class of drugs called anti-thrombotics.

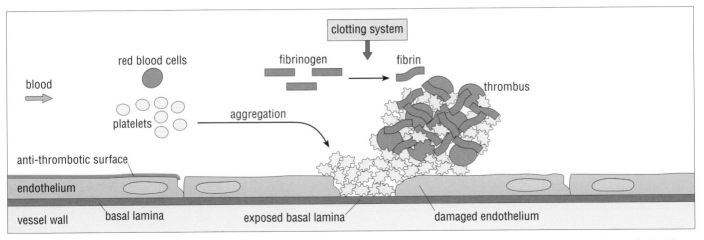

Figure 5.11 The surface of endothelium is anti-thrombotic and normally inhibits blood clotting. If the endothelium is damaged and the basal lamina is exposed, platelets aggregate in the area. The clotting system is also activated and causes the precursor of fibrin (fibrinogen) to be converted into fibrin. A blood clot, consisting of aggregated platelets, trapped red blood cells and fibrin strands, is formed and is attached to the damaged area of the endothelium.

The **clotting system** is a group of proteins normally present in the blood. Damage to tissues, including the blood vessels, activates a chain reaction in which one protein acts on the next, resulting in the precipitation of a fibrous protein called **fibrin**. The precursor of fibrin (fibrinogen) is normally soluble in the blood, but when the clotting system is activated, a meshwork of insoluble fibrin forms, trapping platelets and red blood cells, and stabilising the blood clot. Each step of the reaction that leads to the deposition of fibrin amplifies the reaction, so a small amount of damage can lead very quickly to clot formation. Figure 5.11 summarises how blood clots develop.

There are two main pathways by which the clotting system can be activated:

- through tissue damage: an activator is released from damaged cells
- by contact with activating surfaces.

Damage to endothelial cells will activate the first pathway, whereas loss of the endothelial cells will expose the underlying basal lamina, where molecules (including collagen) will activate the second pathway.

The proteins that form the clotting system are synthesised in the liver and require vitamin K for their production. Preventing their production is one way of inhibiting the blood clotting. Another way is to directly block steps in the chain reaction that leads to fibrin deposition (see Chapter 8).

5.7.2 Laminar and disturbed flow

In arteries, the pattern of blood flow is normally laminar – the blood flows smoothly within the vessel. However, in areas where the inside of the artery is partly obstructed by an atheromatous plaque, or where the vessel branches, disturbed flow with spiralling vortices may occur. Disturbed flow is much less efficient than laminar flow. Moreover, the endothelium is much more susceptible to damage in areas of turbulence. Consequently, blood clotting tends to occur more frequently in such areas, for example on the downstream shoulders of an atheromatous plaque.

5.7.3 Thrombolysis

The formation of blood clots is not an irreversible process. A second group of proteins present in the blood is responsible for dissolving blood clots. This is called the **plasmin system**, and it is required for clearing away blood clots as part of wound healing. The system acts in a series of steps resulting in the formation of an active protein, plasmin, which breaks down fibrin. The process is called fibrinolysis, and the breakdown of the fibrin results in the breakdown of the blood clot, which is called **thrombolysis**. If a person has developed a blood clot inside a blood vessel, one way of getting rid of it is to treat them with something that activates the plasmin system, i.e. using the body's own way of clearing the obstruction. Such thrombolytic agents may be used to treat people who have had an MI, and are referred to as a 'clot-busting' treatment (see Chapter 6).

5.8 Embolism

The formation of a blood clot inside an artery is potentially serious, but enough blood may still flow around the clot to supply the tissue with oxygen. The real problem occurs if the continuing blood flow causes a fragment of the clot to break off and be carried downstream.

● What will happen if a blood clot breaks off from a surface of an artery?

● It will be carried downstream into smaller vessels (arterioles), eventually reaching vessels that are so small that it cannot pass through them. These vessels will be totally blocked, and the tissue that they supply will become severely ischaemic.

This process in which a blood clot is carried through the circulation from one place to another is called **embolism** – or, to be absolutely correct, **thromboembolism**. Other things, such as clumps of tumour cells, may also be carried through the circulation and lodge in arteries in a similar way, and this process is also called embolism, so the term thromboembolism is used specifically when it refers to a detached blood clot being circulated. A detached clump is called an **embolus** (plural emboli), and a detached blood clot is called a **thromboembolus** (plural thromboemboli).

The danger presented by thromboembolism depends on a variety of factors:

*   where the thrombus is formed
*   how big it is
*   where it ends up.

These three factors are interlinked. The smaller an embolus is, the further it will be carried down the vascular tree before it stops. Thromboemboli formed in arteries are carried to the area supplied by that artery, but exactly where this occurs has some element of randomness. For example, a thrombus formed in the aorta could potentially end up in any one of the many tissues supplied by that vessel, whereas thrombi formed in the carotid arteries may well end up in the brain, causing a stroke. In other words, where a thrombus may end up depends on where it is initially formed; where it does end up also depends partly on its size and on an element of chance.

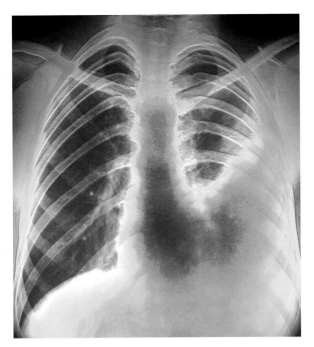

Figure 5.12 Deep vein thrombosis becomes lung thromboembolism. This false-colour X-ray of the chest of a patient with a pulmonary embolism of the left lung shows effusion of fluid into the area affected (orange region at lower right) caused by blockage of the pulmonary artery and associated tissue damage.

5.8.1 Deep vein thrombosis (DVT)

Up to this point, we have been concerned with the formation of thrombi in arteries. However, they can also occur in veins – particularly, in the deep veins that run in the legs, pelvis and arms. You should distinguish the deep veins that run through the muscles in the legs from the superficial veins that are visible just under the skin. Blood may return to the heart via deep or superficial veins, and there is an interconnection between the two types of vein. If a person needs to lose heat, a greater proportion of blood is directed through the superficial veins. If not, a greater proportion runs in the deep veins. The deep veins are greater in diameter than superficial veins, so thrombi that form in them by deep vein thrombosis (DVT) may become quite large. This means that they can potentially block large vessels, if they break off and travel downstream.

● What will happen if a thrombus forms in a deep vein in a leg and breaks off?

● It will move with the blood flow through progressively larger veins until it reaches the heart. At this stage, it may pass through the right side of the heart and out into the arterial circulation of the lung. A clot that has started in a peripheral vein will thus end up blocking a pulmonary artery.

This condition is called **pulmonary embolism** and is potentially very serious. The reduction in blood flow through the lungs may cause breathlessness and ischaemic damage to the lung tissues. In the most serious cases, the blood flow through one or both of the lungs may be blocked, which may be fatal. Pulmonary embolism is diagnosed by a variety of techniques that examine the blood supply to different areas of the lungs. If an area of the lungs is not supplied with blood, it suggests that a thromboembolus is blocking the arterial supply to that area (Figure 5.12).

What causes DVT? The blood flow in veins is much slower than in arteries, which gives thrombi time to grow. Long periods of inactivity can exacerbate this problem – movement of muscles tends to squeeze the veins, pushing blood onwards in the circulation, so a period of inactivity can cause blood to pool in the lower limbs. Hospitalisation or long-haul airline travel are just two of the conditions that can initiate DVT. In addition, some people are genetically more susceptible to the condition.

5.8.2 Thrombosis and embolism

Although a thrombus may break away to form a thromboembolus, this is not always the case. Often, a thrombus may grow and dissolve over a period of days and never become an embolus. Very small fragments (microthrombi) may break off one by one, or they may detach in a single event. The precursors to these events are difficult to predict. The detachment of a deep vein thrombus may relate to sudden movement or constriction of the vein. The detachment of a thrombus in coronary arteries may be triggered by rupture of an atherosclerotic plaque. The sheer unpredictability of such triggering events means that it is nearly impossible to stop them occurring. However, it is possible to undertake long-term preventive treatment to limit the development of atherosclerosis and thrombosis, and these treatments will be discussed further in Chapter 10.

5.9 Summary of Chapter 5

The blood supply to muscle tissue, including the heart, is matched to its energy demand by the adjustment of how much blood flows through the arterioles, a process which is controlled primarily by mediators released in the tissue. Arteries may become gradually blocked by atherosclerotic plaques, producing ischaemia, which causes the symptoms of angina if it affects the coronary circulation. The formation of thrombi and thromboemboli may cause the sudden blockage of the blood supply to an area of tissue and consequent cell death. Smoking, a high-fat diet, stress and genetic predisposition can all increase the rate of atherosclerosis developing and the risk of atherothrombosis occurring.

Questions for Chapter 5

Question 5.1 (Learning Outcomes 5.2 and 5.3)

Which tissues of the body show greatest variation in their energy demand? How is the blood supply to these tissues matched to the variations in their energy demand?

Question 5.2 (Learning Outcomes 5.2 and 5.4)

Why is thrombosis associated with atherosclerosis?

Question 5.3 (Learning Outcomes 5.2, 5.4 and 5.6)

Why does deep vein thrombosis (DVT) not cause people to have strokes?

Question 5.4 (Learning Outcomes 5.2, 5.4, 5.5 and 5.6)

How can a chronic elevation in blood pressure contribute to atherosclerosis? What additional dangers are posed by an acute elevation in blood pressure (e.g. due to excitement)?

Question 5.5 (Learning Outcomes 5.2, 5.3, 5.4 and 5.6)

Consider an area of heart muscle that has been damaged by coronary thrombosis in the vessels that supply it. How can this area recover its function?

Further reading

If you would like to read further, please refer to the following publications.

Berne, R. M., Levy M. N., Koeppen, B. M. and Stanton, B. A. (2004) *Physiology* (5th edition), Section IV, 'The cardiovascular system', St Louis, MO, Mosby.

Kharbanda, R. and MacAllister, R. J. (2005) 'The atherosclerosis time line and the role of endothelium', *Current Medicinal Chemistry – Immunology, Endocrine and Metabolic Agents*, **5**, pp. 47–52.

Lee, R. T. and Libby, P. (1997) 'The unstable atheroma', *Arteriosclerosis, Thrombosis and Vascular Biology*, **17**, pp. 1859–1867.

The Open University (2004) SK277 *Human biology*, Book 3, Chapter 2, 'Circulation', Milton Keynes, The Open University.

Van Gaal, L. F., Mertens, I. L. and De Block, C. E. (2006) 'Mechanisms linking obesity with cardiovascular disease', *Nature*, **444**, pp. 875–880.

HEART DISEASE

6.1 Introduction

The heart is an organ that has essentially only one function – it acts as a pump. Heart failure occurs when the heart is unable to pump sufficient blood around the body to supply nutrients and oxygen to the tissues. This will occur when the coordinated pumping activity of the heart is impaired in some way – a condition that is exacerbated when energy demand from the tissues is greatest, i.e. during exercise.

● Consider all of the elements that contribute to the normal pumping action of the heart – failure in any one of these elements can lead to heart failure. List five possible ways in which the function of the heart could become impaired.

● The normal emptying of the atria could be reduced – for example, because of atrial fibrillation. The filling of the ventricles would be impaired by leakage through the tricuspid or bicuspid valves. The strength of contraction of the atria or the ventricles could become reduced if the heart muscle was damaged. The ability of the ventricles to pump blood into the pulmonary arteries and the aorta would be compromised if the electrical activity of the heart became uncoordinated or a block in atrioventricular conduction had occurred. The cardiac output would also be impaired if the aortic or pulmonary semilunar valves were damaged or leaky.

In other words, the immediate cause of heart failure can be one or more of the following:

* damage to heart muscle
* damage to the chambers or valves
* abnormal electrical activity or conduction.

Such abnormalities may arise in a variety of ways, as a result of damage, aging or infection. In addition, children may be born with malformations of the heart or its conduction system, which impair its ability to pump efficiently or to respond to increased load. Often such congenital heart problems do not give rise to heart failure until later in life or when a higher cardiac output is needed. Indeed, many congenital abnormalities never result in heart failure at all. Nevertheless, the abnormal action or anatomy can often show itself as clinical signs or in diagnostic scans.

Changes in the anatomy of the heart may be a cause of heart failure, or a consequence as the heart tries to adapt to the load placed on it. The term **cardiomyopathy** describes abnormal changes in the heart muscle, such as thinning or thickening of the ventricular wall or damage to the muscle itself. Changes in the heart muscle not only affect the contractility of the heart but also can affect the volume of the ventricles and their elasticity, resulting in decreased cardiac output (Figure 6.1). Because the change is a response to heart failure, different causal events can lead to the same outcome. For example, dilated cardiomyopathy may be due to an infection of the heart muscle, nutritional deficiency or excessive alcohol intake. The causes of hypertrophic cardiomyopathy are less well defined, but some individuals have a genetic predisposition to develop the condition.

● Name two clinical signs and two diagnostic tests which could provide information on the anatomy, function and activity of the heart.

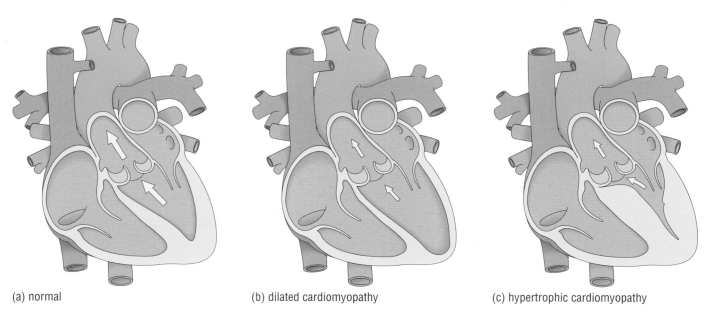

(a) normal　　　　　(b) dilated cardiomyopathy　　　　　(c) hypertrophic cardiomyopathy

Figure 6.1 In dilated cardiomyopathy, the ventricle enlarges, but the force of the systolic contraction is reduced, so a smaller proportion of the blood is pumped into the circulation at each stroke. In hypertrophic cardiomyopathy, the increased thickness of the ventricle wall makes the chamber less elastic so it fills less efficiently and the volume is also reduced.

● Heart sounds (heard via a stethoscope) and blood pressure measurement can each give information on how blood is flowing through the heart and whether the valves are closing properly. An ECG gives information on the anatomy of the heart and its electrical activity. An echocardiogram gives information on how the blood is flowing through the chambers of the heart.

As well as supplying sufficient cardiac output for the tissues, the heart also needs to maintain a minimum blood pressure. The kidney is a site of blood filtration, and a fall in blood pressure stops the filtration system from working normally. Nearly 20% of the cardiac output of a resting person goes to the kidneys. Consequently, heart failure, with a low cardiac output and low blood pressure, can lead to kidney failure. A minimum blood pressure is also needed to get blood to the brain, so low blood pressure can consequently lead to syncope.

In this chapter, you will look at different conditions that can lead to heart failure, and we shall introduce the different diagnostic tests which can help to differentiate each condition.

6.2 Acute and chronic heart failure

Chronic heart failure, also called congestive heart failure, develops progressively over a long period of time, as the capacity of the heart to pump sufficient blood gradually declines. In contrast, **acute heart failure** occurs rapidly, typically as a result of an MI or a failure in the normal coordinated electrical activity of the heart. In practice, these events are often closely interrelated. For example, an MI often produces abnormal electrical activity, and if a person recovers in the short term, there may be residual weakness in the heart muscle, so that it is less effective at pumping blood.

In considering whether the heart is able to pump sufficient blood, we also need to think about the efficiency of the lungs in obtaining oxygen as well as the blood and vascular system in supplying it to the tissue.

Case Study 6.1	Martha Childs develops some troubling symptoms

Martha has recently returned from seeing her mother, who lives in Jamaica. She had spent three uneventful weeks, mostly having a very easy time. She had contracted a bad cold in the last week which had developed into bronchitis, but it was starting to get better by the day of her return. During the return flight, which was 12 hours long and had a stop in Miami, she had taken her shoes off to make herself more comfortable, but when the plane landed she found that she could not get them on again. Her feet and ankles had swollen up. She thought that this was probably due to sitting still for such a long time, and she had had to put on some sandals which were in her hand-baggage in order to get off the plane. When she got home, she put her feet up for a few hours and the swelling went away. However, on the morning of the following day, when she was due to go back to work, she found the same trouble with her feet as she had had on the plane. She had also developed a chest pain, which she thought was probably due to the remains of the cold. Over the next two weeks, these problems persisted with varying degrees of severity. Martha also noticed that she had made one or two mistakes at work in making appointments, which was unusual for her. Her sleep had been a bit irregular after returning, but the tiredness which she had originally ascribed to jet lag did not seem to be getting better, and she had now started taking the bus into work, rather than walking.

After 4 weeks have passed with these symptoms persisting, Martha decides that she should visit the local herbal shop to see if there is something that she could take to reduce the swelling in her feet. Martha has never had much time for doctors, but she has a lot of confidence in traditional remedies. The lady in the shop, who knows Martha well, mentions that Martha is of an age when she may be starting the menopause and that water retention is quite common at this stage of life. She recommends a dandelion extract to be taken over the next 8 weeks and to see then how things have improved. Martha takes the remedy as recommended for 8 weeks and notices that she now has less trouble getting her shoes on. However, the tiredness and chest pain have got no better and are – if anything – slightly worse. Martha thinks that the dandelion treatment for water retention may mean that she is losing salt, so she decides to take a mineral supplement as well, to see if this will help reduce the tiredness.

Activity 6.1   Heart failure

Suggested study time 40 minutes

Now use the Multi-ed Cardiology program to learn more about heart failure and its causes.

Watch the two animations 'What is heart failure?' and 'What causes heart failure?', which can be found by navigating to Animations | Condition | Heart failure, and then answer the following questions.

(a) Of the symptoms that Martha is experiencing, could any of them be related to a heart condition?

(b) Why would heart failure cause breathlessness? Why would lung disease contribute to heart failure?

(c) How can heart failure and kidney failure contribute to each other? Give two mechanisms.

(d) What blood condition can contribute to heart disease?

(e) What do you understand by 'back pressure', and how is it related to the pumping action of the heart?

(f) What is the most common cause of heart failure?

Now watch the two animations 'How is heart failure diagnosed?' and 'How is heart failure treated?', also in Animations | Condition | Heart failure, and then answer the following questions.

(g) Why would a chest X-ray help in the diagnosis of heart failure?

(h) How could an echocardiogram help in the diagnosis of a heart condition?

(i)   Why was it once thought that beta-blockers might be unsuitable for a person with heart failure?

(j)   If Martha does have heart failure, would you expect the dandelion extract (a herbal diuretic) and the mineral supplements to make the condition better or worse?

Comment

(a)   Martha is experiencing swollen feet and ankles and fatigue, both of which are symptomatic of cardiac insufficiency. Chest pain can also be caused by heart failure. The disturbed sleep may be related to jet lag, and indeed none of the other symptoms are necessarily due to a heart problem. A proper examination is needed.

(b)   Heart failure causes fluid to accumulate in the lungs so they work less efficiently – i.e. there is poorer uptake of oxygen in the blood. If there is less oxygen in the blood due to heart failure or lung disease, the cardiac output needs to be greater to supply the tissue.

(c)   The kidneys require sufficient blood flow and blood pressure to work properly. If the kidneys do not work properly, water will be retained, which will put an additional load on the heart.

(d)   Anaemia can contribute to heart disease (see Section 6.2.2).

(e)   If the blood is not pumped out of the heart efficiently, a back pressure is created in the atria and ultimately in the veins, so that the heart does not fill properly. This means that fluid accumulates in the lungs and other tissues.

(f)   Damage to the heart muscle is the most common cause of heart failure. The most common cause of damage to the heart muscle is an MI.

(g)   A chest X-ray can indicate the size of the heart. An enlarged heart can indicate and indeed contribute towards heart failure.

(h)   An echocardiogram can indicate whether the pumping action of the heart and the operation of the valves are normal.

(i)   Beta-blockers make the contraction of the heart less powerful, so one might expect them to decrease cardiac output, which could exacerbate the symptoms of heart failure. In practice, however, this is not necessarily the case.

(j)   It is unsound to treat chronic symptoms, which could arise from a variety of different underlying conditions, without knowing what the actual condition is. Diuretics can be used to treat heart failure, reducing fluid retention and thereby the load on the heart. However, even if the fluid retention is due to heart failure, it is important to know the real cause of the heart condition to treat it appropriately. You do not know what the mineral supplements are and therefore have no idea if they are doing good or harm. For example, sodium will affect water retention, potassium could affect the electrical activity of the heart, and iron could help anaemia if iron deficiency was a problem, but this treatment is as obscure as the original condition is undiagnosed.

6.2.1 Signs and symptoms of chronic heart failure

The heart is, of course, a double pump, in which the output from left and right ventricles is matched in volume. Usually, heart failure involves both sides of the heart, and the symptoms are seen as insufficient cardiac output to both lungs and tissues, with a consequent back pressure in both sides of the venous circulations. However, it is possible for one side of the heart to be more affected than the other, resulting in either **left-sided heart failure** or **right-sided heart failure**. For example, if someone suffered from a pulmonary embolism, then the output of the right side of the heart would be specifically affected. Likewise, if an MI affected one ventricle, but not the other, that side of the circulation would be more affected.

The symptoms of left-sided heart failure are usually more evident than those of right-sided heart failure, because the left side of the heart is supplying critical organs and because blood pressure in the systemic circulation is much greater than in the pulmonary circulation.

So we can distinguish problems that are due to failure of each side of the heart and subdivide these into signs and symptoms. Symptoms are features of an illness that a patient can feel, such as tiredness or a racing pulse. They are not necessarily easily related to the underlying cause. For example, one symptom of left-sided heart failure is a reduced appetite and weight loss. Signs of a disease are things that a doctor can detect on examination or by a diagnostic test or scan. They may not be readily noticed by the person who has the condition. For example, raised blood pressure in the jugular veins (which drain ultimately into the right atrium) is a sign of right-sided heart failure, reflecting the back pressure mentioned above.

Heart failure is classified according to how much it limits a person's activity, i.e. according to the symptoms (Table 6.1). The worse the symptoms, the worse the **prognosis** (probable course and outcome of the disease): mortality at 1 year after diagnosis of grade 4 heart failure is over 60%.

Table 6.1 Classification of heart failure.

Grade	Activity-related symptoms
1	no limitation on physical activity
2	slight limitation on ability to exercise
3	major limitation on any activity
4	symptoms even at rest

6.2.2 Contributory causes of chronic heart failure

Although heart failure is usually due to a problem of the heart itself, a number of other factors can contribute.

● Why might lung infection and **anaemia** (lack of red blood cells) be associated with heart failure?

● In both cases, they affect the ability of blood to supply tissues with oxygen, so the heart will have to provide a higher cardiac output to satisfy the oxygen demands of the tissues.

Conditions that affect the body's metabolism may also place increased demands on the heart. Thyroid disease was mentioned in the animations in Activity 6.1. Thyroid hormones affect the overall rate of metabolism of many tissues, and an overactive thyroid gland is associated with a high metabolic rate of tissues and hence increased load on the heart. Conversely, an inactive thyroid with a low metabolic rate may cause people to put on weight, and being overweight is itself a risk factor for heart failure. Hence thyroid disease may act directly or indirectly to increase the risk of heart failure. It depends on the type of thyroid disease, but the simple point is that normal thyroid activity gives the lowest risk of cardiovascular disease or heart failure.

Diabetes is another condition that has both direct and indirect effects on the risk of heart failure. The direct effects relate to the way glucose is used by the tissues, while indirect effects relate to factors such as the weight gain and high cholesterol levels often associated with diabetes.

6.3 Myocardial infarction

A heart attack is the common term used for acute heart failure. Like chronic heart failure, the severity can vary from an event that is virtually symptom-free to something that is life-threatening or fatal. Because the most common cause of acute heart failure is a myocardial infarction, the two terms are often used synonymously. This is, however, confusing: a number of less common events such as arrhythmias can also result in acute heart failure.

Activity 6.2 Myocardial infarction

Suggested study time 20 minutes

Now use the Multi-ed Cardiology program to learn more about MI.

Watch the three animations 'What is a heart attack?', 'What causes a heart attack?' and 'How is a heart attack diagnosed?', which can be found by navigating to Animations | Condition | Coronary Heart Disease, and then answer the following questions.

(a) What is the difference between angina and an MI, in regard to symptoms, causes and triggering events?

(b) How long can heart muscle survive without a normal blood flow before permanent damage occurs?

(c) How can an MI induce a cardiac arrest?

(d) What value is a blood test in helping to diagnose an MI?

Comment

(a) Angina is due to narrowing of the coronary arteries, often due to atherosclerosis, and is triggered by exercise. The symptoms are of shorter duration and are less severe than for a heart attack, but both cause chest pain. A heart attack is due to blockage of a coronary artery, often by a thrombus. The trigger is usually undetermined.

(b) Heart muscle can survive for a few minutes without its blood supply before permanent damage occurs.

(c) A heart attack may cause the electrical conduction of the heart and the normal wave of depolarisation to be disrupted.

(d) A blood test can detect enzymes released into the blood by the damaged heart muscle.

The treatment of MI has developed considerably in recent years. Previously, the emphasis was centred on making the patient as comfortable as possible, and getting them to hospital quickly. Now, a large amount of diagnosis and treatment is carried out by paramedical staff before the person reaches hospital. The rationale for this change is that the sooner treatment is started, particularly with the use of thrombolytics, the better the prognosis for the patient. Paramedical staff aim to reach the patient within 8 minutes of receiving a category A emergency call, and individual paramedics may be positioned at strategic locations, distant from a hospital, in order to be able to respond quickly to an emergency call. The responses are coordinated from control centres that cover large areas of the country. Even if an ambulance is sent out from a hospital, it may arrive some time after the initial paramedical worker has arrived with the patient and has started diagnosis and treatment (Figure 6.2). The actual times taken to reach a patient will vary, depending on the region – it generally takes longer to reach people in rural areas, where travel distances are correspondingly greater. However, the aim is always to initiate thrombolytic therapy, if appropriate, within 60 minutes of the call – often referred to as the 'call to needle time'.

Activity 6.3   Acute treatment of a myocardial infarction

Suggested study time 90 minutes

Now follow the links on the DVD Guide program to the video sequence 'Heart attack'. Initially, view the entire sequence, uninterrupted. It covers what happens in the 45 minutes between the time that Winifred Fowler starts to develop symptoms and the time she arrives in the coronary care unit at the regional hospital, in Norwich. Take particular care to look out for the following:

Figure 6.2   A paramedic carries out an ECG investigation on Winifred, who is suspected of having an MI.

1   the symptoms of an acute MI, and the series of questions that the ambulance controller asks the bus depot supervisor (Ralph) to establish whether Winifred may be suffering from an MI

2   the diagnostic tests and questions that the first-responder paramedic (Marcus Bailey) uses to confirm the diagnosis

3   the group of drugs/treatments which are given to alleviate the symptoms of MI

4   how the provisional diagnosis of MI is checked with a clinical adviser before the explanation of thrombolytic treatment, and its potential benefit and hazards to Winifred

5   the drugs which are given to Winifred as thrombolytic therapy and to prevent blood clotting, also noting how they are administered

6   the calm and professional way in which the paramedical team work, and the way in which this helps to reassure Winifred

7   the way in which transfer to coronary care staff at the hospital is carried out.

Once you have watched the sequence, answer the following questions. If necessary, skip through the video to find the answers and to pick up points that you might have missed initially.

(a)   Identify four symptoms of an acute MI that affect Winifred.

(b)   Identify four diagnostic procedures that Marcus carries out. Which one of these is most important in confirming the diagnosis of MI?

(c)   What four treatments are used for pain relief and to help stabilise Winifred's condition?

(d)   What hazards are associated with thrombolytic treatment, and in what proportion of people might this occur? Why does Marcus ask Winifred about recent surgery or dental treatment?

(e)   What two drugs are given as thrombolytic therapy? How soon is this given after the MI?

(f)   At what point are the ECG leads put onto Winifred? When are they taken off?

(g)   How do staff at the coronary care unit know what treatment Winifred has received?

Comment

(a)   Winifred has a severe, crushing pain in the centre of her chest radiating to her left arm. She scores it, on a scale of 1–10, as 10: the worst pain she has ever experienced (Figure 6.3). She also has irregular breathing and is pale and clammy. While both Marcus and the ambulance controller ask if she has been sick, this is not a symptom that she reports. However, it is very noticeable how frightened she is by the whole experience. This is very characteristic of a person with an acute MI.

Figure 6.3   Severe, crushing chest pain is a common symptom of MI.

167

(b) Marcus checks her pulse and blood pressure. He also uses a pulse oximeter to measure the oxygen saturation level of the blood (see Section 7.4.2). Most important, he sets up and carries out a full 12-lead ECG. This is essential in establishing the diagnosis of MI, in association with the on-call clinical adviser at the hospital. The ECG trace is transmitted directly to the hospital by the machine, through data-faxing – this is an intrinsic function of the machine and is not seen as a separate event in the video sequence. Consequently, both Marcus and the clinical advisor are able to look at the trace when they are discussing, on the phone, whether Winifred has had an MI, and whether she is a suitable candidate for thrombolysis.

(c) The treatments are morphine, oxygen, nitrate and aspirin – often referred to as MONA, although they are not actually given in this order. Morphine is primarily for pain relief. Oxygen is used to maintain blood oxygen saturation and to give the ischaemic heart muscle the best chance of survival. Nitrate (glyceryl trinitrate) promotes vasodilation, reducing the load on the heart and potentially increasing blood supply in the unblocked coronary circulation (See Section 8.2.1). Aspirin prevents platelet aggregation (see Section 8.2.7) and is given primarily to prevent the clot developing further.

(d) The major hazard of thrombolytic therapy is that it promotes bleeding by dissolving blood clots – and not just those in the coronary circulation. Such problems may occur in 1–2% of people. Bleeding into the brain can cause a stroke, and this is one of the most serious adverse effects that can occur, but does so in less than 0.5% of people given thrombolytic therapy. Marcus asks Winifred whether she has had any surgery or dentistry recently, because these treatments often result in wounds, and the thrombolytic treatment may cause them to bleed. Hence the risk of adverse effects from the therapy is greater in people who have had recent surgery. Having explained the risk of the treatment, Marcus obtains verbal consent from Winifred to carry it out. In less pressing circumstances, doctors generally obtain written consent before carrying out treatment. However, in this case, the urgency of the situation and Winifred's condition mean that verbal consent is appropriate.

(e) The two drugs given are Tenectaplase™ and heparin. Both drugs are given intravenously, once Marcus has confirmed with Jonathan that they are using the correct drugs, that the dose is correct and that the drugs are within their use-by date (Figure 6.4). Only a registered health care worker is allowed to administer this treatment. Tenectaplase™ is the trade name for a preparation of tissue plasminogen activator (t-pa; see Section 5.7.3 and Figure 8.6). Heparin inhibits the activation of the blood clotting system (see Figure 5.11), and the dose that is given depends on the size (weight) of the recipient. Winifred receives thrombolytic therapy within 25 minutes, well within the call to needle time guideline (Department of Health, 2000). The value of thrombolytic therapy reduces as the elapsed time increases. Studies indicate that it has little value in saving lives if it is given more than 3 hours after the MI.

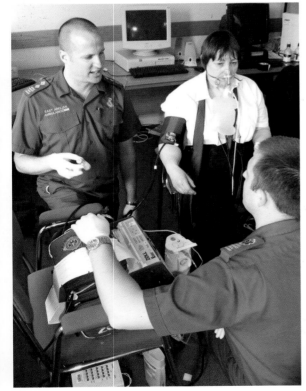

Figure 6.4 Paramedics check the dose and date of the drugs before they are administered.

(f)   The ECG electrodes are put on at the bus depot, and they are not taken off throughout the following sequences. The electrodes are attached to lines which are unplugged from the ECG machine in the office, transferred to a machine in the ambulance and transferred again to another ECG machine in the coronary care unit. The oxygen supplied to Winifred is also maintained as far as is possible. During the transfer on the chair and in the ambulance (Figure 6.5), there is a short period when she is not receiving oxygen, but this relates primarily to the difficulty of moving the chair down narrow staircases, rather than being for any medical reason.

(g)   Winifred is tagged with a yellow wrist-band to indicate that she has had thrombolytic therapy. This ensures that she cannot accidentally receive the same treatment again at the hospital. Marcus, who was the first person to see Winifred and who administered the thrombolytic therapy, is responsible for handover to the staff at the coronary care unit. In this case, a verbal handover was carried out, but in all circumstances, written notes will be made on paper or on a laptop computer, and these would also be transferred to the coronary care staff to form part of the patient's medical record. Marcus is able to discharge his clinical duty of care by means of this handover and by signing to confirm understanding of events, assessment and treatment.

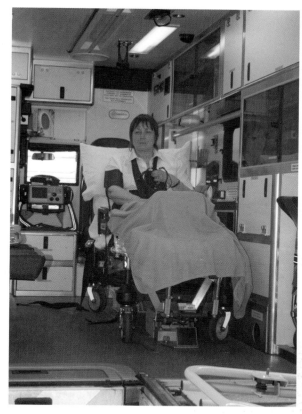

Figure 6.5   Winifred is transferred to the coronary care unit.

Activity 6.4   Developments in the acute treatment of myocardial infarctions

Suggested study time 20 minutes

Follow the links on the DVD Guide program to the audio clip of Alan Bromley, a Senior Training Officer with the London Ambulance Service, in which he describes how the service responds to a person with a suspected MI. Be aware that this recording was made before the video sequence that you have seen above, and that there are differences in ways that ambulances would respond in cities and rural areas. In addition, there have been developments in best practice even within the intervening 2–3 years. When you have listened to the clip, answer the following questions.

(a)   What considerations affect when thrombolysis is given, and how might this vary from an urban region to a rural one?

(b)   How does the practice described with respect to the use of ECG differ from the practice seen in the more recent video sequence?

(c) Under what framework does the ambulance service operate in responding to an MI, and what auditing of their activity takes place?

(d) What option that is not generally available do ambulance crews have in London for treating MI?

Comment

(a) If the appropriate criteria are met, thrombolysis is given at the earliest opportunity by a qualified person. In a rural region, where the time to reach a hospital may be long, there is more incentive to give thrombolysis on the spot, rather than wait until the patient reaches hospital, although treatment before transfer to hospital is increasingly used in all areas.

(b) In the audio sequence the 12-lead ECG is done in the ambulance, and the ECG traces passed to the staff at the hospital as the patient is wheeled in. In the video sequence, the ECG was done in the office where the MI occurred, before Winifred goes to the ambulance, and the ECG was transmitted to the hospital for immediate review.

(c) The service works under the guidelines of the National Service Framework. Alan Bromley has a weekly review with the cardiac care specialist, and hospital accident and emergency (A & E) departments return figures to the Myocardial Infarction National Audit Project.

(d) The London Ambulance Service can take patients directly to the London Chest Hospital for coronary angioplasty. This treatment has a high success rate and is safer than thrombolysis, but such specialist hospitals are not accessible sufficiently quickly in most regions.

6.3.1 Identifying when a person has had a heart attack

In the immediate aftermath of a suspected heart attack, the ECG is particularly valuable in establishing whether the heart beat is normal or abnormal (Figure 6.6). Detailed examination of a full 12-lead ECG is important for establishing exactly what damage has occurred. However, the ECG following a heart attack is not necessarily abnormal, so a normal ECG does not rule out an MI.

A blood test is also useful for establishing whether the heart muscle has been damaged. When cells die due to lack of oxygen, the cell membrane ruptures, releasing the contents of the cell into the bloodstream. Enzymes are proteins that facilitate biochemical reactions inside cells and **cardiac enzymes** are either found only in the heart or are found at much higher levels in the heart than in other tissues. Hence the presence of such proteins in the blood is strongly indicative of heart muscle damage.

● Why would you expect the enzymes in heart muscle to be different from those in other muscle?

● Cardiac muscle is different from skeletal muscle and smooth muscle due to its different sets of proteins, including enzymes (see Chapter 5).

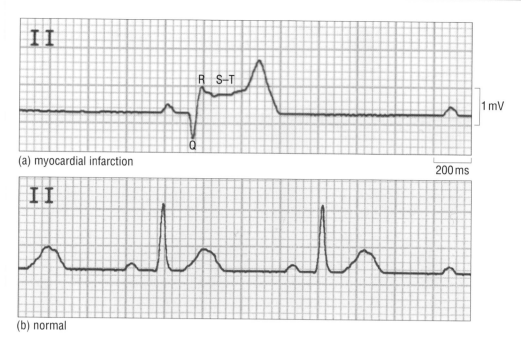

Figure 6.6 The ECG of Winifred Fowler, taken shortly after her MI, shows a number of typical abnormalities. The full ECG produces 12 separate traces, but for simplicity, only trace II is shown here in (a) and is compared with trace II from a normal ECG (b). Note in particular that the Q wave is large and negative, and the R wave is small. These findings suggest that the strength of the ventricular systolic contraction is reduced. Note also that the ST segment does not return to the baseline level and that the T wave is particularly large, which suggests that the myocardium is not repolarising fully after each contraction. As with all the traces in this course, the graph paper sets the scale: one large square horizontally corresponds to a time of 200 ms, and one large square vertically corresponds to a potential of 1 mV. (Variation in the electrical activity of people's hearts – and of the sensitivity and placement of electrodes – means that some graphs show greater variation in potential than others.)

Ideally, a diagnostically useful test would detect an enzyme that is released into the blood early after the MI, and would be specific for the condition – it would not be an enzyme that is released following, for example, an injury to skeletal muscle. A most useful marker is **troponin-T** or **troponin-I**, enzymes which are normally never found in the blood. The heart-muscle-specific forms of these enzymes are released within 1–2 hours of heart damage. **Creatine kinase** is also frequently used, and is elevated in more than 90% of MIs. However, this enzyme is also present in skeletal muscle, so its presence is much less specific for a heart attack. Also increasingly used are heart-specific forms of **creatine phosphokinase**: the isoform called creatine phosphokinase-MB (CPK-MB). (**Isoforms** are variants of an enzyme which occur in a specific tissue.) Other

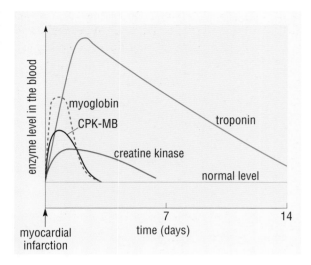

Figure 6.7 Enzymes released from damaged heart muscle typically peak within the first 12–48 hours after an MI and can be detected for several days. Normal level corresponds to different amounts of each enzyme, but has been drawn as one level here for simplicity; the graph therefore indicates only how these enzymes appear and vary in amount with time.

proteins, including myoglobin and lactate dehydrogenase, are also detectable in the blood, but they are much less specific for heart damage (Figure 6.7).

● Why might the measurement of myoglobin be useful even though it is not specific for heart muscle? What is the normal function of myoglobin?

● Myoglobin is elevated earlier than other proteins after the MI (Figure 6.7). It normally stores oxygen in muscle tissues (see Section 5.2).

Because cardiac enzymes may not be elevated during the first few hours following an MI, repeated blood tests are usually taken over the subsequent 24 hours. Because enzymes remain elevated for several days, they are still detectable in a person who has had an MI, but who was not seen immediately by medical staff or who had a symptomless MI. In the latter case, the abnormality would usually be detected during testing for some other condition.

6.4 Cardiac arrhythmias

Changes in the regular heart beat may be part of normal physiology, or may indicate an underlying problem. For example, increased heart rate or **tachycardia** is a normal response to exercise, but may also be due to abnormal electrical activity in the sinoatrial node or another part of the heart's conduction system. Likewise, **bradycardia** or an abnormally slow heart beat is usually defined as fewer than 60 beats per minute when at rest, but healthy older people and athletes may well have a lower heart rate. An abnormally high heart rate may be as dangerous as a low heart rate, because there is insufficient time for the ventricles to fill, so cardiac output actually falls. When a person becomes uncomfortably aware of their heart beat, the symptom is referred to as palpitations and may take various forms – an altered heart rate, particularly forceful heart beats, extra beats (**ectopic beats**) or missed beats. Often, an ectopic beat is followed by an extended period before the next beat (Figure 6.8). Again, these symptoms may be innocent or due to an underlying problem.

● How is the normal heart rate maintained? How is it moderated?

● The intrinsic pacemaker activity of the sinoatrial node maintains the normal heart rate (Section 2.4.1). The activity of the autonomic nervous system and hormones acting on the sinoatrial node moderate its intrinsic rate of depolarisation (Section 2.5).

It follows that alterations in the activity of the sinoatrial node will often result in an arrhythmia. The intrinsic depolarisation rate of the sinoatrial node is faster than that of other parts of the heart, so it leads the wave of depolarisation that causes contraction of the heart. If, however, the sinoatrial node does not provide the pacemaker activity for the heart, other parts of the heart muscle will usually still beat. But the rate is slower, and the normal coordination of the beat is often lost, so that cardiac output is reduced.

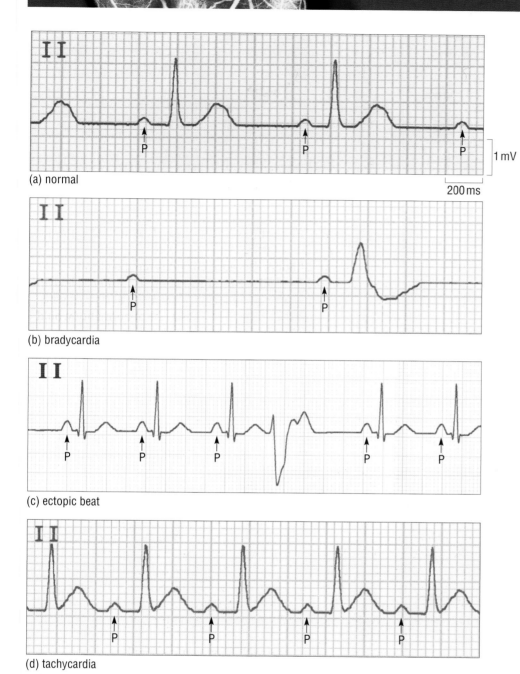

Figure 6.8 ECGs of (a) normal heart function, (b) bradycardia, (c) an ectopic beat with long latency and (d) tachycardia.

Harmless ectopic beats may originate in the sinoatrial node, or in the AVN, without causing any more than a transient change in the heart rate, which quickly reverts to normal. If, however, the abnormal electrical activity persists, treatment with a combination of drugs and/or a pacemaker device is usually required (see Section 9.5.1).

If damage occurs in the conduction systems of the heart, then the wave of depolarisation coordinating the contraction of the atria followed by the ventricles may also be disrupted, so that normal contraction is compromised. Exactly what effect damage to the heart has on the normal heart beat will depend on what the damage is and where it is located. Some examples are considered next.

In **atrial flutter**, the rate of depolarisation and contraction of the atria rises to 250–350 beats per minute, with the rate remaining regular. However, the ventricles do not have sufficient time to recover between beats and so cannot attain this rate. Consequently, the ventricles beat only on every second, third or fourth atrial beat. Nevertheless, the rate at which the ventricles beat is higher than normal, and the combination of poorly coordinated filling and high heart rate puts a continuous load on the ventricular muscle.

In **atrial fibrillation**, the normal contraction of the atria is absent, as waves of uncoordinated depolarisation spread across the atria and lead to an irregular ventricular contraction. Consequently, the atrial contribution to the filling of the ventricles is also absent. The condition may arise for no apparent reason, but is more often associated with other diseases, such as mitral valve damage or rheumatic fever (see Section 6.5.1). The uncoordinated depolarisation may be due to other sources of electrical activity which initiate depolarisation before the sinoatrial node. Getting normal sinus rhythm re-established is the top priority, because of the additional workload put onto the ventricles. This may be achieved within a few hours by appropriate drug treatment. If the condition persists or recurs frequently, the atrial muscle may start to atrophy (waste away), to a point which is not reversible.

An **atrioventricular block**, also called a heart block, describes what happens when the normal depolarisation of the atria does not pass to the ventricles. The degree of the blockage may vary, between a complete block, in which the depolarisation never passes the AVN, to a partial block, in which the conduction is delayed or affects only one branch of the bundle of His. Such problems may be congenital or associated with other heart diseases.

Ventricular fibrillation (uncoordinated waves of contraction in the ventricles) is almost always fatal, as cardiac output falls to zero. This form of arrhythmia produces the clinical features of **cardiac arrest**, and requires that the heart is restarted within 3–4 minutes if the person is to recover. (See the discussion of cardiopulmonary resuscitation in Section 1.8.1.) Myocardial infarction is the most common cause of ventricular fibrillation, but other causes – such as drug overdoses, electrocution or drowning – can also produce this state. If an individual dies within 1 hour of the onset of cardiac symptoms, it is referred to as **sudden cardiac death**, and approximately two thirds of such cases are due to ventricular arrhythmia.

As can be seen in the examples above, although arrhythmias may have congenital or undiagnosed causes, they are often secondary to other conditions, such as MI, valve disease or infection. For this reason, the information that is obtained from an ECG, which directly measures the electrical activity of the heart, can indirectly provide information on the conditions that have produced the arrhythmia. This will be further explored in Chapter 7.

Activity 6.5   Palpitations

Suggested study time 15 minutes

Now use the Multi-ed Cardiology program to gain an overview of cardiac arrhythmias.

Watch the four animations 'What are palpitations?', 'What causes palpitations?', 'What is atrial fibrillation?' and 'What causes atrial fibrillation?', which can be found by navigating to Animations | Condition | Palpitations.

Note that the figure given for the incidence of atrial fibrillation suggests that more than 20% of people over 65 may have this condition, but a more accurate figure would be 10–15%.

Activity 6.6   Valvular heart disease

Suggested study time 15 minutes

Continue with the Multi-ed Cardiology program to watch the three animations 'What is valvular heart disease?', 'What causes valvular heart disease?' and 'How is valvular heart disease diagnosed?', which can be found by navigating to Animations | Condition | Valvular heart disease. Once you have done this, answer the following questions.

(a) Name and define the two principal ways in which heart valves may fail.

(b) What is a heart murmur?

Comment

(a) **Stenosis** describes the condition when a valve becomes restricted so that blood cannot flow through it freely. **Regurgitation** describes what occurs when a valve does not close correctly, and blood flows backwards through it.

(b) A **heart murmur** is an abnormal heart sound, which may signify a problem with blood flow in the chambers of the heart.

6.5 Conditions and diseases that affect the heart valves

Any of the four heart valves may be affected by disease, but those that affect the mitral and aortic semilunar valve are usually of most concern. In North America and Europe, the majority of valvular conditions are seen in older people and are due to progressive degeneration of the heart valves with age. In areas of the world where the average age of the population is lower, and where levels of infectious diseases are higher, valvular disease is more often due to rheumatic fever (not to be confused with rheumatoid arthritis, the joint disease).

6.5.1 Rheumatic fever

Rheumatic fever is a condition that develops following a throat infection with the bacterium *Streptococcus pyogenes* – the most common cause of a sore throat. Typically, the infection happens in childhood, but the damage to the heart valves develops after the initial infection has resolved and progresses over a number of months or years. Only a small proportion of people who get streptococcal throat infection will go on to develop rheumatic fever. The likelihood of progression depends on a number of factors, including the strain of bacteria involved, the person's genetic makeup and their general level of health, which relates to nutrition and the presence of other infections.

Rheumatic fever is an example of an **autoimmune disease**, in which the body makes an immune reaction against its own tissues. Normally, the immune system reacts against anything from outside the body that it identifies both as 'non-self' and dangerous. Conversely, the immune system recognises the body's own tissues as being 'self' and not dangerous, so it does not make an immune reaction against them. Autoimmune diseases occur when this system of self-tolerance breaks down. Note that a molecule that is recognised by the immune system is called an **antigen**. Rheumatic fever is a singularly good example of how an infection can lead to autoimmune disease. It happens that some of the antigens present on the surface of the bacteria are very similar in biochemical structure to antigens that are present on the heart valves. Such antigens are said to be **cross-reactive**, because an antibody that recognises one antigen will recognise the other too (Figure 6.9). If the immune system makes antibodies against the antigens on the bacteria, those antibodies will equally well recognise the antigens on the heart valves. Antibodies are able to activate inflammatory reactions. Ordinarily, it would be very useful to have antibodies directing an inflammatory reaction against bacteria, because it helps to destroy them. However, such reactions directed against heart valves will damage them.

The most common long-term damage in rheumatic fever is stenosis of the mitral valve. This may not become evident until several decades after the initiation of the disease, as a result of recurrent cycles of inflammation, damage and healing.

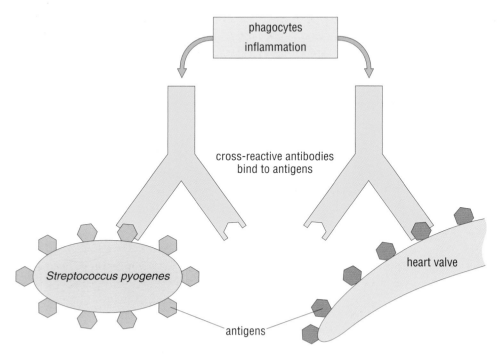

Figure 6.9 Antigens on the surface of bacteria (*Streptococcus pyogenes*) induce the formation of antibodies that coincidentally recognise and bind to similar antigens on heart valves. Antibodies bind to the bacteria, allowing the bacteria to be taken up by phagocytes and potentially inducing inflammation, which is useful in controlling infection. The same antibodies bind to the heart valve and also induce inflammation, but in this case it is potentially damaging.

The narrowing of the valve and increased load on the heart produce an increased risk of arrhythmia – and of atrial fibrillation in particular.

Treatment of rheumatic fever initially involves antibiotics to eradicate the bacterial infection, followed by supportive treatment for potential heart failure. It is standard practice to continue with prophylactic (preventive) antibiotics over many years, because although the disease is not directly due to the bacteria, another streptococcal infection can cause the autoimmune disease to flare up. In the pre-antibiotic era, mortality for rheumatic fever could be as high as 25%, but with best practice this has been reduced to 1%.

6.5.2 Degenerative changes in heart valves

Heart valves, like many other tissues, become increasingly thick and stiff with age. This is due to changes in their protein composition, a process termed **sclerosis**. A similar effect also occurs in arteries as people age. The process can produce both stenosis and/or regurgitation. Thickening of the valves reduces their internal diameter, while loss of elasticity makes it more likely that they will fail to close properly during the cycle of the heart beat. A further complication in older people is **calcification**, a process in which mineral deposits form on the valve tissue, further reducing the elasticity and diameter of the valves. The likelihood of calcification increases in people who have high calcium levels in the blood, possibly as a result of kidney disease. Most often it affects the aortic semilunar valve, and although calcification does not necessarily cause a problem, it has been calculated (using people in the Framingham heart study; see Case Study 3.1) that for each 1 mm reduction in the diameter of the mitral valve as a result of calcification, there was a 10% increased risk of MI. Hence it has been suggested that calcification, which can be detected on X-ray scans (Figure 6.10), may be a good indicator of early cardiovascular disease.

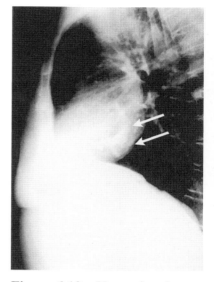

Figure 6.10   X-ray showing calcification of the mitral valve.

6.6 Infections of the heart and aorta

Infections of the heart and valves are uncommon but potentially serious. In these conditions, bacteria or viruses directly infect heart tissue, causing damage to the endocardium, heart muscle or valves.

● Would you consider rheumatic fever to be an infection of the heart?

● No – although it is triggered by a bacterial infection, the infection does not directly affect the heart, and the damage is caused by the immune system.

In **bacterial endocarditis**, bacteria circulating within the blood become lodged on the endocardium, the layer of cells lining the chambers and valves of the heart. This is most likely to happen if there is irregular blood flow through the heart or previous damage causing the surface to be irregular – for example, as a result of rheumatic fever. Bacteria do not normally circulate in the blood, and the route by which they enter the blood is usually unknown, but in some cases it can follow

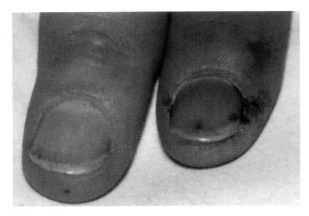

Figure 6.11 Splinter haemorrhages in bacterial endocarditis.

dental treatment. For this reason, susceptible individuals are given prophylactic antibiotics following tooth extractions and other dental surgery.

The symptoms of bacterial endocarditis include those associated with infection (fever, loss of appetite, sweats, weight loss) in addition to any symptoms that may be associated with damage to the heart. Starting from their point of attachment in the heart or on the valves, bacteria can divide, producing 'vegetations' which can break off and spread through the circulation. If these bacterial emboli lodge in small vessels, they can cause local haemorrhage (Figure 6.11). Bacterial emboli in the brain cause small strokes; consequently, neurological symptoms may be the first detected sign of bacterial endocarditis.

Viral infections may affect heart muscle, killing the cells directly and/or inducing an immune response that kills the infected cells. Several viruses may infect the heart muscle, of which the most common is Coxsackie virus – but even this is rare. The loss of heart muscle puts an additional load on unaffected areas (similar to an MI) but, with time, the remaining cells can usually compensate for the loss.

The bacterial infection **syphilis**, which is most often acquired as a venereal infection, may become chronic if not treated early. The bacteria lodge in many tissues throughout the body, including the aorta. The damage caused by the bacteria and the low-grade inflammatory reaction against them, mediated by the immune system, affects the tissues in the aortic wall so that it loses its elasticity. The damage can be detected as a 'sledgehammer pulse', with the pressure rising quickly as the aorta is unable to absorb the pressure wave of systole. The result may be regurgitation in the aortic semilunar valve or the development of aortic aneurysm.

Infections may also affect the pericardium, the sac which surrounds the heart and the roots of the major vessels, protecting the heart and reducing friction with other organs. Infections that affect the pericardium include Coxsackie virus, tuberculosis and a number of other bacteria. However, trauma or autoimmune responses can also cause inflammation of the pericardium (pericarditis). The symptoms are typically a sharp, radiating pain between the shoulders, and the appropriate treatment depends on the underlying cause.

6.7 Congenital conditions that affect the heart

Congenital defects of the heart affect nearly 1% of babies born. There are many different types of defect; some of these are immediately life-threatening, whereas others are less severe and may partly correct themselves. In the more severe conditions, babies show signs that the tissues are not receiving sufficient oxygenated blood (**cyanosis**), and the babies do not develop normally. The great majority of defects are anatomical, i.e. there is something wrong with the plumbing of the heart and/or major vessels. Congenital heart defects may be identified by listening to heart sounds, by an ECG or an echocardiogram. At one time, congenital heart defects were almost exclusively treated by cardiac paediatricians, often with surgery to correct the anatomical defect or at least to compensate for its effects. As surgical treatment has become more effective, an increasing number of children with defects are surviving into adulthood.

6.7.1 Shunts

The heart is a double pump in which the two pumps act in series. If blood can leak between the left and right sides of the circulation in some way, this is described as a **shunt**. Such leaks most often occur between neighbouring parts of the circulation. For example, a defect in the septum between the ventricles can allow blood to shunt between the left and right sides of the circulation. Because the left heart pumps at higher pressure than the right heart, blood usually moves from the left to the right circulation, with mixing of oxygenated and deoxygenated blood and impaired cardiac output. The right heart may also be more heavily loaded than normal, as it would normally be subjected to lower pressures. The severity of such defects greatly depends on the size of the shunt.

Two of the more common conditions are related to special channels in the fetal circulatory system which normally seal up shortly after a baby is born. The circulation in a fetus is slightly different from that in an adult (Figure 6.12), and relates to the fact that babies in the womb receive oxygen from the placenta and not from their lungs. In the fetus, there is an opening called the **foramen ovale** between the right and left atrium, which allows oxygenated blood from the placenta to bypass the right circulation entirely. This opening may fail to close fully (**patent foramen ovale**; also called persistent foramen ovale), and because this occurs in a significant proportion of the population it should be considered to be a normal occasional variation rather than a defect. Although the effect on

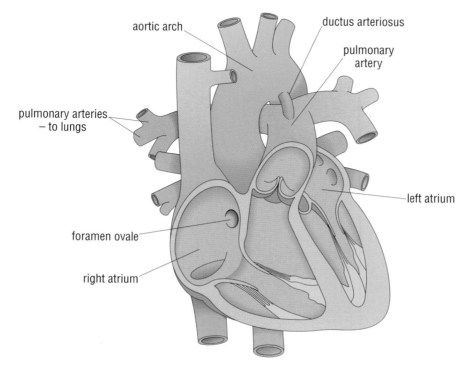

Figure 6.12 Blood circulation in a fetus. The foramen ovale allows blood to move straight from the right to the left atrium. The ductus arteriosus allows blood from the pulmonary artery to supply the systemic circulation. These anatomical bypasses present in the fetal circulation may remain open for a period after birth – and even into adulthood in some people.

blood oxygenation is usually minor, it does allow thromboemboli from the leg veins to move directly from the right atrium into the left circulation, and the condition may therefore manifest itself as a stroke. Another specialisation of the fetal circulation is the **ductus arteriosus**, a connection between the pulmonary artery and the aorta, which allows the right ventricle to pump blood directly into the systemic circulation. Normally this connecting vessel closes off shortly after birth, but if it remains open (**patent ductus arteriosus**; also called persistent ductus arteriosus) the high pressure in the aorta pushes blood into the pulmonary arteries, so that pulmonary hypertension can develop. The overall effect is also to decrease the total blood flow into the systemic circulation.

In some congenital conditions, the ductus arteriosus can act as a life-saver by allowing blood to bypass an anatomical defect and enter the systemic circulation, but as it only remains open for a few days or weeks after birth, the underlying problem needs to be corrected quickly, usually by surgery.

6.7.2 Obstructions and complex conditions

A second major group of defects is obstructions (stenoses) which can affect the valves or the major vessels. Apart from restricting blood flow, such abnormalities potentially provide sites for thrombi to develop, or bacteria to grow.

Some rare conditions involve major transpositions of blood vessels – they establish with the wrong connections during fetal development. For example, in 'transposition of the great arteries', the right ventricle pumps blood into the aorta and the left ventricle pumps blood into the pulmonary arteries.

● What effect would transposition of the great arteries have on the circulation of the blood?

● This transposition would result in two completely separate circulatory systems which are not in series. The systemic circulation would receive no oxygenated blood, unless the ductus arteriosus remains open.

A condition of this severity needs urgent surgical correction shortly after birth. Fortunately, such major abnormalities are rare.

6.8 Summary of Chapter 6

Heart failure describes the inability of the heart to supply the body with an adequate amount of blood at appropriate blood pressure. Heart failure may be caused by damage to the heart muscle, by disturbed blood flow due to stenosis or regurgitation of valves, or may be due to altered electrical activity and an abnormal heart beat. Congenital conditions or infections may lead to heart failure. However, the most common cause of heart failure in adults is MI caused by blockage of the arterial blood supply to an area of heart muscle. Myocardial infarction is usually detected by ECG or blood tests to detect proteins released by the damaged heart muscle. Restoring blood supply to the affected area by treatment with thrombolytic drugs or by coronary angioplasty is the main priority in people who have suffered an MI.

Further reading

If you would like to read further, please refer to the following publications.

Department of Health (2003) *Review of early thrombolysis: faster and better treatment for heart attack patients* [online] http://www.dh.gov.uk/en/Publicationsandstatistics/Publications/PublicationsPolicyAndGuidance/DH_4008531 (Accessed May 2007).

Gray, H. H., Dawkins, K. D., Morgan, J. M. and Simpson, I. A. (2002) *Lecture Notes on Cardiology* (4th edition), Oxford, Blackwell Science.

Hoffman, J. I. E and Kaplan, S. (2002) 'The incidence of congenital heart disease', *Journal of the American College of Cardiology*, **39**, pp. 1890–1900.

Marelli, A. J., Mackie, A. S., Ionescu-Ittu, R., Rahme, E. and Pilote, L. (2007) 'Congenital heart disease in the general population. Changing prevalence and age distribution', *Circulation*, **115**, pp. 163–172.

Mayo Clinic (2007) *Heart disease center* [online] http://www.mayoclinic.com/health/heart-disease/HB99999 (Accessed May 2007).

Morrison, L. J., Verbeek, P. R. and McDonald, A. C. (2000) 'Mortality and prehospital thrombolysis for acute myocardial infarction: a meta-analysis', *Journal of the American Medical Association*, **283**, pp. 2686–2892.

CHAPTER 7

INVESTIGATIONS AND IMAGING

Learning Outcomes

When you have completed this chapter you should be able to:

7.1 Define and use, or recognise definitions and applications of, each of the terms printed in **bold** in the text.

7.2 Outline the main types of investigations available for the diagnosis of cardiovascular disease.

7.3 Understand the differences between invasive and non-invasive investigations.

7.4 Explain the balance between risk and benefit in the medical imaging techniques used to investigate cardiovascular disease.

7.1 Introduction

In this chapter you will be looking at the diagnostic tools available to doctors to investigate cardiovascular diseases. For example, when visiting a health clinic or hospital for a routine check-up, it is usual for them to measure heart rate and then blood pressure, to look at the ears, mouth and eyes, and to listen to heart sounds and those associated with breathing. When diagnosing cardiovascular disease, the types of investigation used are determined by the suspected severity of the disease and whether it is acute or chronic.

Part of the diagnostic process relies on assessing the clinical history of the patient, by discussing: any previous signs suggesting a risk of cardiovascular disease; any breathlessness, especially on exertion; any family history of heart problems; any smoking habit; and issues around weight and obesity. The investigations can also be categorised into: invasive procedures that penetrate or break the skin or enter the body, e.g. those that require an incision or catheterisation; and non-invasive procedures, in which information about the body can be obtained without entering the body in any way.

7.2 Diagnosing angina, valvular disease or heart attack

The complexity and the varied nature of cardiovascular diseases require an equally varied approach to diagnosis. For example, the recommendations for the diagnosis of heart failure are shown in Figure 7.1 as a flowchart. Looking at the figure, you will see that investigation and exploration of the patient's history, symptoms and signs are the first stage in the diagnosis, followed by tests of heart failure (blood tests and urinary analysis). Tests for heart conditions include the ECG, implantable loop recorders, chest X-ray, echocardiogram, radionuclide tests, electrophysiological testing, magnetic resonance imaging, cardiac enzyme tests and coronary angiograms. The list is extensive but not complete, and for the sake of simplicity not all of the tests used to diagnose cardiovascular diseases are included in this chapter.

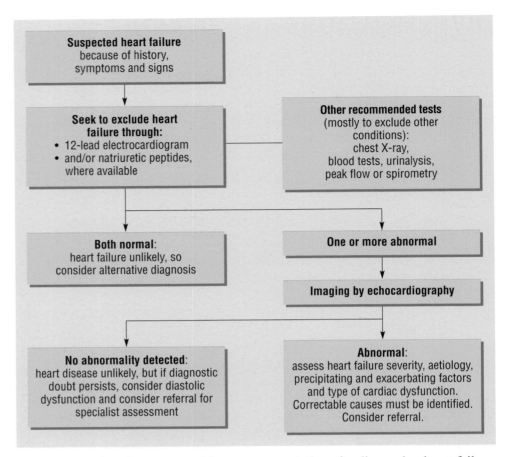

Figure 7.1 Flowchart summarising recommendations for diagnosing heart failure.

7.2.1 Investigating angina

Angina-like symptoms can be brought about by physical activity or emotional upset – or sometimes occur when people are at rest. Remember that Mr Patel's angina (Case Studies 5.1 and 5.2) was brought on by watching football on television. The causes of angina were mentioned in Sections 5.3.4 and 5.6. The main evaluations of patients with angina-like symptoms include:

- a clinical history and examination
- a full blood count
- a test to assess thyroid function (see Section 6.2.2)
- fasting blood glucose and lipoprotein profile
- blood pressure measurement
- resting and exercise ECG (normally using a 12-lead ECG machine).

All of these tests except the 12-lead ECG can be performed in a primary care setting. Hospital appointments are required for further tests such as:

- a radioisotope scan
- a coronary angiogram
- a magnetic resonance imaging (MRI) scan (see Section 7.9)
- an echocardiogram.

Each of these diagnostic tests is explained in greater detail in this chapter. A patient's history should also include an investigation into the causes of an angina attack, the smoking and exercise history of the person, their occupation, dietary history, alcohol intake and family history of coronary heart disease. All these factors contribute not only to a correct diagnosis but also to the long-term prognosis following treatment. The proposed model for the management of patients with stable angina pectoris is shown in Figure 7.2.

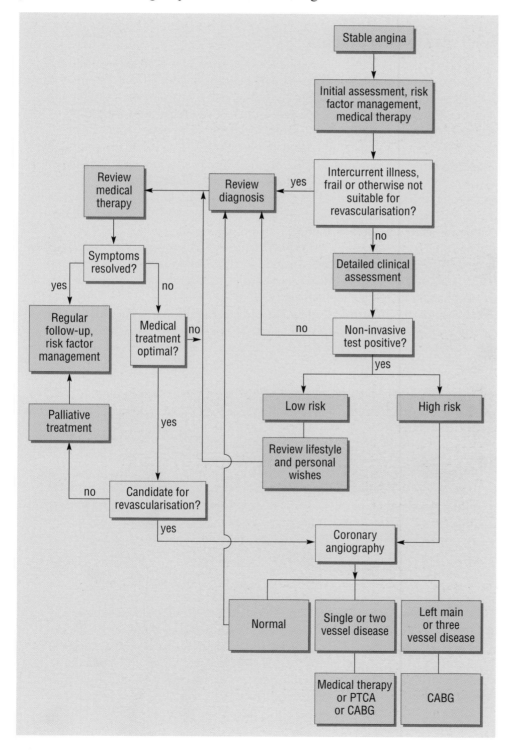

Figure 7.2   Proposed schema for the management of patients with stable angina pectoris.

7.2.2 Valvular heart disease

Valvular heart disease is usually associated with the disturbed flow of blood through a damaged valve. The rushing noise – a heart murmur – can be heard through the chest wall by someone listening through a stethoscope. Murmurs can sometimes be heard in normally functioning hearts when listening to heart sounds (see Section 2.4). Where there is suspicion that a valve is damaged, further tests are required, including a chest X-ray, an ECG and an echocardiogram.

7.2.3 Acute heart failure

Acute heart failure can be a consequence of a heart attack, usually caused by an MI due to atherosclerotic changes in the coronary arteries. For example, in Case Study 6.1, Martha Childs has all the signs of a heart attack. In Section 6.3, Winifred Fowler has a serious MI that is diagnosed on her way to hospital. Winifred's heart attack developed rapidly in a matter of hours, and was of immediate concern to the ambulance and hospital staff as her MI is potentially life-threatening. By contrast, chronic heart failure is a longer-term condition that develops over a matter of months or years and is associated with the heart undergoing adaptive responses (e.g. dilation, increases in size) to a precipitating cause, such as a previous MI, chronic hypertension, underlying genetic defects that cause cardiomyopathy, or progressive coronary atherosclerosis. The diagnosis of heart failure is vitally important in avoiding longer-term disabilities or death as the correct diagnosis can lead to successful management by using drugs (see Chapter 8) or surgical interventions such as replacing heart valves or re-establishing the blood supply to an area of the heart muscle (see Chapter 9). In Case Study 6.3, Winifred Fowler's diagnosis of an MI was based on taking a rapid case history followed by a 12-lead ECG and then a blood test after she was admitted to the coronary care unit. Section 7.3 discusses blood tests in more detail.

Box 7.1 Implied and informed consent

Before any procedure is carried out, the patient will be required to give their consent. Wherever there is a risk attached to a procedure, such as in surgery, consent is obtained formally by the patient signing a consent form. In most other situations, consent is obtained informally by verbally asking the patient's permission. Sometimes this agreement may be implied (unspoken). For example, if the patient were to roll up a sleeve and hold out an arm when told that the health worker wanted to perform a blood pressure measurement, this would be deemed to be consent.

However, it is not enough that a person agrees. The patient should understand what is going to happen and whether there are any risks attached – they should be informed. An individual who is in possession of the relevant facts may not be able to make a reasoned judgement, such as people who are mentally ill at the time of consenting or those defined as minors. If the minor is deemed to be mature, then the Gillick standard may apply (see Activity 7.1). Informed consent is therefore governed by a general requirement of competency. In the UK, 'informed consent requires proof of the standard of care to be expected as a recognised standard of acceptable professional practice' (the Bolam test; see Activity 7.1). Any deviation from this standard may suggest professional negligence and a breach of the duty of care owed to the patient.

Some people may want a detailed explanation before agreeing to anything, while other people are quite happy to agree following a very simple explanation. Every person has the right to as much information as desired before agreeing to a procedure, and needs to be aware of any specific risk involved in a procedure or treatment. It is important that this information is given by someone who has a full understanding of what is involved – and who can answer specific questions from the patient. Written consent must be kept with the records for each patient.

Activity 7.1   The Gillick standard and the Bolam test

Suggested study time 20 minutes

Search the internet for further information about the Gillick standard and the Bolam test.

(a) Which countries apply the same or very similar test of competency as in the UK's Gillick standard?

(b) What is the origin of the Bolam test?

Comment

(a) Countries which apply the same or a very similar test of competency as the UK's Gillick standard include Australia and Canada.

(b) The Bolam test is derived from the legal case *Bolam v. Friern Hospital Management Committee* (1957).

7.3 Cardiac-related blood tests

The presence of acute or chronic cardiovascular disease is often associated with changes in the normal blood chemistry or the presence of substances such as the cardiac proteins troponin I or T, which are not normally found in the blood. Following a heart attack, the damaged heart muscle releases larger-than-normal amounts of cardiac enzymes and proteins into the systemic circulation. The level of these chemicals can be measured over a period of time by taking repeated blood samples.

Blood tests are often used as a key aspect in the diagnosis of MI, acute heart failure or those thought to have high cardiac risk. They are used to confirm the diagnosis of a heart attack even when the person has other obvious signs such as severe angina-like chest pains and disturbances in their ECG. If heart failure is suspected, there are likely to be large changes in plasma electrolyte balance, and these disturbances may lead to arrhythmias which can be recorded using an ECG (see Section 7.4.3).

A list of substances which can be used to forewarn about heart-related problems is shown in Table 7.1.

Table 7.1 Blood tests for cardiovascular disease.

Substance detected in blood	Symptoms	Possible causes
cardiac troponin I*	chest pain/angina	heart attack/injury or chronic failure
cardiac troponin T*	chest pain/angina	heart attack/injury or chronic failure
creatine kinase (CK)	chest pain/angina	heart attack or injury
creatine phosphokinase-MB (CPK-MB)	chest pain/angina	heart attack or injury
myoglobin	chest pain/angina	heart attack or injury
ischaemia modified albumin (IMA)	chest pain/angina	decrease in coronary flow
B-type natriuretic peptide* (BNP)	shortness of breath	congestive heart failure
pro-B-type natriuretic peptide*	shortness of breath	congestive heart failure
cholesterol or LDL cholesterol	none	atherosclerosis
C-reactive protein	none	atherosclerosis/heart injury
lipoprotein phospholipase A2	none	atherosclerosis/heart injury

*specific to the heart.

7.4 Physiological measurements

Physiological measurements are those which record blood pressure, heart rate, oxygen saturation of the blood and the electrical activity of the heart. There are a number of ways of recording blood pressure, either by non-invasive techniques such as using a sphygmomanometer or by the introduction of pressure-measuring devices into various parts of the circulatory system. Heart rate and the electrical activity of the heart can be recorded at the same time using an ECG machine, or heart rate and oxygen saturation of the blood can be recorded simultaneously using a pulse oximeter. ECG machines can detect abnormally low (bradycardic) or high (tachycardic) rates that are an indication that there is a problem with the conducting system of the heart.

7.4.1 Blood pressure measurement

In Section 2.7 you were introduced to the concept of blood pressure, its physiological control and measurement (in Activity 2.5). Its measurement is routinely used as a non-invasive test of the normal or abnormal functioning of the systemic circulation. It is used to determine hypertension, a major risk factor in the development of cardiovascular diseases (see Section 3.2).

The importance of simple, non-invasive tests such as blood pressure measurement using a sphygmomanometer should not be underestimated. There are, however, invasive methods of measuring blood pressure, and these include the insertion of a catheter (guide tube) with pressure-measuring devices at its tip. Such devices are used during cardiac catheterisation (see Section 7.5.3) to diagnose valvular disease.

7.4.2 The pulse oximeter

One of the most important developments in physiological monitoring techniques has been the introduction of pulse oximeters. These devices permit the arterial oxygen saturation (SaO_2) or 'sats' to be continuously monitored non-invasively. These instruments are used routinely by paramedics in emergency situations, in hospitals during general anaesthesia and in intensive care wards to give warning if the oxygenation of the blood of the patient falls below the normal range of 85–99%. This could happen if either gas exchange in the lungs were to be defective for some reason (e.g. the oxygen supply of the anaesthetic machine ran out) or if the circulation were to deteriorate. Pulse oximeters help to ensure that there is minimal delay in detecting and dealing with such emergencies. In Activity 6.3, the paramedic places a pulse oximeter on one of Winifred Fowler's fingers after she has her heart attack while at work.

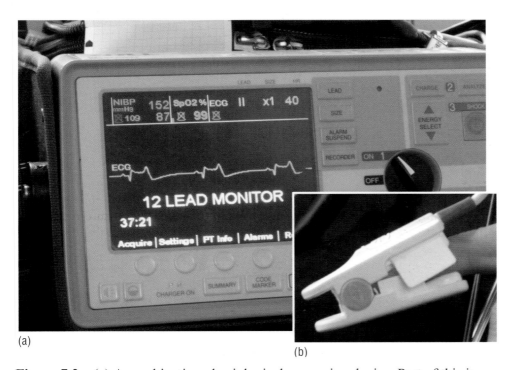

(a)

(b)

Figure 7.3 (a) A combination physiological measuring device. Part of this is a pulse oximeter, with the oxygen saturation shown as 99% (blue reading at the top of the screen). The device also contains a 12-lead ECG and provides non-invasive blood pressure measurements. (b) A finger cuff used as part of the pulse oximeter.

How do pulse oximeters work?

In Section 2.2, you were introduced to the differences in colour of arterial blood and the number of oxygen-binding sites occupied on the haemoglobin molecule. When all four sites are occupied by oxygen, the haemoglobin is described as being saturated (oxyhaemoglobin) and is bright red. Pulse oximeters measure changes in the amount of light absorbed by arterial blood – and therefore its colour. They rely on the differences in light absorption of oxyhaemoglobin and haemoglobin with lower levels of oxygen (deoxyhaemoglobin).

Pulse oximeters operate by shining two sources of light – red and near-infrared – in alternating fashion through part of the body (e.g. fingertip, toe or ear lobe). They use a light-sensitive device (photocell) to record the intensity of the light transmitted through the body when it is illuminated from these two light sources. An example of such a device is shown in Figure 7.3b. When in use, the instrument can be set to beep each time it detects a pulse of blood entering the finger. A similar but continuous sound is produced as an alarm if the saturation signal falls below 85% or if no pulse can be detected.

● If someone has an automatically inflating cuff on an arm to measure blood pressure non-invasively, why should a pulse oximeter not be placed on a finger of the same arm?

● During the inflation phase of the pressure cuff, there will be loss of a peripheral pulse in the finger of the arm and a decrease in arterial oxygen saturation. Under these circumstances, the pulse oximeter will give an incorrect warning of cardiac arrest.

7.4.3 Electrocardiogram

An electrocardiogram, often abbreviated to ECG (and usually EKG in the USA, from the German word) is a painless and harmless test routinely used in clinical environments. ECGs are records of the electrical activity of the heart and are particularly important in diagnosing diseases of the pacemaker cells, the conducting system and cardiac muscle. For example, an ECG is one component in the diagnosis of an MI. The equipment which records the ECG is called an electrocardiograph or, more simply, an ECG machine. ECG machines also pick up the activity of other muscles, such as skeletal muscle, but are designed to filter this out as much as possible. Today, almost every general practice or ambulance has its own machine. The interpretation by a doctor or nurse of the traces produced by the machines is sometimes aided by an in-built computerised diagnostic system.

An example trace from a 12-lead ECG machine is shown in Figure 7.4. Notice that each lead produces a trace, which has a corresponding label. Clinicians use the term 'lead' to mean different viewpoints of the heart's electrical activity. There are:

- six limb leads (I, II and III; aVR, aVL and aVF)
- six chest or 'V' leads (V1, V2, V3, V4, V5 and V6).

These 12 leads are obtained from 10 electrodes connecting various standardised parts of the skin surface to the machine. For example, the region of the myocardium surveyed by each lead varies according to its vantage point: lead aVF has a good view of the lower surface of the heart and lead V3 a good view of the front surface. The interpretation and explanation of the records obtained from each of the limb leads is complex and is considered beyond the scope of this course.

The trace used in Figure 7.4 is from a 45-year-old woman who is attending a clinic for a routine check-up and shows normal sinus rhythm – in other words, nothing obviously wrong with the ECG. Various measurements are automatically made by the machine such as P–R interval and QRS duration. If you look at the trace carefully, you can see that the heart rate is shown as 72 beats per minute, which the machine calculates from the duration of the average R–R interval.

An ECG can be used as part of a routine appointment or to monitor medical emergencies. Leads are placed on the arms, legs and chest and attached to the skin using self-adhesive pads which conduct electrical signals. The ECG machine records the electrical signal which originates from the heart as electrical impulses travel through its conduction system and heart muscle (see Section 2.4.2). The signal is either shown on a screen or it is printed out on graph-like paper. While the ECG is being obtained, patients must keep still, in order to avoid perturbing the readings.

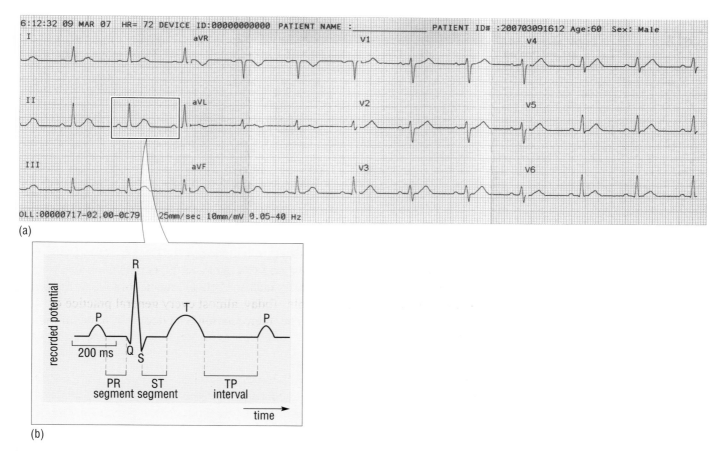

(a)

(b)

Figure 7.4 (a) An ECG trace from a 12-lead ECG machine showing leads I, II, III, aVR, aVL, aVF and V1–6 from top left to bottom right. (b) A stylised representation of the section of the ECG trace shown on lead II in (a).

● Why is it necessary to lie still when an ECG is being obtained?

● ECG machines are very sensitive pieces of equipment which amplify and record very small signals (potential differences) from the skin surface. Muscles of the arms, legs and chest wall also produce small electrical signals which can be recorded from the skin surface and therefore interfere with the ECG signal.

An example of a 12-lead ECG machine being used in a hospital is shown in Figure 2.9. The electrodes on the different parts of the body detect electrical impulses coming via different routes within the heart. The 12-lead ECG machine can be used to diagnose various heart disorders which produce abnormal patterns, for example: bradycardia, tachycardia, irregular and abnormal heart rhythms, an enlarged heart, a recent MI, coronary heart disease, heart enlargements, inflammation of the heart, suspected drug overdose (particularly anti-depressants) and electrolyte imbalance.

● The last of these, electrolyte imbalance, might at first glance seem a rather improbable condition to diagnose using an ECG machine. So why should an electrolyte imbalance affect the rate or force of contraction of the heart?

● The heart is supplied with blood, in the same way as any other organ in the body. If the electrolyte composition of the plasma is changed, then this may alter either the rate of depolarisation of the sinoatrial node, 'the pacemaker', or the force of contraction of the cardiac muscle. If, for example, the plasma potassium concentration ($[K^+]$) is raised, the heart and cardiac muscle will become depolarised and will produce abnormal rhythms. The maintenance of the ideal level of individual electrolytes is part of the body's homeostatic mechanism.

Although the ECG is a valuable and simple test, it does have its limitations. Unfortunately, it is not always possible to diagnose a heart problem with an ECG, and what appears to be a normal ECG does not rule out serious heart disease. If the condition is potentially life-threatening, an ECG trace should not be the only means of diagnosis. Other problems which are not detected using an ECG sometimes include an irregular heart beat, an MI or angina. Sometimes these limitations can be overcome by employing specialised recordings. One example is a 24-hour ECG monitor, which can either be conducted in a hospital environment or as an ambulatory version – one that can be worn as the patient walks around. The Holter monitor is the size of a pack of cards and records heart activity constantly, allowing detection of transient and intermittent abnormal heart rhythms.

Another example is an exercise or stress ECG, in which a record is taken during exercise on a treadmill, an exercise bike or following the injection of a drug that simulates exercise. The ECG traces before and after moderate exercise or stress are compared with each other and any abnormal records noted. This test is particularly useful in assessing the severity of coronary artery narrowing which causes the pain of angina. Standard measures of exercise are used and defined in the Bruce protocol (described later in this section). Occasionally, the exercise tolerance test is not possible, perhaps due to a person's mobility problems or excessive weight. In this case, the person being investigated will have a stress-inducing drug (such as adenosine, dobutamine or dipyridamole) injected into a vein. Dobutamine, for example, mimics the action of adrenalin on the heart, increasing its contractility and cardiac output. The ECG stress test can be combined with other diagnostic tests such as an echocardiogram, radionuclide and stress test. Each of these techniques is described later in this chapter.

Case Study 7.1   Mr Patel has a minor myocardial infarction

At Mr Patel's first hospital visit, when his angina was diagnosed, he can remember the cardiologist asking him how far he could walk without feeling chest pains and lots of other questions about his family history, diet and whether he exercised or smoked. The cardiologist also conducted a couple of tests. In one, they placed ECG electrodes on Mr Patel's arms, legs and chest, and recorded the electrical activity of his heart at rest and when walking on a treadmill. When exercising, Mr Patel achieved 7.2 minutes of the Bruce protocol and his ECG appeared normal. In the other, he had blood tests which revealed slightly elevated cholesterol (5.8 mmol/l). As a result of the visit, Mr Patel was advised to lose weight and to start exercise.

More recently, the pain from his last angina attack had taken over 2 hours to subside and his GP had asked to see him immediately, suspecting unstable angina and a possible heart attack. The GP surgery and King's College Hospital in Denmark Hill were not far from each other, and the doctor phoned the hospital to speak to Dr Price, the same cardiologist that Mr Patel had seen before. Mr Patel was taken to hospital as an emergency admission where Dr Price discovered the resting ECG had (among other things) a raised ST-segment. Dr Price confirmed that Mr Patel had ischaemia of the inferior myocardium (a minor MI). Later that day, Mr Patel had a coronary angiogram.

The Bruce protocol test

The standard Bruce protocol test was developed to evaluate patients with suspected coronary heart disease and also as a measure of cardiovascular fitness in athletes for whom aerobic endurance is important. It is a maximum workload test and comprises three components: a treadmill, a stopwatch and an ECG. The test has 10 stages of fitness which correspond to stepwise increases in treadmill speeds and gradients, with each stage lasting 3 minutes (see Table 7.2). Those taking the test start at stage 1, moving to each subsequent stage if they have performed the previous one safely. The test measures the maximum heart rate and the test score is the time taken to achieve maximum workload in minutes. These measurements can be converted to estimated maximum oxygen score (VO_2 max) using the following formulae, where T is the total time completed (expressed in minutes):

- for men: VO_2 max $= 14.76 - (1.379 \times T) + (0.451 \times T^2) - (0.012 \times T^3)$
- for women: VO_2 max $= (4.38 \times T) - 3.9$

Table 7.2 The levels of work in the Bruce protocol test.

Stage	Speed (km/h)	Speed (mph)	Gradient (%)	Starting minute	VO$_2$ max (ml/kg/min) Men	VO$_2$ max (ml/kg/min) Women
1	2.74	1.7	10	0	0	0
2	4.02	2.5	12	3	14	9
3	5.47	3.4	14	6	20	22
4	6.76	4.2	16	9	30	36
5	8.05	5.0	18	12	42	49
6	8.85	5.5	20	15	55	62
7	9.65	6.0	22	18	66	75
8	10.46	6.5	24	21	74	88
9	11.26	7.0	26	24	76	101
10	12.07	7.5	28	27	70	114

Activity 7.2   Exercise testing

Suggested study time 15 minutes

Use the Multi-ed Cardiology program to familiarise yourself with exercise testing.

The animation to watch, 'Exercise testing', can be found by navigating to Animations | Investigations | Exercise ECG/Isotope scans. As you watch, note down what ECG exercise testing is commonly used for.

Comment

Exercise testing is commonly used:

- to help diagnose if chest pain is due to narrowing in the coronary arteries (angina)
- to identify possible heart-related causes for symptoms such as palpitations and breathlessness
- to assess the need for further investigations after a heart attack and to plan rehabilitation
- to check the effectiveness of some cardiac procedures, for example coronary artery bypass surgery
- to determine the level of exercise a given patient can perform safely.

Implantable loop recorder

An implantable loop recorder is a small electronic box, about the size of a packet of chewing gum, inserted beneath the skin of the chest (under local anaesthetic) and left in place for up to 18 months. It monitors heart rhythms 24 hours a day and is extremely good at detecting arrhythmias missed during a 24-hour ECG. The implantable loop recorder can be useful in determining the cause of fainting, dizziness or palpitations. Implantable loop recorders are used where the opportunity to capture a spontaneous event during testing is very rare.

7.4.4 Cardiac rhythms

The ECG is one of the most widely used and useful techniques to diagnose disorders of the heart and its conducting circuitry (Figure 7.5). Each part of the ECG records the passage of electrical activity from the depolarisation in the sinoatrial node to the repolarisation of the ventricles (see Section 2.4.2). The ST segment shown in lead I in Figure 7.6 is of particular interest in the diagnosis of MI and ischaemia. This is the transient period when no further electrical activity can be passed through the myocardium. The ST segment of the trace is elevated when compared with a 'normal' trace (Figure 7.5).

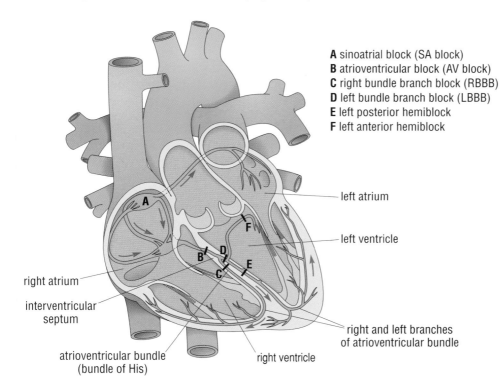

A sinoatrial block (SA block)
B atrioventricular block (AV block)
C right bundle branch block (RBBB)
D left bundle branch block (LBBB)
E left posterior hemiblock
F left anterior hemiblock

Figure 7.5 Transmission of electrical activity (red arrows) through the heart, responsible for the coordinated contraction of the atria and ventricles.

left atrium

left ventricle

right atrium

interventricular septum

right and left branches of atrioventricular bundle

atrioventricular bundle (bundle of His)

right ventricle

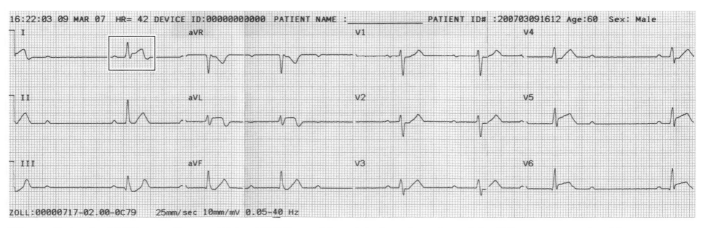

Figure 7.6 An ECG trace from a 12-lead ECG machine showing elevation of the ST segment on lead I (highlighted) in a patient who recently had an acute MI, causing noticeable slowing of the heart from the normal 'resting' value of 72 beats per minute down to 42 beats per minute.

7.5 X-ray investigations

X-rays are used as part of several diagnostic techniques for cardiovascular disease, including the basic 'planar' chest X-ray, fluoroscopy, computed tomography (CT) and cardiac CT angiography. Each of these techniques is used to answer slightly different questions and each one is described later in this section. First of all, so you can understand what is happening in these investigations, we need to explain what X-rays are and why X-ray imaging works.

X-rays are, like light, a type of **electromagnetic radiation**. The physics of electromagnetic radiation is beyond the scope of this course, but Figure 7.7 shows what is known as the electromagnetic spectrum. You will see that X-rays are at the high-energy end of the spectrum, along with gamma rays (γ-rays), which you will come across in Section 7.7. Both X-rays and gamma rays are potentially harmful – they can cause damage to the DNA in cells and this can lead to cell death or to changes that lead to cancer. The chances of this happening are very low and the risks are usually outweighed by the benefits. This will be discussed further in Section 7.10.

X-rays were discovered in 1896 by the German physicist Wilhelm Roentgen (1845–1923) and one of the first things he did with them was to make an image of his wife's hand. He was able to do this for two reasons.

- X-rays can be detected by photographic film.
- The number of X-rays passing through the bone was much less than the number passing through the soft tissues. This meant that, when the film was developed, it was easy to see where the bones had blocked the passage of most of the X-rays.

7.5.1 The chest X-ray

Chest X-rays are often used as a starting point in cardiac diagnosis. For example, if someone has chest pain, a planar X-ray can help determine whether they have heart failure or a collapsed lung, broken ribs or pneumonia. Together with a

Figure 7.7 The electromagnetic spectrum. Note the position of visible light, X-rays and gamma rays.

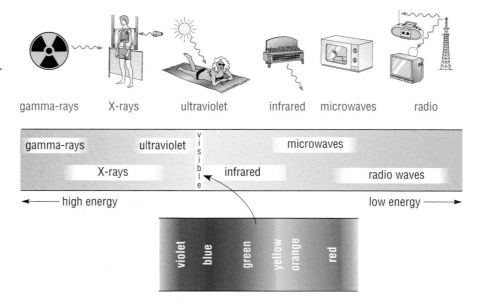

gamma-rays   X-rays   ultraviolet   infrared   microwaves   radio

gamma-rays   ultraviolet   v i s i b l e   microwaves
          X-rays   infrared   radio waves

◀── high energy   low energy ──▶

violet blue green yellow orange red

clinical history and examination, a doctor may request an X-ray as one of the first recommended procedures – particularly if the person has a cough, chest pain, a chest injury or has difficulty breathing.

A chest X-ray is taken by positioning the patient in front of a detector screen (either a specially constructed film or, in modern hospitals, a digital detection system) and passing the X-rays through the chest towards the recording medium while the patient holds a deep breath. Lateral views of the chest can also be taken. Little preparation is required before an X-ray is taken; generally, the only preparation necessary is to remove clothing from the waist upwards and to wear a gown.

The amount of X-ray penetration depends on the density of structures that the X-ray beam has passed through. Within the chest, lungs are mainly filled with air and block little of the radiation, therefore showing as dark on the film. The heart is denser and therefore blocks more of the X-rays, so it appears as a lighter shade on the image.

● In a chest X-ray, what shade of grey would you expect from the image of the ribs?

● The ribs are made of bone, which is very dense when compared with the other structures in the chest, and so would appear white on an image.

Figure 7.8a (overleaf) shows a patient being positioned for a chest X-ray and Figure 7.8b shows the resultant X-ray.

As useful as chest X-rays are in detecting cardiovascular problems, they are just one step in the process of making a diagnosis and are not able to detect all conditions. Suggestions of an abnormality detected by X-rays would usually lead to a patient undergoing a variety of other tests or procedures to help confirm a diagnosis, such as an ECG, an echocardiogram, a coronary angiogram, computed tomography or magnetic resonance imaging.

Chest X-rays have several major advantages: they are painless, quick, inexpensive, non-invasive, and a series of chest images can be recorded over time for comparison. Using this technique, the size and outline of the heart and blood vessels can be determined, for example in heart failure, congenital heart disease, fluid around the heart and valvular disease. Chest X-rays can reveal changes or abnormalities in the lungs that are the result of heart problems due to congestive heart failure such as fluid accumulation in the lungs (pulmonary oedema). X-rays are also useful in locating the position of pacemakers or other implanted devices.

7.5.2 An introduction to fluoroscopy

In Section 7.5, we mentioned that X-rays can be detected by photographic film. They can also be detected by materials known as **phosphors**. These have the property that high-energy radiation falling on them will cause them to emit lower-energy radiation – a property known as **fluorescence**. An example of this is the ubiquitous safety jacket; in that case, ultraviolet radiation (see Figure 7.7) from the sun is absorbed and lower-energy visible radiation is emitted, so that the jacket appears very bright. This property can also be used for medical imaging – the high-energy X-rays cause the production of lower-energy visible radiation.

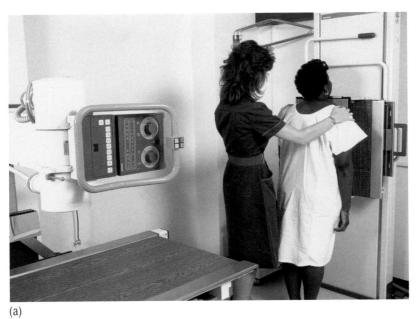

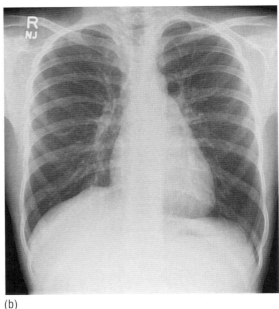

(a)　　　　　　　　　　　　　　　　　　　　　　　(b)

Figure 7.8 (a) A patient being positioned prior to having a chest X-ray taken. Note that the patient is close to the detector plate but some way from the X-ray source. (b) A typical chest X-ray. Note that the lungs appear dark and the bones white.

The equipment used for this type of imaging, which is known as **fluoroscopy**, is known as an **image intensifier** and an example is shown in Figure 7.9. The beam of X-rays is produced in the normal way and, after passing through the patient, the X-rays are detected by a phosphor screen. This image is intensified and displayed on a screen (or can be recorded digitally for later analysis).

The image intensifier has many uses in medicine and is very widely used for investigations of the cardiovascular system – particularly for observing blood vessels.

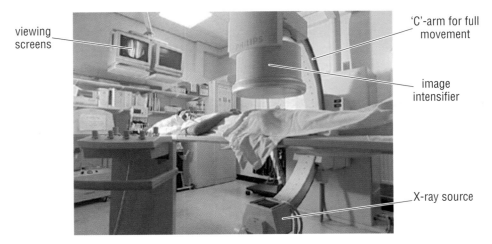

Figure 7.9 An image intensifier. The X-ray beam passes through the patient and onto the phosphor screen. The image produced is then intensified and displayed on a screen or recorded digitally. The X-ray tube and image intensifier can be rotated around the patient to get views from different angles.

● How easy do you think it is to see blood vessels in the X-ray images produced in an image intensifier?

● It is not easy at all! The blood in the vessels and the surrounding tissues have similar densities and will therefore appear as similar shades of grey.

If the blood vessels are to be seen clearly, then there needs to be a way of making them more opaque to X-rays so that they show up more clearly in the image.

● Think back to when you found out why bones show up well on X-rays. How do you think blood vessels could be made to show up clearly?

● A higher-density material (such as bone) will show up as white in the image. A higher density in the blood vessels can be achieved by injecting a denser material into the bloodstream, making the blood vessels look whiter in the image.

Any substance which is used to do this is known as a **contrast medium** – sometimes incorrectly referred to as a 'dye'. You may hear it described as being radio-opaque, meaning that it does not allow many X-rays through. The substance used to show up blood vessels contains iodine, which has a high density. (You may have heard of a barium meal; this is a similar technique used to show up the digestive tract and uses barium, another high-density material.) Images taken after iodine has been injected will show the blood vessels very clearly. This technique is known as **angiography**.

Taking a step further, with modern digital imaging systems it is possible to take an image before – and then again after – the injection of the iodine substance. If the first image is subtracted from the second, then all the bones and other structures will disappear and all that will be left is an image of the blood vessels. This technique is known as digital subtraction angiography (DSA) and is illustrated in Figure 7.10.

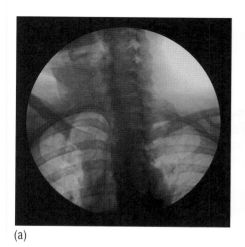
(a)

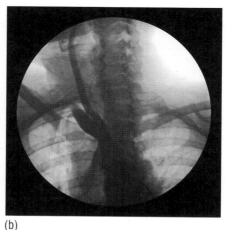
(b)

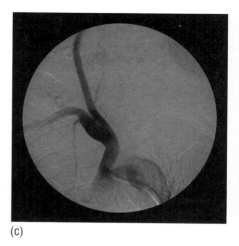
(c)

Figure 7.10 Image of blood flowing through an artery (a) before and (b) after the injection of a contrast medium. (c) This image shows the result when the first image (a) is subtracted from the second (b).

Fluoroscopy exposes the patient to more radiation than a standard planar X-ray but is a useful technique when movement needs to be visualised, such as in the placement of a catheter in cardiac catheterisation and subsequent angiogram (see Section 7.5.3), for coronary angioplasty or when a sample of tissue needs to be obtained, as in a biopsy.

7.5.3 Coronary angiography

A coronary angiogram (sometimes called cardiac catheterisation) involves a contrast medium injected into the coronary arteries where they join the aorta, and usually on the left side of the heart. The person is admitted as a day case patient to have a catheter passed through an incision in either the femoral artery (in the groin) or the radial artery (in the arm) and up towards the heart. Soon after injecting the contrast medium, a series of X-ray pictures are taken to see the route it takes along the heart vessels and into the muscle. The technique is able to determine blocked or narrowed coronary vessels and abnormal contractions of the heart chambers, particularly in patients whose results from non-invasive techniques such as ECG, chest X-ray, echocardiogram or exercise tests are inconclusive.

● In order to push a catheter into the right atrium, would you make an initial entry in a vein or an artery?

● To access the right side of the heart, you need to catheterise a vein.

Once in the heart, atrial or ventricular pressure can be measured, blood samples taken or radio-opaque substance injected. This technique allows X-ray visualisation of the cardiac vascular tree. Different types of catheters (Figure 7.11a) are used to access different chambers of the heart, with one looking like a pigtail used to access the left side of the heart (Figure 7.11b). Cardiac catheterisation is used to assess the severity of coronary artery or valvular disease or heart muscle function. One of the ways to detect valvular disease uses the continuous measurement of blood pressure within the heart chambers and across the valves of the heart. Examples of two pressure traces in Figure 7.11 show a patient with aortic stenosis (Figure 7.11c) and aortic regurgitation (Figure 7.11d).

Case Study 7.2   Katerin Wilcox's arrhythmia is diagnosed

Katerin Wilcox had known for some time that she had hypertension because her GP had diagnosed it after measuring her blood pressure, putting her on an ACE inhibitor. The GP had also noticed that Katerin had a heart murmur that had not caused any symptoms. Katerin hadn't been feeling in the best of health and had suffered repeated headaches, which she treated herself. Now, almost 18 months after her initial diagnosis of hypertension, Katerin has experienced shortness of breath and has been referred by her GP to the cardiologist, Dr Pearson, who diagnoses sinus node disease (an arrhythmia), which is confirmed by 24-hour ambulatory Holter monitor results. However,

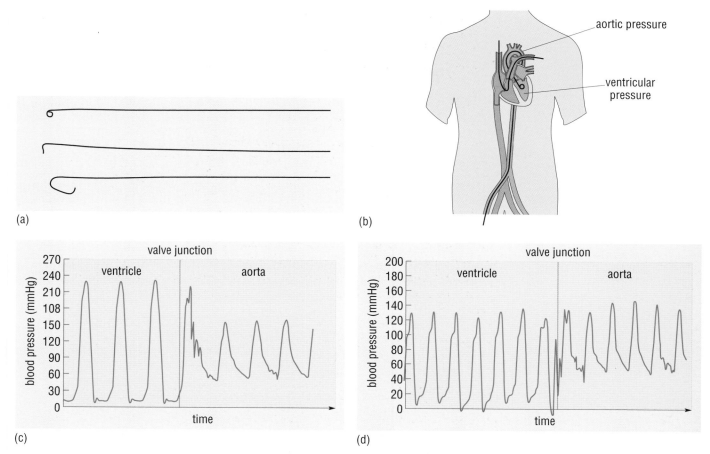

Figure 7.11 Cardiac catheterisation. (a) Examples of catheters used for pressure measurements and angiography. (b) The venous (blue; right side of heart, left of panel) and arterial (red; left side of heart, right of panel) systems, with catheters placed in the right ventricle and pulmonary artery. (c) Ventricular and aortic pressure traces in a patient with aortic stenosis. (d) Ventricular and aortic pressure traces in a patient with aortic regurgitation.

the echocardiogram shows good left ventricular function. Katerin's blood pressure is 170/90 mmHg and a planar chest X-ray indicates moderate enlargement of the heart. The results of the coronary angiogram reveal some minor disease in one of her coronary arteries. Dr Pearson has suggested that Katerin is fitted with a pacemaker because of her sinus node disease.

7.5.4 Interventional techniques

Coronary angiography is an invasive technique and is not usually undertaken unless there is some intention of carrying out a remedial procedure of some sort. This can be done while the patient is catheterised. Examples of techniques usually associated with coronary angiography include angioplasty, valvuloplasty and insertion of a stent. All these techniques are described in detail in Chapter 9.

7.6 Ultrasound investigations

7.6.1 The principles of ultrasound imaging

Ultrasound imaging works rather like radar in that pulses of energy are bounced off objects so that we can detect what we cannot see – because the objects are either far away or are hidden, such as inside the body. However, instead of using the microwaves used in radar (see Figure 7.7), it uses high-frequency sound waves. Humans can hear sounds in the frequency range from about 20 Hz (1 hertz is 1 cycle per second) up to about 20 000 Hz, although this upper limit gets lower as you get older! The frequencies used in medical imaging are usually several megahertz (MHz) – that is, several million cycles per second – and these high frequencies are known as **ultrasound** ('beyond sound'). The device used in ultrasound imaging is a **transducer**. This is a device which produces and sends out pulses of ultrasound and also detects the pulses reflected back (the echoes) from interfaces in tissues – regions where different tissue types meet, such as muscle next to fat. As in radar, the time taken for a pulse to travel out and back allows the calculation of the distance to the reflecting interface. Figure 7.12 shows the principles. For a simple system like this, the returning pulses can be plotted out on a screen.

Ultrasound is often known as a 'kind' technique. Simple investigations can be done quickly and easily, often without moving the patient to a specialist unit or giving injections. Such tests are painless and the potential hazards from ultrasound imaging are almost negligible.

When used for cardiac investigations, ultrasound is often known as **echocardiography** and has a wide range of uses, some of which will be explained in the next few sections.

● At the interfaces between bone and soft tissue, or between air and soft tissue, there is almost complete reflection of ultrasound. What problems do you think this poses for heart imaging?

● It is not possible to receive any signal from tissues beyond these interfaces because hardly any ultrasound passes through. This means that ultrasound imaging is of no use where bone or air is in front of the tissue to be examined. This poses problems because the ribs and the lungs surround and protect the heart. Ways of avoiding these problems will be shown later in this chapter.

Figure 7.12 An ultrasound pulse from the transducer passes into the tissue. Some is reflected back from each interface and the time of arrival at the transducer allows distances to be calculated and representations plotted out on a screen. Signal A corresponds to the reflection from the interface between tissues 1 and 2; signal B to the reflection from the interface between tissues 2 and 3, so has had further to travel and hence taken longer to arrive; and so on.

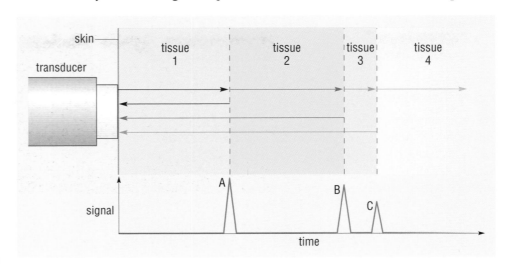

7.6.2 B-mode echocardiography

In **B-mode echocardiography**, a two-dimensional (2D) image is created by scanning the ultrasound beam across the heart using a transthoracic ('across the chest') approach with the ultrasound probe positioned between the ribs (thus avoiding the bone/soft tissue problem mentioned in the previous section). An example of this technique in use is shown in Figure 7.13. The resulting echoes are displayed as a fan-shaped image on a monitor. Stronger echoes appear as brighter areas of the image, and this brightness (B) gives its name to B-mode. An example of such an image is shown in the apical four-chamber ultrasound view of the heart in Figure 7.14. The ultrasound beam can be scanned sufficiently fast that the image can actually be seen in real time, so that the beating of the heart and the opening and closing of the valves can be observed. (The blood flow itself cannot be seen clearly.) The operator carrying out the scan can move the probe and alter its angle to get a series of different planes through the heart.

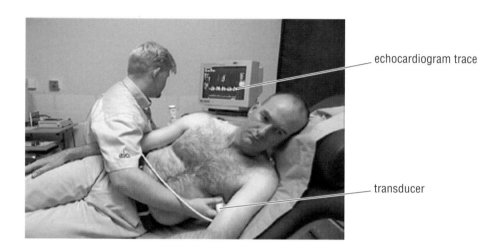

echocardiogram trace

transducer

Figure 7.13   A patient in a hospital having an echocardiogram.

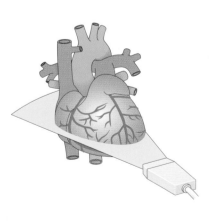

(a)

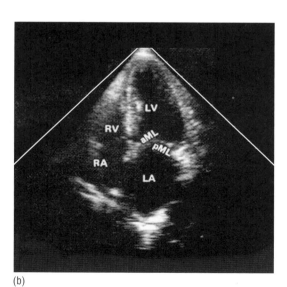

(b)

Figure 7.14   (a) Schematic diagram of an ultrasound probe in use with the fan-shaped beam of ultrasound used to obtain an echocardiogram record. (b) An example apical echocardiogram of the heart showing the heart chambers (LA, left atrium; LV, left ventricle; RL, right atrium; and RV, right ventricle) and mitral valve flaps (aML and pML).

B-mode echocardiography has a wide range of uses. It is useful in determining:

- the size and thickness of the ventricles
- whether the heart valves are working properly
- the condition of the pericardium
- the existence of shunts within the heart
- the way in which the heart muscle pumps.

In essence, echocardiography is uniquely suited to characterise abnormalities in patients at risk of developing heart failure, suspected of having heart failure, and with symptomatic heart failure. It can provide information useful in prognosis and can assist in the management of patients with acute, chronic and end-stage heart failure.

In cases where there is a need to show the blood flow through the heart more clearly, it is possible to use a contrast medium.

● For a contrast medium to be of use in echocardiography, it needs to improve the reflections from the blood. What kind of substance might be useful for this?

● The contrast medium needs to contain some substance which reflects ultrasound well. Several commercial products are on the market and all work on the principle that small bubbles of gas will reflect ultrasound very well.

These contrast media are used in cardiology on occasions when either defects in the septum between the ventricles or shunts are suspected.

7.6.3 Doppler ultrasound

Everyone who has reasonable hearing is familiar with the Doppler effect. You hear it every time a fast car or train comes towards you, passes you and moves away.

● What happens to the sound as the vehicle comes towards you and goes away from you?

● As the vehicle comes toward you, you hear a higher note – the frequency is increased. As it moves away, the frequency is reduced and the note drops.

This effect also works if you as an observer move towards or away from a source of sound: as a passenger on a train moving past the alarm of a parked car, you will hear a similar frequency change. In both cases, the change in frequency depends on the relative speed of the source and the observer: the greater the relative speed, the greater the change in frequency (the difference between notes).

The same effect works for ultrasound: if sound is reflected off blood which is flowing towards or away from the transducer, there is a small shift in the frequency. This change in frequency can be detected and displayed as a change in colour on the image. This is known as **colour flow Doppler**. The usual colours are blue for blood moving away from the probe and red for blood moving towards the probe (Figure 7.15). In Doppler studies, the ultrasound probe and therefore the source of the original signal should be aligned as accurately as possible in parallel with the direction of flow, rather than at right angles to it, so that the speed of blood to and from the ultrasound probe is as great as possible. Figure 7.15 shows an example of a Doppler ultrasound image of blood flow through the heart (within the blue boundary) of the patient in Figure 7.13. The ECG trace can also be seen at the bottom of the image. In addition to investigating

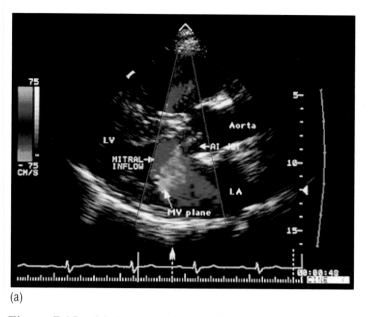

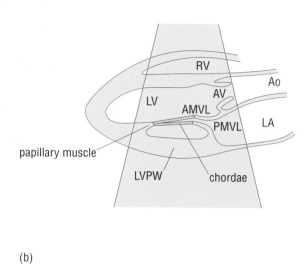

(a)

(b)

Figure 7.15 (a) An example of a Doppler ultrasound image of the heart within the blue fan-shaped boundary in the long axis view of the heart shown in (b). The ECG trace at the bottom of (a) is used to gate the ultrasound image.

the flow of blood through the heart, Doppler ultrasound is also used to diagnose the presence of atheroma in the carotid arteries (carotid atheroma) and to measure blood flow in arteries in different parts of the body.

The Doppler signal can also be used in two other ways. The change in frequency as the heart beats can be used to generate an audio signal. A trained operator will be able to tell from the sound whether the blood is flowing correctly or whether there is stenosis or regurgitation. Alternatively, the speed of the blood (worked out from the frequency shift) can be displayed in the form of a graph (Figure 7.16).

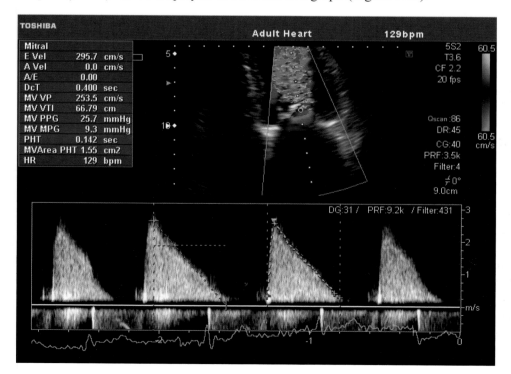

Figure 7.16 A B-scan of the heart with colour Doppler is shown at the top of this image, with the Doppler shift displayed as a graph of frequency shift (proportional to blood speed) against time below.

Case Study 7.3   Martha Childs' mitral regurgitation is identified

At the start of her medical problems, Martha Childs' herbal remedies seemed to be helping to treat her swollen feet, but now the problems were getting worse. She was becoming increasingly short of breath and suffering from fatigue, even with the slightest exercise. She used to walk to work at the council offices half a mile away but now she takes a bus or is driven by one of her friends. At last, Martha's GP convinces her that she should go for diagnostic tests at the local hospital so that they know what is wrong with her. At the hospital, Martha has a chest X-ray and was attached to an ECG machine. Later, she has an echocardiogram performed, including a colour flow Doppler ultrasound. These tests show that Martha's heart is enlarged and she is diagnosed with congestive heart failure with significant mitral valve regurgitation.

Activity 7.3   Using the echocardiogram to diagnose heart ailments

Suggested study time 15 minutes

Use the Multi-ed Cardiology program to investigate how the echocardiogram can be used to diagnose a number of abnormal features of the heart.

The animation to watch, 'Transthoracic echocardiogram', can be found by navigating to Animations | Investigations | Echocardiogram. As you watch, list the uses of the echocardiogram.

Comment

The echocardiogram can be used to diagnose a number of abnormal features of the heart not in the list in Section 7.6.2. These include blood clots within the heart, fluid within the pericardium and shunts within the heart.

7.6.4 M-mode echocardiography

The 'M' in M-mode stands for movement, and **M-mode echocardiography** allows the investigation of the movement of individual structural elements of the heart such as chamber walls and valve flaps. It is usually done in conjunction with a B-mode scan; the echoes from a single narrow beam in a fixed direction (chosen by the operator) are plotted against time along the bottom of the image (Figure 7.17). With this technique, stationary structures are shown as straight lines across the screen while moving structures appear as undulating lines. The addition of an ECG trace to the screen aids in the identification of the phases of the cardiac cycle. An example of an M-mode echocardiogram is shown in Figure 7.17.

M-mode echocardiography is very useful in determining the precise motion of different parts of the heart (e.g. the mitral valve) at different points in the cycle. However, it can only be carried out along one line at a time (see Figure 7.17).

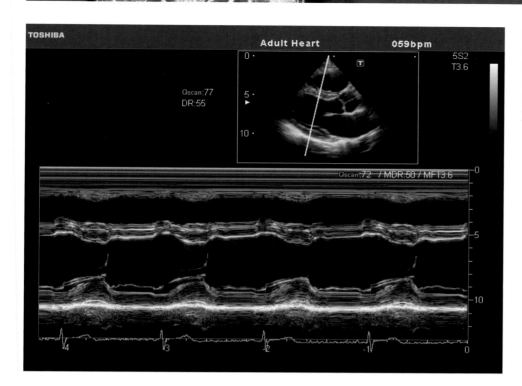

Figure 7.17 An example of an M-mode image. Note the ECG and the movement of the different interfaces along the line chosen (marked on the B-scan above).

7.6.5 Transoesophageal echocardiography

Transoesophageal echocardiography (**TOE**) is a 2D cardiac imaging technique similar to transthoracic echocardiography except that an ultrasound transducer is placed in the oesophagus. The course that the oesophagus takes from the mouth to the stomach brings it into close contact with the heart, and this allows the use of a higher ultrasound frequency (e.g. 5 MHz rather than 2–4 MHz). This proximity allows for the detection of structures located deep within or towards the back (posterior) of the heart, which would otherwise be beyond the scope of the transthoracic method. This technique, although unpalatable, increases the detection of potential cardiac sources of emboli by several fold. It is often used to detect abnormalities associated with the atria and the mitral valve. The main disadvantages of TOE are:

- its invasive nature – some people who are unable to tolerate it need sedation
- the strength of echoes is dependent on the orientation of the beam to the structures being studied, and so correct alignment of the beam is required.

TOE is used to diagnose or investigate:

- heart failure
- ischaemic heart disease
- congenital heart disease
- stenosis or regurgitation of the mitral valve (and other heart valves)
- aortic aneurysm (and dissections; see Section 7.7.1)
- prosthetic heart valve (see Section 9.4.2).

Activity 7.4   Transoesophageal echocardiography

Suggested study time 10 minutes

Use the Multi-ed Cardiology program to learn more about TOE.

The animation to watch, 'Transoesophageal echocardiogram (TOE)', can be found by navigating to Animations | Investigations | Echocardiogram. You can stop at the point where the patient is being told what to do before a TOE.

7.6.6 Intravascular ultrasound

Intravascular ultrasound (IVUS) is one of the methods used to investigate the side walls and narrowed parts of arteries, particularly coronary arteries. A fine ultrasound probe is attached to the tip of a catheter similar to that used in angiography. The probe is passed through an artery (usually the femoral artery) and then advanced towards the heart. The principle is the same as other forms of echocardiography, but in this case the ultrasound source is located at the tip of the probe (as in TOE) and a much higher frequency (at least 20 MHz) is used. Intravascular ultrasound is sometimes used in coronary catheterisation laboratories, where it is able to quantify accurately the amount of arterial plaque, especially within the coronary arteries.

Activity 7.5   The ultrasound video

Suggested study time 20 minutes

Now follow the links on the DVD Guide program to the video sequence on 'Ultrasound'. View the whole sequence and answer the following questions.

(a) Why are ECG electrodes attached to the patient?

(b) Why is coupling gel used between the transducer tip and the patient's skin?

(c) Why is the patient asked to rest on their side?

(d) What does colour flow Doppler echocardiography allow the cardiologist to see?

(e) What does M-mode echocardiography allow the cardiologist to see?

Comment

(a) ECG electrodes are attached to the patient in order to enable the ultrasound images to be linked to the electrical activity of the heart.

(b) The ultrasound will pass through the fluid and soft tissue of the chest but will be reflected by the lungs and the bones of the ribs or sternum. The coupling gel is used between the transducer tip and the patient's skin because even a thin layer of air will reflect the ultrasound signal.

(c) The patient is asked to rest on his left-hand side so that the lungs 'drop out of the way' to avoid the probe coming into contact with air in the lungs.

(d) Colour flow Doppler echocardiography allows the cardiologist to see the speed and direction of blood flow in the heart chambers. It is particularly useful for observing reversed flow (as in Case Study 7.3).

(e) M-mode echocardiography allows the cardiologist to see the movement of different parts of the heart at different stages of the heart cycle. It is especially useful for observing mitral valve deficiencies.

7.6.7 Testing for peripheral arterial disease: the ankle–brachial index

Looking at the heart isn't the only way to diagnose cardiovascular diseases. As you saw in Section 5.5.1, peripheral arterial disease is characterised by inadequate blood flow and, in particular, the loss of pulsatility. Measurements of blood flow in the limbs serve as a reasonably accurate and reproducible non-invasive diagnostic technique.

Examinations of arterial pulses in the feet on their own are an unreliable indicator for the presence of peripheral arterial disease, and the weaker pulses mean that more sensitive equipment is needed to detect the presence of blood flow. So to measure the adequacy of the arterial supply to the limbs, and therefore the ABI, portable Doppler ultrasound apparatus such as a handheld 5–10 MHz unit is used. Coupling gel and a sphygmomanometer with cuffs sized appropriately for the different sites of blood pressure measurement are also required.

To measure the **ankle–brachial index (ABI)**, the patient rests quietly for at least 5 minutes. Cuffs for each limb are placed in appropriate places on the upper arms, thighs and ankles. The systolic arterial pressures are measured in the following order:

- on the right side of the body, the brachial, dorsalis pedis (front of the ankle) and posterior tibial (back of the lower leg) arteries
- on the left side, the dorsalis pedis, posterior tibial and brachial arteries.

The Doppler probe is placed over each artery and angled so that the probe is in line with the blood flow and moved until the strongest pulse is heard through the loudspeaker or earpiece. Once the best pulse is found, a cuff is inflated slowly above systolic pressure until the pulse is no longer audible and then deflated slowly, allowing the pressure to drop at a rate of 2 mmHg per second. The pressure at which the first sustained pulse (more than one beat) reappears is recorded as the systolic pressure at that location. The ABI is the ratio of the leg to arm pressures computed separately for each side of the body, using the higher of the two leg measurements for each side and, for both sides, the higher of the left and right arm measurements. ABI results fall into the following categories:

- 0.91–1.30, peripheral arterial disease highly unlikely
- 0.75–0.90, mild disease
- 0.50–0.75, moderate disease
- <0.5, severe disease.

An ABI value >1.30 suggests that the arteries are not easily compressed and this could be due to arterial calcification similar to the degenerative changes in heart valves (see Section 6.5.2). The ABI test for peripheral arterial disease should be performed in patients over 50 who have diabetes; if the test is normal, it should be repeated every 5 years. Those with diabetes who are younger than 50 should be considered for testing if they have other PAD risk factors (e.g. hypertension, hyperlipidaemia, persistent pain in the legs at rest, or current smoker).

7.7 Computed tomography

Computed tomography (CT) came into being in the 1970s and it is no exaggeration to say that it heralded a revolution in medical imaging. For the first time it allowed images of slices of the body (a technique known as tomography), something which is now commonplace for other imaging methods such as radionuclide imaging (Section 7.8) and MRI (Section 7.9) as well.

We could have included CT in Section 7.5 as it is an X-ray imaging technique. However, it has become so important in the modern hospital that it deserves a section in its own right.

Figure 7.18 shows the basic construction of a CT scanner. The X-ray source rotates around the patient, emitting a fan-shaped beam of X-rays, and a large bank of detectors collects the signal on the opposite side of the patient. The reconstruction of this image from the signals collected requires a large amount of computing power. This was the main reason why the CT scanner could not be developed until the 1970s, even though the mathematics of reconstruction was understood much earlier.

In the early CT scanners, the beam was rotated around the patient and an image of a slice of the patient was formed; then the bed was moved and another slice imaged, and so on. Technological developments then allowed the bed to be

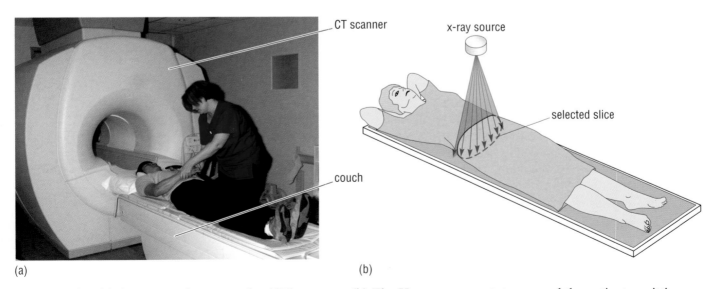

(a) (b)

Figure 7.18 (a) A computed tomography (CT) scanner. (b) The X-ray source rotates around the patient, emitting a fan-shaped beam of X-rays, and a large bank of detectors collects the signal on the opposite side of the patient.

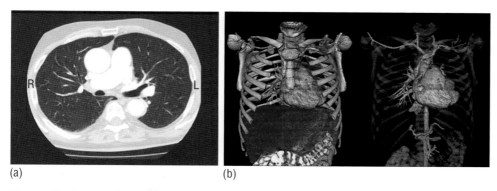

Figure 7.19   Products of a CT scan: (a) an image of a slice through the patient's thorax and (b) a 3D reconstruction of the thorax.

moved continuously so that the beam described a helix (corkscrew shape) around the patient. This allowed for much faster imaging and, crucially for thoracic imaging, imaging in one breath-hold. It also allowed the data to be reformatted in various planes and reconstructed as 3D representations of various body organs and structures (see Figure 7.19), including the heart.

More recently, CT scanners which image many slices at once have made the process even faster. This is known as multislice CT (MSCT). The images obtained have excellent resolution – that is, they show up detail extremely well.

CT is generally a non-invasive imaging technique. However, for many applications, including cardiac investigations, a contrast medium is used. This can be administered by injection into a peripheral vein – only a marginally invasive procedure.

● What properties does the contrast medium need to have?

● It needs to be 'radio-opaque' so that the blood vessels containing the contrast medium show up well on the image. It also needs to be capable of being injected into a vein and passing round in the circulation. And of course it must be non-toxic!

CT can be used to diagnose a variety of cardiovascular abnormalities and is now widely available in hospitals throughout the UK. Scan times vary, but most are in the order of 5–13 seconds so that people with pulmonary disease and congestive heart failure who have impaired breathing can hold their breath for the required length of time. The scans can also be gated (see Section 7.8.2) with the ECG. The ECG is used to trigger collection of data at specific parts of the cardiac cycle.

Technical developments continue at an impressive pace in both MSCT and multi-source CT scanners, and inevitably there is the expectation among health providers to have the latest machine able to perform increasingly complex investigations.

7.7.1 Cardiac CT angiography

CT can be used to generate stunning 3D representations of various structures of the heart, including the coronary vessels. It permits imaging of the heart and

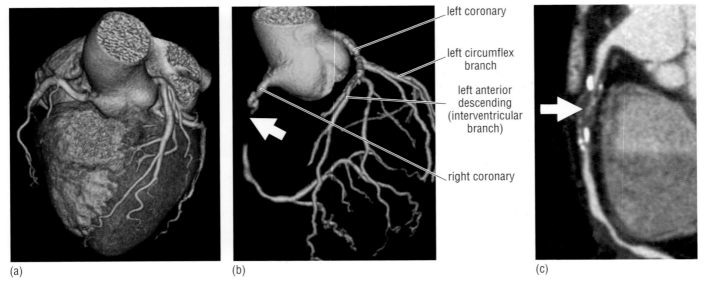

left coronary

left circumflex branch

left anterior descending (interventricular branch)

right coronary

(a)　　　　　(b)　　　　　(c)

Figure 7.20 Cardiac CT angiography. (a) An image of normal coronary arteries obtained using a 64-slice CT scanner (coronary CT angiography) and represented in false colour. (b) A right coronary artery occlusion (indicated by the arrow) on a 3D volume rendered CT angiogram. (c) A reformatted greyscale close-up image showing occlusion in finer detail, with adjacent extensive fatty and calcium-rich plaques (in white) and thrombus (arrow).

the entire coronary arterial tree during one breath of the patient. An example of a CT angiogram and the subsequent diagnosis of a right coronary occlusion (obstruction by a thrombus, for example) is shown in Figure 7.20. Compared with cardiac catheterisation angiography, cardiac CT angiography is much less invasive as it does not involve insertion and movement of a catheter via an artery in the groin – only the injection of a contrast medium into a peripheral vein. Beta-blockers are given to the patient prior to scanning in order to slow their heart rate (see Section 2.2). The technique can be used to identify:

- aneurysms in the aorta or in other major blood vessels (see Section 5.5.3)
- aortic dissections
- atherosclerotic disease and thrombosis, particularly in veins
- narrowing or obstruction of carotid arteries
- the position and effectiveness of a stent (see Section 9.2).

Cardiologists have to decide which technique to use to investigate the coronary circulation. They do this by weighing up the costs (e.g. radiation exposure, financial concerns) against the benefits of that particular technique. At the time of writing (2007), it is uncertain whether cardiac CT angiography will replace invasive coronary catheterisation as the preferred technique. Cardiac CT angiography can be used to rule out coronary artery disease rather than just diagnosing it because a negative test result means that a patient is very unlikely to have coronary artery disease. A positive result is less conclusive and requires invasive angiography to check the diagnosis of coronary artery disease.

7.7.2 The calcium index

The presence of calcium deposits in the coronary arteries is correlated with coronary heart disease and a 'calcium index' is used to quantify the degree of coronary heart disease. The statistical correlation is heavily age-dependent, as calcium deposits appear to be a natural phenomenon of aging. Deposits of calcium can be visualised and used as an added variable in determining the management of disease.

Cardiac calcium scoring (CT cardiac calcium scoring examination) is a simple and painless procedure which is becoming routine in some countries such as the USA, where an assessment can usually be completed in 15–20 minutes. The 'scoring' is used to detect the amount of plaque in coronary arteries or on the valves of the heart (see Table 7.3 for values). For example, the coronary calcium score is known to predict the occurrence of cardiac events, such as fatal and non-fatal MIs, or the necessity for coronary artery bypass surgery or coronary angioplasty (see Chapter 9). Normally, the coronary arteries do not contain calcium, so a score of 0 indicates no detectable plaque; a score of 400 indicates a level of plaque necessitating serious attention (Table 7.3).

Table 7.3 Calcium score ranges with quantifiable risk.

Score	Meaning
0	No detectable atheromatous plaque and therefore no risk of CVD.
1–10	Minimal plaque and a low risk of a cardiac event.
11–100	Definite minimal plaque burden with mild coronary stenosis likely.
101–400	Moderate stenosis. Consider exercise testing.
400	Extensive plaque burden with at least one major stenosis. More investigations necessary, e.g. radionuclide stress test (see Section 7.8.3) recommended together with aggressive risk factor modification.

7.8 Radionuclide tests

Under normal circumstances, the diagnosis of coronary heart disease is established by means of clinical history, an ECG, exercise testing and ultrasound tests. Sometimes, however, radionuclide techniques are used, particularly if the results of the ECG tests are uncertain or inconsistent with the clinical history. However, only some hospitals in the UK have the equipment to carry out radionuclide tests. When they are available, they are useful to show the effectiveness of cardiac contraction, to study myocardial blood flow and to diagnose coronary heart disease.

7.8.1 What are radionuclide tests?

A **radionuclide** is a natural or artificially produced atom with an unstable nucleus that undergoes radioactive decay by emitting gamma rays (see Figure 7.7) and/or other particles. In radionuclide imaging, such a substance is attached to another substance which is known to target the organ that needs to be investigated. This will be different for different organs, even if the radionuclide is the same. This combination of radionuclide and biochemically active substance is known as a **radiopharmaceutical**. The radionuclide is carefully chosen so that it emits gamma rays of a suitable energy and does not emit any other radiation that would not be detected but would be potentially harmful to the patient. There are only a few radionuclides that satisfy these requirements, so the choice is limited.

Once the radiopharmaceutical has reached the organ in question, the patient is placed in front of a gamma camera and imaging takes place (see Figure 7.21).

Consideration has to be given to the **half-life** of any radionuclide used. The half-life is the time taken for half of the radioactivity to decay. So after one half-life, half of the original amount is present, after two half-lives one quarter – and so on.

● What do you think the problems might be if the half-life is either very long or very short?

● If the half-life is very long, then the patient might remain radioactive for a long time. Even if the patient has excreted the radionuclide, it will remain in the environment for a long time. Both of these have a potential for harm. If the half-life is very short, then it does not allow enough time for the imaging to be done with consistent results.

The ideal half-life is a few hours. The most commonly used radionuclide in all radionuclide imaging, not just cardiac imaging, is technetium-99m (Tc-99m for short). Technetium is not a naturally occurring substance and Tc-99m is a by-product of the nuclear power industry. It has a half-life of 6 hours and has the enormous advantage that, unlike many other radioactive substances, it emits gamma rays but no additional harmful particles. Luckily, it is also relatively straightforward to combine it with other substances to make useful radiopharmaceuticals.

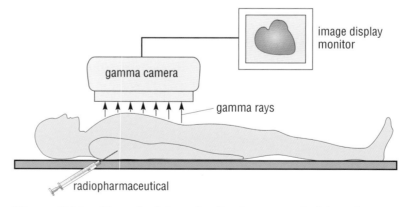

Figure 7.21   The principles of radiopharmaceutical imaging.

Because these substances emit gamma rays, which are high-energy electromagnetic radiation, the patient does receive a dose of potentially harmful radiation. However, the risk from this is small compared with the benefit of a correct diagnosis (see Section 7.10).

Radionuclide imaging cannot produce images of the same resolution as techniques such as CT (Section 7.7) or MRI (Section 7.9). However, it is not directly comparable with these techniques; they are designed to look at the structure of the organ, whereas radionuclide imaging looks at function, as you will see when you read the rest of this section on the most common radionucleotide investigations. This is why radionuclide imaging can be so valuable.

7.8.2 The nuclear ventriculogram: the MUGA scan

The purpose of this scan is to assess left ventricular function and to investigate abnormalities (e.g. aneurysms) in the walls of the ventricles. It is less widely used than it used to be because ultrasound echocardiography is much improved, but it is considered by many to be a more accurate way of assessing ventricular function.

Tc-99m is used to label red blood cells, which are then injected into the patient intravenously. As the labelled red blood cells travel around the body, they mix with unlabelled cells and eventually reach the heart. The patient lies on a couch and the gamma camera is placed over the left anterior chest and used to record the gamma emissions from the labelled red blood cells. The pictures displayed on the monitor are essentially an outline of the major vessels of the body and the chambers of the heart.

The most common scan is a **gated** one known as a **multi-gated acquisition (MUGA)**. ECG electrodes are placed on the patient and the ECG signal is passed to the camera. If the patient has a 'normal' heart rhythm (i.e. a sinus rhythm; see Section 2.4.1), then the length of the cardiac cycle (the interval between two R waves in the QRS complex; see Figure 7.22) can be measured. This is then divided into approximately 20 equal intervals and the images for each segment

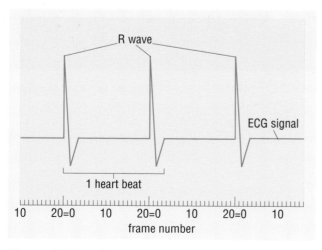

Figure 7.22 The use of an ECG signal to provide gating for a MUGA scan.

of the heart beat are collected over several hundred heart beats. An example of an image produced from a MUGA scan is shown in Figure 7.23.

These images can then be shown in sequence as a movie of the heart beating. A more quantitative analysis can be done if the left ventricle is outlined on each image and the largest and smallest volumes can be compared to give the **left ventricular ejection fraction**. This a measure of how much blood the left ventricle of the heart pumps out with each contraction, and is defined by the formula:

$$\text{left ventricular ejection fraction} = \frac{\text{end diastolic volume} - \text{end systolic volume}}{\text{end diastolic volume}}$$

$$= \frac{\text{stroke volume}}{\text{end diastolic volume}}$$

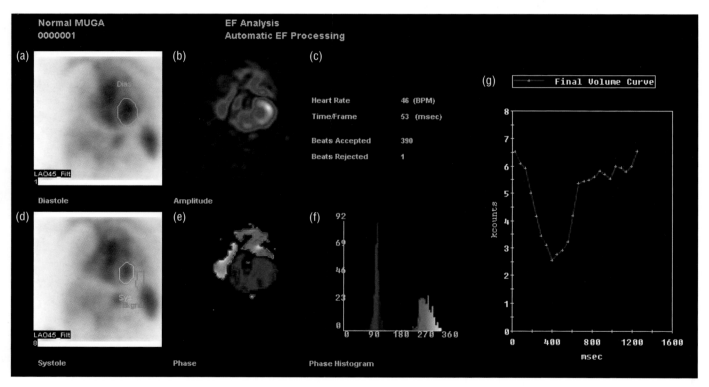

Figure 7.23   A MUGA scan of a normal heart. The heart is shown at end diastole in (a), compared with the heart at end systole in (d). In both cases, the left ventricle has been outlined so that the radioactivity emitted can be measured. (The small green region allows the background radiation to be calculated and subtracted from both values.) The data in (c) shows that these images have been taken from 390 heart beats and that the heart rate was 46 beats per minute – considerably slower than normal. Each beat has been divided into 24 intervals, each being 53 milliseconds (ms) long. The graph in (g) shows the radioactivity detected from the left ventricle (given as the corrected number of counts) at various stages of the heart beat. The maximum (at end diastole) is 6500 counts; the minimum (at end systole) is 2500 counts. This allows the calculation of the left ventricular ejection fraction as ((6.5 − 2.5)/6.5) = 0.61, which is in the normal range. Panel (b) shows the amplitude (the amount of movement) of each part of the heart. Clearly, the centre of the left ventricle moves the most. Panel (e) shows how the different parts of the heart are moving relative to each other. In this case, the left ventricle is moving as one (blue, lower part of image) and the atria (red, upper part of image) are also moving together but out of phase with the ventricle. This is summarised in the histogram in (f).

For example, just after filling with blood from the left atrium, the left ventricle has an average volume of 120 ml and with each heart beat ejects approximately 70 ml, the stroke volume. In this case, the left ventricular ejection fraction is 0.58 (70 ml/120 ml); healthy individuals typically have ejection fractions greater than 0.55.

The left ventricular ejection fraction can also be measured using B-mode echocardiophy. Generally, either an echocardiograph or a MUGA scan is done – not both.

7.8.3 Myocardial perfusion imaging

The MUGA scan is a planar imaging technique – it produces a 2D image of the body. Just as planar X-rays developed into CT scanning in the 1970s, radionuclide imaging has also developed a tomographic version. The nuclear medicine equivalent of a CT scan is a **single photon emission computed tomography (SPECT)** scan. It can be used for imaging any part of the body, but most commonly for myocardial perfusion imaging (MPI) of the heart. (You may also come across the abbreviation SPET. The 'computed' has been left out because everything is computed these days!) For tomographic images to be obtained, the camera must be rotated around the patient; usually two cameras are used set at right angles to each other as shown in Figure 7.24, but different centres may use either one or three cameras.

The radionuclide used is almost invariably Tc-99m, but there are several possible radiopharmaceuticals; Tc-99m tetrofosmin is the most commonly used. The take-up in the myocardium is dependent on the efficiency of perfusion. Brighter areas of the images indicate areas of greater take-up, and therefore more efficient perfusion.

The images are reconstructed using the same mathematical techniques as in CT (Section 7.7). However, whereas CT images are usually displayed as axial slices

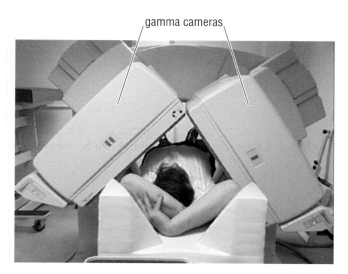

gamma cameras

Figure 7.24   A view of a patient under investigation using a SPECT scanner. The two gamma cameras rotate around the patient.

Figure 7.25 The planes used to display SPECT MPI images.

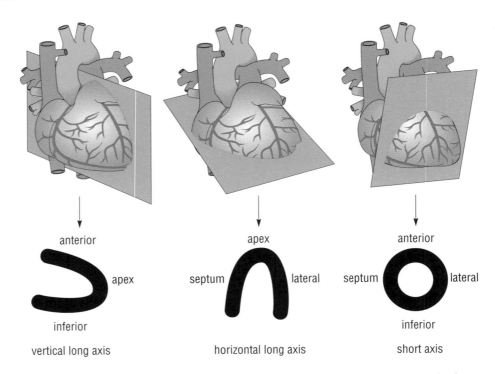

anterior

apex

inferior

vertical long axis

apex

septum — lateral

horizontal long axis

anterior

septum — lateral

inferior

short axis

(across the body), MPI images are shown as slices in three planes across the heart. Figure 7.25 shows the way these planes relate to the heart anatomy.

To obtain quantitative information about the perfusion of different parts of the myocardium and to establish whether defects are reversible, the SPECT technique is used both at rest and when the heart is under stress. These two scans are usually performed on two consecutive days, with the stress test performed after exercise – or, more commonly, after chemical cardiac stimulation to simulate stress. For this, drugs such as adenosine, dobutamine or dipyridamole are used, being administered intravenously. These stimulants are the same as those used in one of the options of the ECG stress test.

● Why is the stress test usually performed first?

● Usually the stress test is first because if this image is normal, it is unnecessary to perform rest imaging, as it too will be normal.

Typical stress and rest images are shown in Figure 7.25. Note the different planes used and how these relate to Figure 7.26, which shows a defect in the inferior and lateral walls of the ventricular muscle. Any decision on whether to proceed to surgery such as coronary bypass grafting or coronary angioplasty (see Chapter 9) can be taken at this point.

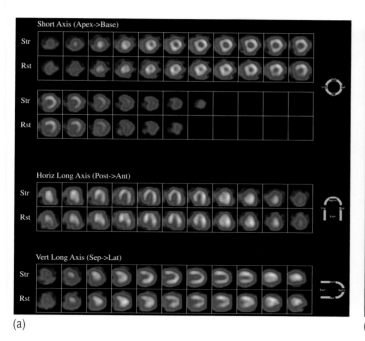

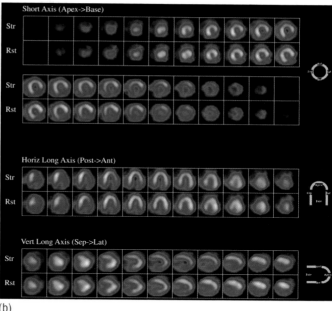

(a)

(b)

Figure 7.26 Myocardial perfusion SPECT images in different planar views (see Figure 7.25) acquired using Tc-99m tetrofosmin. The defect in the abnormal case is most clearly seen in the short axis views at the top of the image. There is a clear defect in the inferior and lateral walls of the ventricular muscle in both stress and rest images.

In SPECT, as with other imaging methods, it is possible to gate that records are obtained about the heart in various parts of its

- What other gated techniques have been discussed already in How is gating carried out?

- Both CT and the MUGA scan can be gated. Gating is carried the ECG output to the imaging system so that the images parts of the heart cycle are collected separately.

Gated imaging allows the presentation of the type of images Figure 7.26 as a movie of the beating heart. Alternatively, the presented in 3D as in Figure 7.27.

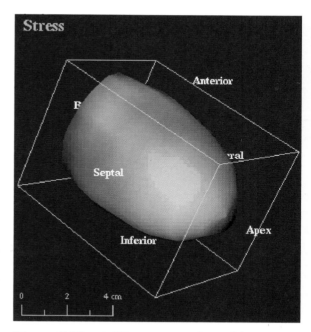

Figure 7.27 A 3D representation of the perfusion images shown in Figure 7.26. This can be displayed as a movie of the beating heart.

Activity 7.6   SPECT in use

Suggested study time 30 minutes

Follow the links on the DVD Guide program to the video resources. View the SPECT imaging sequence and answer the following questions.

(a) How is the patient's heart stressed?

(b) Which radiopharmaceutical is used in the procedure?

(c) How long does the radio-labelled tetrofosmin take to reach the heart?

(d) What position does the patient adopt on the scanning bed, and why?

Comment

(a) The patient's heart stressed using a vasodilating pharmaceutical and, in addition, the patient is asked to squeeze a dumbbell.

(b) The radionuclide used in the procedure is 99m-technetium-labelled tetrofosmin.

(c) The radio-labelled tetrofosmin takes up to an hour to reach the heart.

(d) The patient is lying on his back with his arms rested above his head. This is to allow the cameras to get as close to his heart as possible.

7.9 Magnetic resonance imaging

Magnetic resonance imaging (MRI) is based on a technique which has been well known to physicists and chemists for many decades: nuclear magnetic resonance. However, it only became possible to use it as an imaging technique in the 1980s, thanks to the work of Peter Mansfield and Paul Lauterbur, who were awarded the Nobel Prize in Physiology or Medicine in 2003 for their work.

7.9.1 The MRI scanner

The first prerequisite for MRI is a very strong and very uniform magnetic field. The fields used for imaging are commonly 20 000 times stronger than the Earth's magnetic field. Creating a magnetic field that is big enough to contain a patient is not cheap and is usually brought about using superconducting materials, so the first thing to say about MRI scanners is that they are very expensive!

The human body contains a very large number of hydrogen atoms – in fat, in muscle, in water and in all other tissues. When a patient is in the MRI scanner, the nuclei of these hydrogen atoms will tend to line up either parallel to the magnetic field or anti-parallel (at right angles) to it. The next step in creating an image is to apply a rapidly varying magnetic pulse (known as a radiofrequency pulse). What this pulse does can be described as 'flipping' the hydrogen nuclei over; when the pulse ends, the nuclei will quickly return to their original orientation (parallel or anti-parallel to the field). MRI only works because the time taken for this return process ('relaxation' to a physicist) depends on the differences in the surroundings of these nuclei. So, for example, a hydrogen nucleus in water will relax back to its original orientation much more slowly than one in fat. Using a very complicated system, which involves yet more varying magnetic fields, it is possible to identify the signals from different parts of the body and create an image. Figure 7.28 shows a magnetic resonance scanner in use.

Contrast medium can be used, which in this case contains gadolinium, which affects the local magnetic field and therefore the relaxation of the nuclei. As with other methods, the contrast medium is injected into a vein.

MRI scanning has some very strong advantages:

- the images are excellent, with very good discrimination of detail
- the images can be produced showing planes in any direction
- there are no X-rays or gamma rays involved, so there is less potential for harm.

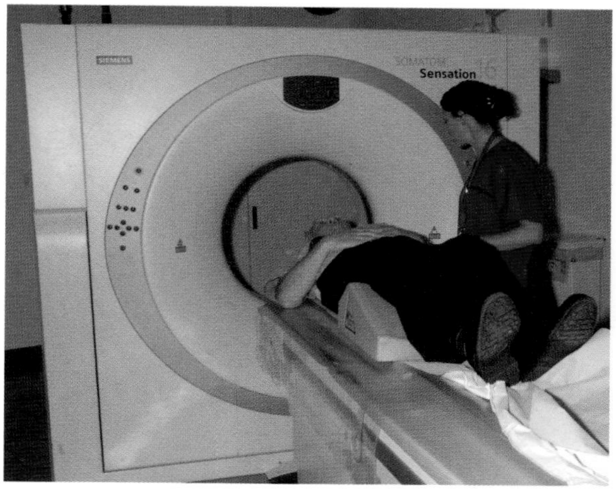

However, there are also some disadvantages.

- MRI scans take longer than CT scans. The time is reducing as new techniques are used, but it can take 30 minutes to carry out an investigation.

- The long procedure time, combined with the expense – and therefore scarcity – of MRI scanners, means that waiting times can be long and that MRI scans are not an option for emergency cases.

- Patients with heart pacemakers and other metal implants cannot be placed in the magnetic field.

- Some patients suffer claustrophobia in the scanner and have to be sedated. However, MRI technology is improving and becoming more patient-friendly, with machines which are wider and shorter and do not fully enclose the patient, whereas other units are open at the sides.

Figure 7.28 A magnetic resonance scanner. The patient lies inside the scanner with the part to be imaged in the centre of the magnetic field.

7.9.2 Cardiac MRI

MRI can be used in the diagnosis of a broad range of cardiovascular diseases, including heart and vascular disease (particularly coronary heart disease) and stroke. It can create detailed images of blood vessels without the normal use of contrast medium (with the occasional exception of gadolinium). MRI requires specialised equipment and expertise and allows evaluation of some body structures which may not be as visible with other imaging methods. When the chambers of the heart and coronary vessels need to be viewed in high contrast then contrast material is injected through an intravenous line placed in a peripheral vein (such as an arm) and the investigation continued for up to 45 minutes.

MRI can be used to determine:

- the size and thickness of the chambers of the heart
- the extent of damage caused by MI or cardiomyopathy
- the efficiency of the heart
- whether the myocardium is damaged or the pericardium is swollen.

It can also be used to:

- detect blocked or damaged heart chambers or major vessels
- detect the build-up of plaque
- investigate the function of the heart muscles, valves and vessels – movies of the beating heart can be created.

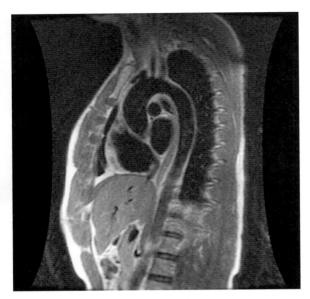

Figure 7.29 An image of a human torso showing the aortic arch extending down through the abdomen obtained with the MRI technique. The blood within the aorta is shown in black.

Figure 7.29 shows the sort of images that can be obtained using cardiac MRI.

7.10 Risks of investigative techniques

A health professional recommending any procedure must always try to balance the possible risks of that procedure against the benefits. Some procedures are apparently virtually risk-free. Others – especially invasive or interventional procedures – have more obvious risks. However, there are some procedures, such as those using X-rays, where the potential for damage is not obvious to the patient but is known to the health professionals.

● Which of the investigative procedures discussed in this chapter would you describe as very unlikely to cause harm to the patient?

● Listening to the patient's heart with a stethoscope, taking blood pressure measurements, pulse oximetry and ECG measurements all involve minimal harm. You might also have added echocardiography, but this procedure involves a slight risk associated with few potential hazards (see Section 7.10.2).

The remaining techniques are the imaging techniques, each of which has its possible dangers.

7.10.1 Techniques involving X-rays and radioactivity

As you can see in Figure 7.7, both X-rays and gamma rays are at the high-energy end of the electromagnetic spectrum. As mentioned previously, this type of radiation has the potential to cause damage to cells. The possible damage due to what is known as **ionising radiation** (X-rays and gamma rays in this case) has been and continues to be the subject of extensive study. One of the problems is that, because most of the available data are from people who have had large doses of radiation (from nuclear accidents or the atomic bombs dropped over Hiroshima and Nagasaki), it is difficult to know the effect of small doses.

The effects due to radiation can be divided into two categories – early effects and late effects. Early effects occur in the hours and days after exposure to a large dose of radiation. They include radiation sickness, skin reddening and (if the eyes are irradiated) cataracts. Apart from a few (thankfully rare) cases of skin reddening after long fluoroscopy sessions, these effects are never seen in diagnostic procedures.

Late effects, as their name suggests, occur many years after exposure. There are two types of effect:

• the development of cancer, many years after the radiation was received

• genetic effects in the next generation due to irradiation of the reproductive organs.

Genetic effects are only relevant if the patient is of an age to reproduce; the most likely effect from any diagnostic procedure is cancer induction. However, there are three points to emphasise.

- The risks from any procedure are very low indeed, especially when compared with the 1 in 3 risk that we all have of developing cancer for some other reason.

- Any cancer induced is not likely to develop until about 20 years after exposure to radiation. Because many heart patients are already in their 60s, this is not a major consideration.

- All women of child-bearing age will be questioned before imaging to establish whether there is any possibility of their being pregnant. If they are, then the procedure will be postponed until after they have given birth, or else very careful calculations will be carried out to estimate the possible risks to the fetus and the matter will be discussed carefully with the patient before proceeding.

In order to estimate the risks of developing cancer, scientists have worked out a way of calculating what is known as the **effective dose** of ionising radiation. All procedures involving X-rays or gamma rays will give the patient a dose of radiation which must be compared with the dose of natural background radiation to which everyone is subjected every day. This background radiation comes from radioactive materials in rocks and from cosmic rays, as well as a very small amount from man-made sources. Table 7.4 compares the effective doses from background radiation and from some medical procedures. It also shows the approximate dose received from cosmic rays during commercial airline flights from the UK.

Table 7.4 Approximate effective dose received (in units of millisieverts, mSv) from some medical procedures and flights, together with the average time required to receive the same amount of background radiation.

Procedure	Approximate effective dose (mSv)	Time to receive same amount of background radiation
standard dental X-ray	0.005	less than 1 day
flight to Spain from the UK	0.005*	less than 1 day
chest X-ray	0.02	2.8 days
flight to Australia from the UK	0.05*	7 days
coronary angiography	5–10 (depending on time)	2–4 years
Tc-99m MPI	7	2.7 years
MUGA scan	7	2.7 years
barium enema	7.2	2.8 years
CT scan (chest)	10	4 years

*These figures are very approximate because the effective dose depends on the altitude as well as on solar flares.

These figures should reassure you that the doses received from most cardiac investigations are low and very unlikely to cause any harm. None the less, health professionals are always aware of the risk due to ionising radiation, and all possible measures are taken to ensure that only the necessary radiation is received. The need to repeat a scan – because the original does not show the information required, for example – is kept to a minimum.

7.10.2 Ultrasound imaging

There is no ionising radiation involved in an ultrasound scan. If a large amount of energy is supplied to a small part of the body, then there is a risk of either heating or of cavitation (the formation and collapse of small bubbles). Of these, heating is the most likely in diagnostic ultrasound. All modern ultrasound scanners are equipped with devices to calculate two variables which indicate to the operator that there is a possibility of heating or cavitation. There are limits on these variables, above which machines must not be operated. So the potential for harm due to ultrasound imaging is very low – it really is a 'kind' imaging technique.

7.10.3 MRI

Again, there is no ionising radiation involved in an MRI scan. However, the very strong magnetic field required for MRI comes at a cost. Any ferrous (iron-containing) object on the body or anywhere in the MRI investigation room will be attracted to the magnetic core of the machine with frightening speed. This is not an effect to be dismissed lightly – there have been some horrendous accidents with ferrous gas cylinders taken into an MRI room by mistake. Also, it is not possible to wear a heart pacemaker or implanted defibrillator as these will be affected by the very large and constant magnetic field.

Metallic implants which do not contain iron are not affected by the constant field, but the radiofrequency field will induce currents in them which can lead to heating. This is not a problem in parts of the body where there is a good blood supply to cool the tissues, but it is a problem in the eye, where there is no blood supply. Anyone who has worked with metal will need to be checked for small metal fragments in their eyes as heating of these can cause serious damage.

All of these risks can be minimised by careful preparation of the patient. But the one potentially harmful effect for every patient is the possible effect of the loud noise to which they are subjected while in the scanner. This is due to the constant and fast movement of the coils producing the magnetic fields that locate the signals from different parts of the body. Much research is being carried out to try to find ways to reduce this, but at present the most effective way is to supply each patient with ear defenders.

7.10.4 Summary

In this section, we have summarised the possible harmful effects of the various investigative procedures used in cardiology. You should have concluded that in most cases there is very little potential for harm, provided that the correct procedures are followed. The overriding concern of the clinician is always to obtain the diagnostic information needed to treat the patient successfully, and this will normally be the prime consideration in choosing a diagnostic procedure.

7.11 Summary of Chapter 7

The method used to investigate cardiovascular diseases depends on the initial clinical assessment, including the history of the patient. You can see from this chapter that these methods of investigation are numerous and in some cases complex. More emphasis has been given to techniques that, as a patient or a health care professional, you are more likely to come across when you visit a general practice, health clinic or hospital – or when you watch television or read an article in a magazine or newspaper. There are a range of non-invasive to invasive techniques covered together with their advantages and associated risks. For example, X-rays as used in cardiology range from the reasonably safe, simple, non-invasive chest X-ray to coronary angiography and interventional techniques carried out using fluoroscopy. Computed tomography is an even more sophisticated X-ray technique that produces images of slices of the body as well as 3D reconstructions of organs. With increasing technological advances, the techniques in this chapter are likely to evolve with time, to increase in complexity and to provide far more detailed analysis of potential and actual cardiovascular diseases. MRI is the most recent imaging technique and can produce stunning images with a wide range of diagnostic uses.

Questions for Chapter 7

Question 7.1 (Learning Outcomes 7.2 and 7.4)

Complete Table 7.5 to summarise in your own words the basic method, the uses and the advantages and disadvantages of some of the different imaging techniques introduced in this chapter.

Table 7.5 A summary of imaging techniques: the basic method, the uses and the advantages and disadvantages.

Technique	Fluoroscopy	B-mode ultrasound with colour flow Doppler ultrasound	CT angiography	Myocardial perfusion imaging with Tc-99m tetrofosmin
Basic method				
Main uses				
Advantages				
Disadvantages				

Question 7.2 (Learning Outcome 7.2)

Section 7.6.2 described the use of small bubbles of gas as a contrast medium in ultrasound imaging. If this medium is to be used to image the left ventricle but is injected into a peripheral vein, what can you say about the size and durability of these bubbles? (Hint: think of the path the bubbles will need to follow.)

Question 7.3 (Learning Outcome 7.3)

Complete Table 7.6 by placing a tick in either the non-invasive or invasive category for each of the techniques.

Table 7.6 A list of invasive and non-invasive diagnostic techniques used to investigate cardiovascular diseases.

Technique	Invasive	Non-invasive
fluoroscopy		
B-mode ultrasound with colour flow Doppler ultrasound		
CT angiography		
myocardial perfusion with Tc-99m tetrofosmin		
12-lead ECG		
cardiac-related blood tests		
pulse oximeter		
chest X-ray		
MRI		

References

Adams, J. and Apple, F. (2004) 'New blood tests for detecting heart disease', *Circulation*, **109**, pp. 12–14 [online] Available from: http://circ.ahajournals.org/cgi/reprint/109/3/e12 (Accessed May 2007).

Department of Health (2000) *National Service Framework for coronary heart disease*, Chapter 4 [online] Available from: http://www.dh.gov.uk/en/Publicationsandstatistics/Publications/PublicationsPolicyAndGuidance/DH_4094275 (Accessed May 2007).

Elhendy, A., Bax, J. J. and Poldermans, D. (2002) 'Dobutamine stress myocardial perfusion imaging in coronary artery disease', *Journal of Nuclear Medicine*, **43**, pp. 1634–1646 [online] Available from: http://jnm.snmjournals.org/cgi/content/abstract/43/12/1634 (Accessed July 2007).

Packard, C. J., O'Reilly, D. S. J, Caslake, M. J., McMahon, A. D., Ford, I., Cooney, J., Macphee, C. H., Suckling, K. E., Krishna, M., Wilkinson, F. E., Rumley, A., Lowe, G. D. O., Docherty, G. and Burczak, J. D. (2000) 'Lipoprotein-associated phospholipase A2 as an independent predictor of coronary heart disease', *New England Journal of Medicine*, **343**, pp. 1148–1155.

CHAPTER 8

MEDICAL MANAGEMENT OF CARDIOVASCULAR DISEASES

Learning Outcomes

When you have completed this chapter you should be able to:

8.1 Define and use, or recognise definitions and applications of, each of the terms printed in **bold** in the text.

8.2 Outline what types of treatment are available for different types of cardiovascular diseases.

8.3 Understand how treatment options are assessed for individuals.

8.4 Describe the main groups of therapeutic drugs used to treat cardiovascular diseases.

8.5 Relate the use of different treatments to the underlying physiology and pathology.

8.6 Understand how different drugs can help prevent the progression of cardiovascular diseases.

8.7 Outline how drugs are evaluated.

8.8 Outline the factors that affect the bioavailability and efficacy of drugs.

8.1 Introduction

In the remaining chapters of this course, you will learn about the various ways in which cardiovascular disease may be treated. There are several aims in treating cardiovascular diseases:

- Symptom control: people with cardiovascular disease can experience symptoms such as chest pain, shortness of breath, ankle swelling and palpitations.

- Preventing progression of disease: a person with cardiovascular disease will be encouraged to take measures aimed at preventing deterioration of their condition.

- Preventing deaths: various medications can reduce the risk of death from cardiovascular disease.

- Treating conditions associated with cardiovascular disease: in particular, hypertension and high cholesterol levels.

- Adapting to living with cardiovascular disease.

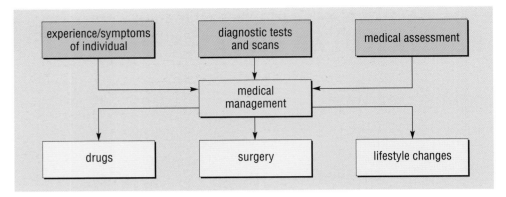

Figure 8.1 Medical management of someone with a cardiovascular condition involves assessment of signs, symptoms and diagnostic tests and advising treatment with a combination of drugs (Chapter 8), surgery (Chapter 9) and lifestyle modifications (Chapter 10).

The main types of treatment for cardiovascular disease are summarised in Figure 8.1. This chapter focuses on the medical management of cardiovascular disease and the various ways in which different drugs can be used in a person with cardiovascular disease.

Case Study 8.1 Winifred Fowler's medication

Winifred has been discharged from hospital one week after her heart attack and has gone home in a taxi with her husband, Frank. Before leaving the hospital she went to the pharmacy to collect several packs of tablets, some of which she recognises from her stay on the ward, whereas others are unfamiliar. There is a detailed plan telling her which tablets should be taken at what time of day and how many should be taken each time. The pharmacist checked everything carefully and said that there is enough to last for 2 weeks, but did not have time to explain what each of the tablets does.

The journey home is uneventful and Winifred is very glad to be back with her family. She finds that she feels reasonably well when she is just pottering around the house, and the next morning she tries to walk to the newsagent, which is about 100 metres along the road, down a slight hill. She takes it slowly, but even so is a bit breathless and has to stop once on the way back. Although she is trying very hard to be positive, she is terrified that she will have another heart attack and die, especially because the staff at the hospital told her that this was a definite possibility. Frank tells her to take it very carefully, and asks her if she has taken all the pills that she should have done. She is not so sure, because so much has been happening with people visiting to see how she is. She looks at the packs and bottles of tablets to try to work out how many she has taken. She thinks about taking a double dose to make up for the ones she might have missed, but Frank tells her that is not a good idea. He makes her put all the tablets she is supposed to take that day into eggcups and lines them up on the kitchen window-sill – one for each time. 'From now on,' he says, 'you will have to do this until we can find a better way. I am sure you can get special boxes which hold a whole week's supply of pills with a separate compartment for what you have to take at each time. I'll drop into the chemist this afternoon and see if they've got some.'

● What do you think are Winifred's main concerns, and what might she want to discuss with her doctor? What aims will her doctor have in devising treatment?

● Winifred's main concern is likely to be the symptoms she is still experiencing. A key aim for the doctor is to control Winifred's symptoms – getting rid of her chest pain and improving her breathing. Another aim is to prevent her from having a second MI, and a further aim is to lower her high blood pressure to reduce her risk of further cardiovascular disease.

8.2 Types of drugs used to treat cardiovascular diseases

This section outlines the different drugs used to treat cardiovascular disease, their mechanism of action and why certain treatments are chosen for individual patients. You will also learn how drugs can help prevent the progression of cardiovascular disease.

8.2.1 Nitrates

This group of drugs includes compounds such as glyceryl trinitrate, which work by stimulating the release of nitric oxide (NO) from endothelial cells. They are often taken as sublingual tablets or as sprays (see Section 8.5.1).

● What effect will the release of NO have on the arterioles?

● NO causes the smooth muscles of the arterioles to relax, resulting in an increase in the blood flow through the capillary beds (Section 5.3.2).

Nitrates have two main effects on the circulation:

- They act as coronary vasodilators, increasing the blood flow through the capillary beds supplying the heart. Recall that in the coronary circulation, nearly all the available oxygen is used during the passage of blood through the capillaries, so the only way to increase oxygen supply to the heart is to increase coronary blood flow.
- They reduce the workload of the heart by reducing the rate at which blood returns to the heart from the rest of the body. The reduction in venous return enables the heart to pump more efficiently.

The increased coronary blood supply and reduced venous return caused by nitrates result in an increase in the proportion of the blood ejected from the ventricles at each heart beat – the left ventricular ejection fraction, which reflects how efficiently the heart is pumping.

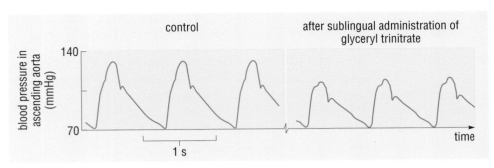

Figure 8.2 Pressure waves recorded in the ascending aorta (upper traces) and brachial artery (lower traces) in a 54-year-old man under control conditions (left) and after sublingual administration of glyceryl trinitrate 0.3 mg (right). The pressure trace was obtained from catheters placed inside the vessels.

Nitrates are used to treat angina and can also be used to treat heart failure.

● What effect will nitrates have on blood pressure?

● Nitrates cause peripheral vasodilation and thus a reduction in blood pressure (Figure 8.2).

A common side effect of nitrates is **hypotension** (abnormally low blood pressure), which can cause dizziness or fainting – hence nitrates may not be suitable for individuals with very low blood pressure.

8.2.2 Beta-blockers

Heart muscle cells contain receptors on their cell membranes known as **beta-adrenoreceptors**. When the body produces adrenalin, this binds to the receptors, causing the heart to beat more strongly and more rapidly (see Section 2.5).

● In which cardiovascular condition could adrenalin release cause a worsening of symptoms?

● In angina, where the flow of blood, and hence oxygen, to the heart muscle is restricted. If adrenalin is released, the heart muscle beats more strongly, which requires more oxygen. Blood flow cannot be increased through the narrowed arteries, so insufficient oxygen is supplied to the heart cells, resulting in ischaemia.

Beta-blockers may be used to treat angina by blocking the action of adrenalin on the heart muscle (Figure 8.3). Beta-blockers are also prescribed following MI, because they have been shown to improve survival rates and reduce the incidence of a second MI, by 20–40% (Aronow, 1997, Everly et al., 2004). Traditionally, beta-blockers were avoided in any person with heart failure, as it was believed that that their effects on the rate and strength of the heart contraction could cause deterioration in symptoms. However, several clinical trials have demonstrated that beta-blockers improve survival, reduce hospital admissions due to heart failure and improve symptoms in people with heart failure.

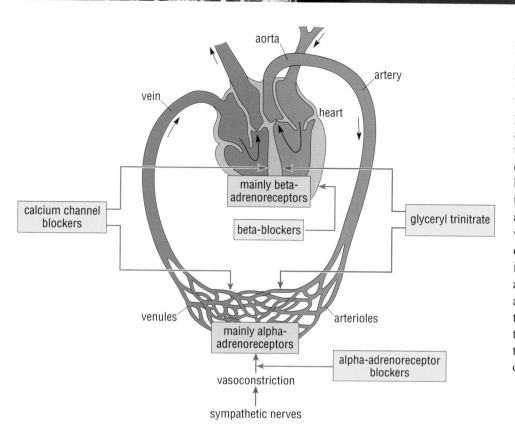

Figure 8.3 The heart has beta-adrenoreceptors that, when stimulated, make it beat more strongly. Blocking these receptors reduces blood pressure. Blood pressure is also reduced by increasing the dilation of peripheral and coronary vessels. This can be brought about by using glyceryl trinitrate or by blocking the action of sympathetic nerves, which cause constriction of the arterioles. Vessels in the periphery also have adrenoreceptors (primarily alpha-adrenoreceptors) but, as they are of a different type from those in the heart, it is possible to use drugs selectively to target one type or the other.

Beta-blockers can also be used to treat hypertension. Some of their effect on blood pressure is explained by the reduction in cardiac output and the blocking of beta-adrenoreceptors in peripheral blood vessels. However, their exact mechanism of action is not fully understood.

Beta-blockers are contraindicated (not recommended for use) in anyone with asthma. The lungs also contain beta-adrenoreceptors; if these receptors are blocked, the airways can constrict, causing breathing difficulty. In a person who does not suffer from asthma, this may cause some transient wheezing and breathlessness. In an asthma sufferer, this additional breathing difficulty can be severe and even life-threatening. The other common side effects of beta-blockers are headache, fatigue, sleep disturbance, and cold hands and feet.

8.2.3 Calcium channel blockers

Muscle cells depend on the movement of calcium across their cell membranes through calcium channels to cause them to contract. **Calcium channel blockers** prevent calcium from entering the smooth muscle cells of arteries and arterioles, causing the muscle cells to relax.

● What effect will this have on blood flow through the capillary bed?

● The calcium channel blockers will increase blood flow through the capillary beds by relaxing arteriolar smooth muscle.

So calcium channel blockers can be used to treat angina because they cause an increased blood flow through the capillary bed supplying the heart (Figure 8.3). Elsewhere in the body, they have the effect of reducing blood pressure. In Chapter 3 you learned that hypertension is a risk factor for developing heart disease. If a person has established heart disease, hypertension will increase the likelihood of the disease progressing. Calcium channel blockers are one of a number of drugs which can be used to treat hypertension.

However, calcium channel blockers can have a similar relaxing effect on the heart muscle cells, which may reduce the strength with which the heart can contract and make heart failure worse. People with heart failure may be unable to take a calcium channel blocker for this reason, and even people without heart failure may develop ankle swelling when taking these drugs. The vasodilation caused by calcium channel blockers may cause headaches, dizziness and flushing, which also limits their use.

Figure 8.3 summarises where nitrates, beta-blockers and calcium channel blockers act within the body.

8.2.4 Diuretics and ACE inhibitors

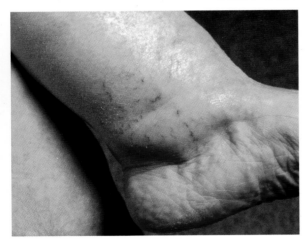

Figure 8.4   Fluid retention in heart failure (oedema): swelling in the legs.

Diuretics and **angiotensin-converting enzyme inhibitors (ACE inhibitors)** are mainly used in the treatment of heart failure. In heart failure, the heart contracts with less strength. This can result in fluid retention in the lungs, causing breathlessness, especially on exertion; and in the legs, causing oedema (Figure 8.4; see Section 6.2).

The salt and water balance of the body is controlled by a group of interacting hormones and enzymes referred to as the **renin–angiotensin–aldosterone axis** (Figure 8.5). ACE inhibitors, aldosterone antagonists and diuretics all cause the body to lose salt and water. (An **antagonist** is a compound that blocks the normal action of the mediator.) This loss improves the symptoms of breathlessness and oedema associated with heart failure. ACE inhibitors also cause peripheral vasodilation, which further reduces strain on the heart. Thus ACE inhibitors can be used to treat hypertension. However, like nitrates, they can cause hypotension, especially with the first few doses. Because some people do not tolerate ACE inhibitors well, some treatments use angiotensin receptor blockers (A-II blockers) to inhibit the action of angiotensin on the kidneys.

- Can you think of any adverse effects which may be caused by the loss of salt and water?

- People taking these medicines may become dehydrated and the amount of sodium (from salt) in the body may become low, while the level of potassium becomes relatively high, which can increase the risk of developing an arrhythmia.

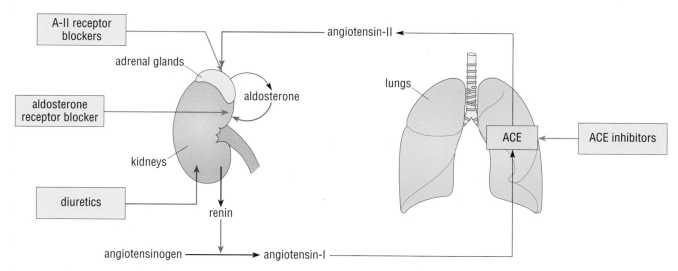

Figure 8.5   The salt balance of the body is controlled by the kidneys, which secrete an enzyme (renin) that converts the precursor, angiotensinogen, into angiotensin-I, which is converted to angiotensin-II in the lungs by the action of angiotensin-converting enzyme (ACE). This step can be blocked with ACE inhibitors. Angiotensin-II acts on the adrenal glands to cause the secretion of aldosterone, a hormone that causes salt retention by the kidney. The production of aldosterone can be blocked using an A-II receptor blocker, which prevents the adrenal glands from responding to angiotensin-II. The effects of aldosterone can be interrupted by drugs that block its receptor. All of the drugs shown with blue arrows (A-II receptor blockers, aldosterone receptor blockers and ACE inhibitors) can therefore reduce salt retention and promote water loss. Diuretics act directly on the kidney to promote water loss. Decreasing water retention reduces the load on the heart.

Alterations in the salt/water balance also affect kidney function, and people taking these drugs may ultimately develop kidney failure. Therefore anybody taking an ACE inhibitor or diuretic should have regular blood tests to monitor kidney function and sodium and potassium levels in the blood.

ACE inhibitors are also important in secondary prevention of cardiovascular diseases and it has been recommended that they are taken for at least 6 weeks following an MI. ACE inhibitors also improve long-term survival in heart failure, as does an aldosterone antagonist (spironolactone).

It is worth emphasising at this point that the recommendations for the use of different drug combinations after an MI and to treat heart failure have changed periodically as new drugs and new studies become available. It is important therefore to check any recommendations that are found in printed texts (including this one) against the most up-to-date guidelines available from NICE and similar bodies. It is also important to understand that any recommendations have to be viewed in the context of the individual patient (see Section 8.6). As you have seen, particular drugs may be contraindicated in people who have characteristics such as low blood pressure, or who may have other concurrent medical conditions.

8.2.5 Anti-arrhythmics

In Chapter 2 you learned how the regular contraction of the heart is initiated by an electrical impulse, which flows from the sinoatrial node through the conductive pathways of the heart, causing regular contraction of the heart. The disturbance of this regular flow of electricity can cause an arrhythmia, resulting in a reduction in cardiac output. In addition, arrhythmia often causes disturbed blood flow within the heart, which can lead to the formation of thrombi and thromboemboli (see Sections 5.6 and 5.7).

There are several aims in treating an arrhythmia:

- to restore the normal rhythm of the heart
- if normal heart rhythm is restored, to prevent further episodes of arrhythmia
- if normal heart rhythm cannot be restored, to keep the heart rate under control in order to minimise symptoms
- to reduce the risk of complications – in particular, stroke or a **transient ischaemic attack**.

Various drugs can be used in the management of arrhythmias, including some you have encountered already. We will briefly examine the four main types of drugs.

Beta-blockers reduce the action of adrenalin on the heart, which reduces the excitability of the sinoatrial node and minimises abnormal electrical conduction within the heart. Beta-blockers are often used to treat arrhythmias following an MI, for which they are particularly effective.

Calcium channel blockers reduce the movement of calcium into the heart cells. **Verapamil** is a calcium channel blocker which exerts a similar effect on the cells of the heart's conductive pathways, suppressing the formation of extraneous electrical impulses within the heart. Other calcium channel blockers are less effective as anti-arrhythmic drugs because they act less on the conductive pathways than verapamil.

Amiodarone is a drug which is used for a wide range of different arrhythmias because it has several effects on the conduction of electricity through the heart. It slows down the speed at which electricity is conducted through the heart, reduces the rate at which electrical impulses are fired from the sinoatrial node and delays repolarisation (the rate at which the heart's electrical system recharges itself ready for another contraction). These effects reduce the heart's ability to contract rapidly, and hence will help control an arrhythmia.

Digoxin modulates the heart rate and is used to treat atrial fibrillation, a condition in which the electrical activity of the atria is disorganised and irregular (Section 6.4). If the heart's electrical activity cannot be returned to normal, digoxin may be given to slow the heart down, as this will enable it to contract more fully. Digoxin acts on the AVN to reduce conductivity, and hence slows down the rate at which the ventricles can contract. Digoxin is now used less frequently than it was, and it is no longer a first-line treatment choice.

Prevention of thromboembolism is an important part of treating arrhythmias. Normally either aspirin or warfarin (see Section 8.2.7) will be prescribed. The choice of treatment will depend on the age of the patient and the risk of thromboembolic stroke.

8.2.6 Thrombolytic drugs

● When a person has an MI, what process occurs in the coronary arteries?

● The coronary arteries are narrow due to a build-up of atheromatous plaques. Disturbed blood flow or rupture of the fibrous cap of an atheromatous plaque causes the formation of thrombus, which completely obstructs the blood supply to a part of the heart.

Once a person has had an MI, immediate treatment is aimed at restoring blood flow to the damaged heart tissue to minimise cell death. This is achieved by administering drugs which accelerate the breakdown of the thrombus.

● Which group of chemicals in the body are normally involved in breaking down blood clots?

● The plasmin system, a group of proteins which act in a series of steps to form plasmin, which breaks down the fibrin in a blood clot (Section 5.7.3).

As soon as possible after an MI, a patient will usually be treated with a **thrombolytic drug**. This will either activate the plasmin system, causing a more rapid breakdown of the thrombus obstructing the coronary artery, or will act directly on fibrin to break down the thrombus (Figure 8.6). The sooner these drugs are administered after an MI, the less the amount of damage to the heart and the greater the prospects are for recovery. The most common serious adverse effect of thrombolytic drugs is bleeding into the brain, resulting in a stroke, although this is still very uncommon. Because they can cause bleeding from anywhere in the body, a person who has recently suffered trauma, haemorrhage or recently had any teeth removed cannot

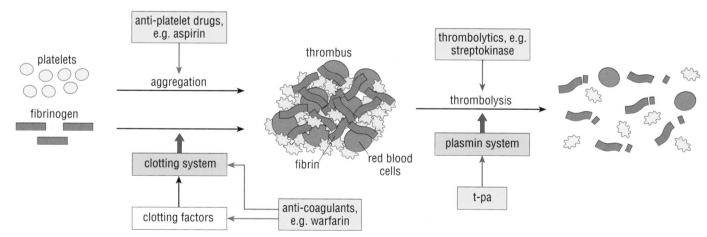

Figure 8.6 Blood clots are formed by aggregated platelets, fibrin and trapped red blood cells. Anti-platelet drugs inhibit the ability of platelets to aggregate. Anti-coagulants interfere with the ability of the liver to make clotting factors, or with the activation of the clotting system, which produces fibrin. Blood clots are normally dissolved (thrombolysis) by the plasmin system, which breaks up fibrin into fragments. This process can be accelerated by factors such as t-pa (tissue plasminogen activator) which activate the plasmin system. Fibrin can also be directly broken down by thrombolytic enzymes. Notice how treatments are aimed at inhibiting blood clotting (anti-platelet drugs and anti-coagulants, blue arrows) or promoting clot breakdown (thrombolytics and t-pa, thin green arrows).

be given thrombolytics. (In Chapter 6, Winifred Fowler was treated with the tissue plasminogen activator tenecteplase as an acute treatment for MI. Before administering the thrombolytic, the health care worker checked that Winifred did not have any of the excluding criteria, was careful to outline that the procedure was potentially hazardous and then obtained Winifred's consent before proceeding.)

8.2.7 Preventing blood clotting

● Which two processes are involved in the formation of blood clots and what are the major components of a blood clot?

● Platelet aggregation and activation of the blood clotting system are the two major processes involved in blood clotting. Blood clots consist of aggregated platelets, fibrin and trapped red blood cells (see Figures 5.11 and 5.12).

Certain medications can reduce platelet aggregation and so reduce the risk of thrombosis and MI. These drugs are called **anti-platelet drugs**. By far the most widely used and well researched anti-platelet drug is **aspirin**, which works by inhibiting the production of signalling molecules (thromboxanes) that trigger platelet aggregation. (Related molecules are involved in producing pain.) If a person is suspected of having an MI, they will be given a high dose (300 mg) of aspirin because this has been shown to reduce damage to the heart. A low dose of aspirin (75 mg) is prescribed to all patients with cardiovascular disease – this reduces the risk of further MI by up to 30%. Aspirin is also given to patients with certain arrhythmias to reduce the risk of stroke and transient ischaemic attacks. It can also be prescribed to healthy patients who are at high risk of developing cardiovascular disease to try to reduce this risk (Hayden et al., 2002).

Aspirin can increase acid production by the stomach, so can lead to a worsening of symptoms in a person with a stomach ulcer. Other side effects of aspirin are indigestion, nausea, bleeding from the stomach and wheezing if the person is susceptible to asthma.

Clopidogrel is a newer anti-platelet drug which can be used if a person is unable to take aspirin because of side effects or if aspirin is contraindicated, although there is a risk of bleeding with this drug too. Clopidogrel can also be used alongside aspirin after an angioplasty and stent insertion (see Chapter 9) and after certain types of MI.

The group of drugs that inhibits the blood clotting system are the **anti-coagulants**, of which the most often used is **warfarin**. Warfarin prevents the utilisation of vitamin K, which is required by the liver to produce some of the proteins of the blood clotting system. It can be used if a person cannot take aspirin or clopidogrel. It is also used in patients with some arrhythmias who are at high risk of suffering a stroke. The effectiveness of warfarin is monitored by regular blood tests and the dose is adjusted according to the results. Any person who takes warfarin will need frequent blood tests to determine the correct dose. Figure 8.6 indicates where anti-platelet drugs and anti-coagulants act.

8.2.8 Lipid-lowering drugs

● Why is a raised level of cholesterol in the bloodstream a cause for concern in a person with cardiovascular disease?

● Cholesterol contributes to the development of fatty deposits in arterial walls; these may develop into atheromatous plaques, which can narrow the coronary arteries and lead to angina or MI.

● What is the main source of cholesterol in the bloodstream?

● A diet with a high fat content can lead to a raised cholesterol level. A person's cholesterol level will also be determined by the liver's ability to synthesise and internalise cholesterol, which is genetically determined (see Figure 3.3).

There are two main groups of drugs which reduce cholesterol levels. These are the **statins** and the **fibrates**. Statins reduce the production of cholesterol by the liver, and cause an increase in the uptake of LDL cholesterol from the blood, resulting in a reduction in levels of LDL and total cholesterol, with a proportional increase in HDL cholesterol levels (Figure 8.7). Taking a statin has been shown in trials to reduce the risk of developing an MI by approximately 29% (Thavendiranathan et al., 2006), and, in people with established heart disease, to reduce the likelihood of disease progression.

Fibrates work by increasing the proportion of HDL in the blood, but have a less marked effect on cholesterol levels than statins. They may be prescribed if a person cannot take statins because of side effects, if a statin alone is not reducing cholesterol levels sufficiently, or for certain familial conditions in which triglyceride levels are raised. If statins and fibrates fail to bring the blood cholesterol down to target levels, a number of other options are available, including ezetimibe, which inhibits the uptake of lipids from the intestine.

The commonest side effects of statins are pain in the muscles (myalgia), headache, abdominal pain, diarrhoea, flatulence, nausea and, occasionally, liver damage. Fibrates may also cause myalgia and gastrointestinal side effects. Taking a fibrate and a statin together significantly increases the risk of myalgia and muscle breakdown (rhabdomyolysis), which can damage the kidneys.

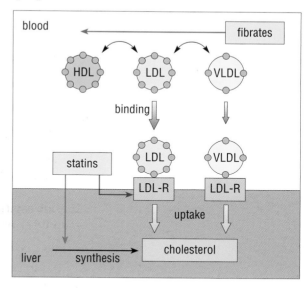

Figure 8.7 Statins inhibit the synthesis of cholesterol in the liver and increase the number of LDL-receptors, thus reducing the level of serum cholesterol. Fibrates produce a shift in the distribution of serum lipids towards the HDL form, resulting in a decrease in LDL and VLDL.

8.2.9 Summary of drugs used to treat cardiovascular diseases

The ways in which the various cardiovascular drugs exert their effects are summarised in Table 8.1, together with their side effects and specific examples in each group. It is important to distinguish between the general classes of drugs and specific formulations, which often have proprietary names from different companies.

Table 8.1 Drugs used to treat cardiovascular disease.

Class of drug	Examples	Main effect	Side effects
nitrates	glyceryl trinitrate Imdur™	stimulate NO release from vascular endothelium, causing vasodilation	headaches, flushing, hypotension
beta-blockers	carvedilol bisoprolol nebivolol atenolol	block beta-adrenoreceptors, reducing the effect of adrenalin on the heart	wheezing, headache, fatigue, sleep disturbance, cold extremities
calcium channel blockers	verapamil diltiazem amiodarone	prevent movement of calcium into arterial muscle cells, causes vasodilation as muscle cells relax	ankle oedema, headaches, dizziness, facial flushing
diuretics	furosemide bumetanide bendroflumethiazide	act on the cells of the kidney to cause salt and water loss	dehydration, electrolyte (ion) imbalance, frequent urination
ACE inhibitors	captopril ramipril lisinopril	prevent the production of ACE, causing salt and water loss and vasodilation	kidney failure, electrolyte (ion) imbalance, frequent urination, coughing
anti-arrhythmics	amiodarone digoxin verapamil	in general, reduce the electrical activity of the heart's conducting system	nausea, vomiting, taste disturbance, visual disturbance
thrombolytics	tenecteplase alteplase reteplase streptokinase	activate the plasmin system and break down fibrin	bleeding from elsewhere in the body
anti-platelet drugs	aspirin clopidogrel	inhibit platelet aggregation, reducing thrombus formation	bleeding, indigestion, nausea, wheezing
anti-coagulants	warfarin	prevent use of vitamin K, so that blood clotting proteins cannot be made	bleeding, rash, nausea, diarrhoea, hair loss
statins	simvastatin pravastatin atorvastatin lovastatin	reduce the liver's ability to make cholesterol, and increase the number of LDL receptors, hence increasing LDL breakdown	muscle pain, muscle breakdown, altered liver function, nausea, diarrhoea, headache
fibrates	bezafibrate ciprofibrate	cause shift in lipids from LDL to HDL	muscle pain, headache, diarrhoea, nausea

8.2.10 Drugs used to treat diabetes

Because diabetes is a risk factor for hypertension and cardiovascular disease, individuals may also be taking drugs to control their diabetes. These drugs act in a variety of ways to regulate the metabolism of glucose and the production and action of insulin, the hormone which controls how glucose is taken up by cells. They are described in SK120 *Diabetes care* (Chapter 4 of *Living with Diabetes*).

8.3 Secondary prevention of cardiovascular diseases with drugs

Any person with ischaemic heart disease is at risk of their condition deteriorating; this can result in worsening symptoms from angina or heart failure. A person who has had an MI or a transient ischaemic attack is more likely to have another. Some drugs can be taken to reduce the risk of progression of cardiovascular disease and can help protect the heart from damage if a person has already had an MI. It might seem obvious that drugs which can prevent the development of cardiovascular disease will be useful in treating the condition once it has developed, and vice versa. This may be true, but the assumption is unwarranted unless there is evidence to support it, based on drug trials in two different groups of people.

The recommendations in the next section are based on guidelines issued by NICE in 2001. They were revised in 2003 and are subject to periodic review. It should also be emphasised that the recommendations would be modified for individuals according to age, gender, ethnicity, and in light of other medical conditions.

8.3.1 Types of treatment

Beta-blockers

People with ischaemic heart disease are recommended to take a beta-blocker unless there is a specific contraindication, such as asthma. Beta-blockers reduce the risk of a person with heart disease having an MI. They also reduce the damage to the heart muscle cells if a person does have an MI, by reducing the strength of contraction and energy demand of the heart muscle.

Statins

In patients with heart disease, statins reduce the risk of further MI. It has been recommended that patients with ischaemic heart disease should take a statin even if their cholesterol level is not unduly high. The level of cholesterol should be reduced to less than 5 mmol/l or by 30% – whichever is the greatest reduction. The benefits from the use of statins are most evident in patients with the highest risk factors, so this recommendation is very much dependent on the individual (see Section 8.4.3; Manuel et al., 2006).

Anti-platelet drugs

In Section 8.2.7 you learned how aspirin and clopidogrel can reduce platelet aggregation and thrombus formation. In 1994, the Anti-platelet Trialists' Collaboration demonstrated that taking anti-platelet therapy (in particular, aspirin) helped prevent MI, strokes and deaths in people who have had an MI, angina, a stroke or transient ischaemic attack, coronary artery bypass graft surgery or angioplasty. People with any of these conditions are now routinely prescribed an anti-platelet medication.

ACE inhibitors

Taking an ACE inhibitor improves the prognosis of many patients who have had an MI. There is also evidence that any patient with cardiovascular disease should be prescribed an ACE inhibitor.

8.3.2 Evidence for secondary prevention

A large amount of research has been undertaken in the area of secondary prevention and there is much evidence about which medications will reduce the risk of disease progression. Some examples of these trials are summarised in Table 8.2.

Table 8.2 Drugs used for secondary prevention.

Type of drug	Trial	Date	Findings
aspirin	Anti-platelet Trialists' Collaboration	1994	after an MI, taking 75 mg of aspirin reduces risk of further MI by 30%
beta-blockers	First International Study of Infarct Survival (ISIS-1)	1986	following MI, beta-blocker therapy reduces mortality by 20% over 2 years
statins	Scandinavian Simvastatin Survival Study (4S)	1994	after an MI, reducing cholesterol level to <5 mmol/l or by 30% reduces risk of further MI by 30%
ACE inhibitors	Fourth International Study of Infarct Survival (ISIS-4)	1995	following MI, an ACE inhibitor reduces the incidence of heart failure, recurrent MI and death from heart disease

Activity 8.1   Identifying which drugs are used for different conditions

Suggested study time 30 minutes

Fill in Table 8.3 to show which drugs are used to treat which conditions. Put a tick if you think a drug is used to treat a particular condition, a cross if a drug can make a condition worse and leave the square blank if a drug has no effect on the condition. Use this activity to review and revise everything that you have learned about the different drug treatments for the various conditions.

Table 8.3 Revision of uses of drugs to treat and prevent cardiovascular disease.

Type of drug	Angina	Heart failure	Arrhythmias	Secondary prevention
nitrates				
beta-blockers				
calcium channel blockers				
digoxin				
diuretics				
ACE inhibitors				
anti-platelet drugs				
amiodarone				
statins				

Comment

Compare your completed table with the one given in the answers to questions for this chapter.

8.4 How drugs are evaluated

● Which aspects of a drug need to be evaluated before it can be prescribed for a particular medical condition?

● A drug's safety, effectiveness and optimum dose need to be established before it can be prescribed.

To assess these aspects adequately, drugs are required to undergo different stages of evaluation in clinical trials. Once a drug has been developed in the laboratory, it will normally be tested on animals for safety and efficacy. If there are no adverse effects, the drug may proceed to clinical trials.

Phase 1 trials normally last several months and are designed to test the safety of drugs in humans and the best route of administration (for example, by mouth or by injection). These studies investigate how well the body processes the drug and any side effects which may result from increasing the dosage.

Phase 2 trials test the effectiveness and safety of a drug. Most phase 2 trials are randomised controlled trials (RCTs), which are described in more detail in Section 8.4.1. The experimental drug is given to one group of volunteers, while another group is given a placebo (a 'dummy' pill with no active ingredient).

Phase 3 trials are also RCTs but are carried out on a much larger number of people. These studies aim to measure how well a drug works on larger populations, and to fine-tune doses and safety procedures.

Of the numerous drugs which are developed in the laboratory, only a very small fraction will make it as far as phase 3. If phase 3 trials are successfully completed, a licence can be granted for the drug, which may then be prescribed for certain conditions.

Even after a drug has been licensed for use, doctors will be alert to the possibility of unexpected adverse effects in particular patients. Systems are in place in many countries to report such adverse effects to licensing authorities.

Why might a drug, which has been successively tested in many patients and shown to be safe and effective, have unexpected adverse effects in some individuals? Some individuals will have uncommon genetic variants, which means that they do not metabolise the drugs or respond to them in the same way as most other people. Some people will be taking other drugs, which may interact with the treatment. Although the phase 2 and 3 trials will aim to identify such drug interactions, individuals may self-medicate, use inappropriate amounts of other drugs, or use untested herbal remedies that contain active ingredients. The potential variety of such interactions is so enormous that it is not possible to anticipate and test every combination. In addition, clinical trials take place over a limited period of time, and long-term effects of the treatment may not become apparent during this period.

8.4.1 Randomised controlled trials (RCTs)

An RCT is the most rigorous way of testing the effectiveness and safety of any treatment. Volunteers are randomly assigned to receive either the drug being tested or a control drug (either a placebo or the drug currently being used to treat the condition). Their response to the drug is then monitored and recorded.

To explain the steps in an RCT, we will follow an imaginary new ACE inhibitor, openopril, through an RCT designed to assess its effect on blood pressure.

- A group of 500 volunteers are selected, all of whom have high blood pressure.
- The volunteers are randomly assigned to receive either openopril or a placebo. Those receiving the placebo are known as the **control group**.
- The trial is **double-blind**. This means that neither the volunteers nor the researchers are aware which drug each volunteer is receiving. This is often achieved by a computer program allocating each volunteer a random number to determine which drug will be used. The 'code' of random numbers is only revealed at the end of the trial, indicating whether a placebo or an active treatment has been used.
- Each volunteer's blood pressure is measured before starting treatment and at monthly intervals.
- At each blood pressure check, each volunteer is asked to record anything which they feel may be a side effect from taking the medication.
- At the end of a 6-month period, the data are collated to give an assessment as to whether openopril has had a significant effect on blood pressure and whether it has caused any significant side effects.

- Why is it important for a trial to be double-blind?

- To eliminate any bias which a volunteer or researcher may have. A volunteer may believe they are gaining greater benefit if they are aware that they are taking the active drug. (This may be more important for drugs where the measured response is subjective, for example anti-depressants or painkillers.) Likewise, a researcher may treat a volunteer differently knowing that the volunteer is taking an active drug. If a trial is double-blind, this potential source of bias is eliminated.

Occasionally, RCTs can demonstrate additional benefits of a drug. The anti-smoking drug bupropion (see Section 10.2.4) was originally developed as an anti-depressant. During trials, smokers who were taking buprorion reported less desire to smoke. Further tests showed the drug was effective in helping smokers quit, and buproprion is now licensed as a smoking cessation drug.

Activity 8.2   Investigating a drug treatment

Suggested study time 1 hour

Use the internet to find out about a specific drug used in the treatment of cardiovascular disease. This could be one of the drugs mentioned in Table 8.1, or it may be a drug which someone you know has taken for heart disease. Try to find out as much as you can about your chosen drug – for example, any prescription recommendations, doses, dosing regimes, costs, side effects and contraindications.

Once you have established how the drug is used, take a step back to establish which authority has licensed it for use or recommended it for use in your country.

Using an advanced internet search is an effective way of finding this type of information. For example, if you want to know how warfarin has been evaluated, use Google's advanced search by typing 'randomised controlled trial' into the box entitled 'with the exact phrase' and typing 'warfarin' into the box entitled 'with all of the words'.

Comment

There is lots of information out there, which can be found using a suitable search strategy. You should look carefully at the provenance of the information supplied. Information from independent sites is likely to be more balanced than those with a vested interest, such as drug companies or specific patient groups. Misinformation can find its way onto the internet, including wikis, so it is important to cross-check important findings with original documents if at all possible.

8.4.2 Cost-effectiveness of drugs

The cost of prescription drugs for cardiovascular disease is staggering. In 2004, the spending in the UK was greater than £2 billion, while in the USA more than US$12 billion was spent on controlling blood pressure alone. Since the closing years of the twentieth century, there has been a progressive rise in the cost of prescribing, mostly due to lipid-regulating drugs, ACE inhibitors and anti-platelet drugs. Table 8.4 shows the costs of prescribing drugs for cardiovascular disease in the UK in 2003.

Table 8.4 The number of prescriptions of drugs for cardiovascular disease in the UK in 2003.

Type of drug	Prescriptions	Total cost
diuretics	32 million	£50 million
renin/angiotensin system drugs	26 million	£460 million
nitrates and potassium-channel activators	10 million	£80 million
anti-platelet drugs	26 million	£120 million
beta-blockers	24 million	£90 million
other anti-hypertensive drugs	4 million	£110 million
calcium channel blockers	18 million	£310 million
lipid-regulating drugs	22 million	£770 million

● What is the cost per prescription for each of the types of drug, based on these figures?

● As one example, the figures for diuretics are £1.56 per prescription (£50 million/32 million).

Clearly, there is a big difference between the average cost of a diuretic prescription (£1.56) and lipid-regulating drugs, including statins (£35). Given that health resources are limited, it therefore is necessary for clinicians and policy-makers to analyse what drugs are most cost-effective. Let us take the example of statins – drugs that are expensive, but have also been shown to be effective in reducing the incidence of MI. Analysis of a number of different studies (meta-analysis) indicates that treatment with statins is cost-effective in populations with a high annual risk of cardiovascular disease (>4%), and is not cost-effective in populations with a low annual risk (<1%). For groups with intermediate risk (1–4%), it depends on the particular cohort under study, including their age and country of origin (Franco et al., 2005). In fact, the cost–benefit analysis for different drugs may vary from year to year, as specific drugs come off patent and more generic equivalents become available.

Such arguments are important in evaluating whether it would be cost-effective to use a polypill for primary prevention in a large section of the population (see Section 4.8, Table 4.2). The benefits are comparatively limited for individuals in low-risk populations, but the possibility of adverse effects remains.

8.5 Treating the individual

The previous sections have explained the treatments that a person with cardiovascular disease may be recommended. In practice, however, not all people with heart disease are able to take the treatments recommended for them, and not all choose to take them. Studies on people with chronic conditions have shown that adherence to drug regimes is surprisingly low (Schroeder et al., 2004). Often, less than 50% of individuals adhere to their prescribed drug regime. The level of adherence depends on the group of people; for example, older people are more likely to take a prescribed course of drugs for cardiovascular disease than younger people. It is important, however, that people do take their prescribed drugs. Unsurprisingly, mortality after an MI is lower in people who adhere to their prescribed course of statins and beta-blockers (Rasmussen et al., 2007). In the last 10 years, there has been a progressive change in attitude, from 'compliance' to 'concordance', meaning that clinicians will try to engage their patients in the process of medication, rather than telling them what to do. It is hoped that engaging patients will mean that they are more likely to adhere to their prescribed drug regimes, although the evidence for the effectiveness of this approach is still doubtful (McDonald et al., 2002).

● Can you think of any reasons why a person may be unable to or may choose not to take a recommended medication?

● A person may experience, or worry that they may experience, side effects from a medication. Some people find it difficult to swallow tablets, and it may also be difficult to remember to take tablets on a regular basis. Certain medications may interact with other medications which may be necessary for other medical conditions.

Case Study 8.2   The side effects of Winifred Fowler's medication

After the initial lapse with her medication, Winifred has resolved to be more careful about taking her tablets at the right time and to keep track of what she should be taking. On the second day, shortly after taking her morning tablets, Winifred starts to feel peculiar. She becomes flushed and dizzy, and has a dreadful headache. She has to rush to the toilet to pass urine very often during the morning and is beginning to think that she would rather have the breathlessness than feel this way. Winifred was expecting to visit her doctor in four days' time anyway, but Frank persuades her to ring the surgery to ask if this is what she should expect with these tablets. She is not able to get through to Dr Chivers immediately, but speaks to the practice nurse, who is not sure what has been prescribed by the hospital. He explains that it is very important that she continues to take the tablets prescribed, partly because that is what the cardiologist thinks is needed, and partly because starting or stopping a series of prescribed medicines can have unexpected side effects. He does his best to reassure her, and asks her to discuss her symptoms with Dr Chivers when she sees her. Winifred is not wholly convinced by these reassurances. She decides to stop taking the tablets, at least until she has spoken to Dr Chivers.

By the third day, Frank is becoming increasingly worried about Winifred. Since stopping her tablets, she is getting a lot more chest pain and cannot walk to the local newsagent because she gets so out of breath. She is also spending a lot of time brooding about the possibility of having another heart attack. The following day, she sees Dr Chivers, explaining her symptoms and that she has stopped the tablets as they made her feel unwell.

Dr Chivers spends some time talking to her about the reasons for taking her tablets. She suggests that Winifred starts taking the tablets prescribed by the hospital and explains that these are to reduce her risk of having any further heart attacks. She also prescribes a nitrate to help with her chest pain, but advises her to start at a low dose and to increase gradually the amount she takes. She arranges to see Winifred the following week to see how she is getting on and makes her an appointment with the practice nurse to discuss diet, exercise and smoking. She also arranges for Winifred to see the cardiac rehabilitation nurse in two weeks' time.

● Considering the side effects of the drugs that are prescribed for cardiovascular disease, what medication do you think the cardiologist has prescribed for Winifred Fowler?

● The side effects of various drugs are listed in Table 8.1. In view of the prescribing recommendations for a person who has had an MI (Section 8.3), it is likely that she has been prescribed a beta-blocker (headache) and an ACE inhibitor (frequent urination).

People often do not know exactly why they have been prescribed a particular type of medication, nor the implications of stopping. A lack of information and communication by health care professionals is a common problem with taking tablets. In addition, many people forget what they are told by a doctor or nurse – it can be helpful to have written information about any treatment.

Some people find it difficult to remember to take tablets, particularly if they have never had to take any tablets before. A doctor or pharmacist may be able to give advice about ways of remembering, such as putting the tablets in a prominent place, setting an alarm or mobile phone to go off when a dose of tablets is due or using dosette boxes. These are boxes in which tablets are placed a week in advance, forming an easy way to check at the end of the day if tablets have been taken (Figure 8.8).

Figure 8.8   A dosette box with a week's supply of pills for cardiovascular disease.

A further problem is that of interactions between different tablets. Winifred may be on several tablets which lower her blood pressure. Each tablet on its own may not cause a problem, but, taken together, the combination of tablets may be lowering her blood pressure excessively and causing her to feel dizzy.

There may also be practical problems with taking medicines. Some people find it very difficult to swallow tablets, whereas others work shifts and so find it hard to take tablets at regular intervals. Some tablets have to be taken with food, and people may be reluctant to do this if, for example, they are going out for a meal. This list is by no means exhaustive, and other problems may occur.

● Why is it important for people who are taking medicines to understand why they are taking them? Think of both practical and psychological reasons.

● Knowing what medicines they are taking – and why they are taking them – will allow people to feel more in control of their own condition, and possibly more aware of their health in the broadest sense. Knowing the potential effects and side effects of a medication will allow the person to identify them if they occur and distinguish them from symptoms of the medical condition. Understanding how the medicine works will allow the person to relate their treatment and the dose regimes to their condition, with a greater likelihood of adherence to the course of treatment.

8.5.1 Methods of taking medicines

● What different methods can you think of to take a medicine?

● There are several different routes of administration for medicines. The most common way of taking a medicine is orally, as a tablet or liquid. Medicines can also be injected – into a vein, a muscle or just below the skin. Some medicines can be inhaled, whereas some are given as a patch to be applied to the skin. Others can be put under the tongue or administered as suppositories.

There are various factors which determine the best route of administration for a drug. For example, some drugs are not well absorbed from the gut. In addition, enzymes in the stomach may break down a drug before it can be absorbed. An example of this is insulin, used to treat diabetes, which has to be injected because it is broken down in the stomach.

Some drugs may be well absorbed by the digestive system but are then broken down by the liver – this is known as **first-pass metabolism**. An example of this is glyceryl trinitrate, used for the relief of angina. If taken by mouth, glyceryl trinitrate will be almost entirely metabolised by the liver, leaving virtually no active drug. Hence, glyceryl trinitrate is given **sublingually** – meaning that either a tablet or a spray is put under the tongue and the glyceryl trinitrate is absorbed directly into the bloodstream via blood vessels located under the tongue (Figure 8.9). Glyceryl trinitrate may also be given as a **transdermal patch** to be applied

Figure 8.9   Glyceryl trinitrate being administered as a sublingual spray.

to the skin – this provides a gradual release into the circulation, again avoiding first-pass metabolism.

Compare this with a different type of nitrate called isosorbide mononitrate. This is well absorbed from the digestive system. Its chemical makeup is different from glyceryl trinitrate and it is not metabolised by the liver. Isosorbide mononitrate is taken as a tablet and almost all of the active ingredient in the tablet is absorbed into the circulation.

These different variables mean that for certain drugs, not all of the drug which is taken is actually used by the body. The **bioavailability** of a drug refers to the difference between the amount of the drug administered and the actual dose received at the target site in the body, often recorded as a percentage.

- Which drug will have the greater bioavailability when taken as a tablet: glyceryl trinitrate or isosorbide mononitrate?

- Isosorbide mononitrate will have greater bioavailablity. If glyceryl trinitrate is taken as a tablet, most of it will be broken down by the liver. The bioavailablity of oral glyceryl trinitrate is <1%, whereas that of oral isosorbide mononitrate is nearly 100%.

8.5.2 Dosing regimes

The frequency with which a drug should be taken varies considerably, depending on exactly what the drug is. Some drugs are absorbed much more quickly than others. Moreover, the rate at which drugs are broken down (metabolised) or passed out in the urine (excreted) also varies greatly. Hence the level of a drug that is present in the blood will depend on the rate of uptake, breakdown and excretion. In addition, some drugs move from the blood into cells or tissues more quickly than others. The science that underlies what happens to drugs within the body is called **pharmacodynamics**, and each drug is a study in itself. These differences explain why some drugs need to be taken more frequently than others. For example, warfarin is taken once a day, whereas nitrates often need to be taken several times a day. The aim in devising the dosing regime is very often to maintain the amount of the drug in the blood at a level which is therapeutically effective. This means that the level of the drug is maintained above the effective dose (the minimum dose producing the desired effect), but below the **toxic dose** (the minimum dose producing a damaging effect) – i.e. in the **therapeutic range** of the drug.

- For a person who is taking a drug regularly, what determines the frequency with which the drug has to be taken?

- The speed with which the drug is eliminated from the body, either by being broken down or by excretion.

The half-life of a drug is the time taken for the concentration of the drug in blood plasma to reduce to half of its original level, assuming that the person has not taken another dose of the drug in the meantime. The most common ways in which a drug is eliminated from the body are to be broken down by the liver or excreted by the kidneys in the urine.

A drug with a half-life of a few hours (for example, isosorbide mononitrate, which has a half-life of around 6 hours) will fall below the effective dose in the bloodstream fairly quickly. It therefore needs to be taken more than once during a 24-hour period to try to keep the level of the drug within the therapeutic range.

● If the concentration of isosorbide mononitrate in a person's blood at 8 a.m. is 60 µg/l (60 millionths of a gram per litre), and they do not take any further tablets during the day, what will be the concentration in the blood at 8 p.m. on that day?

● The level is approximately 15 µg/l. The concentration halves in the first 6 hours and halves again in the next 6 hours, becoming one quarter of the original level.

By comparison, warfarin has a half-life of between 40 and 70 hours. Warfarin is given as a single daily dose, and has to be taken for several days before the level of the drug reaches the therapeutic range. Figure 8.10 compares the rate at which warfarin and aspirin are lost from the blood.

The half-life of a drug may vary from person to person, meaning that some drugs may need to have their doses varied in different people. An example of this is elderly people, when their kidneys become less efficient at filtering the blood. Drugs which are normally excreted by the kidneys, such as lisinopril and digoxin, can build up in the blood. For this reason, many drugs are given at lower doses in older people.

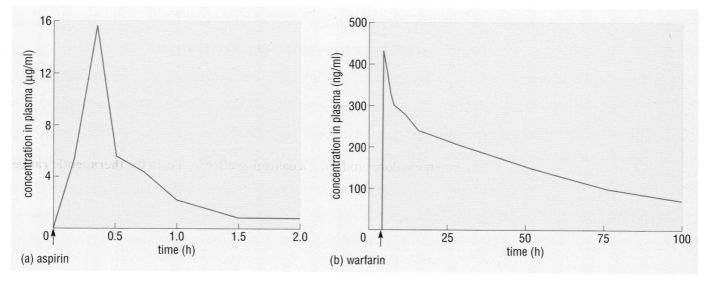

Figure 8.10   Average concentrations of (a) aspirin (soluble tablet, 500 mg) and (b) warfarin (tablet, 7.5 mg) in blood plasma over time. Aspirin is lost quickly and therefore needs to be taken every 4 hours to maintain the effective dose. Warfarin is lost slowly, and a daily dose regime is sufficient. Note that the biological effects of aspirin in inhibiting platelet aggregation continue for some time after the plasma level has fallen below the therapeutic range.

8.5.3 Drug interactions

You have already learned about the various side effects that certain medications may cause. A further problem, particularly when several medications are taken together, is that of **drug interactions**. We will now look at some examples of drug interactions and the reasons why they occur.

● What effect do beta-blockers and calcium channel blockers exert on heart muscle cells?

● Both groups of drugs cause a reduction in the strength with which the heart cells can contract.

If two drugs that cause a similar effect are given to someone, this effect may be exaggerated. In the case of beta-blockers and calcium channel blockers, it may cause an episode of heart failure, which may be serious enough to warrant hospital admission. If verapamil is given with a beta-blocker, the heart may stop completely.

A similar effect can be seen if two drugs are given that cause hypotension. For example, a beta-blocker given with an ACE inhibitor can cause profound hypotension.

Once absorbed into the circulation, a drug may be bound to a protein in the blood. Administering another drug which also binds to the same protein may affect the level of the first drug in the bloodstream. An example of this is warfarin and aspirin, which both strongly bind to plasma proteins. If a patient taking warfarin starts to take aspirin, both drugs will compete to bind with the plasma proteins. Some of the warfarin will be displaced from its protein, which will increase the amount of free warfarin in the blood and can significantly increase the risk of bleeding.

8.6 Choosing the right treatment

General recommendations for the treatment of cardiovascular disease are based on studies of large groups of people, who will usually differ in age, gender, ethnicity and, to some degree, in their medical condition. Within these large cohorts, some people will respond better to particular drugs than others; some will suffer side effects, whereas others will not. For these reasons, general recommendations on prescribing need to be modified according to the particular medical condition and characteristics of an individual. There is an increasing understanding that the genetic makeup of a person will affect how their condition develops, how they respond to drugs and whether they are susceptible to adverse side effects. It therefore follows that drug treatment should ideally be tailored according to an individual's genetic makeup. This approach is called **pharmacogenetics** or **pharmacogenomics** (Johnson and Cavallari, 2005).

Genetic variation (see Section 3.4) particularly affects the way in which different drugs are metabolised. For example, the breakdown of warfarin is primarily controlled by an enzyme that varies between individuals. Up to 40% of Caucasian people have variants (SNPs) which cause the enzyme's activity to be reduced. Consequently, warfarin breaks down more slowly in these people and a lower dose is required to maintain the therapeutic level in the blood. The variants are much less common in non-Caucasian individuals. Genetic variation also affects the metabolism of diuretics, beta-blockers and aspirin. In addition, the target molecules of drugs (e.g. receptors) may also vary between individuals, so that a drug which is effective in one person is either more effective or less effective in another – even when the level in the blood is the same in both people.

Often, our understanding of the genetic basis of disease and drug treatment is incomplete. In other cases, the appropriate genetic tests are not generally available, so knowledge of pharmacogenetics is not used to devise individual treatment plans. Nevertheless, the principle still applies that general medication guidelines need to be adapted to the individual.

8.6.1 Assessing treatment options for an individual

Symptoms

The symptoms a person is experiencing may give some indication of what is wrong with them and suggest the most appropriate treatment. For example, a person experiencing chest pain when walking uphill may have angina, and so may be advised to take a nitrate or a beta-blocker. A person with breathlessness may have heart failure, which may improve with an ACE inhibitor.

Signs

A doctor or nurse may be able to tell what the problem is by examining a person. For example, an irregular heart beat could be a sign of an arrhythmia, and an anti-arrhythmic may be recommended for this. Ankle swelling could mean heart failure, and an ACE inhibitor or diuretic may help ease this.

Investigations

Certain tests can be carried out in a GP surgery to determine the best treatment.

- A blood pressure test can determine whether someone has hypertension, in which case medication may be suggested to reduce it. If it reveals hypotension, certain drugs cannot be given.
- A cholesterol test can assess the need for a cholesterol-lowering treatment.
- An ECG can determine whether someone has an arrhythmia, in which case medication may be offered to restore normal heart rhythms.

Other tests may require a visit to hospital.

- An exercise tolerance test is used to determine whether a person has angina – and, if so, to assess its severity.
- An angiogram will assess the extent of blockage of the coronary arteries and whether this can be overcome by angioplasty, stent insertion or coronary artery bypass grafting (see Chapter 9).
- An echocardiogram can determine the severity of heart failure. It can also show whether a person with an arrhythmia has a problem with their heart valves, which may make the arrhythmia more difficult to treat.

General health

If surgery is contemplated, the general health and wellbeing of a person must be assessed. Having an anaesthetic can be dangerous and an operation may be too risky for a person with severe damage to the heart. Occasionally, other conditions (e.g. asthma or diabetes), if severe, may make the use of anaesthetic too much of a risk. A health assessment is likely to involve a full physical examination, blood tests, an ECG and a chest X-ray.

8.6.2 General recommendations

Although medication needs to be adapted to the individual, general guidelines on the use of drugs are extremely valuable because they are based on evidence from many different studies – RCTs, usually. In the UK, NICE provides guidance to health care professionals on the appropriate treatment and care of people with specific diseases and conditions, and also advises on health promotion. It does this by examining evidence from trial data about different treatments in order to decide which treatments will give the most benefit in terms of symptom relief and long-term outcome. Some of NICE's decisions may also be based on the cost-effectiveness of different treatments.

In terms of cardiovascular disease, NICE has issued guidelines on a variety of subjects, including treatment after an MI, treatment of heart failure and treatment of hypertension. The information and findings are freely available from their website (see Activity 8.3).

Activity 8.3   The scientific basis for recommending medicines

Suggested study time 1 hour

In Sections 8.2 and 8.3, you have learned that certain drugs are recommended to treat a particular condition. For this activity, use the internet to investigate the evidence that supports the recommendation given by NICE that people who have had an MI should be treated with a beta-blocker in order to reduce the risk of a further MI. To begin with, you could visit the NICE website at http://www.nice.org.uk, perhaps looking at the patient summary of their guidance for patients who have experienced an MI or a similar piece of the NICE guidelines. Try to identify the evidence upon which the recommendation to take a particular drug is based. Aim to answer the following questions.

(a) How many double-blind trials were made of the long-term effects of beta-blockers in unselected people who had had one MI between 1975 and 2000 – fewer than 5 trials, 5–10 trials or more than 10 trials?

(b) In 1993, a study was reported in the *Journal of the American College of Cardiologists* on the effects of continuing digoxin treatment or withdrawing it from patients who had suffered an MI. The first author of the paper was Dr B. F. Uretsky. Locate the abstract (summary) of this paper, which can be readily found through an internet search. How many individuals were included in the study, and what was its conclusion? Write down the full reference of the paper, including authors, date, title, journal, volume and page numbers.

Comment

(a) There are at least 25 double-blind trials on the long-term use of beta-blockers in people who have had an MI.

(b) In total, 88 people took part in the study: 46 were in the control group, taking a placebo, and 42 continued taking digoxin. The study gave strong evidence for the benefit of taking digoxin (higher capacity for aerobic exercise and fewer treatment failures), provided that patients had a normal sinus rhythm, mild to moderate chronic heart failure, and were also treated with diuretics. The reference is:

Uretsky, B. F., Young, J. B., Shahidi, F. E., Yellen, L. G., Harrison, M. C. and Jolly, M. K. (1993) 'Randomised study assessing the effect of digoxin withdrawal in patients with mild to moderate chronic congestive heart failure: results of the PROVED trial. PROVED Investigative Group', *Journal of the American College of Cardiology*, **22**, pp. 955–962.

8.7 Summary of Chapter 8

In this chapter, you have learned about various aspects of the medical management of cardiovascular disease. You should have a good understanding of the different groups of drugs used to treat heart disease, the ways in which these drugs act on the various tissues of the body, and the net effects the drugs have on the heart and circulation. You should also understand how drugs are developed and some of the factors to be taken into account when treating individuals and populations.

As you learned in the introduction, treatment with medication is only one aspect of the management of cardiovascular disease. A person with heart disease may benefit from surgery and will certainly be offered advice about their lifestyle. You will learn about these aspects of treatment in the final two chapters of this book.

Questions for Chapter 8

Question 8.1 (Learning Outcomes 8.1, 8.2, 8.4 and 8.8)

Explain why aspirin tablets (taken for secondary prevention of MI, for example) have to be taken several times each day, whereas warfarin needs to be taken only once per day.

Question 8.2 (Learning Outcomes 8.2, 8.4, and 8.5)

Why is dizziness a possible side effect of taking calcium channel blockers?

Question 8.3 (Learning Outcomes 8.1, 8.2, 8.4, 8.5 and 8.6)

Where in the body do ACE inhibitors have their effect, and what is their function in treating heart disease?

Question 8.4 (Learning Outcomes 8.2, 8.4, 8.5 and 8.6)

Where in the body do statins act, and what is their function in treating cardiovascular disease?

Question 8.5 (Learning Outcomes 8.2 and 8.3)

Why would giving an explanation of a drug's actions to a post-myocardial-infarction patient produce an improved chance of preventing a further MI in that patient?

Question 8.6 (Learning Outcomes 8.3, 8.7 and 8.8)

Outline how drugs are evaluated, and explain why a drug that passes a phase 3 clinical trial may still have adverse effects in some people.

Further reading

If you would like to read further, please refer to the following publications.

National Institute for Health and Clinical Excellence (2007) *NICE guideline on prophylaxis for patients who have experienced a myocardial infarction* [online] Available from: http://www.nice.org.uk/guidance/CGA (Accessed April 2007).

Rang, H. P., Dale, M. M. and Ritter, J. M. (1999) *Pharmacology* (4th edition), London, Churchill Livingstone.

References

Aronow, W. S. (1997) 'Postinfarction use of beta-blockers in elderly patients', *Drugs Aging*, **11**, pp. 424–432.

Everly, M. J., Heaton, P. C. and Cluxton, R. J. (2004) 'Beta-blocker underuse in secondary prevention of myocardial infarction', *Annals of Pharmacotherapy*, **38**, pp. 286–293.

Franco, O. H., Peeters, A., Looman, C. W. N. and Bonneux, L. (2005) 'Cost effectiveness of statins in coronary heart disease', *Journal of Epidemiology and Community Health*, **59**, pp. 927–933.

Hayden, M., Pignone, M., Phillips, C. and Mulrow, C. (2002) 'Aspirin for the primary prevention of cardiovascular events', *Annals of Internal Medicine*, **136**, pp. 161–172.

Johnson, J. A. and Cavallari, J. H. (2005) 'Cardiovascular pharmacogenomics', *Experimental Physiology*, **90**, pp. 283–289.

Manuel, D. G., Lim, J., Tanuseputro, P., Anderson, G. M., Alter, D. A., Laupacis, A. and Mustard, C. A. (2006) 'Revisiting Rose: Strategies for reducing coronary heart disease', *British Medical Journal*, **332**, pp. 659–662.

McDonald, H. P., Garg, A. X. and Haynes, R. B. (2002) 'Interventions to enhance patient adherence to medication prescriptions', *Journal of the American Medical Association*, **288**, pp. 2868–2879.

Rasmussen, J. N., Chong, A. and Alter, D. A. (2007) 'Relationship between adherence to evidence-based pharmacotherapy and long-term mortality after acute myocardial infarction', *Journal of the American Medical Association*, **297**, pp. 177–186.

Schroeder, K., Fahey, T. and Ebrahim, S. (2004) 'How can we improve adherence to blood pressure-lowering medication in ambulatory care? Systematic review of randomized controlled trials', *Archives of Internal Medicine*, **164**, pp. 722–732.

Thavendiranathan, P., Bagai, A., Brookhart, A. and Choudhry, N. K. (2006) 'Primary prevention of cardiovascular diseases with statin therapy. A meta-analysis of randomized controlled trials', *Archives Of Internal Medicine*, **166**, pp. 2307–2313.

CHAPTER 9

SURGICAL MANAGEMENT OF CARDIOVASCULAR DISEASES

Learning Outcomes

When you have completed this chapter you should be able to:

9.1 Define and use, or recognise definitions and applications of, each of the terms printed in **bold** in the text.

9.2 Describe how a patient needs to prepare for cardiovascular surgery and how surgery affects a patient's lifestyle.

9.3 Outline the different types of surgical treatments available to someone with cardiovascular disease.

9.4 Understand the differences between invasive and non-invasive treatments.

9.5 Locate information on the internet and multimedia resources. Understand and interpret data on surgical treatments.

9.6 Describe the range of implantable devices used to treat cardiovascular disease.

9.7 Relate the use of different surgical procedures to the severity of cardiovascular disease.

9.8 Understand the complications associated with surgery for cardiovascular disease.

9.9 Describe the surgical methods used to increase coronary blood flow.

9.1 Introduction

In Chapter 8 you read about the medical management of cardiovascular diseases. Unfortunately, heart failure, vascular and valvular diseases cannot always be controlled by drugs, and often some form of surgery is advised – particularly when devices have to be implanted into the body. In some people where heart failure is very severe and drug therapy has been unsuccessful, a heart transplant may be an option.

Surgical treatments for angina, breathlessness or heart attacks usually follow unsuccessful drug therapy. This is because, with the possible exception of MIs, surgical procedures carry a higher risk of damage to the patient and are therefore not the first choice of treatment. Where facilities exist, such as in urban areas, the use of angioplasty is associated with lower mortality and is better than thrombolysis, as long as it can be carried out quickly after the MI.

So what surgical treatments will be considered? This depends very much on the severity of the problem and whether it is a chronic (long-term) or acute (sudden and life-threatening). Treatments range from the more 'routine' ones such as angioplasty, in which the patient is awake during the procedure, to cardiac transplantation, in which the patient is deeply anaesthetised and their life is entirely dependent on various external and internal devices such as heart–lung machines and ventilators. The surgical treatment plan follows a well proven path preceded by thorough investigations such as those described in Chapter 7.

The surgical procedures described in this chapter follow a broadly logical progression from the least invasive to the most invasive surgery. However, you will soon see that technological advances in the last few years mean that the division is often blurred. In addition, advances are so rapid that even heart valve replacement can now be performed following relatively minor surgery – often referred to as 'keyhole' surgery by the media. Any technical advance that removes the need for deep anaesthesia and opening up the chest is to be welcomed because the chances of survival are improved and the complications are minimised.

About 39 000 people in the UK have heart surgery each year (Society of Cardiothoracic Surgeons of Great Britain and Ireland, 2003). Of these, 25 000 have coronary bypass surgery, 9 500 have surgery on the heart valves and about 4000 have surgery to correct congenital abnormalities of the heart. On the whole, operations on the heart are routine and safe, although risks vary depending on the person's state of health.

If you are waiting for heart surgery, you must use the time wisely to increase your level of fitness. If you smoke, you should stop; if you are overweight, you should lose some weight. However, you may not be in a position to keep physically active because of your condition (British Heart Foundation, 2005a).

As with words in the rest of medicine, it is commonplace for the names of surgical procedures to be derived from Latin or Greek. It was mentioned in Chapter 1 that it is difficult – if not impossible – to work out what these terms mean without knowledge of how they break down into parts and what these parts mean. The more familiar you become with the subject, the easier this analysis becomes. As an example, the surgical term 'cardiac angioplasty' breaks down into 'cardiac' (of the heart) 'angio-' (blood vessel) and '-plasty' (shaping or forming). Therefore, cardiac angioplasty means surgery to widen a blood vessel in the heart; analogously, aortic valvuloplasty means surgery to repair a valve in the aorta.

9.2 Coronary angioplasty and stent placement

Coronary angioplasty is an invasive procedure used to stretch coronary arteries that have been narrowed due to build-up of plaques (see Sections 5.5 and 5.6). It is used to treat patients with angina or those who have had a heart attack. It is also called **percutaneous transluminal coronary angioplasty** (**PTCA**). The technique is carried out in hospitals in the catheter laboratory, usually under local anaesthesia and sedation, and its intended outcome is to improve regional coronary blood flow. The technique is similar to coronary angiography (see Section 7.5.3).

The widest parts of the coronary arteries are those that are proximal – a term used to describe the part of the artery that is closest to its origin in the aorta. If, after

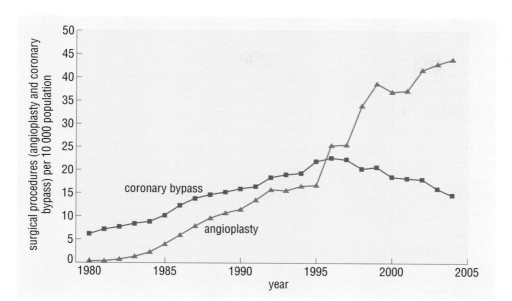

Figure 9.1 The numbers of angioplasty and coronary bypass operations per 10 000 of the population in the USA between 1980 and 2005.

initial investigations, the proximal parts of a coronary artery are found to be stenosed (narrowed) then this places a large area of the myocardium at risk, and someone in this state is a potential candidate for coronary angioplasty.

The first successful angioplasty was reported in 1977. Since then, the numbers of less invasive procedures, including angioplasty, have risen noticeably. In contrast, the numbers of more invasive procedures, such as coronary bypass (see Figure 9.1) and cardiac transplantation, have tended to decrease or level off.

The coronary angioplasty procedure takes about an hour and requires a specialist team including a cardiologist, a radiographer, a cardiac technician and a nurse. The area on the skin where the catheter will be inserted is cleaned and covered in sterile drapes. The team selects the artery to be used – most commonly the femoral artery. Local anaesthetic is injected into the area in the groin where a small incision is made to enable the catheter to enter the femoral artery and be pushed in the direction of the heart (see Figure 9.2). If the person having the angioplasty is agitated, the nurse may give them a sedative. During the procedure, the patient has to lie still on a special table and have ECG leads attached to them to allow the electrical activity of the heart to be monitored.

The patient has a cannula (a small, flexible tube) inserted into a vein in their arm, to which an intravenous line (also referred to as an IV line) is attached. Heparin, a short-acting anticoagulant drug, is given to prevent the formation of blood clots that would otherwise form. Other drugs that affect platelet aggregation for a longer period of time (up to 12 hours) may also be administered via the intravenous line as well as a contrast

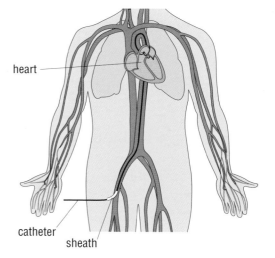

Figure 9.2 Cardiac catheterisation. A catheter is inserted into the femoral artery through an incision in the groin and is pushed towards the narrowed coronary artery. After administration of a contrast medium, fluoroscopy involves a series of short pulses of X-rays to produce a moving image showing the position of the catheter against the backdrop of the surrounding tissues. Precise detail is not needed, so each pulse gives a low radiation dose.

medium. The administration of the contrast medium can sometimes cause a person to feel sick, have a headache, experience palpitations or have various other sensations. These symptoms are all transient and resolve quickly. The contrast medium allows the vascular system to be viewed using X-ray techniques so that the surrounding tissues are shown in contrast – a technique called fluoroscopy (see Section 7.5.2).

A catheter containing a guide wire and another catheter with an inflatable balloon at the end is placed into the artery and pushed along its interior under X-ray guidance until the narrowed coronary artery is reached. The guide wire is pushed so that it is either side of the narrowing, i.e. it is extended beyond the narrowed area (see Figure 9.3a). The balloon at the tip of the catheter is then inflated for up to a minute in order to widen the interior of the artery and eventually allow the normal passage of blood through it and on to the ventricular muscle. During this period, the plaque deposit is flattened onto the wall of the artery, allowing the coronary artery to remain widened. To achieve optimum results and an adequate widening of the coronary artery, the balloon may need to be inflated several times.

Figure 9.3 Coronary angioplasty and stenting procedures. (a) Angioplasty involves stretching the affected artery by (i) inserting a balloon along a guide wire, (ii) inflating it at the site of the blockage and (iii) withdrawing the balloon. (b) Sometimes a fine wire mesh stent is used to hold the artery open and prevent any recurrence, shown here (i) around the balloon, (ii) being expanded as the balloon is inflated and (iii) remaining in place as the balloon is withdrawn.

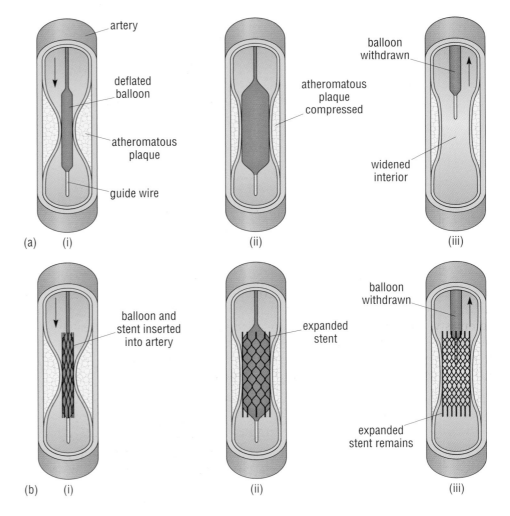

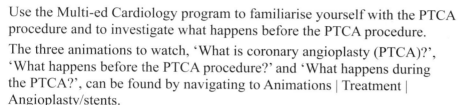

- Why is it not unusual to have angina-like symptoms during the angioplasty procedure?

- During the inflation of the angioplasty balloon, the normal blood flow through the coronary artery is interrupted for up to a minute on each occasion. This is sufficient time for pain-causing substances that are a by-product of metabolism to build up in the parts of the heart that the vessel perfuses. The pain disappears soon after the balloon is deflated. Angina is described in more detail in Chapter 6.

Activity 9.1   The PTCA procedure

Suggested study time 15 minutes

Use the Multi-ed Cardiology program to familiarise yourself with the PTCA procedure and to investigate what happens before the PTCA procedure.

The three animations to watch, 'What is coronary angioplasty (PTCA)?', 'What happens before the PTCA procedure?' and 'What happens during the PTCA?', can be found by navigating to Animations | Treatment | Angioplasty/stents.

Comment

Before the PTCA procedure you will be asked to fast and bring with you any medication. You will also be asked if you have any allergies or kidney problems and be advised when to stop or start your medications. It is particularly important that you should follow the advice on the use of warfarin.

- What does PTCA mean?

- PTCA is percutaneous transluminal coronary angioplasty. Percutaneous means through the skin, transluminal means that it is inside the artery, coronary means the heart and angioplasty to shape or extend a blood vessel.

After the balloon catheter is withdrawn, coronary angiography is undertaken immediately to assess the degree of arterial dilation and to look for complications. Occasionally, small tears in the inner wall of the coronary artery occur following angioplasty. These tears are called coronary dissections and must be treated immediately before they encourage the formation of blood clots that may block the artery completely. This occurs in about 3% of cases and sometimes requires emergency coronary bypass surgery (Greene et al., 1991).

An alternative to widening coronary arteries using angioplasty involves the placement of a **stent** in the restricted section of the artery (see Figure 9.3b). Stents are made of metal or polymer tubular mesh and are kept in a compressed state until they are expanded at the site of a narrowing in a coronary artery. A balloon is used to expand the stent and provide structural support for the artery wall, allowing it to remain open. Metal stents are left in a person's artery for the rest of their lives, whereas polymer stents dissolve away over a period of two to three years.

At the end of the operation, the balloon catheter, guide wire and guiding catheter are removed from the femoral artery and pressure is placed over the incision site until the bleeding stops. People who have this procedure will sometimes stay in hospital overnight. For the two weeks following angioplasty or the placement of stents, the person takes anticoagulation medication such as aspirin or clopidogrel to reduce the risk of blood clots forming. Current guidelines recommend taking aspirin and clopidogrel for several months after stent insertion (National Institute for Health and Clinical Excellence, 2007). Following successful angioplasty or placement of a stent, it is hoped that the symptoms of chest pain associated with angina will be substantially reduced. On a long-term basis, the rates at which arteries return to their narrowed state (a process known as restenosis) appear to be lower with stents than with coronary angioplasty. In addition to the two types of stents already mentioned, one of the latest types is called a drug-eluting stent. It is coated with a time-release drug that prevents cell proliferation and has been shown to lead to an increased success rate beyond a year in patients who have stents inserted (Holmes et al., 2004).

If the angioplasty is unsuccessful at widening the artery or a dissection occurs, a stent is usually inserted. In practice, however, stents are often inserted after successful angioplasty, based on evidence that this improves longer-term patency (the state of being expanded and unblocked), especially in smaller vessels.

Although the use of angioplasty and the placement of stents are routine, safe and normally successful, these procedures do carry certain risks. The risks are either a direct effect of the surgery or the anticoagulation medication necessary to stop the formation of blood clots. Bleeding from the point of incision in the groin into the surrounding tissue may occur, causing the area to look bruised. Following angioplasty, the risk of having a stroke is 1 in 1000 or loss of life 2–3 in 1000. These risks are lower if the procedure is elective rather than being carried out as an emergency operation. Each member of the clinical team will weigh up the risks against the likely benefits and always err on the side of caution. In a small number of cases (fewer than 1 in 100), both procedures are unsuccessful and an alternative surgical approach is required. One that is commonly used is the coronary artery bypass.

9.3 Coronary artery bypass surgery

Coronary artery bypass surgery is also referred to as coronary artery bypass grafting (or CABG for short, pronounced 'cabbage'). The surgery uses a graft taken from a healthy blood vessel somewhere else in the body to bypass the blocked or narrowed coronary arteries that have not responded to angioplasty or stents. Each coronary artery that has become narrowed receives its own coronary bypass, so a person could have a single, double or triple bypass operation depending on their needs (Figure 9.4). Significant atherosclerotic narrowing in the left anterior descending, circumflex and right coronary arteries would require a triple bypass. The objective remains the same, however, and that is to maintain adequate perfusion of the heart muscle to allow it to function properly. In about 80–90% of cases, coronary artery bypass grafting is a highly effective treatment for the prolonged relief of angina, and those patients with the most severe angina

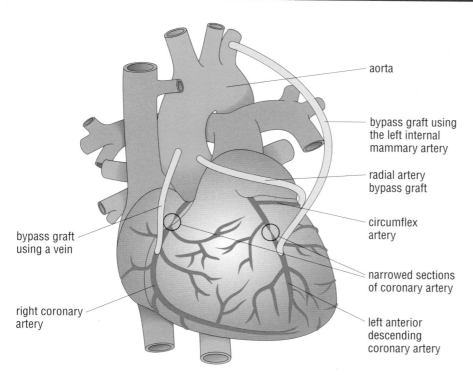

aorta

bypass graft using the left internal mammary artery

radial artery bypass graft

circumflex artery

narrowed sections of coronary artery

left anterior descending coronary artery

bypass graft using a vein

right coronary artery

Figure 9.4 Examples of coronary bypass surgery. Grafts are taken from healthy blood vessels elsewhere in the body and are used to bypass the blocked or narrowed coronary arteries in a single, double or triple bypass operation, depending on the number and location of the blockages.

symptoms derive the greatest benefit. A major part of the surgery requires the normal function of the heart and lungs to be replaced by a heart–lung machine (cardiopulmonary bypass) and the heart stopped. Techniques that allow 'beating heart' surgery or ('keyhole' surgery) are now in routine use in several UK centres, although as yet there are limited controlled trial data to prove its effectiveness.

Bypass surgery requires direct access to the heart during general anaesthesia, which is achieved by a mid-line incision of the sternum. A separate surgical procedure is performed to remove a healthy blood vessel to use as a graft, usually by a different surgeon. The most commonly harvested vessel is the saphenous vein. This is superficial and is one of many veins in the leg; the graft is taken from the portion in the upper leg. The venous drainage from the leg is not compromised in any way unless there is a history of deep vein thrombosis or previous leg surgery. Other vessels used in bypass grafts include the radial and mammary arteries. Once the bypass grafts are in place, the heart–lung machine is stopped, the heart restarted, the incisions closed and the person admitted to the intensive care unit. During the initial stages of recovery, the lungs continue to be inflated via a tube placed in the trachea (windpipe) and are artificially ventilated using oxygen-enriched air. While in the intensive care unit, patients are very closely monitored; pacing wires (external pacemaker) are placed on the chest, a catheter in the urethra allows the passage of urine, blood pressure is measured using an indwelling arterial catheter, an ECG is recorded and the patient is placed on an intravenous drip to give fluids or blood. As long as the recovery process goes to plan, patients are usually discharged after a week. Between 6 and 10 days after an operation, the non-dissolvable stitches are removed by a nurse or doctor.

It is not uncommon to feel unwell after cardiac surgery; however, a GP should be contacted if the patient has the following symptoms:

- shortness of breath
- severe palpitations
- a fever or profuse sweating
- dizziness
- blood oozing from the incision sites.

Having a coronary artery bypass is major surgery but, depending on the person's state of health, the risk associated with it is low: about 2 in 100 patients do not survive the surgery and about 4 in 100 have a stroke. The survival benefit of surgery over medical therapy becomes greater with the increased number of diseased coronary arteries (Allen et al., 2004). In the European Coronary Surgery study of men less than 65 years old with mild to moderate angina, normal left ventricular function and at least two diseased coronary arteries were followed over an 8-year period. At the projected 5-year follow-up interval, there was a significantly higher survival rate in the group that was assigned to surgical treatment (92.4%) than in the group assigned to medical treatment (83.1%; Varnauskas, 1988).

Coronary artery bypass surgery is unlikely to provide long-term therapy if the risk factors for atheroma are not addressed both before and after an operation. Smoking, hypertension, diabetes and high cholesterol levels all contribute to the build-up of atheromatous plaques in the first place and must be controlled to prevent the re-occurrence of symptoms in the long term. Indeed, having a heart attack or having cardiac surgery is often sufficient shock to encourage someone to dramatically change their lifestyle. Cardiac rehabilitation programmes (see Chapter 10) stress the need to lead a healthy life.

9.4 Heart valve surgery

Heart valve surgery is a common operation to repair or replace leaky or narrowed heart valves. The procedure depends on the severity of the condition and on the result of investigations (see Chapter 7), and most surgery is performed under general anaesthesia.

● What are the valves in the heart?

● There are four valves in the heart: two on the right, lower-pressure side, the pulmonary and tricuspid valves; and two on the left, higher-pressure side, the aortic and mitral valves.

If the investigation shows that the coronary arteries are also narrowed, valve surgery can be combined with angioplasty, stents or coronary bypass.

9.4.1 Valvuloplasty

Valvuloplasty, as its name suggests, involves distending (expanding) the valves to allow a more effective flow of blood. The normal task of a valve is to allow the blood to flow in one direction between different chambers of the heart or between the heart and the great vessels. Just as with angioplasty (Section 9.2), valvuloplasty involves placing a catheter into an artery in the groin and passing its tip into the heart until the narrowed valve is reached. The balloon at the end of the catheter is then gently inflated to stretch the valve. The most common valve treated in this way is the mitral valve when mitral stenosis (hardening and narrowing of the mitral valve) is diagnosed. The big advantage of valvuloplasty is that invasive cardiac surgery is avoided, and it is the only heart valve surgery performed under local anaesthesia.

9.4.2 Heart valve replacement surgery

Heart valve replacement surgery involves the removal of a valve and replacing it with a new prosthetic (artificial) valve that takes on the role of the original valve. As in coronary bypass surgery, the surgery is performed under general anaesthesia and access to the heart is made through the sternum. The heart beat is stopped and the functions of the heart and lungs taken over by a heart–lung machine. The technique is therefore invasive and requires prolonged hospitalisation of up to a week.

There are two types of replacement valve: mechanical and tissue (Figure 9.5). There are many different types of mechanical valves, including caged-ball, tilting-disc and bi-leaflet. The tilting-disc and bi-leaflet types of valve have been designed to mimic the natural pattern of blood flow through the heart. The main advantage of a mechanical valve is its high durability; when placed in young patients, it will usually last a lifetime. The main disadvantage of mechanical valves is the increased risk of blood clots, with a high probability of a heart attack or stroke. To prevent blood clots, mechanical valve recipients must take anticoagulant drugs for the rest of their lives.

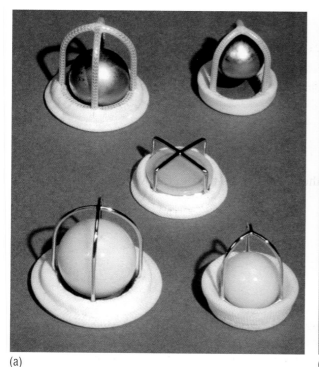

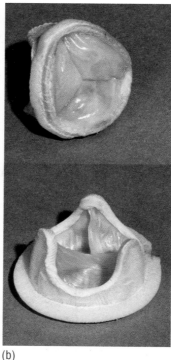

Figure 9.5 Examples of (a) mechanical heart valves (caged-ball designs) and (b) a prosthetic tricuspid heart valve.

(a)

(b)

● Can you think of other problems that could be associated with mechanical heart valves?

● There are several disadvantages of replacement mechanical heart valves. For example, the design of a caged-ball mechanical valve (Figure 9.5) requires more energy to allow blood to flow around the ball, and in the process also damages red blood cells. The mechanical parts of the valves are not as responsive as human tissue and so limit the rate of valve opening and closing to about resting heart rate.

Tissue valves are so named because they are made from either human or animal tissue. They can either be crafted from animal tissue (from a pig or cow) and mounted on a cloth-covered ring, or be obtained in their entirety from a human donor or a pig whose valve size closely matches that of the recipient. Either type has many advantages over mechanical valves and is closer to the design of a natural heart valve.

● What major disadvantages would you want to avoid when designing a replacement for a natural heart valve?

● You would want to avoid the long-term requirement for anticoagulants, improve the haemodynamics (blood flow), ensure that red blood cells are not damaged and have an assurance of longevity.

Case Study 9.1   Martha Childs has emergency surgery on a mitral valve

In the last few months, Martha's medical condition had started to deteriorate rapidly. After a recent flight from Jamaica, she found that her feet and ankles had swollen up and she felt tired more often than usual. For the last two months she had tried herbal remedies and mineral supplements to help her symptoms, but although her swollen feet seem better, her tiredness and chest pain were, if anything, worse. At last, after seeking medical help, she has been diagnosed with mitral regurgitation as a result of rheumatic fever she had contracted as a teenager while still living in Jamaica.

At the hospital that diagnosed Martha's condition, the cardiologist Dr Starling had recommended that Martha had heart valve surgery because the rheumatic fever had caused scarring of the mitral valve flaps. By this time, Martha had severe mitral valve regurgitation which had weakened her heart. In response, the left ventricle had enlarged so that it could pump more blood with each heart beat. At first, this adaptation had helped Martha's heart beat with more force. Eventually, however, the change had weakened her heart and had caused congestive heart failure and heart rhythm irregularities, such as atrial fibrillation.

There had been about two weeks between diagnosis and the admission to hospital. Under normal circumstances, people attending hospital for heart valve replacement would have to wait much longer than that, but Martha was failing fast and even she had noticed a marked deterioration in her condition. There was also insufficient time for Martha to take the advice of the hospital staff to lose weight and take up more physical activity, although she had at last given up smoking at the time of diagnosis. For the hospital staff, the chances of her survival were in the balance. Martha was to have valve replacement surgery, where the damaged mitral valve was to be replaced by a prosthetic valve. The surgeon had discussed the type of heart valve with Martha, and it was felt on balance that she should have a tissue valve because she was not happy with taking anticoagulation medication (such as warfarin) for the rest of her life to prevent blood clots from forming on the valve. Even though her new valve would wear out over time and would need replacement in another operation, she felt that this was the easiest option.

Martha was admitted to the surgical ward of her local hospital two days before the operation. Even though Martha's condition was severe, the chances of survival were in her favour because of her age (48). Unfortunately, the operation to replace the valve did not quite go to plan. She survived 24 hours in the intensive care unit but died 3 days later in the cardiac surgical ward after what the hospital had described as 'complications following surgery'. Needless to say, her husband and teenage daughter are distraught and are waiting to hear the outcome of the post-mortem.

Look at the ETHRISK calculations in Activity 3.3 and Martha's case history in Chapters 4, 6 and 7.

● What are the main risk factors that contributed to Martha's medical condition?

● Martha led a rather sedentary lifestyle, was obese, smoked 10 cigarettes a day and ate an irregular, high-fat diet. These factors and a history of rheumatic fever as a child all predispose someone to heart disease. The rheumatic fever triggered an immune response that damaged the heart valves – and the mitral valve in particular. (See Section 6.5 for more information on conditions and diseases that affect the heart valves.)

The risks associated with heart valve surgery are low: the risk to life is about 5 in 100 people. These risks increase if more than one valve needs to be replaced. People should prepare for heart valve surgery by stopping smoking, taking moderate exercise, losing weight and visiting the dentist.

● Why should someone visit the dentist before having cardiac surgery?

● Many patients requiring cardiac surgery are considered to have poor oral health. Decayed teeth, untreated abscesses, inflamed gums and accumulated dental plaque all represent a potent potential cause of bacterial infection, which may have catastrophic consequences during or soon after surgery. A study carried out in Scandinavia by Hakeburg et al. (1999) showed a clear trend of benefit for patients who had dental treatment prior to cardiac surgery.

Once the heart valve operation is completed, patients need to recuperate at home. Full recovery from heart valve surgery takes anywhere from two to three months, but this will vary from one person to another and will depend on other surgery carried out at the same time.

9.5 Surgery to correct congenital abnormalities

Congenital abnormalities involving the cardiovascular system (including the heart) can become apparent during childhood or give rise to heart failure later in life. These can include problems with the heart valves, heart rhythm (such as atrioventricular block), shunts or vascular obstructions (see Section 6.7). Congenital heart conditions are associated in particular with Down's syndrome: about 40% of the babies born with the syndrome have a heart problem.

The most common congenital defects of the heart involve the septum or a failure to close fully the foramen ovale or ductus arteriosus (see Section 6.7.1). Children born with ventricular septal defects risk getting bacterial endocarditis (see Section 6.6) and developing other severe conditions such as pulmonary hypertension, so early repair is often necessary. If the defect in the septum is small, surgery may not be needed as it often closes on its own. Closing a larger defect in the septum requires **open heart surgery** (surgery requiring access to the ventricles and atria). This is usually performed in infancy or childhood and often a cloth patch is sewn over the hole to close it completely. Such repairs usually restore the blood circulation to normality and the long-term outlook is good. If pulmonary hypertension exists in an infant as a result of an abnormality and the child is too small to perform open heart surgery, a band is placed around the pulmonary artery so as to reduce the blood flow to the lungs. This procedure allows the child to grow sufficiently until the defect can be corrected with open heart surgery, during which the band is removed. Open surgical procedures are invasive because they require a mid-line incision in the chest and use a heart-lung machine. Repair of ventricular septal defects is complicated because the conducting system of the heart is in the immediate vicinity (see Section 2.4.1). Severe congenital abnormalities such as those where the great arteries are transposed require urgent surgical correction (see Section 6.7.2).

In certain patients requiring repairs to the atrial septum, surgery can be avoided and a less invasive technique can be performed on the beating heart. In this technique, an implantable closure device is placed inside a catheter that is inserted into a peripheral vein, and the catheter is advanced as far as the defect. At this point, the closure device is pushed out of the tip and bridges the atrial defect to produce a blood-tight seal, effectively restoring the normal function of the atria. Such a technique can also be used to close a patent ductus arteriosus.

9.6 Surgery for peripheral arterial disease

Peripheral arterial disease has the same causes and receives the same surgical treatment as coronary artery disease. In both cases, the cause is primarily atherosclerosis of the vessels supplying part of the body with clinical signs that are due to limitations in blood supply to the affected area. Indeed, someone who has peripheral arterial disease is likely to also have coronary artery disease. The treatment of peripheral arterial disease is almost wholly surgical, with balloon angioplasty and/or bypass surgery providing marked benefits. In severe cases, amputation may be necessary if symptoms persist even at rest and there is evidence of infarction in the extremities of the limb.

Angioplasty treatment for peripheral arterial disease is performed under local anaesthetic. As with coronary angioplasty, a catheter is inserted into an artery in the groin, but this time it is moved in the direction of the limb until it reaches the vessel with the restriction. Angioplasty treatment of a limb is usually combined with stent placement at the same time. One alternative to angioplasty is called **cryoplasty**, which is another minimally invasive treatment for peripheral arterial disease. Instead of the saline–contrast solution used to inflate the balloon in angioplasty, in cryoplasty, pressurised liquid nitrous oxide is delivered into a special angioplasty balloon. As the nitrous oxide expands to a gas, the balloon cools the arterial wall to a temperature of –10 °C. The cooling effect appears to limit re-occurrence of restenosis by reducing tearing and subsequent inflammation of the affected vessel. At the time of writing (2007), cryoplasty has not received official approval by vascular surgeons and health services in Europe or the USA.

If the circulation to the affected area is severely affected, bypass surgery is an option, just as with coronary artery bypass grafting. Unlike angioplasty, bypass surgery of the limb is a major operation as it involves obtaining suitable veins from the limb to be used in the bypass, involves general anaesthesia and a hospital stay of 8–10 days.

9.7 Implantable devices for correcting or maintaining normal heart rhythm

Implantable devices require surgery for implantation and use electrical depolarisation of the heart to correct or maintain normal heart rhythm. These devices take two forms: pacemakers and cardioverter defibrillators.

9.7.1 Pacemakers (resynchronisation therapy)

Implantable pacemakers (Figure 9.6) take over the role of the sinoatrial node and AVN, the natural pacemakers of the heart (see Section 2.4.1). Whenever the natural pacemakers (or their electrical conducting pathways through the heart)

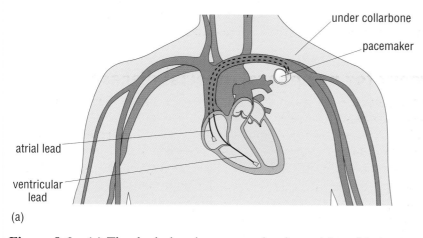

under collarbone

pacemaker

atrial lead

ventricular lead

(a)

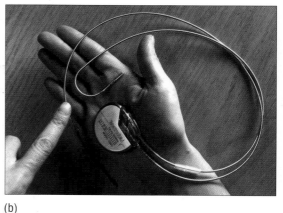

(b)

Figure 9.6   (a) The dual-chamber pacemaker in position. (b) An example pacemaker, approximately 4 cm at its widest and 8 mm thick.

malfunction, implantable pacemakers become a necessity. In order to coordinate the contractions of the heart, pacemakers enable both ventricles to contract at the same time by means of one or more electrical leads. Certain arrhythmias also require an electrical lead in the right atrium. Once inserted, the leads rest against the walls of the heart chambers and in time are held in place by scar tissue, a process called passive fixation. Sometimes, leads have some means of being secured to the heart muscle – typically by a screw device.

Activity 9.2   Cardiac resynchronisation therapy

Suggested study time 5 minutes

Use the Multi-ed Cardiology program to find out what cardiac resynchronisation therapy is.

The animation to watch, 'What is Cardiac Resynchronisation Therapy (CRT)?', can be found by navigating to Animations | Treatment | Pacemakers.

Comment

Cardiac resynchronisation therapy is a treatment for people who have heart failure where the timing of the heart contractions is abnormal. This is also termed dyssynchrony as it results in inefficient pump action. The treatment is the implantation of a specialised biventricular pacemaker that re-establishes normal timing and can lead to significant improvement in symptoms.

Implantable pacemakers are used to correct a variety of conditions associated with malfunctioning electrical conducting pathways through the heart, such as atrioventricular block (see Section 6.4). In complete atrioventricular block, the ventricles revert to their intrinsic rhythm of about 40 beats per minute. At this level, someone will feel breathless, may faint or have periodic blackouts or become confused. In an extreme case, slow heart rhythms can be life-threatening and need immediate surgical intervention. Pacemakers are occasionally recommended for people with irregular or fast electrical activity of the heart.

Case Study 9.2   Katerin Wilcox has a pacemaker fitted

In Case Study 7.2, Katerin Wilcox was referred to a cardiac specialist (Dr Pearson, a cardiologist) for tests on her heart. Katerin keeps herself healthy by eating a good, mixed diet and exercising regularly by walking and swimming, but her age has eventually caught up with her. She is now 71 and is worried that her blood pressure, measured by her cardiologist and found to be 170/90 mmHg, is going to get worse now that Dr Pearson has said that her hypertension has probably contributed to the palpitations she experiences. (She was diagnosed with sinus node disease.) Katerin knows that there is a family history of stroke and she is happy that the medication she was given following her diagnosis (an ACE inhibitor) has controlled her hypertension. However, Dr Pearson has suggested that Katerin should be fitted with a pacemaker as her own pacemaker 'does not seem to work properly'. Katerin's operation to fit a single-chamber pacemaker with a lead connected to the right atrium is arranged for the following week.

Katerin prepares for her operation by fasting overnight. Her son Ivan will be driving her to the hospital and staying in the visitor's room until the operation is over. Once in the hospital, Katerin is shown to a room, where she is asked to sign a consent form and is then given a sedative and a local anaesthetic. A trolley takes her into the operating theatre, where she is covered with sterile drapes from head to foot. Katerin's pacemaker is a type that can be inserted by transvenous implantation following an incision which is about 5 cm long just under her collarbone. She is awake throughout the whole operation but has trouble remembering much. Just before the start of the operation, Katerin could remember being connected to three different monitors:

- an electrocardiogram, where several sticky electrode patches were placed on her chest to monitor her heart beat throughout the procedure

- an oximeter monitor attached to the tip of her finger to monitor the oxygen level of her blood

- a blood pressure monitor which consisted of a blood pressure cuff placed around Katerin's forearm to automatically check her blood pressure throughout the operation.

The operation goes quite smoothly, according to Ivan, who says that it took about an hour. He is also told that because of her age and because she lived alone at home, the hospital would like to keep Katerin in for a couple of days until they have done further tests and given her sufficient time to get used to the pacemaker.

- Is there any reason why Katerin's recollection of the operation to place the pacemaker is a blur?

- Katerin was given a sedative, which has the side effect of producing amnesia (loss of memory).

How does a pacemaker work?

Artificial pacemakers weigh between 20 and 50 g and consist of two main parts: a case containing the electronics, including the lithium battery, sealed in metal; and a collection of one, two or three electrode leads. The type of pacemaker and the function of the electronics are determined by its use. Pacemakers with one lead are called single-chamber pacemakers, those with two leads are dual-chamber pacemakers (see Figure 9.6b), and the three-lead versions are called biventricular pacemakers. Examples of each type of pacemaker can be found on the British Heart Foundation website (British Heart Foundation, 2005c). Each electrical impulse sent by the pacemaker leads to the contraction of the heart and the rate of depolarisation is called the 'discharge rate'. Artificial pacemakers can either discharge at a steady rate or 'on demand' when exercising. Some are sophisticated enough to sense the rhythm of the heart and respond appropriately – and even to stop pacing if the heart beat becomes normal.

The most common type of pacemaker is the 'demand type', which only comes into its own if the heart misses a beat. Pacemakers are designed so that they can be checked occasionally by placing a magnet over the skin covering the pacemaker. There is an internal magnetic sensor in the pacemaker that allows its program to be changed using this method. Occasional complications of pacemakers include a small risk of infections, the leads coming out of position (particularly with vigorous exercise) and a leak of air into the space between the lungs and chest wall (the pneumothorax).

The type of pacemaker that is fitted to an individual depends on the type of heart rhythm abnormality. Table 9.1 lists the options.

Table 9.1 The options for the type of pacemaker implanted.

Electrical abnormality	Type of pacemaker required
the atria always beat irregularly	single-chamber, with the lead connected to the right ventricle
intermittent atrial fibrillation	single-chamber
sinoatrial node not working normally and no atrioventricular block	single-chamber, with the lead connected to the right atrium
atrioventricular block, but with the sinoatrial node working normally	dual-chamber
heart failure	biventricular, with leads to the right atrium and one to each of the two ventricles

How is a pacemaker fitted?

Pacemakers are usually fitted by transvenous implantation. In Case Study 9.2, a transvenous approach has been used to implant a single-chamber pacemaker with the lead connected to the right atrium. Under X-ray guidance, the lead is inserted into a vein at the shoulder or the base of the neck. The surgeon will then push the leads into the correct heart chamber. Once all the leads are in place, the 'pacing' procedure is started to ensure that the leads and pacemaker are working correctly. Patients sometimes feel as though their heart is racing as the pacemaker increases the heart rate. After the leads are tested, they are connected to the pacemaker and the cardiologist adjusts the rate of the pacemaker. The pacemaker is then fitted into a pocket between the skin and the muscle over the chest. After the implantation, the final pacemaker settings are programmed according to the needs of the patient. This is done through the skin by an external programmer that alters the settings using radiofrequency signals.

The second, less common method of implantation uses the epicardial approach. Unlike the transvenous route, epicardial implantation is performed under general anaesthesia using sterile procedures and an intravenous line started. An incision is made in the chest to expose the exterior surface of the heart (the epicardium) and the leads are attached directly to the outside of the heart muscle. The pacemaker is then placed under the skin in the upper abdomen. Occasionally, a telemetry monitor will be used to record the function of the pacemaker and to monitor the heart rate when the patient is in the recovery room. Telemetry monitoring allows some pacemakers to transmit ECG data using radiofrequency signals to a remote monitor (either in the recovery room or at the patient's home) where the data can be recorded and analysed. There is no advantage of the epicardial over the transvenous route; the former is usually only performed if a person is having heart surgery at the same time.

It is important that patients are prepared for the placement of pacemakers. Patients should not eat or drink after midnight on the day of the procedure until the operation is over. If on medications, these should be taken as prescribed with a small sip of water unless directed otherwise by the cardiologist. The patient should alert the cardiologist if:

- they have an allergy to seafood, X-ray contrast medium or iodine
- they are pregnant or suspect they are
- they are taking anticoagulants
- they have a history of bleeding problems
- they have diabetes.

Living with a pacemaker

Once a pacemaker has been implanted into a patient, they will soon realise that the device is comfortable and reliable, and that with appropriate regular checks very little can go wrong. Most recipients do not give it another thought and find them comfortable and very reliable. Often, having a pacemaker will allow someone to lead a normal lifestyle free of the fear of fainting or becoming dizzy. Even though there is a tendency for a person to forget that they have a pacemaker, it is important for them to carry the details of the make and model of the pacemaker on a registration card at all times. Further information on driving after cardiac surgery is discussed in Section 10.5.1. There are very few restrictions to your lifestyle when you have a pacemaker. Almost any sport is possible, except when the pacemaker is likely to be damaged, as in contact sports such as football or kickboxing.

There are a few precautions that someone should take if they are fitted with a pacemaker. They should not stand too close to a strong electromagnetic field such as those found in airport screening facilities, hospital diagnostic magnetic resonance imaging equipment or spot-welding equipment. People should always tell airport security operators if they have a pacemaker and should not use a mobile phone less than 15 cm from the device.

It is essential that pacemakers are regularly checked by a cardiac nurse to see that they are working correctly. Depending on the type of pacemaker, the interval between hospital checks could be anything from 3 to 12 months. The batteries in pacemakers last up to 10 years, so the electronics box will eventually need to be replaced as part of a simple operation; the leads can be reused.

Activity 9.3   Catheter (radiofrequency) ablation therapy

Suggested time 5 minutes

Use the Multi-ed Cardiology program to find out what radiofrequency ablation therapy is.

The animation to watch, 'What is radiofrequency ablation?', can be found by navigating to Animations | Treatment | Ablation.

Comment

Radiofrequency ablation therapy is sometimes also called **catheter ablation therapy**. It is used to treat certain types of palpitation where abnormal electrical signals are confined to a part of the heart that is easily accessible to a radiofrequency probe. The probe is used to ablate (to functionally remove) the anomaly by destroying its cause. In order to locate the exact area to destroy, an electrophysiological study using specialised catheters precedes ablation.

9.7.2 Cardioverter defibrillators

Implantable cardioverter defibrillators (ICDs) are similar to pacemakers and are surgically implanted when a person's heart is likely to be at risk of developing life-threatening heart rhythms that render the heart unable to pump blood normally. ICDs monitor the heart continuously and intervene to restore normal heart rhythm should the need arise.

ICDs are used for two types of arrhythmias, ventricular tachycardia and ventricular fibrillation – most commonly resulting from an MI or cardiomyopathy, although sometimes there are no other signs of heart disease. The symptoms may include palpitations, feeling faint or collapsing, but not chest pain or breathlessness. The most common use of ICDs is for people who have had a cardiac arrest and have needed to be resuscitated, and who are at high risk of ventricular tachycardia or ventricular fibrillation. Before ICDs are implanted, the options of drug treatment and catheter ablation therapy need to be considered and the person needs to undergo extensive tests including prolonged heart rhythm monitoring, echocardiography and cardiac catheterisation.

ICDs are similar to pacemakers in the way they work, their method of implantation and the care and complications that might arise. They deliver one of the following treatments if the device senses a rhythm disturbance.

*   In less serious situations, the ICD will deliver 'pacing' electrical pulses that correct the heart beat.
*   If pacing does not work or the ICD senses that the rhythm is seriously disturbed, it delivers a bigger electrical shock to get the rhythm back to normal. Under these circumstances, the ICD can be a life-saver; without it, ventricular fibrillation would be fatal.

Activity 9.4 The use of implantable cardioverter defibrillators for arrhythmias

Suggested study time 25 minutes

Visit the National Institute for Health and Clinical Excellence website and look for the most recent advice on ICDs for arrhythmias.

What ICDs are recommended for different patient categories?

Comment

ICDs are recommended for the following categories.

Secondary prevention, that is, for patients who present, in the absence of a treatable cause, with one of the following:

- having survived a cardiac arrest due to either ventricular tachycardia (VT) or ventricular fibrillation
- spontaneous sustained VT causing syncope or significant haemodynamic compromise (reduced blood flow)
- sustained VT without syncope or cardiac arrest, and who have an associated reduction in left ventricular ejection fraction (LVEF < 35%).

Primary prevention, that is, for patients who have a history of previous (> 4 weeks) MI, left ventricular dysfunction with LVEF < 35%, and one of the following:

- non-sustained VT on 24-hour ECG monitoring, and inducible VT on electrophysiological testing
- left ventricular dysfunction with LVEF < 30% and QRS duration of equal to or more than 120 milliseconds (120 thousandths of a second).

9.8 Ventricular assist devices and artificial hearts

Left ventricular assist devices (LVADs) are used for those people awaiting a heart transplant or who have heart failure due to an acute infection of the heart tissue and are therefore not eligible for a transplant. LVADs are mechanical devices used to support the pumping action of a failing heart and, in the case of infection, to allow the heart muscle time to recover. The devices take blood via a cannula inserted into the atria or ventricular apex (the lowest superficial part of the heart – the pointed end) and pump it into the pulmonary artery or aorta. As a consequence of their use, the ventricles do not have to work as hard, and at the same time the pulmonary and systemic circulations are supported.

The intended use and clinical assessment of a patient before the implantation of an LVAD has a very significant influence on the type of device used. LVADs vary considerably in their complexity and there have been rapid technological advances in this area. Mechanical circulatory support devices can be either extracorporeal (lying outside the body) or implantable, and can be either pulsatile or non-pulsatile – or there is the option of the total artificial heart. Temporary total artificial hearts are only used in patients with failure of left and right ventricles (end-stage biventricular failure) as a way to improve life expectancy while they are waiting for a heart transplant. These devices pump more blood (up to 9.5 litres per minute) than a ventricular assist device. This helps patients regain their strength, making them better heart transplant candidates.

Before an LVAD is employed, the following questions need to be considered.

- Has there been cardiac arrest with advanced chronic heart failure?
- How much is the function of the heart impaired?
- What is the likelihood that the heart muscle will recover?
- What is the duration of support required?
- Does the pump need to assist the left and the right ventricles?
- How heavy is the person?
- What device will offer the patient the greatest mobility and potential for rehabilitation?

The application of these devices is limited to the short term because their use is accompanied by high rates of complications such as haemorrhage, thrombus formation, infection and neurological and kidney problems. However, people with LVADs have been shown to have an increased chance of survival and a better quality of life (Rose et al., 2001). Several studies have demonstrated that long-term support using LVADs can restore a previously dilated heart and improve the function of the heart cells (Nakatani, 1996).

Activity 9.5　Ventricular assist devices

Suggested study time 30 minutes

Use the internet to look for websites that provide lists of ventricular assist devices approved by your national health service. (Some example links are included on the course website.) Once you have identified a list of websites, search their content to answer the following questions.

(a) What types of devices are available?

(b) Are there any studies ongoing that are looking at the effectiveness of ventricular assist devices?

(c) Who are the surgical team members and what are their roles?

(d) Are there any patient testimonials?

Comment

The answer to this question depends on the search engine that you use and the particular country's health service. For example the US Food and Drug administration gives a list of 'Recently approved VADs' on their website and NICE has similar recommendations in the UK.

9.9 Heart transplantation

Heart transplantation is an option for people with advanced heart disease, including those with uncontrollable angina, severe heart valve problems or those with congenital abnormalities (British Heart Foundation, 2005b). The diseased heart is removed and replaced with a donor heart, and the person receives medication that prevents the donor heart being rejected (immunosuppressant drugs). Before a patient is placed on the heart transplant list, they undergo a series of tests to determine their suitability and the chances of a successful outcome or prognosis. People are not normally placed on the list unless their estimated remaining life expectancy with their current heart is less than a year.

Since the 1960s, cardiac transplantation has evolved from the sensational experiments of the pioneering surgeons such as Christiaan Barnard (who in 1967 conducted the first cardiac transplant) to the conventional therapy for **end-stage heart disease**. This is heart disease that progresses to an advanced form where the patient is gravely ill, possibly disabled, and generally unable to function at even limited levels of activity. Someone in this state would often have a history of multiple heart attacks and possibly have had previous surgical intervention. Even after a successful transplant the patient has to be monitored regularly for the rest of their lives. The transplanted heart has been dissociated from its nerve supply that normally regulates its rhythm and pairs of pacing electrodes have to be placed onto the atria and ventricles in order to control the heart beat. The new heart is also foreign to the host's body and so it would normally be rejected by their immune system – hence the need for immunosuppressant drugs.

The early human heart allografts (a graft between two individuals who are of the same species but have genetic differences) were a proven success in that they provided evidence that the transplanted heart could sustain the recipient's circulation. However, the main obstacles were the immunological reactions the donor heart produced and the complications of infections. Subsequent advances in the prevention, diagnosis and treatment of infectious pathogens in patients receiving immunosuppressants and in the initial selection of patients resulted in an increase in the proportion of patients surviving a year after surgery – from 20% at the end of the 1960s to 70% in 1980 (Kaye et al., 1985). Figure 9.7 shows the comparison of survival following heart transplantation in recipients grouped according to the period in which the data were analysed. You can see a noticeable improvement in outcomes since the first half of the 1980s. Survival rates have remained roughly the same over the years since the second half of the 1980s, which is possibly evidence of better patient management strategies. This period does, however, coincide with the discovery and clinical development of the safe and effective immunosuppressant cyclosporin A. The new pharmacological management combined with regulation of the immune response lifted the one-year survival rate from approximately 60% in 1980 to 80% in 1990.

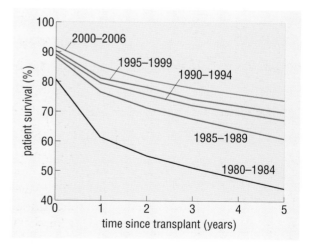

Figure 9.7 Heart transplant survival in the USA, 1980–2006.

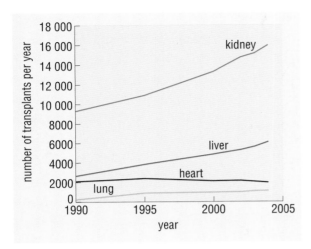

Figure 9.8 Organ transplants in the USA, 1990–2004. This graph shows major single-organ transplants, excluding bone or skin grafts and transplants of the cornea, pancreas and intestine.

The number of heart transplants (at least in the USA) is small when compared with the number of transplants of other organs. Analysis of the major organs routinely transplanted shows that the number of heart transplants has levelled off over time when compared with those of the lung, liver or kidney (US Census Bureau, 2006; see Figure 9.8).

A further analysis of the US heart transplant statistics (Organ Procurement and Transplantation Network, 2007; see Figure 9.9) shows that the downward trend is almost entirely due to a decrease in heart transplants for those in the age group 50–64 years, and that the trend for the age groups 18–34 and 35–49 years is either static or falling slightly. The only group where there is a continued rise is the 65+ category, where there is less of a chance of long-term success. The major reason for the levelling off is the lack of acquisition of donor hearts – not the lack of need.

Recently, a series of internationally agreed guidelines on the rationale and process (Mehra et al., 2006a), selection criteria (Mehra et al., 2006b), use of ventricular assist devices (Gronda et al., 2006) and pharmacological treatment of cardiac transplant patients has been agreed. Generally, someone who is a suitable candidate for a heart transplant is likely to have end-stage heart disease with the following indications (signs that make a particular treatment advisable) and with a high chance of success.

- general indications and absence of a non-cardiac condition likely to: limit survival independent of cardiac function or lead to life-threatening infection following administration of immunosuppressants

- specific indications of heart failure, including: cardiomyopathy (e.g. due to viruses or alcohol; see Section 4.9.1), valvular or congenital heart disease or a failed transplant due to rejection

- non-specific indications including: angina that has not responded to bypass surgery and arrhythmia that has failed conventional therapy.

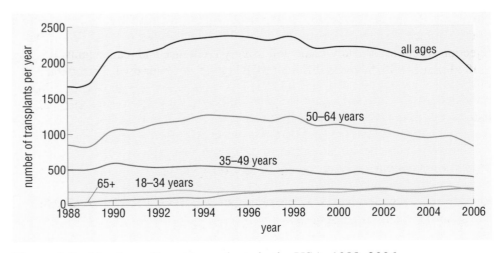

Figure 9.9 Number of heart transplants in the USA, 1988–2006.

Someone who is an unsuitable candidate for a heart transplant is likely to have end-stage heart disease with the following contraindications.

- conditions ruling out a heart transplant: poor lung or kidney function, an active viral or bacterial infection, active peptic ulcer disease, diabetes with multi-organ damage, vascular disease, malignancy (cancer, as opposed to benign) in the last two years or inability to follow treatment plan

- conditions where caution is indicated: older than 65, diabetes without organ failure or disease of another organ that would limit quality of life.

The selection of a suitable donor is critical for a successful outcome. First and foremost, the ideal donor should, before death, have been a young, fit and healthy person without cardiac disease or hypertension and someone who is reasonably well matched to the intended recipient. Tissue typing, the time-consuming process that checks that donor and recipient are matched for shared transplant antigens, is not normally used for hearts because of the extremely low probability of a close match. However, where it is possible to tissue type, three main categories are used to determine blood and tissue compatibility: blood type, tissue type and cross-matching.

Blood type

There are four blood types, defined by the presence or absence of two antigens: the A antigen and the B antigen. Blood type A has the A antigen, type B has the B antigen, type AB has both antigens and type O has neither antigen. Ideally, the donor should have a blood type compatible with the recipient:

- type O can donate to types A, B, AB and O
- type AB can donate to type AB
- type A can donate to types A and AB
- type B can donate to types B and AB.

Tissue type

'Tissue type' refers to genetic variation that occurs in a specific position on a chromosome (gene locus) called the major histocompatibility complex (MHC). All mammals have this gene locus and in humans it is called HLA. The genes are highly variable between individuals and are essential for the normal function of the immune system. However, they are coincidentally responsible for graft-rejection reactions, so individuals will usually recognise and react against grafted tissues which have a different MHC type from their own. Transplant surgeons aim to match HLA-type as closely as possible to reduce rejection, but the development of more effective immunosuppressant drugs has reduced the importance of the HLA matching.

Cross-matching

This third blood test assesses further antigen compatibility.

- Can you think of other important consideration when assessing a suitable donor for heart transplantation?

- The donor–recipient heart size match is important, as is matching the donor's height with the recipient's height.

The medical management of the person due to receive a donor heart has improved very significantly since the late 1980s. Failing hearts often have to work harder at rest than healthy hearts. The use of drugs (see Chapter 8) such as diuretics, anticoagulants and beta-blockers, coupled with improved mechanical support for the heart, has reduced the mortality rate for patients waiting for a transplant. The mechanical support includes ventricular assist devices (see Section 9.8).

9.9.1 Drug-induced immunosuppression

The clinical objective of immunosuppression therapy is to prevent the immune-mediated injury to the transplanted heart while minimising associated complications, including opportunistic infections. Most transplant centres use a triple therapy approach of a calcineurin inhibitor (a drug preventing the formation of certain cells of the immune system), an antimitotic agent (a drug preventing cell division) and steroids (anti-inflammatory and immunosuppressant drugs). Table 9.2 gives a list of commonly used drugs in each of these categories, together with their side effects.

Table 9.2 Drugs used in the triple therapy approach to immunosupression after cardiac transplantation, together with their side effects.

Drug type	Examples	Side effects
calineurin inhibitors	cyclosporin A tacrolimus	hypertension, reduced renal (kidney) function, muscular tremors, hirsutism (excessive body hair; cyclosporin A only), gingival hyperplasia (excessive gum growth), diabetes mellitus (tacrolimus only)
antimitotic agents	azathioprine mycophenolate	suppression of bone marrow function, nausea, diarrhoea, stomach cramps
glucocorticoids	methylprednisolone prednisolone	hypertension, insulin resistance (Type 2 diabetes), osteoporosis, emotional changes, obesity

● Why is the prognosis for a cardiac transplant patient with diabetes likely to be worse than one without?

● At least two of the common immunosuppressants produce symptoms of diabetes and are likely to make someone with a predetermined diagnosis of diabetes more difficult to manage their condition.

The drugs used in immunosuppression therapy all have side effects that cause particular complications in patients who are debilitated or whose hearts are insufficiently well-managed before the transplanted heart is in place (Bourge et al., 1993). Following surgery, the common complications include: bleeding from the wound in the skin and around the new heart; liver or kidney malfunction; and bacterial pathogens (disease-causing micro-organisms) that predominate in the lung and sites of vascular or surgical intervention. Opportunistic fungal and viral infections usually occur later.

● Why are bacterial, viral and fungal pathogens such a problem following cardiac transplantation?

● The normal response of the body to the presence of these disease-causing agents is suppressed by the immunosuppressant drugs used to control the new heart.

9.10 Returning to work after cardiac surgery

How soon someone returns to work after cardiac surgery will depend on the type of work they do, the surgical procedure and its success. In the case of coronary angioplasty and someone who has a desk-based job, this is likely to be about a week. In all cases, the cardiologists or cardiac specialist nurse will advise on when the patient can return to full-time employment. Recovery from major heart surgery such as a coronary bypass is likely to take several months. During this time, the person may have depression, exhibit emotional changes or suffer from memory loss. In most cases, these symptoms are transient and the patient will make a full recovery. In the UK, recovering patients should not drive for the first four weeks following cardiac surgery; if a bus or commercial vehicle driver, this is mandatory and extended to six weeks. (Restrictions on driving are covered in more detail in Section 10.5.1.) Everyone who has had cardiac surgery has an outpatients' appointment around 4 to 6 weeks after the operation, at which the surgeon checks that all the wounds are healing and that they are not suffering too much discomfort.

Activity 9.6   Cardiac procedures

Suggested study time 30 minutes

Most large district hospitals perform a variety of cardiac procedures including surgery. A good example of information for patients waiting for cardiac surgery can be found on the website of King's College Hospital in London. Locate this using an internet search, search their website for 'cardiac surgery' and look for a list of surgical treatments available. Download the patient information that describes CABG. What advice is given about activities to avoid following coronary artery bypass surgery?

Follow this by searching for the nearest hospital to you to see if they provide information for patients waiting for cardiac surgery.

Comment

At the time of writing (2007), the list of surgical treatments at King's College Hospital includes aortic surgery, coronary bypass surgery, heart valve surgery, surgery for heart failure, surgical treatment for arrhythmia and thoracic surgery. The advice given on activities to avoid for the first six weeks include excessive pulling, pushing, lifting, upper arm movement or holding your breath, as this may stop your chest wound healing properly.

9.11 Summary of Chapter 9

In this chapter, you have learned about various aspects of the surgical management of cardiovascular diseases and of the variety of techniques that surgeons employ to treat defects in the blood supply to the heart and the peripheral circulation. You should have a reasonably good understanding of the different types of implantable devices used to replace damaged heart valves and to correct abnormal heart rhythms. You should also understand the differences between invasive and non-invasive treatments. You have learned about routine surgical treatments, ranging from angioplasty, in which the patient is awake during the procedure, to cardiac transplantation, in which the patient is deeply anaesthetised and their life is entirely dependent on various devices. In the next and final chapter you will learn more about living with cardiovascular diseases.

Questions for Chapter 9

Question 9.1 (Learning Outcome 9.4)

Referring to Figure 9.1, how many people per 10 000 of the USA population had angioplasty or coronary bypass surgery in: (i) 1980; (ii) 1995; and (iii) 2004? Make sure that you multiply the value on the y-axis (labelled 'surgical procedures per 10 000 population') by 10 000.

Question 9.2 (Learning Outcome 9.2)

How should you prepare yourself for heart surgery and what are the likely changes to your lifestyle afterwards?

Question 9.3 (Learning Outcome 9.5)

Name two different types of implantable electronic devices used to treat cardiovascular diseases.

Question 9.4 (Learning Outcomes 9.2, 9.3, 9.4 and 9.6)

Distinguish between acute and chronic conditions. Give examples of the least invasive and most invasive surgical approaches to treating cardiovascular diseases.

Question 9.5 (Learning Outcome 9.8)

List the surgical methods used to increase coronary blood flow.

Question 9.6 (Learning Outcome 9.4)

List the short-term complications associated with cardiovascular surgery.

References

Allen, K. B., Dowling, R. D., Schuch, D. R., Pfeffer, T. A., Marra, S., Lefrak, E. A., Fudge, T. L., Mostovych, M., Szentpetery, S., Saha, S. P., Murphy, D. and Dennis, H. (2004) 'Adjunctive transmyocardial revascularization: five-year follow-up of a prospective, randomized trial', *Annals of Thoracic Surgery*, **78**, pp. 458–465.

Bourge, R. C., Naftel, D. C., Costanzo-Nordin, M. R., Kirklin, J. K., Young, J. B., Kubo, S. H., Olivari, M. T. and Kasper, E. K. (1993) 'Pretransplantation risk factors for death after heart transplantation: a multiinstitutional study. The Transplant Cardiologists Research Database Group', *Journal of Heart and Lung Transplantation*, **12**, pp. 549–562.

British Heart Foundation (2005a) *Having heart surgery*, Heart Information Series Number 12, London, British Heart Foundation.

British Heart Foundation (2005b) *Heart transplantation*, Heart Information Series Number 13, London, British Heart Foundation.

British Heart Foundation (2005c) *Pacemakers*, Heart Information Series Number 15, London, British Heart Foundation.

Greene, M. A., Gray, L. A., Slater, A. D., Ganzel, B. L. and Mavroudis, C (1991) 'Emergency aortocoronary bypass after failed angioplasty', *Annals of Thoracic Surgery*, **51**, pp. 194–199.

Gronda, E., Bourge, R. C., Costanzo, M. R., Deng, M., Mancini, D., Martinelli, L. and Torre-Amione, G. (2006). 'Heart rhythm considerations in heart transplant candidates and considerations for ventricular assist devices: International Society for Heart and Lung Transplantation guidelines for the care of cardiac transplant candidates', *Journal of Heart and Lung Transplantation*, **25**, pp. 1043–1056.

Hakeburg, M., Derenvik, L. and Gatzinsky, P. (1999) 'The significance of oral health and dental treatment for the postoperative outcome of heart valve surgery', *Scandinavian Cardiovascular Journal*, **33**, pp. 5–8.

Holmes, D. R., Leon, M. B., Moses, J. W., Popma, J. J., Cutlip, D., Fitzgerald, P. J., Brown, C., Fischell, T., Wong, S. C., Midei, M., Snead, D. and Kuntz, R. E. (2004) 'Analysis of 1-year clinical outcomes in the SIRIUS trial: a randomized trial of a sirolimus-eluting stent versus a standard stent in patients at high risk for coronary restenosis', *Circulation*, **109**, pp. 634–640.

Kaye, M. P., Elcombe, S. A. and O'Fallon, W. M. (1985) 'The International Heart Transplantation Registry: the 1984 report', *Journal of Heart Transplantation*, **4**, pp. 290–292.

Mehra, M. R., Jessup, M., Gronda, E. and Costanzo, M. R. (2006a) 'Rationale and process: International Society for Heart and Lung Transplantation guidelines for the care of cardiac transplant candidates', *Journal of Heart and Lung Transplantation*, **25**, pp. 1001–1002.

Mehra, M. R., Kobashigawa, J., Starling, R., Russell, S., Uber, P. A., Parameshwar, J., Mohacsi, P., Augustine, S., Aaronson, K. and Barr, M. (2006b) 'Listing criteria for heart transplantation: International Society for Heart and Lung Transplantation guidelines for the care of cardiac transplant candidates', *Journal of Heart and Lung Transplantation*, **25**, pp. 1024–1042.

Nakatani, S., McCarthy, P. M., Kottke-Marchant, K., Harasaki, H., James, K. B., Savage, R. M. and Thomas, J. D. (1996) 'Left ventricular echocardiographic and histologic changes: impact of chronic unloading by an implantable ventricular assist device', *Journal of the American College of Cardiology*, **27**, pp. 894–901.

National Institute for Health and Clinical Excellence (2007) *Acute coronary syndromes: clopidogrel* [online] Available from: http://guidance.nice.org.uk/TA80 (Accessed June 2007).

Rose, E. A., Gelijns, A. C., Moskowitz, A. J., Heitjan, D. F., Stevenson, L. W., Dembitsky, W., Long, J. W., Ascheim, D. D., Tierney, A. R., Levitan, R. G., Watson, J. T., Ronan, N. S., Shapiro, P. A., Lazar, R. M., Miller, L. W., Gupta, L., Frazier, O. H., Desvigne-Nickens, P., Oz, M. C., Poirier, V. L. and Meier, P. (2001) 'Long-term use of a left ventricular assist device for end-stage heart failure', *New England Journal of Medicine*, **345**, pp. 1435–1443.

Scottish Intercollegiate Guidelines Network (1996) *Obesity in Scotland: integrating prevention with weight management* [online] Available from: http://www.sign.ac.uk/pdf/sign8.pdf (Accessed May 2007).

Society of Cardiothoracic Surgeons of Great Britain and Ireland (2003) *The 5th National Adult Cardiac Surgical Database* [online] Available from: http://www.scts.org/sections/audit/Cardiac/ (Accessed May 2007).

US Census Bureau (2006) *Statistical abstract of the United States: 2006*, Section 3 [online] Available from: http://www.census.gov/prod/2005pubs/06statab/health.pdf (Accessed February 2007).

US Department of Health and Human Services (1990) *The health benefits of smoking cessation: a report of the Surgeon General*, pp. 239–240 [online] Available from: http://profiles.nlm.nih.gov/NN/B/B/D/H/_/nnbbdh.pdf (Accessed May 2007).

Varnauskas, E. (1988) 'Twelve-year follow-up of survival in the randomized European Coronary Surgery Study', *The New England Journal of Medicine*, **319**, pp. 332–337.

USA Organ Procurement and Transplantation Network (2007) *View data reports* [online] http://www.optn.org/latestData/viewDataReports.asp (Accessed May 2007).

CHAPTER 10

LIVING WITH CARDIOVASCULAR DISEASES

Learning Outcomes

When you have completed this chapter you should be able to:

10.1 Define and use, or recognise definitions and applications of, each of the terms printed in **bold** in the text.

10.2 List different ways in which progression of vascular disease can be minimised, and the risk of heart attack reduced.

10.3 Evaluate the contribution that can be made, by changes in lifestyle or by the use of therapeutic drugs, to risk reduction in different people.

10.4 Understand the potential changes that a heart attack, vascular disease or surgery can make to the psychological outlook of an individual.

10.5 Understand the potential changes that these conditions can make to relationships with friends, family and colleagues.

10.6 Evaluate the potential for a healthy life, and any limitations on lifestyle that may have arisen.

10.1 Introduction

Throughout this course, you have studied the biological and medical aspects of managing cardiovascular disease. You should have a good understanding of the causes of cardiovascular disease; the processes that occur in the heart and blood vessels in health and disease; the ways in which a person with suspected cardiovascular disease is investigated; and the various medical and surgical treatments, together with the reasons for using them.

Of equal importance is that you recognise the impact which cardiovascular disease can have on a person and the changes which may be needed. This chapter will consider what it means to live with cardiovascular disease, and examines lifestyle changes, practical considerations and the psychological implications of having heart disease. You will study various sources of help available for a person with heart disease so that they are able to deal with these changes. A large component of living with a chronic disease is medical management, so you will learn about the monitoring and check-ups that a person with heart disease would be encouraged to have.

Activity 10.1　How a heart attack affects people's lives

Suggested study time 30 minutes

Now follow the links on the DVD Guide program to the audio clip of Michael and his wife, in which they describe the changes they have made to their lifestyle since Michael had an MI. While you are listening, write down the main areas in which their lives have changed. Some of these changes are related directly to Michael's condition and some to psychological adjustments which they have made.

This chapter explores several dimensions of the changes Michael has made to his life, so keep the notes you have made to hand.

Comment

Michael and his wife mention significant changes to their lives. Michael describes symptoms which he experiences and how these limit him. They discuss the help they have had from the heart failure nurses, who are a source of advice and support and whom they trust as experts in Michael's condition. They also detail the losses and limitations on their lives, and Michael describes his feelings of apprehension of going anywhere different. He briefly mentions the use of medication, worries about driving and his concerns for his wife.

10.2 Lifestyle

Lifestyle can be defined as 'the way of life that is typical of a person, group or culture'. Individuals do not necessarily have the same lifestyle as the culture in which they live. The course uses a fairly broad definition, covering any aspect of the way in which a person leads his or her life.

In terms of health and disease, we tend to think of aspects of behaviour such as diet, exercise, smoking and drinking when discussing lifestyle – behaviours that can influence a person's risk of developing cardiovascular disease (see Chapters 3 and 4). A person who has cardiovascular disease may be encouraged to modify their behaviour in order to improve their condition and prevent progression, as considered below.

10.2.1 Diet

In medical terms, the word **diet** refers to everything a person eats and drinks. A healthy, balanced diet is recommended for all people, not just those with heart disease (Figure 10.1). There are several main groups of food, all of which should be included in the diet.

Complex carbohydrates such as rice, pasta, bread and potatoes are broken down slowly by the body to provide sugar, which is used as fuel. Approximately a third of food intake should be made up of complex carbohydrates.

Fruit and vegetables should form around a third of a person's intake of food. The current nutritional guidelines, produced by the UK's Department of Health, recommend at least five portions of fruit and vegetables each day. Findings suggest that each portion eaten is associated with a risk reduction of 4% for coronary heart disease (Joshipura et al., 2001).

fruit and vegetables

complex carbohydrates

meat, fish and pulses

dairy foods

foods containing
fat and sugar

Figure 10.1   A healthy, balanced diet.

Protein is essential for the growth and maintenance of the cells of the body. It is found in foods such as meat, fish, eggs and pulses. Dairy products also contain significant amounts of protein. These items should be included in the diet but in moderation as excessive intake of protein may lead to weight gain.

Foods containing fat and sugar can be eaten by most people as part of a healthy balanced diet. They should be included in moderation and their intake may need to be restricted if a person is trying to lose weight.

Some people with cardiovascular disease may be encouraged to alter their diet in order to lose weight (see Section 10.2.3).

The Mediterranean diet was briefly discussed in Section 3.13. It includes fats and oils rich in unsaturated (particularly monounsaturated) fatty acids, which seem to reduce the risk of coronary heart disease compared with similar quantities of saturated fatty acids.

The omega-3 fatty acids contained in the oily fish consumed in many areas of the Mediterranean are also thought to have a beneficial effect on the heart. In addition, antioxidants, including flavonoids, polyphenols and vitamins C and E, are believed to be beneficial in preventing the progression of cardiovascular disease, by protecting important proteins from oxidative damage. However, the evidence that antioxidants (particularly antioxidant vitamins) protect against heart disease is limited. Because people are so varied in their constitution, diet and habits, obtaining a clear picture of the contribution of particular nutrients (or even the diet as a whole) to health is very difficult. For example, the observations on the Mediterranean diet seek to explain why people in this area have a surprisingly low incidence of cardiovascular disease. However, these groups also have distinctive genetic types and patterns of work and lifestyle as well as their diet.

It is possible to see how monounsaturated fats affect the ratios of HDL, LDL and chylomicrons, and thus slow the formation of atheroma. However, there is no clear explanation for how antioxidants might do so. Despite the limited evidence, the claims of protection against cardiovascular disease are widely propagated for antioxidant vitamins, mineral supplements and fats containing essential fatty acids. It is also essential to point out that to obtain any health benefit from unsaturated fats, people must eat them instead of saturated fats. Not eating saturates is probably as important as the effects of the unsaturated lipids themselves.

10.2.2 Exercise

The benefits of exercise have been demonstrated in a number of studies (reviewed by Press et al., 2003):

- it helps reduce blood pressure and can stop high blood pressure from developing
- it can assist in weight loss or in keeping a person's weight steady
- it reduces the risk of developing diabetes and, in a person with diabetes, can help improve blood sugar levels
- it causes an increase in the levels of HDL cholesterol
- it can help prevent thrombus formation
- it increases the strength of heart contraction and the cardiac output
- it can reduce levels of stress, depression and anxiety, all of which can slow recovery from heart disease.

Regular exercise reduces the risk of developing heart disease by half. In a person who already has heart disease, exercise can improve health and wellbeing, and reduce the risk of the disease progressing.

In the UK, most people are recommended to take at least 30 minutes of physical activity of moderate intensity on at least 5 days per week. The recommendation is made by the Department of Health, and supported by various health-related organisations such as the British Heart Foundation and Diabetes UK. This can involve activities like going for a run, going to exercise classes, going to the gym or playing a game such as tennis, football or badminton. However, exercise can be included in day-to-day activities such as walking the dog, taking the stairs rather than the lift, mowing the lawn, or cycling to work. Any activity which makes you slightly sweaty and out of breath counts as exercise (Figure 10.2).

Figure 10.2   Exercise for prevention of cardiovascular disease.

Activity 10.2   What limitations does a heart attack place on exercise?

Suggested study time 10 minutes

Think back to Michael, whom you heard in Activity 10.1 describing his life after his MI. What problems may a person with heart disease have when attempting to exercise? Make a list of four potential problems and how these problems may be overcome.

Comment

Michael states that he cannot exercise because he gets short of breath just by walking upstairs. This is a common problem in people with heart disease.
A person with angina may suffer chest pain on exercising, and certain arrhythmias may be triggered by exercise. Some of the tablets used to treat heart disease can affect the body's ability to respond to exercise, such as beta-blockers, which slow the heart down. Mobility and lack of access to suitable facilities may be a problem if a person is no longer confident about travelling. You may have thought about problems with confidence – Michael describes feeling weak, easily tired and lacking in motivation, but also apprehensive about undertaking new activities.

After an MI, people will often be referred for cardiac rehabilitation (see Section 10.7.2). This will include a programme of exercise specially designed to take a person's limitations into account. It may involve starting with gentle exercise for a short period of time, then gradually increasing the intensity and duration of exercise until a person is able to do 30 minutes of moderate intensity exercise at a time. It is normally carried out under supervision, which can increase confidence.

A person with severe symptoms which cannot be controlled with medication, or after surgery, may not be able to exercise. However, even small activities, such as walking upstairs or walking around the house or garden will give some benefits. A cardiac rehabilitation nurse (see Section 10.7.1) may be able to help them work out what they can do without exacerbating any symptoms.

10.2.3 Weight management

Being overweight or obese increases the risk of developing heart disease and disease progression. Several changes are more likely to occur in a person who is overweight:

- total cholesterol and triglyceride levels may be higher
- HDL cholesterol may be lower
- blood pressure may be higher
- the risk of developing diabetes will be higher
- the heart will work under more strain, which can result in enlargement of the heart and eventually in heart failure.

Whether or not a person is overweight can be estimated by measuring a person's BMI (see Section 4.12). Tables correlating weight, height and BMI make it easy to determine whether a person is normal, overweight or obese (Figure 10.3).

Directions: Find your weight in kilograms (or pounds) along the top of the table and your height in metres (or ft and inches) along the left-hand side. Your BMI is the value at the point in the table where they intersect. **_NB The chart does not apply to athletes, children, pregnant or lactating women._**

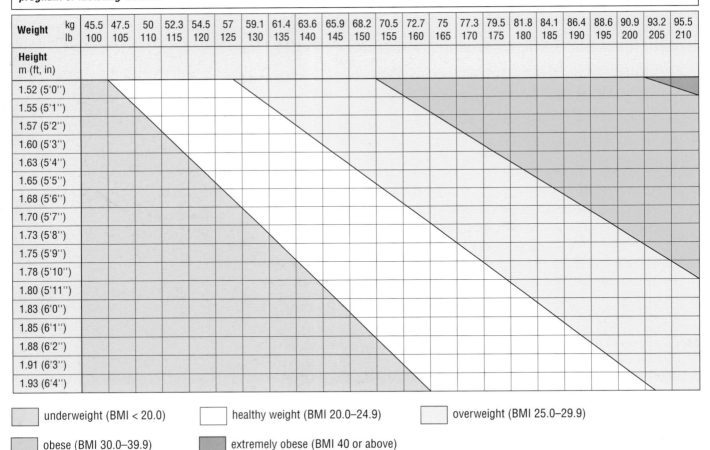

Weight	kg	45.5	47.5	50	52.3	54.5	57	59.1	61.4	63.6	65.9	68.2	70.5	72.7	75	77.3	79.5	81.8	84.1	86.4	88.6	90.9	93.2	95.5
	lb	100	105	110	115	120	125	130	135	140	145	150	155	160	165	170	175	180	185	190	195	200	205	210
Height m (ft, in)																								
1.52 (5'0'')																								
1.55 (5'1'')																								
1.57 (5'2'')																								
1.60 (5'3'')																								
1.63 (5'4'')																								
1.65 (5'5'')																								
1.68 (5'6'')																								
1.70 (5'7'')																								
1.73 (5'8'')																								
1.75 (5'9'')																								
1.78 (5'10'')																								
1.80 (5'11'')																								
1.83 (6'0'')																								
1.85 (6'1'')																								
1.88 (6'2'')																								
1.91 (6'3'')																								
1.93 (6'4'')																								

underweight (BMI < 20.0)   healthy weight (BMI 20.0–24.9)   overweight (BMI 25.0–29.9)

obese (BMI 30.0–39.9)   extremely obese (BMI 40 or above)

Figure 10.3 Cross-refer a person's weight on the *x*-axis with their height on the *y*-axis to determine whether they are normal, overweight or obese. Consideration is also taken of the fat distribution in estimating the risk of cardiovascular disease.

Activity 10.3   What is a healthy weight?

Suggested study time 10 minutes

Winifred Fowler has a mass of 86 kg and is 167 cm (1.67 m) tall. Recall that BMI is calculated using the following equation:

$$\text{BMI} = \frac{\text{mass (kg)}}{\text{height (m)} \times \text{height (m)}}$$

(a) Based on this information, calculate Winifred's BMI. Is she a healthy weight, overweight or obese?

(b) How much weight would Winifred need to lose in order to have a healthy weight?

Comment

(a) Winifred's BMI is 30.8, so she would be classified as obese. This puts her at increased risk of her heart disease progressing further. She will be encouraged to achieve a healthy body weight as part of her recovery. Initially, attention will be given to her diet and activity levels.

(b) A healthy BMI is in the range 20–25. The upper healthy weight limit for a person of height 1.67m is therefore $25 \times 1.67 \times 1.67 = 69.7$ kg. Consequently, Winifred needs to lose 16.3 kg (= 86 kg – 69.7 kg) in order to attain a healthy BMI.

Diet is an important part of weight management. Anybody trying to lose weight will be encouraged to stick to a healthy, balanced diet. Certain changes may be recommended, aimed at reducing the overall energy intake from food and drink. This may involve:

- Reducing portion sizes: often a person's diet is not especially unhealthy in terms of content, but the portion sizes are large.

- Encouraging regular meals: a person may attempt to skip meals to try and reduce energy intake. In practice, most people make up for this at other times during the day and overall energy intake is not normally reduced.

- Having healthier snacks: for example, eating fruit, raw vegetables or diet yoghurts instead of crisps or chocolate bars.

More structured diets, such as Weight Watchers or Slimming World, are likely to result in weight loss if a person can stick to them. They normally encourage healthier eating patterns and, as they often involve attending meetings, can provide support and encouragement, which many people find essential if they are to lose weight successfully.

Meal replacement plans and products can help to achieve short-term weight loss. However, many people find it very hard to stick to these diets because normal food is not usually allowed.

Exercise, when combined with dietary change, can result in weight loss. Increasing exercise to the recommended level (Section 10.2.2) without any changes in diet can result in some mass loss, but this is often limited (on average, 0.5 to 1 kg per month). Combining exercise and dietary changes can significantly increase weight loss. People who persist with regular exercise as part of their daily life are more likely to maintain any weight loss than those who do not exercise.

Drugs can be given to promote weight loss in certain individuals. NICE have recommended that weight loss drugs can be prescribed to people with a BMI over 30 or a BMI over 27 if they have other conditions such as diabetes or high cholesterol. There are two main drugs used in the UK to help with weight loss:

- Sibutramine (Reductil) acts on the brain to reduce appetite – it makes a person feel full more quickly than normal. It can be prescribed for a maximum of a year and can cause raised blood pressure.

- Orlistat (Xenical) reduces fat absorption by preventing the actions of enzymes in the gut which would normally break down fat. It can cause diarrhoea and fatty stools. It is thought that some weight loss occurs because individuals taking orlistat reduce their fat intake to avoid the side effects.

Surgery can be used for people with a BMI of more than 40 when other methods of weight loss have been unsuccessful. The techniques used involve either reducing the volume of the stomach so that less food can be eaten, or bypassing the stomach so that there is reduced absorption of nutrients by the body.

10.2.4 Smoking

In Chapters 3 and 4, you learned that smoking is the most significant single cause of death due to cardiovascular disease. Around half of all lifelong smokers will die from smoking-related diseases, and a person who smokes has approximately twice the risk of developing heart disease as a person who does not, and will die on average over 10 years younger. Anybody with cardiovascular disease will be encouraged to give up smoking to prevent any progression of their condition.

There are several ways in which health care professionals can help a person to give up smoking, and there has been much research to try and establish which method is the most effective (reviewed in West et al., 2000).

Advice from a doctor or nurse can encourage a person to stop smoking. Simply briefly explaining the risks of continuing to smoke and the health benefits of stopping has been shown to cause around 2% of people to stop smoking.

Nicotine replacement therapy (**NRT**) increases the success rate of people giving up smoking to approximately 18%. Nicotine is the addictive chemical in tobacco and replacing it can reduce cravings for cigarettes. Nicotine can be given as patches to be applied to the skin, lozenges, nasal spray, chewing gum, tablets to be placed on the tongue and via an inhaler designed to mimic smoking a cigarette (Figure 10.4).

Bupropion (zyban) is a medication which is thought to work by suppressing the part of the brain which is active in addiction. It should be taken for a week before a person stops smoking, then

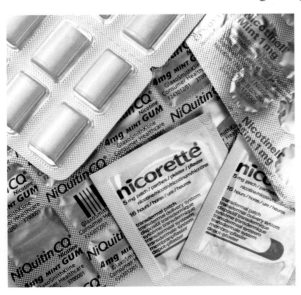

Figure 10.4 Different types of nicotine replacement therapy.

continued for a maximum of 9 weeks. The main concern with taking bupropion is that it increases the risk of a person having an epileptic fit. In trials, the risk of having a fit was found to be 1 person in every 1000. It cannot be given to anyone who has ever had a fit, or who is taking certain medications which, when combined with bupropion, will increase the risk of a fit. As with NRT, bupropion increases the success rate of people stopping smoking to around 18% when measured 1 year later. This compares with ≈3% for people who receive advice only, and ≈10% for people who have a specific programme of counselling.

Activity 10.4 Advice on how to quit smoking

Suggested study time 30 minutes

Use the internet to find the NICE website and then locate the summary of the advice NICE gives about the use of NRT and bupropion in stopping smoking.

(a) Under what circumstances should NRT or bupropion be prescribed?

(b) What additional measures do NICE recommend to increase the chances of success when giving up smoking?

(c) What groups of people (in addition to those noted above) should not be prescribed bupropion or NRT?

(d) Is there any evidence that buproprion is more effective or less effective than NRT?

(e) Is there any advantage to using NRT and buproprion together?

Comment

(a) NICE recommend that NRT and bupropion should be available on prescription to smokers who say they wish to stop smoking. They should only be prescribed once a date has been agreed to stop smoking and advice and encouragement should be offered to a person trying to stop smoking. NICE suggest prescribing enough to last for 2 weeks after a person's target date and more should be prescribed after this only if a person is still trying to give up smoking. If a person is unable to give up smoking, they should not be prescribed NRT or bupropion until 6 months have passed.

(b) NICE stress the importance of advice and encouragement from the doctor and the level of motivation of the subject to quit smoking.

(c) People under the age of 18 and women who are pregnant or breast-feeding are specifically excluded.

(d) The evidence that NRT or bupropion is more effective is inconclusive.

(e) There is no evidence that combining the two treatments is more effective than either used separately.

10.3 Problems with changing a lifestyle

A person who has had a heart attack will be assessed by their doctor and a plan for recovery and rehabilitation will be recommended, which may well include changes in lifestyle alongside the use of drugs. The plan will be different for each person, depending both on their medical condition and on their personal and domestic circumstances. However, making some of these changes can be quite difficult.

Case Study 10.1   Winifred Fowler's lifestyle changes

Winifred goes to visit her doctor to get advice on how best to recover following her MI. She realises after talking to staff in the hospital that her work as a bus driver is quite stressful, and that she has not helped herself by overeating and taking little exercise. She is worried that she might get another heart attack. Nevertheless, she is anxious to get back to work if at all possible: she enjoys the company of her colleagues, and the money is really useful – especially because she and Frank like to take a holiday in Italy each year. She has already rung the bus depot to see whether she can restart work with them, and also asked if there was any possibility of working fewer hours, at least to begin with. Her controller at the bus depot says that they are very sympathetic to people returning to work, but it has to be on the recommendation of her doctors, and the earliest she can possibly be considered is 6 weeks after her heart attack.

Dr Chivers has received letters from the cardiac specialist at the hospital, advising on Winifred's condition, and has spent some time explaining to Winifred what her various medicines do and when she should take them. Dr Chivers sits down with Winifred to discuss changes she should make in her lifestyle, advising her to look at her diet, level of physical activity and smoking. Winifred is obese and is encouraged to eat a healthy balanced diet, incorporating oily fish, antioxidants and monounsaturated fats, while reducing her overall energy intake to try and lose weight. Winifred understands about fish, but not about antioxidants, which she thinks are something to do with face cream. It takes some time to explain which foods make up a balanced diet. Fortunately, Dr Chivers has some leaflets that Winifred can take home with her.

Winifred should also try to incorporate exercise into her daily routine, aiming for 30 minutes of moderate-intensity exercise on 5 days each week. They discuss the possibility of going swimming, which Winifred has always enjoyed (at least when she is on holiday), or going to the gym.

Winifred should also give up smoking, and Dr Chivers explains that this is really the most important thing she can do to help herself. Winifred comes away from the Doctor's thinking that there are an awful lot of changes she needs to make.

Activity 10.5   Translating good advice into healthy living

Suggested study time 10 minutes

What problems might Winifred encounter in trying to change her lifestyle and how might she try to overcome these problems? Make a table as in Table 10.1 and put your answers in the empty boxes.

Table 10.1 The difficulties Winifred Fowler will encounter in trying to change her lifestyle and ways she can work round them.

Lifestyle change	Difficulties	Ways of working around them
improving diet		
losing weight		
taking exercise		
giving up smoking		

Comment

Winifred may encounter various problems in trying to change her lifestyle. A few examples are:

- lack of knowledge about new, healthier foods
- lack of time to cook and exercise
- financial concerns: new foods may be expensive and joining a gym or going swimming costs money
- she may not enjoy the new foods
- because she is overweight, she is more likely to have arthritis of the back and knees, which can make exercise more difficult
- she may feel self-conscious about exercising, especially if she is surrounded by fit people at a gym or swimming pool
- she still has symptoms from angina and heart failure, which may limit her ability to exercise
- giving up smoking can be difficult because nicotine is addictive.

There are several ways Winifred could try to overcome these problems and your answer will depend on what you felt the problems were. A few examples are:

- to ask for advice about eating healthily, possibly from a dietician
- to try one new food every day, rather than trying to change her diet all at once
- to do exercise which can be incorporated into daily life, such as walking to work or taking the stairs rather than the lift
- to start exercising gradually and build up her exercise levels
- to discuss her life changes with the cardiac rehabilitation nurse, to try to develop a plan which will not exacerbate her symptoms
- to join a group of people who are stopping smoking and possibly try NRT.

Figure 10.5 The cycle of change. This model, developed by Prochaska and Declemente (1983), illustrates normal patterns when attempting behavioural change. The model was originally developed in relation to attempting to stop smoking, but can be applied to any aspect of behaviour which an individual attempts to modify. It is normal for an individual to go through the various stages of the cycle several times before successfully maintaining their change in behaviour.

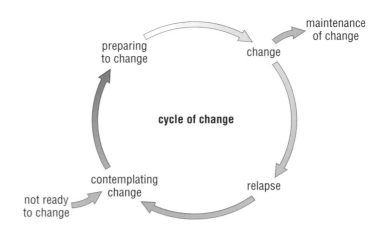

You may have come up with several other answers to Activity 10.5. The main point is that Winifred may find changing her lifestyle much easier if she breaks these changes down into manageable chunks, rather than trying to change everything at once, which can be daunting (Figure 10.5).

10.4 Returning to work

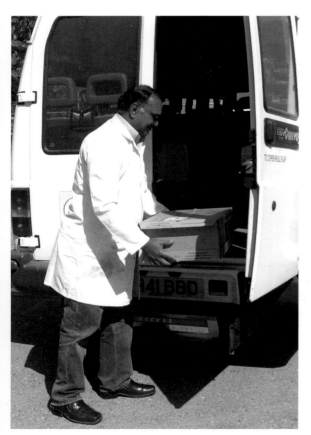

Figure 10.6 You can return to work after an MI.

It is a common belief that stress at work can increase the risk of heart disease – in particular, MI – and this thought alone may act as a barrier to returning to work, with many patients and even doctors believing that the heart is worn out and needs a rest. In fact, there is no evidence that stress in the workplace directly causes cardiovascular disease, although the Whitehall studies showed a link between lack of control at work and various diseases, including heart disease (Section 3.15). Additionally, some of the behaviours associated with stress – in particular, smoking – increase the risk of heart disease.

Depression increases a person's risk of heart disease. This seems to be due to a combination of biological factors, such as increased platelet aggregation, and behavioural factors, such as being sedentary and not taking medication as recommended.

Most people who have had an MI will be advised to stay off work for at least 6 weeks to give themselves a chance to recover. People in sedentary jobs may be advised that they can return to work sooner than those in more physical jobs. Again, while it is popularly believed that physical work could strain the damaged myocardium, there is no evidence to support the view that delaying a return to work is beneficial. The British Heart Foundation advise that, in general, people with cardiovascular disease who return to work quickly and can continue working have a better quality of life than those who cannot (Figure 10.6).

There are very few occupations which a person with heart disease may not do. A person with ischaemic heart disease may not work as a deep sea diver, and certain limitations apply to professions which involve driving. People may not return to work as airline pilots or air traffic controllers. However, in general, most people may be able to return to their previous occupations after developing heart disease.

● What barriers may face Winifred in returning to work?

● Winifred works as a bus driver, so there will be restrictions on her driving, depending on her physical health and rate of recovery (see Section 10.5).

● What barriers may face Michael in regaining an enjoyable lifestyle in retirement?

● Michael continues to experience some symptoms of angina. He also describes a feeling of apprehension and anxiety if he is required to travel outside the immediate vicinity of his home or the local hospital. Previously, he enjoyed concerts and operas, but he would find this difficult now owing partly to practical limitations, such as needing to pass urine frequently, and partly to his worries about being anywhere unfamiliar. The potential psychological limitations of cardiovascular disease will be explored in Section 10.6.

10.5 Limitations on lifestyle
10.5.1 Driving

Driving is often important in maintaining independence. Being able to drive allows people mobility without relying on public transport or family and friends. However, a person with cardiovascular disease may find themselves unable to drive or lacking the confidence to do so.

● Look back at the notes you made about Michael or listen again to the audio clip. Why is Michael concerned about driving following his MI?

● Michael voices two concerns about driving. He is worried that he may experience an attack of angina while he is driving and he worries about what may happen to his wife if this were to happen.

The law

The rules regarding driving with any medical condition are designed to protect drivers, their passengers and other members of the public. Anyone who is experiencing symptoms which may affect their ability to control a vehicle safely should not be driving. The specific laws vary in detail between countries; the description in Activity 10.6 applies to the UK.

● What symptoms may a person with cardiovascular disease experience which could cause problems driving?

● An episode of angina may impair the concentration of people such as Michael. You may also have thought of symptoms such as dizziness or fainting (syncope), which could be caused by arrhythmias. These symptoms can happen in anyone with cardiovascular disease but are more common in the weeks following an MI.

Activity 10.6　Driving with cardiovascular disease

Suggested study time 30 minutes

The rules about driving with a medical condition are set in the UK by the Driver and Vehicle Licensing Agency (DVLA). Use the internet to find their website and then find the guidance on medical standards of fitness to drive. What are the recommendations regarding driving after an MI?

Comment

The standards document refers to group 1 vehicles (cars and motorbikes) and group 2 vehicles (lorries, buses and minibuses). At the time of writing, the rules state that driving a group 1 vehicle is not allowed if a person suffers angina at rest, within 4 weeks of an MI or coronary artery bypass graft, or within 1 week of an angioplasty. A group 2 licence will be revoked for at least 6 weeks following an MI, angioplasty or angina at rest. An exercise tolerance test must then be performed which must show no angina, having first stopped all anti-anginal medication for 48 hours.

Case Study 10.2　Winifred Fowler's work and travel considerations

Winifred has a follow-up appointment with her cardiologist, Dr Jeffries, 6 weeks after her MI. She has stopped driving, as instructed by Dr Chivers, and is hoping to be told she can drive again because she is keen to get back to work as a bus driver. She has taken things fairly gently for the few days preceding the tests, and has not experienced any angina. Her cardiologist arranges an exercise tolerance test, in which an ECG is taken while Winifred walks on a treadmill.

Within a few minutes of starting the test, Winifred develops chest pain and has to stop and take her GTN spray. She is told that she cannot be recommended to drive class 2 vehicles because she is still experiencing angina. This comes as a serious blow to Winifred, as she thinks that it will place limitations on her ability to travel – not just on work. Dr Jeffries explains that the restrictions on driving passenger vehicles are much more severe than on personal driving. Although Winifred is not allowed to drive a passenger vehicle at the moment, it may be possible for her to drive a car. However, Dr Jeffries does not recommend that just yet – at least not until her tolerance to exercise improves. He also reminds her that she should have a further check-up before she starts to drive the car. In addition, she will have to be in contact with her car insurance company because having an MI may be seen as a substantial change in the conditions of motor insurance.

Winifred had previously booked a holiday in Rome to see her sister, and the flight is due in 3 weeks. She asks whether she should cancel the flight and claim on her travel insurance. Dr Jeffries says that this should not be necessary and she can go ahead with the holiday as planned, as long as she can manage the flight of stairs in her own house and can walk 100 m on level ground without any discomfort. It would be a good idea to check this with the airline or with her travel agent. He also reminds her not to carry too much baggage and to make sure that she travels with all her medications.

● What do you think are the implications of this discussion with the cardiologist for Winifred and her family?

● On a practical level, Winifred will be unable to work in her current job, which has financial implications. As she continues to experience angina, she may require further medical or surgical treatment. She may find it difficult to obtain life insurance, which could affect the family's finances in the future.

There may also be psychological and social implications for Winifred and her family. She may worry about the family's finances. She may become anxious and depressed, which is more likely if she continues to experience symptoms that affect the quality of life. She may be bored at home, as she is used to going out at work, and may miss the social contact with her colleagues. We will explore the psychological aspects of living with cardiovascular disease in Section 10.6.

Case Study 10.3   Katerin Wilcox's driving and leisure activities

Katerin has been discharged from hospital 2 days after having her pacemaker fitted, and is collected by her nephew, who drives her home. Despite the minor surgery to implant the pacemaker, she is feeling excellent. For the first weekend at home, she has a lot of friends and family calling in to make sure that she is alright. Monday is her music night with the local orchestra, and she wonders if it would be possible to go round to join them as usual to play the violin. Of course she enjoys meeting up with friends, but she also has a sense of pride and wants to show them that a short stop in hospital has not set her back at all. She is a little concerned that playing the violin might disturb her stitches – she has had an incision which is about 6 cm long, just beneath her collarbone, and is healing well. She is also not too sure about whether she is allowed to drive, so she decides to ring her doctor for advice.

Dr Karlsen is very encouraging, and says that it is excellent that Katerin has such a positive attitude about getting back to doing things that she enjoys. However, he does say that it is a bit too early. 'Give it a miss for at least 2 weeks until the incision has healed over, especially as playing the violin involves lifting your arms, which may disturb the stitches,' he says. 'The other thing is that you are not allowed to drive for at least a week. After that, see how you feel, and you will probably be able to start driving again in 2 weeks' time.'

10.5.2 Finances and insurance

Activity 10.7   Changes in financial circumstances

Suggested study time 10 minutes

Make a list of the potential financial changes that could affect a person, such as Winifred Fowler, who has recently had an MI. After each item, write down why their condition affects the financial circumstances of that person.

Comment

Winifred is unable to return to work in her old job as a result of her condition, and may have a direct loss of earnings and be less well off. This circumstance may change as she recovers and makes the lifestyle changes identified by Dr Chivers. Certain insurance policies, such as life insurance or critical illness cover, may require higher premiums or be impossible to obtain. Obtaining a mortgage may require a medical report from a person's GP, who is obliged to report any medical conditions, including cardiovascular disease. Omitting details of any illness is likely to result in life/medical insurance or finance being refused. The reason is that anyone who has had cardiovascular disease is at increased risk of further MI or cardiovascular event, and hence will be at increased risk of premature death. Insurance companies are thus more likely to have to pay out in the event of a person dying or being unable to work, and so will increase the premiums to cover this likely additional cost. Activities such as joining a gym or attending an exercise class may be expensive, and a healthier diet may also be more expensive than her current diet.

10.6 Adjusting psychologically

10.6.1 Changes in lifestyle

● Think again about Michael, referring back to the notes you made earlier. What limitations does Michael have on his lifestyle following his MI? Which of these limitations is psychological, and which is practical?

● Michael and his wife mention several limitations. Before his MI, Michael travelled to various concerts and operas. Now he restricts himself to going to the local supermarkets and to visiting friends who live locally. Michael's wife mentions an example of deciding to cancel a trip to the opera, while Michael explains that he is reluctant to travel to the Bath Festival – something he did every year before he became unwell.

The main reason for these limitations is Michael's feeling of apprehension if he travels far from home. He worries about what would happen if he was unwell while away from home or while driving, or if he needed to be admitted to a hospital where he does not know the cardiology team. These restrictions on Michael's lifestyle are his way of adapting psychologically to the feelings of anxiety he experiences following his MI. He finds it more comfortable to remain within familiar surroundings just in case he is taken ill. He describes days when he feels generally unwell and is comforted by being in his own home and being able to go to bed if he wishes.

Michael also mentions some limitations of a practical nature. This includes worries about having to go to the toilet frequently because of the diuretics he takes. This may be difficult if he has to go up and down stairs because he gets so breathless on any exertion.

● Winifred Fowler has been advised to make a number of changes in her lifestyle. What are they, and how do you think she will feel about this?

● Winifred has been advised to modify her diet, take up exercise and give up smoking. She may feel unhappy and resentful about being forced to change her lifestyle, or deprived of the foods and cigarettes she enjoys. However, she may feel more positive about her new, healthier lifestyle, as she is given a lot of helpful advice about ways of improving her health. This is more likely if she starts feeling better in herself as a result of her new lifestyle. She finds she is unable to work in her previous job as a bus driver, which could have financial implications, but Winifred may also have feelings of loss. She may feel guilty that she can no longer provide for her family, and may feel socially isolated because she no longer sees her work colleagues.

All of the changes described above may increase a person's chances of becoming depressed – we will now look at this in more detail.

10.6.2 Psychological problems following myocardial infarction or surgery

Depression and anxiety are common in patients who suffer an MI. Almost all patients are anxious on admission to and discharge from hospital, and most will suffer low mood on coming home from hospital. Unless a person suffers a further MI, these symptoms are likely to slowly resolve over the following weeks. However, around a quarter of patients will remain depressed or anxious a year after their MI.

Traditionally, doctors believed that depression was a fairly normal reaction to heart disease, but recent research has shown that patients who suffer depression in the weeks after an MI or surgery are twice as likely to have a further MI or to die during the first year after their MI as those who are not depressed. They are also less likely to return to their normal levels of activity than non-depressed people. Patients who become depressed after cardiac surgery tend to have smaller improvements in the functioning of the heart than those who are not depressed (Rumsfeld and Ho, 2005).

● Can you think of any reasons why depression may be bad for the heart?

● People with depression may be less likely to take their medication than those without depression. A depressed person may be more likely to continue behaviours which are harmful to the heart, such as smoking, drinking heavily and remaining physically inactive. It is also known that depression can cause platelet activation, which increases the risk of thrombosis.

The best way to treat depression and anxiety has not been clearly established. Symptoms may be improved by cognitive behavioural therapy, by anxiety and stress management techniques, and by certain anti-depressant medications. Studies originally demonstrated that treating depression and anxiety did not reduce the risk of further MI (ENRICHD investigators, 2003, 2004). However, analysis of the trial data actually showed that treatment improved the prognosis of white men, but not women and ethnic minority groups, suggesting that treatment of depression and anxiety needs to be better adapted to the needs of different sexes and cultural groups.

10.6.3 Relationships with friends and family

● How do you think relationships with friends and family may change following an MI or cardiac surgery? Think again about Michael and Winifred when answering this.

● Partners are often concerned for each other if one of them has heart disease. This affects each partner in different ways. Michael is concerned about how his wife will cope if he has an angina attack while driving, or is admitted to hospital a long way from home. Winifred's husband is very worried about Winifred, especially when her symptoms deteriorate.

If a person is very unwell, their partner or another family member may have to take on the role of carer. Even if this is not necessary, they may be more dependent on their partner – for example, in remembering to take medication or being driven to hospital or doctor's appointments.

Other members of the family may feel guilty that they are not sufficiently involved in the person's care, especially if they live a long distance away when it is very difficult for them. They may also feel that they have neglected their relative, perhaps by not phoning or visiting as often as they should have.

Friends may find it difficult to know how to deal with someone following an MI. Michael finds it difficult to go away from home and some of his friends may not understand the reasons for this. Others may be overprotective, for example not allowing the person with heart disease to help clear the plates or wash up after a meal, which may make the person feel socially isolated and different to everybody else.

Often the most important way of overcoming these difficulties is by good communication (Figure 10.7). Partners who are aware of each other's concerns tend to feel less anxious as a result. Explaining what has happened to other family members and friends can make it easier to socialise, knowing that people are aware of any limitations a person may have. Sometimes discussing concerns with health care professionals can be reassuring, and Michael's wife found it helpful to talk to someone who had been through a similar experience.

Figure 10.7 Communication and social support are important for rehabilitation.

10.6.4 Sex and myocardial infarction

Following an MI, patients may be reluctant to resume sex for fear of triggering a further MI or angina. Studies have shown that while there is an increase in the heart rate during sex, which potentially increases strain on the heart, this increase is no more than that caused by moderate exercise or becoming angry. In fact, as moderate exercise is beneficial to the heart, sex may help prevent further MI. People should be informed that there is no evidence that sex is dangerous and that they may resume having sex when they feel able to do so (Thompson and Lewin, 2000).

10.6.5 Relationships with work colleagues

A person who has had an MI may well experience subtle or overt changes in their relationships with colleagues, which may be due to:

* Colleagues worrying about the person's ability to do their job or the possibility of further absences through ill health: 'Will I have to work harder to make up for their inability?'

* Worrying about what happens if the person has a heart attack at work.

* The belief that work caused the person's heart disease (this belief may be shared by the person with heart disease).

* Oversympathy: being steered away from stressful aspects or harder manual labour.

* 'Social outcast' syndrome: some colleagues may not know how to treat someone with heart disease and so may find it easier to ignore them altogether.

When returning to work, people may develop their own methods of coping with these problems. Some may simply soldier on with the job, hoping that their colleagues will realise they are still capable of doing their work. Some will gradually return to their normal working life, starting off with lighter duties and part-time work and building up gradually to their previous levels of activities. Others will try to explain their condition, together with any limitations, to their colleagues.

Sadly, a number of people will take early retirement following an MI or other heart disease, often fuelled by the belief that they are no longer able to do their job because of their weakened heart.

10.7 Facilities and help available for readjusting lifestyle

Activity 10.8 Identifying sources of help and support

Suggested study time 10 minutes

Think back to Winifred and Michael and their experiences in hospital and during their recovery from MI. Who has been important in helping support and advise them?

Michael and his wife seem to have found most support from the heart failure nurses, who can advise on symptoms and treatment, and discuss Michael's care with his cardiologist. Michael and his wife feel reassured that they can phone the nurses in an emergency, or simply for advice and reassurance if he is feeling unwell.

Winifred is seen by her GP and cardiologist, both of whom advise on different medications to help her symptoms and to improve her prognosis. She is referred to the cardiac rehabilitation team to aid her recovery. She also has an exercise tolerance test, which would be administered by a cardiac technician.

10.7.1 The multidisciplinary care team

This term is used to describe the team of health care professionals involved in the care of a person with cardiovascular disease. A patient may see a number of people, each of whom has a specific role to play within the team. These staff may be based mainly in the hospital (secondary care) or in general practice and the community (primary care). We will now look at the roles of some of these people.

A **cardiologist** is a hospital-based doctor who specialises in heart disease and advises on the medical aspects of care, including the organisation and interpretation of investigations, advice on medication, performing complex investigations such as an angiogram and angioplasty, and referring a patient for surgery when this would be beneficial.

Coronary care unit (CCU) nurses are specially trained nurses who work on the CCU. They are responsible for the care of patients admitted to the CCU, most of whom will have suffered an MI. They have special training in the management of MI and of the common complications in its immediate aftermath, such as heart failure and arrhythmias.

Cardiac rehabilitation nurses assess and coordinate rehabilitation needs for the patient.

Cardiac specialist nurses, including the **heart failure nurses** mentioned by Michael and his wife, have specialist knowledge in different aspects of heart disease and will often be the first point of contact for a patient needing advice.

Cardiac technicians are responsible for administering different investigations, such as electrocardiograms, echocardiograms and exercise tolerance testing, and may assist at more complex procedures such as angiograms and angioplasty.

The **cardiothoracic surgeon** is the consultant surgeon responsible for performing any surgery on the heart (see Chapter 9).

A **general practitioner (GP)** is a patient's family doctor. They may advise on various aspects of cardiovascular disease, including work, psychological issues, lifestyle and medication, and coordinate referrals to other members of the team.

Practice nurses work in general practice. A person with heart disease may be referred to the practice nurse for advice on aspects of lifestyle such as giving up smoking or losing weight. In addition, many practice nurses carry out monitoring of patients with heart disease in special cardiovascular clinics.

A **dietician** will advise on various aspects of a person's diet. A person with heart disease may see a dietician for advice on weight loss or on specific diets such as the Mediterranean diet.

A **fitness instructor** may see a person with heart disease as part of their cardiac rehabilitation. Their role is to devise an exercise programme which will safely improve a person's physical fitness while taking into account any limitations caused by heart disease.

While patients may come into contact with particular members of the team more often than others, two important points should be made here:

- All members of the multidisciplinary team carry out an important role. Without all the different members, the team would be unable to function and look after the person with heart disease.

- The person who is being treated is at the centre of the team and should be involved in all aspects of their care.

Activity 10.9   Communication in the multidisciplinary team

Suggested study time 10 minutes

Communication is vitally important within the multidisciplinary team. Look at Figure 10.8, in which various members of the team are arranged around the patient. Draw a line connecting two people where you think these people would need to communicate with each other. For example, you may think that a patient would talk to a cardiologist, so you could draw a line connecting the patient to the cardiologist. You may then think that a cardiac specialist nurse would talk to the cardiologist, so they could also be connected. Keep doing this, thinking about the various reasons why these team members would need to communicate with each other as you do it.

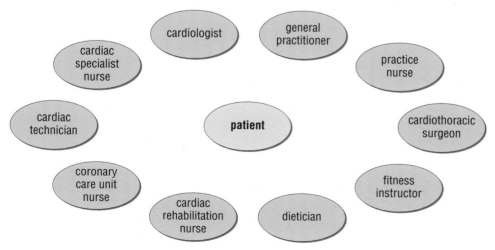

Figure 10.8   Lines of communication within the multidisciplinary team.

The aim of this exercise is to get you thinking about the vital role of communication within the team, and of teamwork, with no individual member of the team being more important than any other. The patient would talk to every member of the team, but most members of the team would need to communicate with several other team members.

10.7.2 Cardiac rehabilitation

Cardiac rehabilitation (CR) is defined as:

> '…the sum of activities required to influence favourably the underlying cause of the disease, as well as to provide the best possible physical, mental and social conditions, so that patients may, by their own efforts, preserve or resume when lost, as normal a place as possible in the community.'

(World Health Organization)

Who should have cardiac rehabilitation?

The National Service Framework for coronary heart disease was introduced in Chapter 1. One of the aims of the National Service Framework is to increase the provision of CR to patients with heart disease. Traditionally, only a handful of patients were referred for CR following an MI. The National Service Framework stated that by 2002, 85% of patients who have suffered an MI or undergone angioplasty or coronary artery bypass graft should receive CR. It also stated that, once this had been achieved, CR should be offered to people with angina and heart failure, and following other surgical interventions such as transplantation and valve replacement.

Unfortunately, comparatively few people are referred for CR after an MI: in 2006, less than half the people who suffered an MI were referred, falling far short of the National Service Framework target. This is partly due to lack of provision of CR in certain areas of the country, but also because certain groups of people, such as older people and some ethnic groups, are less likely to accept CR if it is offered.

● Considering the WHO definition of CR, what sort of 'activities' might be involved in a CR programme for Michael or Winifred?

● Winifred may benefit from some help to give up smoking and lose weight. Because she is unable to work, she may need some advice on retraining or claiming benefits. Michael feels unable to exercise and so may benefit from developing a gentle exercise programme under the supervision of the hospital. Winifred and Michael both feel stressed and anxious at times; each may benefit from seeing a psychologist or counsellor and from learning ways of managing their anxiety.

Traditionally, CR was a standard package of interventions based in a hospital outpatient department and was exactly the same for each individual. It mainly consisted of structured exercise under supervision, education about heart disease and group relaxation exercises.

Since the publication of the National Service Framework for coronary heart disease, CR is much more focused on the needs of the individual. Winifred and Michael have very different needs and these will be taken into consideration in developing a programme for each of them. Each person will be assessed medically, socially and psychologically and an individualised programme is developed based on this assessment. CR may be carried out mainly in a hospital setting, mainly in the community, or a mixture of both. Examples of activities include:

- smoking cessation clinics
- referral to a dietician
- exercise programs based in the hospital or in the community, which may involve exercise in a gym, swimming, walking or other forms of exercise
- weight loss groups, which may be run by a GP surgery, a hospital clinic, or may be unconnected (for example, a Weight Watchers group)
- stress and anxiety management, which can be individual work or as part of a group
- psychological support from counsellors or psychologists.

A person's medical needs will also be considered, both in terms of symptom control and in trying to prevent progression of the condition. This may be monitored by the cardiologist and cardiac specialist nurses, by the GP and practice nurses – or a mixture of the two. All GP surgeries should offer a full medical review of each patient with heart disease at least annually.

Does CR work?

In a word, yes! Although there is no evidence that CR reduces deaths from heart disease, people who receive CR are more likely to improve their lifestyle, quality of life, blood pressure and cholesterol levels. They are also more likely to have a reduced risk of re-admission to hospital, an improved psychological wellbeing and a better knowledge of heart disease.

10.7.3 Other sources of help

While the multidisciplinary team and CR have a role to play in improving a person's health and wellbeing, they cannot be available 24 hours a day. So people with heart disease largely have to find additional sources of help and support.

● What other sources of help, support and advice are available for a person with heart disease?

● Perhaps the most important source of help and support is from family and friends. Help is also available from support groups and job centres.

Often the family are involved when a person has an MI and will go along to the hospital with them, then attend outpatient and CR appointments with them. But think of the role Michael's wife plays in his life: she is his constant companion and he feels reassured that she understands the way he is feeling and will not push him into doing anything about which he feels uncomfortable. Michael also mentions his friends as a source of support: he and his wife will go for dinner with friends who live locally, and his wife found it helpful to talk to a friend who had also suffered an MI because it reassured her that Michael's feelings of apprehension were entirely normal.

Support groups are organisations where people with heart disease can meet a range of other people with similar conditions with whom they can share experiences, ask advice and possibly make friends. These groups may be run by a hospital or a GP surgery and may form part of a CR programme. Other support groups may be run by organisations such as the British Heart Foundation or may be set up by an individual or a group of people.

Because Winifred can no longer work as a bus driver, she may gain support and advice from organisations such as the job centre, who can advise her on retraining and on any benefits she is entitled to claim. Michael has found solace in his computer – so he may gain support from online resources. This could include accessing information about his condition, or possibly meeting other people with heart disease in online chat rooms.

This list is by no means exhaustive. The point is that most people will gain help, support and advice from a variety of sources, only a handful of which will be medical.

10.8 Prospects for a healthy future life

10.8.1 Supportive medication

In Chapter 8, you learned about the different medications used to treat heart disease. Many of these play an important role in controlling symptoms – for example, from angina or heart failure. Other medications are used to treat conditions associated with heart disease and to reduce the risk of the disease progressing.

● Which risk factors for heart disease can be modified by medication?

● The two main modifiable risk factors which can be helped by medication are high blood pressure (hypertension) and raised blood cholesterol (hyperlipidaemia).

Anyone who has developed cardiovascular disease will be at increased risk of suffering a further event, such as an MI or stroke. It is of vital importance to reduce their risk as much as possible by treating any modifiable risk factors. Some risk factors can only be altered by a change in lifestyle, for example by losing weight, taking up exercise or giving up smoking. The risk can be further reduced by taking various medications which can reduce the risk of further MI and also reduce the risk of death should a person suffer a subsequent MI. Secondary prevention such as this is described in Section 8.3.

10.8.2 Monitoring and check-ups

All people with cardiovascular disease should be monitored regularly. This may be carried out by various different members of the multidisciplinary team, depending on a person's state of health. A person whose symptoms are not easily controlled by medication may be under regular review by a cardiologist, whereas someone like Michael may be seen most often by the heart failure nurses or other specialist nurses.

The majority of people with heart disease are monitored in the community by their GP, practice nurse and other primary care staff. For this reason, this section will finish with a more detailed examination of the annual review in the GP surgery. The investigations and areas of discussion will be similar for all patients, whether they are seen in primary or secondary care.

● Keeping in mind the various risk factors for heart disease and the discussion of secondary prevention, what should be discussed or carried out at an annual review for heart disease?

● Symptoms, medication and lifestyle should all be discussed.

The National Service Framework for coronary heart disease states that GPs and primary care teams should 'identify all people with established cardiovascular disease and offer them comprehensive advice and appropriate treatment to reduce their risks' (Department of Health, 2000, 2004). Most GP surgeries offer an annual review to all people with heart disease, which consists of an initial appointment, at which investigations are carried out, followed by a longer appointment where a variety of topics will be discussed, including medication.

Examples of investigations carried out include:

* blood pressure
* height, weight and BMI
* blood cholesterol level
* kidney function, if a person is on an ACE inhibitor or diuretic
* liver function, if a person is taking a statin or other cholesterol-lowering drug
* full blood count (a measurement of the numbers of red blood cells, leukocytes and platelets in the blood; see Table 2.1), to check for anaemia if a person is taking an anti-platelet agent (anaemia may indicate that the medication is causing some damage to the stomach or bleeding elsewhere in the body)
* an ECG to detect any changes in the electrical activity of the heart, which could indicate worsening ischaemia.

Examples of topics covered at the follow-up appointment include:

* discussion of any symptoms, such as chest pain, shortness of breath, oedema, dizziness or palpitations
* recording whether or not a person smokes and, if appropriate, offering advice and help on giving up smoking
* discussion of diet and exercise, with referral to a dietician or the local supervised exercise scheme if necessary

Figure 10.9 An annual review with a practice nurse.

- discussion of alcohol intake
- discussion of medication, to ensure that a person is prescribed the correct medication for their condition and that they remember to take it; the doctor would also enquire about any side effects and check that the medication is having the desired outcome, for example by looking at blood pressure and cholesterol levels
- enquiry about a person's psychological wellbeing, which may include asking about depression, anxiety and stress, sometimes using specially designed questionnaires such as the hospital anxiety and depression scale (HADS)
- open-ended questions, to see if the person has anything else they wish to discuss.

An annual review is broad-reaching, covering symptoms, lifestyle, medication and psycho-social areas of a person's life. These are often run by the practice nurse, with referrals made to other members of the multidisciplinary team if necessary (Figure 10.9). Practice nurses will often make adjustments to medication if, for example, blood pressure or cholesterol levels are elevated, and they will arrange a further blood pressure or cholesterol check a few weeks later.

If all is well, a person is likely to be offered a further appointment 6 months later in which their blood pressure and cholesterol levels are measured. Each patient should also be encouraged to come back sooner if they experience any problems with worsening symptoms, side effects from medications or any other difficulties.

These regular reviews have been shown to help maintain the general health of people who attend regularly, with reduction in their symptoms and improvements in their general health and survival rates (Murchie et al., 2004). However, the long-term benefit of these clinics has not yet been fully assessed.

10.9 Summary of Chapter 10

This chapter has focused on the experience of living with cardiovascular disease. You have seen the various changes in lifestyle which are recommended to anybody with heart disease and the difficulties in achieving these changes. You have also explored the psychological difficulties which a person with heart disease may face, and ways of overcoming them. There are many different people who may be involved in the care of someone with heart disease; their roles and the importance of cardiac rehabilitation have been discussed. Finally, the ways in which the risk of disease progression can be minimised have been explored, as part of routine monitoring, which also involves assessment of lifestyle and psychosocial aspects of care.

Although living with cardiovascular disease causes a wide range of difficulties and challenges, this chapter has given you an insight into various ways in which these problems can be overcome, enabling a person to live with – rather than be controlled by – cardiovascular disease.

We hope that you have enjoyed this course. Coronary heart disease and cardiovascular disease are important both for health care professionals and planners, as well as for individuals who may be affected by the conditions. The incidence of coronary heart disease in the under-65 age group has fallen by more than half in the UK over the last 25 years, and more than 90% people who have an MI will be alive a year later. An understanding of risk factors has been as important as advances in medical science in producing these changes, but there are still many challenges for controlling these conditions, as lifestyles change and life expectancy increases.

Questions for Chapter 10

Question 10.1 (Learning Outcomes 10.5 and 10.6)

Evaluate what limitations are placed on the following people in regard to their potential to return to work following an MI:

(a) a school teacher who drives the school football team to matches once a week in a minibus

(b) a despatch rider who carries small parcels and letters by motorbike

(c) a ship builder who is engaged in moderately heavy manual work, rivetting steel plates

(d) an airline traffic controller.

Question 10.2 (Learning Outcomes 10.2 and 10.3)

Evaluate what are the most important changes that Winifred Fowler can make in her lifestyle, and place them in order of priority for reducing her risk of another MI.

Question 10.3 (Learning Outcomes 10.4 and 10.5)

What risk is there that Michael will develop depression over the next year, and how could you determine whether this had actually occurred?

Further reading

If you would like to read further, please refer to the following publication.

Rippe, J. M., Angelopoulos, T. J. and Zukley, L. (2007) 'Lifestyle medicine strategies for risk factor reduction, prevention and treatment of coronary heart disease: Part II', *American Journal of Lifestyle Medicine*, **1**, pp. 79–90.

References

Department of Health (2000) *National Service Framework for coronary heart disease* [online] Available from: http://www.dh.gov.uk/en/Publicationsandstatistics/Publications/PublicationsPolicyAndGuidance/DH_4094274 (Accessed February 2007).

Department of Health (2004) *Winning the war on heart disease* [online] Available from: http://www.dh.gov.uk/prod_consum_dh/groups/dh_digitalassets/@dh/@en/documents/digitalasset/dh_4077158.pdf (Accessed May 2007).

ENRICHD investigators (2003) 'Effects of treating depression and perceived low social support on clinical events after myocardial infarction', *Journal of the American Medical Association*, **289**, pp. 3106–3116.

ENRICHD investigators (2004) 'Psychosocial treatment within sex by ethnicity subgroups in the enhancing recovery in coronary heart disease clinical trial', *Psychosomatic Medicine*, **66**, pp. 475–483.

Joshipura, K. J., Hu, F. B., Mason, J. E., Stampfer, M. J., Rimm, E. B., Speizer, F. E., Colditz, G., Ascherio, A., Rosner, B., Spiegelman, D. and Willett, W. C. (2001) 'The effect of fruit and vegetable intake on risk for coronary heart disease', *Annals of Internal Medicine*, **134**, pp. 1106–1114.

Murchie, P., Campbell, N. C., Richie, L. D., Deans, H. G., and Thain, J. (2004) 'Effects of secondary prevention clinics on health status in patients with coronary heart disease: 4 year follow-up of a randomized trial in primary care', *Family Practice*, **21**, pp. 567–574.

Press, V., Freestone, I. and George, C. F. (2003) 'Physical activity: the evidence of benefit in the prevention of coronary heart disease', *Quarterly Journal of Medicine*, **96**, pp. 245–251.

Prochaska, J. and Declemente, C. (1983) 'Stages and processes of self-change of smoking: towards an integrative model', *Journal of Consulting and Clinical Psychology*, **51**, pp. 390–395.

Rumsfeld, J. S. and Ho, P. M. (2005) 'Depression and cardiovascular disease: a call for recognition', *Circulation*, **111**, pp. 250–253.

Thompson, D.R. and Lewin, R.J. (2000) 'Management of the post-myocardial-infarction patient: rehabilitation and cardiac neurosis', *Heart*, **84**, pp. 101–105.

West, R., McNeill, A. and Raw, M. (2000) 'Smoking cessation guidelines for health professionals: an update', *Thorax*, **55**, pp. 987–999.

ANSWERS TO QUESTIONS

Question 1.1

(i) 10; (ii) 8; (iii) 7.

Question 1.2

Two of the following: heart or coronary arteries; blood vessels in brain; blood vessels in periphery, e.g. arms, legs.

Question 1.3

Age (increasing); smoking; gender (being male); diet (unhealthy or unbalanced); family history (genetic); inactivity (sedentary lifestyle); race/ethnicity; excess alcohol consumption; high blood cholesterol; psychosocial factors, e.g. stress, depression and anger; high blood pressure; diabetes (types 1 and 2); obesity and being overweight.

Question 1.4

Your table should look like Table 1.6 below.

Table 1.6 Risk factors for cardiovascular diseases.

Biological risk factors: non-modifiable	Biological risk factors: modifiable by treatment or altered lifestyle	Lifestyle risk factors: modifiable
age (increasing)	high blood cholesterol	smoking
male	high blood pressure (hypertension)	diet (unhealthy or unbalanced)
family history (genetic)	overweight and obesity	inactivity (sedentary lifestyle)
race/ethnicity	diabetes (Type 2)	excess alcohol consumption
diabetes (Type 1)	psychosocial factors, e.g. stress, depression, anger	

There are two types of diabetes. Type 1 would be classed as a biological non-modifiable risk factor, but Type 2 can be improved with appropriate management and so is modifiable – especially if it has arisen as a result of lifestyle, developed following weight gain.

Suggestions to positively influence modifiable risk factors could include:

* reducing or give up smoking and alcohol intake
* improving diet by following healthy eating guidelines
* becoming more active, e.g. by taking the stairs instead of the escalator or lift or starting an exercise programme after a medical assessment.
* taking measures or obtaining advice on how to manage psychosocial factors.

Question 1.5

Angina pectoris; ischaemia; pericarditis; myocardial infarction; musculoskeletal problems; indigestion (acid reflux); gallbladder disease; coronary artery disease.

Question 1.6

Primary prevention strategies for developing cardiovascular diseases involve preventing the onset of disease in individuals without symptoms. Secondary prevention strategies refer to the prevention (or delay) of death or recurrence of disease in individuals with pre-existing symptoms. This distinction is made because recommendations are slightly different, depending on whether cardiovascular diseases have already been established in the patient. For example, the 'Sheffield table' to estimate cardiovascular disease risk is not appropriate for secondary prevention, that is, in people with established cardiovascular diseases such as myocardial infarction and angina.

Question 1.7

Following successful surgery, it remains essential to control the symptoms and further development of cardiovascular diseases by reducing the risk factors that contributed to the development of disease in the first place. For instance, a diet high in saturated fat would need to be modified.

Question 1.8

Hypertension and high blood cholesterol levels are early indicators, common to the development of many cardiovascular diseases. Regular monitoring of blood pressure and blood cholesterol levels is important so that medical interventions can take place to keep the levels of both under control.

Question 2.1

The droplet of blood enters the right atrium via the inferior or superior vena cava and then passes through the tricuspid (atrioventricular) valve into the right ventricle (assisted by atrial contraction). The droplet is then pumped from the right ventricle into one of the two branches of the pulmonary arteries and travels to the lungs. Backflow into the right side of the heart is prevented by the closure of the pulmonary semilunar valve. The droplet returns to the heart from the lungs via one of the two pulmonary veins into the left atrium. From the left atrium it passes through the bicuspid (mitral) valve into the left ventricle and is subsequently pumped out of the heart into the aorta and then around the body. Backflow in the left side of the heart is prevented by closure of the aortic semilunar valve.

Question 2.2

Your trace should look like the example shown in Figure 2.10a. The P wave corresponds to the wave of atrial depolarisation arising from the sinoatrial node, the pacemaker node which initiates the heart beat. The QRS complex represents the wave of ventricular depolarisation that initiates contraction of the ventricles. The T wave corresponds to the period of repolarisation when the ventricular cells return to their normal resting membrane potential.

Question 2.3

Starling's law states that the force of contraction is related to the degree the heart is stretched before it contracts. Contractility is an increase in the contractile strength of the muscle, and is under the control of the sympathetic nervous system and circulating hormones, such as noradrenalin and adrenalin.

The relationship described by Starling's law is dependent on the degree of muscle stretching, whereas contractility is independent of muscle length.

Question 2.4

The sympathetic nervous system innervates the heart, where it increases the heart rate (by exciting the SAN) and increases the contractility of the heart muscle. The parasympathetic nervous system slows the beating of the heart via the vagus nerve, which also innervates the SAN. In addition, the sympathetic nervous system can regulate peripheral resistance (and hence blood pressure) by controlling vasoconstriction of the arteriole smooth muscle. The sympathetic nervous system exerts its action via direct neural control (using the neurotransmitter noradrenalin) or via the release of the 'fright, fight or flight' hormones adrenalin and noradrenalin. The parasympathetic nervous system uses the neurotransmitter acetylcholine.

Question 2.5

Cardiac output is calculated using the following relationship:

Cardiac output = heart rate × stroke volume

Thus, the cardiac output in litres per hour (= 60 minutes) is:

Cardiac output = 72 beats per minute × 70 ml × 60 minutes

= 5040 ml per minute × 60 minutes

= 5.040 litres per minute × 60 minutes

= 302.4 litres per hour

Cardiac output can be influenced by changes in heart rate or stroke volume.

Question 2.6

The baroreceptor reflex plays an important role in the homeostatic regulation of blood pressure. Baroreceptors are located in the carotid sinus and the aorta and are capable of detecting small changes in the blood pressure. Information concerning changes in blood pressure is relayed back to the vasomotor and cardio-inhibitory centres in the brain, where it is processed. The output from the brain to the heart, via the sympathetic and vagus nerves, is altered accordingly to change heart rate (and in the case of the sympathetic system, contractility) to return blood pressure back to its normal level. The baroreceptor reflex also regulates peripheral resistance via the sympathetic nervous system.

Question 3.1

Epidemiological research indicates that smoking continues to be the most important modifiable risk factor for the future development of cardiovascular disease. People who stop smoking will eventually have virtually the same cardiovascular risk as non-smokers. Research to determine the effect of risk factors such as smoking is always done by comparing the health outcome of large numbers of people who have the risk factor against those who do not.

Question 3.2

Although it is important not to generalise about all women, it has been found in many studies that heart-related symptoms in women are often treated as less important than when men complain. For this reason, it does appear that the outcome of cardiovascular disease in women is worse than in men.

Question 3.3

As countries develop economically, the habits of the population change. In general terms, increased affluence brings greater risk from declining levels of physical activity and from additional fat in the diet. Some developing countries have a complex pattern of disease: 'diseases of affluence' affect the richest sectors of society, whereas the poorest sectors continue to have all the disease problems associated with poverty and malnutrition.

Question 3.4

The Mediterranean diet contains many of the components that appear to be beneficial to cardiovascular health. This includes a healthy balance of protective lipids as well as the inclusion of large amounts of fruit and vegetables. The outlook for people with established cardiovascular disease will improve if they eat the components associated with a Mediterranean diet.

Question 3.5

Research on individuals and on populations has shown that high salt intake leads to increased blood pressure levels, which in turn increases the risk of cardiovascular disease. Populations that include large amounts of salt in their diet will develop an increased incidence of cardiovascular disease compared with those with more modest intakes. This relationship also seems to hold for individuals, and current recommendations include the suggestion of restricting dietary salt intake in order to avoid high blood pressure and the development of cardiovascular disease in the future.

Question 4.1

Reducing the incidence of cardiovascular disease relies on large numbers of people reducing their risk factors. You will be aware that using tobacco is the most important risk factor for individuals and for communities as a whole. Increasing taxation as well as direct restrictions on smoking that are introduced by governments have been demonstrated to be effective in reducing tobacco consumption throughout their communities.

Question 4.2

The constituent chemicals in 'environmental tobacco smoke' seem particularly dangerous to health because they include the chemicals released by the slow-burning ash at the tip of the cigarette. Often people inhale these dangerous products for many years – for example, workers in bars or clubs – without being aware of the potential dangers. Many governments are introducing restrictions on the use of tobacco in public spaces in order to protect workers in these environments.

Question 4.3

This chapter has focused on some of the ways in which individuals are able to reduce their personal risk of developing cardiovascular disease. Every one of us can make adjustments to our lifestyle in order to reduce our cardiovascular risk. The most important change is for people who smoke to stop, but all of us can reduce our intake of harmful fats and make sure that our exercise levels increase as well as maintaining as low blood pressure as possible.

Question 4.4

The precise role of diet in the development of cardiovascular disease is still being researched. Current opinion focuses on the role of different lipids, but it seems as though there are many other potentially protective as well as possibly harmful constituents in our diet. Over and above this it seems increasingly likely that the balance of various constituents (carbohydrates, fibre, trace elements, etc.) is important.

Question 4.5

Exercise is enormously important for many health-related reasons. People who exercise almost every day have a reduced incidence of many different diseases, including cardiovascular disease. This protective effect has been studied in individuals and also in whole communities using a wide range of epidemiological research methodologies.

The beneficial effects of exercise can be determined by following matched groups of people who undertake different levels of exercise. Over a period of time, it can be anticipated that the amount of cardiovascular disease experienced within each group will be different. If sufficient numbers of people are followed up for long enough, it can be demonstrated that those with greater levels of exercise will have fewer cardiovascular events and live longer than those who are more sedentary.

Question 5.1

Skeletal muscle and heart muscle show great variation in energy demand, depending on a person's level of physical activity. Energy is supplied primarily by aerobic metabolism, which requires oxygen. Arterioles determine how much blood can enter the vascular beds supplying the muscle, and the dilation of arterioles depends on products of metabolism released from the active tissue and on factors produced by the local endothelium.

Question 5.2

An atherosclerotic plaque causes disturbed blood flow, which may lead to damage to the endothelium. Both factors tend to promote platelet aggregation. If the plaque ruptures, then the blood comes into contact with the damaged tissue. This activates platelets, and factors released by the damaged tissue activate the clotting system, starting thrombosis.

Question 5.3

Thromboemboli which have broken away from veins enter the right side of the heart and are pumped into the circulation of the lungs. The circulation to the brain comes from the left side of the heart, not the right side.

Question 5.4

Chronic elevation of blood pressure can lead to prolonged minor damage to the arterial wall with the accumulation of fats and macrophages. Acute elevations may cause plaques to rupture (shear stress) or cause thrombi to break off and block vessels downstream.

Question 5.5

The muscle cells are not necessarily killed by lack of oxygen, because they may receive some supply from neighbouring blood vessels, in which case the cells can survive and recover their function. If the thrombus is dissolved by the plasmin system, supply may be restored through the vessel that was blocked. Over time, new blood vessels may be formed in response to the energy demand of the tissue, sufficient for the cells to function again. Furthermore, areas of heart muscle that have not been damaged may gradually increase in size and strength to compensate to an extent for the damaged area.

Question 7.1

The completed table is shown in Table 7.7.

Table 7.7 Answer to Question 7.1.

Technique	Fluoroscopy	B-mode ultrasound with colour flow Doppler ultrasound	CT angiography	Myocardial perfusion imaging with Tc-99m tetrofosmin
Basic method	Based on differential penetration of X-rays in different tissues Contrast medium used to highlight blood vessels	Based on reflection of pulses of ultrasound from interfaces, with 2D image built up by scanning Change in frequency due to the Doppler effect can be used to superimpose colour	Tomographic technique, based on differential penetration of X-rays in different tissues Contrast medium used to highlight blood vessels Images produced are 2D slices with excellent soft-tissue discriminations	Radiopharmaceutical injected into patient targets the heart muscle Tomographic images produced show high activity in regions of good perfusion Images viewed in different planes or 3D
Main uses	Cardiac angiography and interventional techniques	Assessment of heart chamber size and flow of blood through valves	Cardiac angiography	Assessment of myocardial perfusion to identify regions well-perfused at rest but poorly perfused under stress
Advantages	Allows constant imaging of the blood vessels as interventional techniques performed	Very low hazard Wide range of uses Cheap and readily available Most techniques non-invasive	Fast technique Less invasive than fluoroscopy because contrast medium injected into vein	Good accurate assessment of perfusion Often used prior to coronary bypass operations
Disadvantages	Uses ionising radiation	Images not as good definition as X-ray techniques or MRI	Uses ionising radiation CT machines are costly	Uses ionising radiation

Question 7.2

The bubbles will have to pass from the vein to the right atrium of the heart, then to the right ventricle and on to the lungs via the pulmonary artery. They then have to pass through the very small blood vessels in the lungs before they reach the left side of the heart via the pulmonary vein. So the bubbles must be small enough to pass through the capillaries in the lungs or they will not reach the left side of the heart. In practice, this means they must be less than 8 μm (8 millionths of a metre) in diameter. They must also last long enough for the blood to reach the left ventricle.

Question 7.3

Table 7.8 Answer to Question 7.3.

Technique	Invasive	Non-invasive
fluoroscopy	✓	
B-mode ultrasound with colour flow Doppler ultrasound		✓
CT angiography	✓	
myocardial perfusion with Tc-99m tetrofosmin	✓	
12-lead ECG		✓
cardiac-related blood tests	✓	
pulse oximeter		✓
chest X-ray		✓
MRI		✓

Activity 8.1

Table 8.5 Answer to Activity 8.1.

	Angina	Heart failure	Arrhythmias	Secondary prevention
nitrates	✓	✓		
beta-blockers	✓	✓	✓	✓
calcium channel blockers	✓	✓	✓	
digoxin		✓	✓	
diuretics		✓		
ACE inhibitors		✓		✓
anti-platelet drugs	✓		✓	✓
amiodarone		✗	✓	
statins	✓			✓

Question 8.1

The half-life of aspirin is much shorter than that of warfarin (Figure 8.10), so to maintain a therapeutic dose, aspirin must be taken more frequently.

Question 8.2

Calcium channel blockers cause vasodilation and consequently a drop in blood pressure. If the fall in pressure causes insufficient blood to be pumped to the brain, then dizziness may ensue.

Question 8.3

ACE inhibitors act in the lung to reduce the conversion of angiotensin-I to angiotensin-II. This results in reduced production of aldosterone by the kidney, increased excretion of water as urine – and therefore a reduced load on the heart.

Question 8.4

Statins act primarily on the liver to increase LDL uptake and reduce cholesterol synthesis. By reducing blood cholesterol, they slow the progression of cholesterol and lipid accumulation in atheromatous plaques.

Question 8.5

The ACE inhibitors and beta-blockers given for secondary prevention of myocardial infarction both have potential side effects. A patient who is not aware of the side effects, or the reason for taking the drugs, is more likely to stop taking them, and hence have a higher risk of a second myocardial infarction.

Question 8.6

Drugs are evaluated in randomised controlled trials. Some individuals may have specific characteristics (e.g. slow drug metabolism or high activity) which means that the drug is more effective or less effective in them. Some individuals may have other medical conditions or may be taking other medication which affects how the prescribed drug interacts.

Question 9.1

The approximate values are: (i) angioplasty 0, coronary bypass 60 000; (ii) angioplasty 160 000, coronary bypass 210 000; and (iii) angioplasty 440 000, coronary bypass 140 000. Note that these values are approximate.

Question 9.2

You should try to increase your level of fitness before heart surgery, seeking medical advice before attempting exercise so that an appropriate level and frequency of exercise can be determined. If you smoke, you should stop; if you are overweight, you should lose some weight. Following surgery, you are likely to require a period of recovery. This is dependent on your physical fitness, the type of surgery performed, your age and type of job that you have. During the recovery period you may have depression, exhibit emotional changes or suffer from memory loss.

Question 9.3

Pacemakers and cardioverter defibrillators.

Question 9.4

'Acute' describes as an event that is sudden and life-threatening, such as a myocardial infarction. 'Chronic' describes something that is long-term, such as angina. The least invasive surgical approaches include coronary angioplasty, and the most invasive include heart transplants.

Question 9.5

Angioplasty, stenting and coronary artery bypass grafting all increase coronary blood flow.

Question 9.6

Short-term complications include bleeding from wounds, blood clots forming in blood vessels, amnesia, dissections, pain, heart attack, stroke and rejection (for transplants).

Question 10.1

(a) Without the appropriate group 2 driving licence, the school teacher may not drive the minibus with passengers. However, because driving is such a minor element of their work, someone else can do it. There is effectively very little limitation.

(b) The despatch rider should be able to take up their previous occupation, following appropriate check-ups and advice.

(c) Moderately heavy manual work is certainly possible for people who have had a myocardial infarction. However, the precise nature of this work should be evaluated. For example, if the ship builder normally works on scaffolding or gantries, there are additional hazards associated with angina or a further myocardial infarction, so such situations are ruled out.

(d) An airline traffic controller is a specific occupation that a person who has had a myocardial infarction may not hold.

Question 10.2

The most important change she can make is to stop smoking. After this, the linked goals of weight reduction and increased exercise will also produce a clear reduction in risk. Finally, weight reduction may be linked to an improved quality of diet, with an increasing proportion of foods that have some protective actions against cardiovascular disease.

Question 10.3

Up to half of people who have a myocardial infarction develop some level of depression. Michael also shows some indications of anxiety and a lack of motivation to engage with the activities he previously enjoyed. Therefore he is at a considerable risk of developing depression. Set against this risk, he has a caring and supportive wife, and says that he wants to keep his mind active. Whether he does develop depression may be monitored by his GP at follow-up appointments, perhaps with the aid of questionnaires. Family and colleagues may also notice changes in his behaviour, but whether they identify these as depression is doubtful unless they are aware of the psychological aspects of cardiovascular disease.

ACKNOWLEDGEMENTS

Grateful acknowledgement is made to the following sources for permission to reproduce material within this product.

Cover

Cover image and title page © Science Photo Library.

Figures

Figures 1.1, 1.3, 1.4, 1.5, 1.7, 1.12 Based on Mackay, J. and Mensah, G. (2004) The Atlas of Heart Disease and Stroke, The World Health Organisation; *Figure 1.2* The Stroke Association (2007) Know your blood pressure, The Stroke Association; *Figure 1.6, 9.1* Kahn, J. (2007) 'Healing the heart', *National Geographic*, **211** (2), February 2007; *Figure 1.9* Swanton, K. and Frost, M. (2007) Lightening the load, tackling overweight and obesity, Department of Health. Crown copyright material is reproduced under Class Licence Number C01W0000065 with the permission of the Controller of HMSO; *Figure 1.10* Reproduced with kind permission of the British Heart Foundation; *Figure 1.13* NICE Guidance notes, National Institute of Clinical Excellence; *Figure 2.1* Professors P.M. Motta & S. Correr/Science Photo Library; *Figure 2.2* Anaesthesia UK; *Figure 2.5* Vilee, C. A. (1989) Biology, 2nd ed., Saunders College Publishing; *Figure 2.7* Source unknown; *Figure 2.11* Gangong, M.D.F., Lange, J. and Lange, D. (1983) *Review of Medical Physiology*, 11th ed., Appleton and Lange; *Figure 2.12a* Yoav Levy/photolibrary.com; *Figure 2.12b* van Wynsberghe, D., Noback, C. R. and Carola, R. (1995) Human Anatomy and Physiology, 3rd ed,, McGraw-Hill Inc; *Figure 3.1* NHLBI/Framingham Heart Study; *Figure 3.2* PRIMIS+, University of Nottingham; *Figure 3.6* Elliott, P. (2005) 'Role of salt intake in the development of high blood pressure', *International Journal of Epidemiology*, **34** (5), Oxford University Press; *Figure 3.5* Victor De Schwanberg/Science Photo Library; *Figure 3.7* © Visual Arts Library (London)/Alamy; *Figure 3.8* Doll et al. (2004) 'Mortality in relation to smoking:50 years observations on male British doctors', *British Medical Journal*, **328**; *Figures 3.9, 3.10* Adapted from Strong, K., Mathers, C., Leeder, S. and Beaglehole, R. (2005) 'Preventing chronic disease-how many lives can we save?', *The Lancet*, **366**; *Figure 3.11* Belgin, U. et al. (2004) 'Explaining the decline in CHD mortality in England and Wales between 1981 and 2000', *Circulation*, **109**; *Figure 3.12* BSIP, Chassenet/Science Photo Library; *Figure 3.13* Sue Sharples; *Figure 3.14* The British Journal of Diabetes and Vascular Disease, Medinews (Diabetes) Limited; *Figure 3.15* Tonkin, A. (2004) 'The metabolic syndrome, a growing problem', European Health Journal Supplements, **6**; *Figure 4.1* Townsend, J. et al. (1994) 'Cigarette smoking by socioeconomic group, sex and age', *British Medical Journal*, **309**; *Figure 4.2* AFP/Getty Images; *Figure 4.3* Steve Percival/Science Photo Library; *Figure 4.4* Image courtesy www.adbusters.org; *Figure 4.5b* © Jon Sparks/Alamy; *Figure 4.6* National Public Health Institute, Finland; *Figure 4.7* Pater, C. (2005)

'The blood pressure uncertainty range: a pragmatic approach to overcome current diagnostic uncertainties', *Current Controlled Trials in Cardiovascular Medicine*, **6**; *Figure 4.8* US Department of Health and Human Services Food and Drug Administration; *Figure 4.10* Heller, T. D. et al. (2001) 'Treating the patient or the population', *Western Journal of Medicine*, **175** (2); *Figure 4.11* Cristina Pedrazzini/Science Photo Library; *Figure 4.13* Hu, F. B. (2003) 'Plant based foods and prevention of cardiovascular disease: an overview', *American Journal of Clinical Nutrition*, **78** (3); *Figure 4.14* A J Photo/Science Photo Library; *Figure 4.15* Murphy, et al. (2006) 'Long-term cardiovascular consequences of obesity', *European Heart Journal*, **78**; *Figure 5.5* Eye of Science/Science Photo Library; *Figure 5.6* Science Photo Library; *Figure 5.7a* Dr P. Marazzi/Science Photo Library; *Figure 5.7b* © geldi/Alamy; *Figure 5.10* Prof. P. Motta/Dept. of Anatomy/University "La Sapienza", Rome/Science Photo Library; *Figure 5.12* ZEPHYR/Science Photo Library; *Figures 6.10, 6.11*: Gray, H. H. et al. (2002) *Lecture Notes on Cardiology*, 4th ed., Blackwell Publishing Limited; *Figure 7.1* National Institute for Health and Clinical Excellence; *Figure 7.2* Department of Health. Crown copyright material is reproduced under Class Licence Number C01W0000065 with the permission of the Controller of HMSO and the Queen's Printer for Scotland; *Figure 7.8* Chris Priest/Science Photo Library; *Figure 7.8b* Department of Medical Physics and Radiology, Oxford Radcliffe Hospitals; *Figures 7.16, 7.17, 7.19*:Toshiba; *Figures 7.18, 7.28* Malcolm Sperrin, Royal Berkshire Hospital; *Figure 7.20* Fairfax Radiological Consultants; *Figures 7.23, 7.26* Nigel Williams, University Hospitals Coventry and Warwickshire NHS Trust; *Figure 8.4* Alain Dex, Publiphoto Diffusion/Science Photo Library; *Figure 9.5* © Medical-on-line/Alamy; *Figure 9.6b* Sipa Press/Rex Features; *Figure 10.1* Balanced diet photograph © British Nutrition Foundation, www.nutrition.org.uk, concept for the Balance of Good Health model, © Food Standards Agency; *Figure 10.2a* Peter Menzel/Science Photo Library; *Figure 10.2b*: Ian Hooton/Science Photo Library; *Figure 10.4* Cordelia Molloy/ Science Photo Library; *Figure 10.7* CC Studio/Science Photo Library; *Figure 10.9*: Mark Thomas/Science Photo Library.

Tables

Table 1.3 Department of Health (2006) Coronary heart disease: national service framework for coronary heart disease – modern standards and service models: executive summary. Crown copyright material is reproduced under Class Licence Number C01W0000065 with the permission of the Controller of HMSO and the Queen's Printer for Scotland; *Table 4.1* National Public Health Institute, Finland.

INDEX

Entries and page numbers in **bold** refer to glossary terms. Page numbers in *italics* refer to items mainly, or wholly, appearing in tables, figures or boxes.